1989

THE
CHALLENGE
OF EFFECTIVE
SPEAKING

THE CHALLENGE OF EFFECTIVE SPEAKING

SEVENTH EDITION

RUDOLPH F. VERDERBER

University of Cincinnati

Wadsworth Publishing Company
Belmont, California
A Division of Wadsworth, Inc.

Communication Editor: Kristine Clerkin
Editorial Assistant: Melissa Harris
Production Editor: Vicki Friedberg
Designer: Donna Davis
Print Buyer: Karen Hunt
Copy Editor: Phyllis Cairns
Photo Researcher: Lindsay Kefauver
Compositor: Typothetae
Cover: Craig Frazier

p. xxii: Oscar Williams © 1987. p. 5: Cary Wolinsky/ Stock, Boston. p. 25: Rose Skytta/Jeroboam, Inc. p. 42: UPI/Bettmann Newsphotos. p. 59: George Bellerose/Stock, Boston. p. 86: Rick Smolan/Stock, Boston. p. 113: AP/Wide World Photos. p. 134: Robert George Gaylord/Jeroboam, Inc. p. 150: Ellis Herwig/Stock, Boston. p. 155: George Bellerose/ Stock, Boston. p. 174: Michael Hayman/Stock, Boston. p. 187: Karen R. Preuss/Jeroboam, Inc. p. 210: Bruce Davidson/Magnum Photos. p. 225: Reuters/Bettmann Newsphotos. p. 244: Suzanne E. Stock, Boston. p. 287: Michael Rothstein/Jeroboam, Inc. p. 308: AP/Wide World Photos. p. 330: Jim Pickerell/Stock, Boston. p. 340: Vince Compagnone/ Jeroboam, Inc. p. 364: © Susan Lapides/Design Conceptions. p. 371: AP/Wide World Photos.

Printed in the United States of America   34

1 2 3 4 5 6 7 8 9 10—92 91 90 89 88

Library of Congress Cataloging-in-Publication Data

Verderber, Rudolph F.
  The challenge of effective speaking.

  Bibliography: p.
  Includes index.
  1. Public speaking.   I. Title.
PN4121.V4   1988   808.5′1   87-16056
ISBN 0-534-08478-8

CONTENTS

PART ONE
ORIENTATION   1

PART TWO

**FUNDAMENTAL
PRINCIPLES   43**

CHAPTER THREE
Selecting Topics and Finding Material   45

CHAPTER FOUR
Organizing Speech Material   71

CHAPTER FIVE
Speech Wording   97

CHAPTER SIX
Practicing the Delivery   121

CHAPTER NINE
Explaining Processes   185

CHAPTER TEN
Descriptive Speeches   199

CHAPTER ELEVEN
Speeches of Definition   209

CHAPTER TWELVE
Expository Speeches:
Using Resource Material   219

PART FOUR

PERSUASIVE
SPEAKING   245

CHAPTER THIRTEEN
Principles of Persuasive Speaking   247

CHAPTER FOURTEEN
Reasoning with Audiences:
Speeches of Conviction   277

CHAPTER FIFTEEN
Motivating Audiences:
Speeches to Actuate   297

CHAPTER SIXTEEN
Critically Evaluating Arguments:
Speeches of Refutation   317

Part Four SUGGESTED READINGS   339

PART FIVE

ADAPTING TO OTHER OCCASIONS AND FORMATS   341

CHAPTER SEVENTEEN
Speaking in Problem-Solving Groups   343

CONTENTS

I am pleased that through the years both students and faculty have found that *The Challenge of Effective Speaking* has met their expectations for a fundamentals-of-effective-speaking book. As times change, however, different needs emerge, which an author must meet if that book is going to continue to be a worthwhile teaching tool. In this seventh edition, I have tried to make the kinds of changes that will meet those needs.

As we approach the 1990s, issues of assessment, critical thinking, critical listening, and effective speaking are causing students and faculty to hold even higher standards for text material. This seventh edition of *Challenge* has been revised with these issues in mind.

In **Chapter 2,** "Listening Critically to Speeches," there is greater emphasis on using listening skills to analyze speeches. I have also added a narrative speech assignment that can be used either for critical listening training during the first two days of the term or as a simple first assignment to help diagnose students' strengths and weaknesses. In **Chapter 7,** "Preparing Informative Speeches," the organization has been changed from a general topical organization to a chronological organization that builds on the steps of speech preparation established in Part Two, "Fundamental Principles." The chapter now focuses on how newness, relevance, organization, and creativity can be incorporated into a first informative speech. In **Chapter 13,** "Principles of Persuasive Speaking," the organization has been changed to build on the steps of speech preparation established in Part Two and contrasts with the steps of preparation of the informative speech. The revision emphasizes how reasoning, motivation, and credibility fit into steps of preparation and how they can be used in a persuasive speech. In **Chapter 16,** "Critically Evaluating Arguments: Speeches of Refutation," all the material has been rewritten to emphasize critical thinking.

All other chapters have been revised to emphasize that a course in public speaking is also a course in critical listening and evaluation. **For every speech assignment, there is a clear set of questions that provides a basis for critical listening and critical evaluation. Moreover, this edition contains seven new speeches and analyses.**

But changes in a book are only meaningful if the basic structure and philosophy of a book are sound. The needs of public speaking students provide the author of a textbook with at least two special challenges: (1) In theory, students must master a great deal of basic information before they give a first speech; yet at the same time, students need to start early giving speeches and present as many as possible during the term. (2) Instructors are likely to want to proceed somewhat differently from what an author might envision, so a book must be flexible. Through six editions students and faculty alike have stressed that the practical approach of *The Challenge of Effective Speaking* meets both of these needs.

After the two introductory chapters you will find a four-chapter unit presenting the fundamental principles of speech making (Chapters 3–6). Although this section is long enough to cover the material, it is short enough to be read and assimilated during the first or second week of classes. The remainder of the book is organized to allow instructors flexibility in their assignments. Chapters and units can be presented in any of several orders; some chapters can be used as the basis for speech assignments, others for general information. Let us now preview the organization in more detail.

In **Part One,** "Orientation," we lay the foundation for the study of speech principles. In Chapter 1, we examine the importance of public speaking and consider basic speaker responsibilities; in Chapter 2, we focus on listening and on why becoming a good listener is essential to becoming a good speaker. These two chapters can be read as one assignment.

In **Part Two,** "Fundamental Principles," we emphasize the step-by-step procedure used to prepare speech purposes and thesis statements, find material, outline the organization, word the speech, and practice the delivery. The eleven exercises included in this unit will guide the student in preparing and delivering a first speech early in the term.

In **Part Three,** "Informative Speaking," we build on the fundamentals but focus on information exchange. The first chapter in this unit (Chapter 7) focuses on principles of informative speaking; the remaining chapters consider the separate skills of using visual aids, explaining processes, and of defining, describing, and using research material. The material in the unit can be applied in a single informative speech, or in one or more speeches, each concentrating on a specific skill.

In **Part Four,** "Persuasive Speaking," we build both on fundamental principles and principles of information exchange. The instructor can tailor the unit to students' needs. The opening chapter of the unit (Chapter 13) focuses on principles of persuasion; the remaining chapters consider the separate skills of reasoning, motivation, and critical thinking and refutation. The material in the unit can be applied in a single persuasive speech, or in one or more speeches, each concentrating on a specific skill.

In **Part Five,** "Adapting to Other Occasions and Formats," we present material designed for special occasion speech making and for group projects.

There is and always will be only one justification for the use of a textbook in a public speaking course: to help students understand and use basic rhetorical theory to prepare and deliver better speeches. I believe students can and will use this seventh edition to help them give the very best speeches possible.

Although I am responsible for what appears in this book, the content reflects the thoughts of a great number of people. I would like to acknowledge the students who contributed speeches and outlines to this edition. Also, I would like to thank the many instructors who offered feedback and insights gained through their use of the sixth edition: Rachael C. Allstatter, Southern Ohio College; Gene Anderson, California State University, Fresno; Rev. Robert Bargen, Gonzaga University; Thomas L. Bottone, Los Angeles Harbor College; James M. Brines, Community College of Rhode Island; Robert Brown, Southern Ohio College; John Cease, University of Wisconsin; Sharon Keech Chase, San Jose State University; Gil Clardy, East Texas State University; Marvin Coates, El Paso Community College; Sharon B. Covitz, Augusta College; Jane Cushing; Steven Dayton, Orange Coast College; Lesley DiMare, California State University, Los Angeles; Karen Durst, University of Minnesota; William David Elkins, Tarleton State University; Betty Fair, Scott Community College; Benjamin Fisher, Glassboro State College; Don Friar, American River Junior College; Dorothy Greene, Community College of Rhode Island; Lillian J. Hall, Louisiana State University; Charlene Handford, Louisiana State University; Frank Harnish, College of Lake County; Jennie Harrison, North Harris County College;

Richard Haven, University of Wisconsin, Whitewater; Charles R. Hill, Austin Community College; Ruby T. Johnson, Wallace State Community College; William Johnson, Augusta College; Dan Julien, Northern Arizona University; Ben Kanter, De Anza College; Michael Kelley, California State University, Los Angeles; Marilyn Kelly, McLennan Community College; Barbara Kordenbrock, Belleville Area College; Deborah J. Kraut, Santa Monica College; Joseph Laine, University of Wisconsin, Oshkosh; Jo Ann Lawlor, West Valley College; Rich Leigh, Georgetown College; Gerald Lewis, Southern Ohio College; E. G. McNealey, Claflin College; Robert F. Martin, Western Oregon State College; Richard A. Parker, Northern Arizona University; Lonnie Polson, Bob Jones University; Joe Probst, Pasadena City College; Russ Proctor, Elmhurst College; Sharon A. Ratliffe, Golden West College; C. Reichert, Pasadena City College; Laura Kaye Roth, Lamar University, Port Arthur; R. Salzberg, Pasadena City College; Inge Schmidt, Butte College; Marion T. Shea, St. Petersburg Junior College; Sherwood Snyder, Chicago State University; Cindy M. SoRelle, McLennan Community College; Fred Sternhagen, Concordia College; Mary Ellen Tirpak, Lackawanna Junior College; James E. Towns, Stephen F. Austin State University; Patricia A. Townsend, University of Wisconsin, Whitewater; Barbara Wenner, Southern Ohio College; Elizabeth S. Willey, Southern Ohio College; S. Clay Willmington, University of Wisconsin, Oshkosh; Roger Wilson, Virginia Western Community College; and Christiane Ziolo-Hoelle, Southern Ohio College. In addition, a number of key reviewers played an important role in reviewing the changes made for the seventh edition: David J. Blackim, Hutchinson Community College; Samuel C. Gant, Nashville State Technical Institute; Ruth L. Goldfarb, Nassau Community College; Nancy Goulden, Kansas State University; Marilyn J. Hoffs, Glendale Community College; E. Joseph Lamp, Anne Arundel Community College; Roger Smith, Harrisburg Area Community College; and Susan Thomas, University of Illinois, Urbana.

Finally, I express my gratitude to my wife Kathie, who continues to provide both valuable insight and inspiration.

ORIENTATION

Personal Experience Speech by Andy Gilgoff

FUNDAMENTAL PRINCIPLES

Classifications of Nursery Rhymes by Susan Woistmann

INFORMATIVE SPEAKING

Truman Capote: The Four Stages of His Career by Terry Loftus

Juggling by Nancy Grant

The Cape Hatteras Lighthouse by Karen Zimmer

A Definition of Fossils by Frank Ettensohn

Dyslexia by Kelley Kane

PERSUASIVE SPEAKING

Television and Children by Mary Heintz

Learn to Speak Spanish by Mary Jo Cranley

Open Your Eyes by Kathleen Sheldon

NOTE: Except for the personal experience speech, student speeches, in the first four groups at left, are accompanied by outlines prepared by students and commentaries prepared by the author of this book.

ADAPTING TO OTHER OCCASIONS AND FORMATS

THE CHALLENGE OF EFFECTIVE SPEAKING

PART ONE

ORIENTATION

The material in this section lays the groundwork for your study of public speaking.
Chapter 1, an introduction, examines the
nature, importance, and responsibilities of
public speaking. Chapter 2 shows that speaking and listening are part of the same process
and that listening improvement is not a
separate skill, but should be developed to
help you speak more effectively.

ONE

INTRODUCTION TO PUBLIC SPEAKING

A successful, responsible, productive citizen must know how to read critically, how to write coherently, and how to speak effectively. Public speaking is a major part of deciding who becomes the president of the United States, or who becomes senator or chairman of the board or a leader of a business, political, or social organization. Moreover, your public speaking will directly affect your ability to lead a successful career.

You are now beginning your study of an art form that is nearly as old as humanity itself. Throughout the centuries famous speakers have changed the history of the world: Pericles, Demosthenes, and Cicero in classical times; Patrick Henry, Daniel Webster, Abraham Lincoln, Susan B. Anthony, and Booker T. Washington during the early years of our nation; and John F. Kennedy, Martin Luther King, Jr., Billy Graham, Betty Friedan, and hundreds of others in our recent history.

Yet in every period of history some people have tried to lessen the importance of the spoken word. In every age people have heard such statements as "We need less rhetoric and more action," or "That was only empty rhetoric," or "Don't pay any attention to what they say. . . ." It's as if what a person says is totally unrelated to what a person really believes or what a person does. More often than not, however, the oral record is a clear statement of both the speaker's philosophy and the speaker's action. Of course, there are and have been deceitful and immoral speakers—just as there are and have been deceitful and immoral doctors, lawyers, scientists, and teachers. But in every art and science we look for and depend on the best of the group to guide us.

Through the study and mastery of public speaking principles, you will not only increase your own effectiveness, but you can also influence the decision making that affects us all. Moreover, you can do it within the moral, ethical framework of our society.

We begin our book by analyzing public speaking as communication, public speaking as conversation, public speaking in decision making, and public speaking responsibilities.

PUBLIC SPEAKING AS COMMUNICATION

Public speaking, like writing a letter to your folks or like saying to that special man or woman, "I love you," is a form of communication. To begin our analysis of public speaking, let us consider public speaking as a communication process.

Public speaking is a communication process that involves the sharing of meaning. Although the process is a dynamic one, for purposes of identifying and explaining the variables involved let us isolate one specific segment. Tom concludes his speech to the student senate by saying, "So, I believe this senate should petition the administration to reinstate a two-day reading period prior to the beginning of final exams." As he concludes the sentence, many student senators show their approval of his plan by applauding or by nodding or by saying such things as "right on" or "yes." In his speech, Tom, the *source,* presented a *message,* through the *channel* of speech, to a group of *receivers,* who gave Tom a great deal of verbal and nonverbal *feedback.* Let us take a closer look at these variables of source, message, channel, receiver, and feedback, along with one additional variable, noise, and consider how they relate to each other to form a communication transaction.

The Source

The *source* is the sender, the originator of the communication message. The source may be a group of people—a committee, a company, or even a national government. As the author of this book, I am the source of the communication you are reading. In speeches you prepare and deliver for this course, you will be the source.

What the source elects to communicate depends on the field of experience that affects the thoughts and feelings of that source. Thus

Famous speakers throughout history have helped shape the course of world events. Martin Luther King, Jr., inspired the civil rights movement with his passionate speeches.

all of us, I as the author of this book and you in your speeches, are affected by our past and present experiences, feelings, ideas, moods, sex, occupation, and religion, as well as the aspects of our total environment. You are best able to understand another's perspective by analyzing that person's field of experience. Similarly, how you have lived your life determines what you say and how you say it.

Public speakers send messages to their audience. The *message* is the content that the source, the speaker, communicates. In this book, my message is how to prepare speeches. What you say in your speeches in and out of the classroom will be your message. Messages have at least three components: meaning, symbols expressing the meaning, and a form or organization of those symbols.

The Message

Meanings are ideas and feelings. You have ideas about how to study for your next exam, where to go on vacation, and whether taxes should be raised or lowered. You also have feelings such as hunger (for something to eat), anger (toward your roommate), and love.

We express these ideas and feelings through symbols. *Symbols* are words, sounds, or actions that represent meaning. Symbols can be communicated with both voice and body. As you speak, you choose words to convey your meaning. At the same time, your facial expressions, gestures, and tone of voice—all nonverbal cues—accompany your words and affect the meaning that people receive. Listeners take both the verbal symbols and the nonverbal cues and assign meanings to them. *Encoding* is the process a speaker uses to transform ideas and feelings into symbols; *decoding* is the process listeners use to transform symbols and the accompanying nonverbal cues into ideas and feelings.

You have been communicating for so long that you probably don't consciously think about either the encoding or the decoding processes. When your eyes grow bleary and you say, "I'm tired," you aren't thinking, "I wonder what symbols will best express the feeling I am now having." When you hear the words, "I'm tired" and see the bleary eyes of the other person, you are not likely to think, "*I* stands for the person doing the talking, *am* means that the *I* is linked to some idea, and *tired* means growing weary or feeling a need for sleep; therefore, the person is feeling a need for sleep and the bleary eyes confirm the accuracy of the statement." At the same time, you are not likely to consider whether you have the same mental picture of "tired" as the person using the word. You are probably aware of the encoding process only when you must grope for words, especially when you feel the right word is just on the tip of your tongue. Similarly, you are aware of the decoding process when you figure out the meaning of an unfamiliar word by the way it is used in a sentence.

When you speak you may communicate meaning intentionally or unintentionally. Intentional meaning occurs when you make a conscious effort to select symbols to communicate. Under these circumstances you are acting purposefully. Yet, at the same time, you may be unintentionally sending a conflicting message through nonverbal cues. For instance, when you attempt to compliment your audience for its contribution to a charity effort you led, you may notice that some members of the audience show signs of irritability. You may have intended to be very gracious with your compliments to the audience, but the unintentional nonverbal messages you sent may have given away your belief that the group did not do all it could have in helping you. As a result of the negative thought, your voice may have had an "edge" to it that the audience perceived as sarcasm.

Although unintentional communication can be either verbal or nonverbal, it is more likely to be nonverbal. People do on occasion blurt out something they were not intending to say, but most of us are far better able to control verbal reaction than nonverbal. When unintentional messages compete with intentional ones, listeners are more likely to pay attention to the unintentional because they believe that spontaneous reaction is more likely to be honest. When you deliver speeches, you should make sure that both the verbal and the nonverbal communication send the same message.

The third component of the message is its *form* or *organization.* Form or organization includes the message's syntax and grammar. For instance, when Tom gives his speech to the student senate about the need for reinstatement of a two-day reading period prior to the beginning of final exams, his symbols take a certain form. If his argument moves logically from reason to reason, meaning is likely to be clearer than if he presents bits and pieces of argument and evidence at random.

At first, organizing statements clearly will take time and may seem quite difficult. As you gain experience, you will find that you can organize even your spur-of-the-moment thoughts clearly.

The *channel* is both the route traveled by the message and the means of transportation. Your words are carried to others by air waves; your facial expressions, gestures, and movement are carried by light waves. Usually the more channels that you can use to carry a message, the more likely your communication is to succeed. Although our everyday communication is carried intentionally and unintentionally by any of the sensory channels—a fragrant scent and a firm handshake may both communicate—public speaking is basically two-channeled, that is, carried by sound and sight.

The Channel

The *receiver* is the message's destination: the listener or reader. When you speak in public, the receiver is your audience. The audience receives your message in the form of symbols that have been carried by sound and light waves. The receiver (the audience) turns these symbols back into meaning. This process of turning symbols back into meaning is called *decoding.*

The Receiver

Just as the speaker's experience affects the character of the message being sent, so does the audience's experience affect the way the message is received. Thus, the meaning that an audience gets from your message may be different from the meaning you sent. For instance, if you were to say, "Company sales representatives make really good money," the meaning of "really good money" may differ considerably from one person in your audience to another.

Feedback

Whether your audience decodes the meaning of your messages properly or not they will have some mental or physical response to your messages, and that response often enables you to determine whether your audience really understands you. Audience response—called *feedback*—tells you whether your message was heard, seen, or understood. If the verbal or nonverbal response tells you that your message was not received or was received incorrectly or was misinterpreted, you can send the message again, perhaps in a different way, so that your intended meaning is the same as the meaning your audience got.

Different kinds of public speaking situations provide for different amounts of feedback. A *zero-feedback* situation is said to exist when it is virtually impossible for the source to be aware of a receiver's response. Suppose that right now I stated, "Stop what you are doing and draw a rectangle resting on one of its longer sides." I would have no way of knowing whether you understood what I was talking about, whether you actually drew the rectangle, or, if you drew it, whether you drew it correctly. As the source of that message—as well as the other messages in this textbook—I cannot know for sure whether I am really communicating. The lack of direct feedback is one of the weaknesses of any of the forms of mass communication. The source has little or no immediate opportunity to test the impact of the message.

Suppose, however, that instead of being the author of a book, I am your instructor in a class of twenty students. Now suppose that I asked you to draw a rectangle resting on one of its longer sides. Even if you said nothing, my presence would enable me to monitor your nonverbal feedback directly. If you drew the rectangle, I could see it; if you refused, I would know; in some cases I could see exactly what you were drawing. A public speaker must be sensitive to nonverbal feedback.

Now suppose that as I asked you to draw the rectangle, you were free to ask me any direct questions and I were free and willing to respond. The free flow of interacting communication that would take place represents the highest level of feedback. Free flow of interaction that occurs in your conversation is less likely to occur when you give a speech.

How important is feedback to effective speaking? Leavitt and Mueller conducted an experiment similar to the one just described.[1] They reported that communication improved markedly as the situation moved from zero feedback to complete interaction. In your speeches, you want to stimulate as much feedback as possible.

Noise

Noise often hurts the audience's ability to interpret, understand, or respond to symbols. *Noise* is any stimulus that gets in the way of sharing meaning. Much of your success as a speaker depends on how you cope with external, semantic, and internal noises.

External noises are the sights, sounds, and other stimuli that draw people's attention away from intended meaning. For instance, during a student's explanation of how a food processor works, your attention may be drawn to the sound of an airplane overhead. The airplane sound is external noise. External noise does not have to be a sound. Perhaps during the explanation, a particularly attractive classmate glances toward you, and for a moment your attention turns to that person. Such visual distraction to your attention is also external noise.

Internal noises are the thoughts and feelings that interfere with meaning. Have you ever found yourself daydreaming during a speech? Perhaps you let your mind wander to thoughts of the good time you had at a party last night or to the argument you had with someone this morning. If you have tuned out the words of the speaker and tuned in a daydream or a past conversation, then you have created internal noise.

Semantic noises are those alternate meanings aroused by certain symbols that inhibit meaning. Suppose a speaker mentioned that the salesperson who sells food processors at the department store seems like a "gay fellow." If you think of "gay" as a word for homosexual, you would miss the speaker's meaning entirely. Since meaning depends on your own experience, others may at times decode a word or phrase differently from the way you intended. When this happens, you have semantic noise.

Model of Public Speaking as Communication

Let us look at these variables of public speaking in model form. Figure 1.1 illustrates the communication process in terms of a one-to-one relationship, that is, a speaker to one person in an audience. The left-hand circle represents the sender. In the center of that circle is a

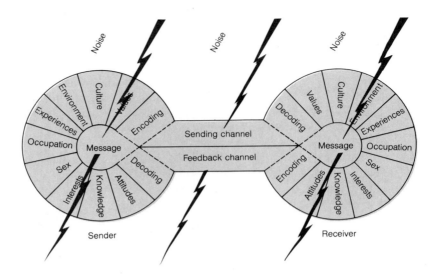

Figure 1.1. *A model of communication between two individuals.*

message—a thought or feeling that a person sends. The nature of that thought or feeling is created, shaped, and affected by the speaker's total field of experience, represented in the outer circle by such specific factors as values, culture, environment, experiences, occupation, sex, interests, knowledge, and attitudes. The bar between the circles represents the channel. By words and actions the person sends the message through the sending channel (upper half of the bar).

The right-hand circle represents the receiver. The message moves to the center of the circle. The receiver decodes the message, giving it meaning. The receiver's total field of experience affects the decoding process—that is, values, culture, environment, experiences, occupation, sex, interests, knowledge, and attitudes. Upon decoding and interpreting the message, the receiver sends verbal and nonverbal reaction back to the sender through the receiving or feedback channel (lower half of the bar). The sender receives and decodes the feedback to interpret the receiver's response.

The area around the sender and the receiver represents the physical and psychological context. At the same time this process is taking place, external, internal, and semantic noise may be occurring at various places in the model. These noises may affect the ability of sender and receiver to share meanings.

In a public speech this model is repeated for every person in the audience.

Now let us relate a simple communication act and trace the variables in operation. As the professor looks at her watch she sees she has only five minutes left. She frowns because she still has one major point to cover; but, aware that time is too short, she says, "That's enough for today." As she speaks various members of the class look surprised, many smile, and a few cheer. All of them gather their books, pencils, paper, and coats and begin filing out.

As the *source,* the professor conveys her *message* in verbal symbols and nonverbal signs. Her language, "That's enough for today," is the verbal representation of her thoughts; her frown and dejected tone are the nonverbal representation of her frustration at not having more time. Air waves carry her words and tone of voice, light waves her facial expression and bodily action (the *channel*) to each member of the class. As *receivers,* the class members record the sound and light waves and then interpret (decode) the verbal symbols and nonverbal signs that carried the message. As a result of their interpretation of the message, the class responds, gives *feedback,* by looks of surprise, smiles, and a few cheers. They further respond to the message by gathering materials and leaving. In this example there were no barriers (*noise*) to the satisfactory completion of the communication.

PUBLIC SPEAKING AS CONVERSATION

You are likely to be most comfortable with the kind of informal speaking you engage in daily—conversation. *Conversation,* a form of interpersonal communication, is the person-to-person interaction we have with another individual or with a small group of people. So, talking to a friend on campus, talking on the phone with a classmate about an upcoming test, and discussing a movie with the gang over a beer are all examples of conversation. Yet, in many ways, public speaking is conversation. Giving a speech involves many of the conversational skills with which you are already familiar. Still, public speaking differs from conversation in a few significant ways. Let's see how.

First, public speaking is relatively uninterrupted speech. Some books refer to public speaking as "one to many" communication. In short, this means that a public speaker talks to many people at one time; moreover, the talk is relatively uninterrupted. Occasionally, a listener will ask a question or even heckle a speaker. But more often, a public speaker talks continuously until the speech is over.

Second, public speaking is better organized than conversation. Conversation occurs on the spur of the moment. Your friend asks, "How do you make an omelet?" In your conversation you are not likely to say, "Good question. I'm going to go to my room now to think about an answer—I'll be back in about half an hour to tell you." No, if you know how to make an omelet, you start immediately to tell your friend how to do it. Because you are speaking on the spur of the moment, your wording is likely to be relatively rough, and the steps may not be as well organized as you might like. In contrast, if you were assigned to give a public speech on how to make an omelet, you would have the preparation time necessary to make sure that the steps were clearly identified, in their proper order, and that each step was well developed and used the most expressive language. Listeners expect some mistakes in presentation during conversation. Likewise, listeners expect good, clear organization in a public speech.

Third, public speaking calls for more formal language. In everyday conversation your language use varies. At times you may use slang; at other times your language may be informal, or occasionally, formal. When talking with friends you might say, "Keep your eyes open going up Carson Hill; last week I was going five miles an hour over the speed limit and the cops nailed me!" But giving such advice in a formal speech you would be likely to say, "The police are keeping a close watch in various places during the holiday season. The other day I was stopped on Carson Hill even though I was going only five miles an hour more than the forty-mile-per-hour limit." Public speakers shouldn't be pompous, nor should their language be obscure. But public speaking language should be on a level similar to the level of the language you would use in writing a theme paper for your English class.

Fourth, public speaking requires broader or more pronounced nonverbal behavior than conversation. When you are talking to your friends, you talk loud enough to be heard, but not loud enough to be heard down the street. Likewise, you are likely to talk with variations in pitch levels. And you are likely to use your face, hands, and body to show your feelings. But in a public speech, each of these would be enlarged. You must talk louder to reach an entire audience. Your pitch levels must be more pronounced to communicate subtle differences in meaning, and your facial expression, gestures, and movement must be broader to be seen easily by everyone.

Yet, even with these differences, public speaking has more in common with conversation than it has aspects that differ. In fact, in Chapter 6, we will speak of the importance of a "conversational quality" in speech delivery.

PUBLIC SPEAKING IN DECISION MAKING

Although public speaking is difficult for some people, it is a necessary part of modern life, and to succeed you need to equip yourself with public speaking skills. Why? For one crucial reason—public speaking plays a vital role in decision making. We recognize the importance of the words of our political and religious leaders in making decisions, but every day people in all walks of life use words to achieve their goals.

All human beings are decision makers. Starting with whether you want to get up this morning, through what you have for breakfast, to whether you decide to go to class, you make countless personal decisions each day. Some of these decisions you make alone; others you make in consultation with one or more persons. And some of these decisions you make as a result of the information you get from people speaking to you. Many of the decisions you make affect large numbers of people. Whether we are talking about personal decisions or decisions that affect the community in which you live, your state, your business, your church, or the entire nation, public speaking can be and often is very important in making those decisions.

One important decision-making function of public speaking is to provide people with information. Without data it is impossible to make wise decisions. Much good data may be communicated through speeches. For instance, when we are trying to make a decision on whom to vote for in a coming election, we can learn a great deal about the candidates by listening to what they have to say on the issues. In their speeches they are giving information that tells how they might behave under certain circumstances and where they will put their energies if elected. Since decisions generally are better when they are based on information, anything that you can do to improve the accuracy of your information exchange is to your benefit in decision making.

Providing Information

Changing Attitudes and Behaviors

A second important decision-making function of public speaking is to change attitudes and behaviors—something with which you already have experience. For instance, you may have spent time convincing your friends to go to a play rather than to a movie or persuading your parents to let you use the car this weekend. Some scholars go so far as to argue that the primary purpose of all speech effort is to influence the behavior of others.

There is a direct relationship between public speaking and decision making. The better you understand how to present information and to persuade, the more likely you are to be able to effect good decisions. Likewise, the more understanding you have of the problem-solving method, the more likely you are to cope with your problems systematically and to arrive at the best possible decisions.

RESPONSIBLE PUBLIC SPEAKING

We have stressed the importance of public speaking to us personally and to the society in which we live. Although the First Amendment to the Constitution guarantees freedom of speech, it is interpreted by the courts as carrying certain legal and ethical responsibilities. As a student of public speaking, you bear many legal and ethical responsibilities. In 1972, the Speech Communication Association, the national association of teachers of speech communication in America, endorsed the Credo for Free and Responsible Communication in a Democratic Society. Two paragraphs of the document lay a foundation for an understanding of your speech responsibilities:

> We accept the responsibility of cultivating by precept and example, in our classrooms and in our communities, enlightened uses of communication; of developing in our students a respect for precision and accuracy in communication, and for reasoning based upon evidence and a judicious discrimination among values.
>
> We encourage our students to accept the role of well-informed and articulate citizens, to defend the communication rights of those with whom they may disagree, and to expose abuses of the communication process.

These two paragraphs provide the overall approach to speech responsibilities; now let us take a look at some specific legal and ethical responsibilities.

The public speaker has at least three major legal responsibilities.

Legal Responsibilities

First, a speaker must refrain from any communication that may be defined as a clear and present danger. Speech behaviors that present a clear and present danger are those that incite people to panic, to riot, or to overthrow the government. From the time you began studying civics you learned that a person can't yell "fire" in a public place just to see what might happen. Such behavior is an example of speech designed to incite panic. You could also be prosecuted for giving a speech that incited a mob of students to riot against the administration or a mob of citizens to riot against the government.

Second, a speaker must refrain from using obscene language. Despite a relaxation of society's attitude toward the use of vulgar language, a person can still be prosecuted for obscene public speaking. Since the Supreme Court has defined obscenity as behavior that is outside the boundary of "community standards," what is considered illegal may vary from one place to another.

Third, a speaker must refrain from using language that will defame the character of another person. *Defamation* is harming another person by making statements that convey an unjust unfavorable impression. So, if in a political campaign Carson calls Simpson a card-carrying communist, Simpson can sue Carson for defamation. If Carson made a statement on the basis of hearsay or solely to cast doubt on the political aims of Simpson, then Carson will be held guilty of defamation. If, however, Carson can *prove* that Simpson is a communist, Carson will be acquitted. Truth is the best defense of any charge of defamation. So, if you are planning to say anything that could be interpreted as defamation, you will want to make sure that you have the evidence to uphold your opinion.

Ethical Responsibilities

"Ethical issues," according to Richard Johannesen, "center in value judgments concerning degrees of rightness and wrongness, goodness and badness, in human conduct."[2]

Although legal responsibilities are codified, what is ethical is far more likely to be a personal matter. Still, we expect the society in which we live to hold to certain standards that can be used to help with our personal value judgments. The family, schools, and church all share the responsibility of helping the individual develop ethical standards that can be applied to specific situations. Yet, as we are all aware, ethical judgments are seldom easy. In this initial look at ethical responsibilities for the public speaker, we will present two broad guidelines that were reflected in the Speech Communication Association Credo and that are endorsed by most, if not all, communication scholars. Then, in Chapter 13, on principles of persuasion, we will look at several specific behaviors that are considered unethical.

1. *You as a public speaker are responsible for what you say.* Your audience has the right to hold you accountable for what you say. If, for instance, you say that Peters (your opponent in a hotly contested political election) received campaign funds from illegal sources, your audience holds you responsible for the truth and accuracy of that statement.

    You uphold this ethical responsibility in at least two ways. First, you should have solid evidence, not personal opinion or hearsay on which to build your arguments. Before you make any statement about Peters's campaign funds, you are responsible for finding the facts. If you have not found facts to support your claim, it is unethical to present such a claim as if you have the facts.

    Second, you should present the facts for your audience to examine. You have the right to advocate a position—however unpopular it may be—but the listener has the right to examine the bases for the conclusions you have drawn. If you state that Peters received funds from illegal sources, you should share with the audience the facts that led you to that conclusion. Although an audience may be willing to trust your judgment on such matters, you owe them, and Peters for that matter, the right to examine the facts for themselves.

2. *You as a public speaker have a responsibility to allow free choice on the part of your audience.* Often this means allowing the other side to be heard. Freedom of speech applies equally to both sides of an issue or controversy. You do not have the right to suppress the speech of those who hold different views from your own. If you have accused Peters of getting illegal campaign funds, you have the responsibility for allowing Peters to reply to your accusations. Any effort to suppress that right or to deny Peters access to the same audience is unethical.

Everything we say or do in our speeches has a potential effect on our audience. If we know that we have a solid basis for what we say, are willing to share the facts on which our statements are based, and are willing to listen to opposing views, we are reasonably certain that our public speaking will meet our ethical responsibilities.

Ethical speaking helps you build respect for yourself and others.

NOTES

1. H. J. Leavitt and Ronald A. H. Mueller, "Some Effects of Feedback on Communication," *Human Relations* 4 (1951), 403.
2. Richard L. Johannesen, *Ethics in Human Communication* (Columbus, Ohio: Charles E. Merrill, 1975), 11.

TWO

LISTENING CRITICALLY TO SPEECHES

You are likely to ask why a book on effective speaking begins with a chapter on critical listening. First, becoming a better speaker depends on your becoming a better listener. Second, critical listening is by itself essential to effective communication.

WHY IS LISTENING IMPORTANT?

Improving your listening will help make you a better speaker in at least three ways. First, the better you listen the more you will be able to learn about effective speech making. Everyone in class, including your professor, is trying to model effective speaking characteristics in their classroom speeches and lectures. In contrast to the five to ten speeches you will give in this class, you can expect to hear from one hundred to two hundred speeches—more than you are likely to hear during the next several years outside the classroom. Because you will see a much wider selection of methods and techniques in operation than you could hope to try out yourself in your comparatively few classroom speeches, you can use the experience of others to help you. By learning to listen effectively, you can identify elements of effective speaking that you can try in your speeches as well as mistakes you want to avoid.

Second, the better you listen, the better critic you will become. Although your instructor may do much of the critiquing of speeches, you will be asked your opinion about the effectiveness of other speakers' methods. Good criticism—honest, accurate evaluation—is essential to learning how to get better. To make more than very obvious, superficial comments, you must listen carefully.

Third, as a bonus, the better you listen, the more you will learn about a great number of subjects. Since much of what your classmates say will be new information or will give you new insights, you will find that this speech class is truly a liberal arts course. In addition, you may find the information you learn as a listener today may be useful to you later as a speaker.

WHAT KIND OF LISTENER ARE YOU?

Perhaps you believe you are already a good listener. Although that may be true, most college students are not. In fact, studies indicate that college students listen at only about a 50 percent level of effectiveness. When a short delay occurs between when students listen and when they are tested, average listening efficiency drops to nearly 25 percent. For the past twenty years, Ralph Nichols, a leading authority on listening, has conducted numerous studies and has reported the research of others. All of his studies point to the same sad figures: 25 to 50 percent efficiency.[1] These low percentages are especially important when we realize that up to half of our daily communication time is spent listening.[2]

One of the problems that students have is that they don't understand the difference between listening and just hearing. *Hearing* is the ability to record the sound vibrations that are transmitted; *listening* involves making sense of what we hear. Most students hear well enough to be good listeners. Yet most students aren't able to understand, accurately report, or remember what they have heard.

Suppose you are attending a classroom lecture. At least five different things can prevent you from listening efficiently.

1. You may totally miss what the professor is saying. Many times we miss key ideas and even long sections of a speech because of a

physical or psychological problem of the moment. Something as small as a simple head cold can be a distraction. If you've had some deep emotional trauma like a death in the family, the loss of a friendship, or a low grade on an assignment you can be completely distracted when your professor is trying to explain the task.

2. You may hear what is said but not understand it. For instance, in a foreign language class you might hear every word the professor is saying, but if she is speaking in French and you haven't been studying, you may have no idea what is being said. But the speaker need not be talking in a foreign language for this to occur. If the professor uses words that you don't know or uses them in a way that you don't recognize, then the result is the same: You don't understand. If your professor tells you that "your implementation is obfuscatory," you may not understand that he's telling you that what you are doing gets in the way.

3. You may hear what is said, but you may assign a meaning different from what was intended. This happens because you hold different meanings for words or you perceive something in the communication process that alters your meanings. For instance, the professor may announce that a hotel is "within walking distance" of the convention center. When you get to the hotel you may discover that your understanding of "walking distance" is much different from your professor's. Or when the professor says, "Watch what you're doing," you may see the professor wink and decide that the professor is really kidding when he is not.

4. You may listen accurately, but as time passes your mind may change the meaning. For instance, your professor may say that the paper is due on the fifth. You listen and understand. But a few days later you may think he said the fifteenth.

5. You may listen accurately and then forget. You may hear the professor say that the paper is due on the fifth, but by the end of the class session you have no memory of the statement—and later you deny that it was ever mentioned.

In each of the five situations, the speaker, your professor in this case, has some responsibility for the outcome. But it is unfair to put the entire burden of effective listening on the speaker. You, as the listener, have as much responsibility, and in some cases more, than the speaker.

There are at least three factors that can be used to predict what kind of listener you are likely to be.

WHAT FACTORS DETERMINE YOUR LISTENING LEVEL?

Your listening is a product of many factors; you have only minimal control over some, but others you can change if you want. Let us consider three factors that are a function of your heredity and environment: hearing acuity, vocabulary, and an "ear for language."

Hearing Acuity

Some people have real hearing problems. Nearly 15 million Americans suffer some hearing impairment.[3] If you are among this number, you may wear a hearing aid or you may have learned to adapt to the problem. If you are not aware of the problem, however, poor hearing alone may limit your listening effectiveness.

If you suspect you may have a hearing problem, have a complete hearing test. Most schools have facilities for testing hearing acuity. The test is painless and is usually provided free or at minimal cost to the student.

Vocabulary

Listening and vocabulary are definitely related. If you know the meaning of all the words a person uses, you are likely to have a better understanding of the material and, as a result, retain more. However, if you do not know the meaning of words used in a conversation or if you are not familiar with the specialized vocabulary used in a particular field of study, you may not understand, and your listening may be affected. Many "poor students" have average or better intelligence but may be handicapped by a poor vocabulary. If you have a below-average vocabulary, you may have to work harder on listening.

When a person uses a word you do not understand, what do you do? People are often shy about calling attention to their lack of understanding of a particular word. Why? They do not want to appear foolish.

But isn't it foolish to respond to a person as if you understand when you really do not? If your professor told you your speech reached the "nadir" and you smiled because you didn't know what he or she was talking about, that behavior would be foolish. *Nadir* means the low point—the pits. Although you may *feel* embarrassed when you need to ask what a word means, you are likely to *behave* foolishly if you do not ask.

One way to enlarge your vocabulary is to work through a basic vocabulary book such as Agel's *Test Your Word Power,* noted in the suggested readings at the end of Part One. Another way is to take a more active role in working with the words you hear and read every day. Begin by noting words that people use in their conversations with you that you are not able to define precisely. For instance, suppose Jackie says, "I was inundated with phone calls today!" If you can't give a precise definition for *inundated,* you could ask Jackie what she meant by that word. But if for some reason you don't wish to ask Jackie, you can still make a note of the word, look up its meaning at the first opportunity, and then review what Jackie said to see whether the dictionary meaning seems to be what Jackie meant. Most dictionaries define *inundated* with synonyms such as *overwhelmed* and *flooded.* If you then say to yourself, "Jackie was inundated—overwhelmed or flooded—with phone calls today," you will tend to remember that meaning and apply it the next time you hear the word. You can follow the same procedure in your reading. As you are reading one of today's course assignments, circle any words about which you have a question. After you have finished the assignment, go back to those words and look them up.

An Ear for the English Language

If members of your family carry on meaningful conversations about world events, the arts, and what is happening around them, you will probably have a natural "ear for language," a grasp of good language structure, and experience in a variety of kinds and levels of listening. If you have not developed an ear for language at home, then your ear may not be attuned to the more difficult kinds of listening that you may encounter in adult relationships. Although an adult cannot suddenly make up for years of lack of practice with language, you can use your classroom experiences to help you improve, even if your former environment has been a source of your listening problems.

WHAT CAN YOU DO TO IMPROVE?

Assuming that your listening efficiency is about average, what can you do about it? With determination, an average listener can almost double listening efficiency in a few months. In fact, by following a few simple steps, you will note immediate improvement in your listening.

Adopt a Positive Listening Attitude

The first step to improving your listening is to *adopt a positive listening attitude.* There's no reason why you cannot improve your listening *if you want to.* It's up to you to decide that listening is important and that you are going to do whatever it takes to listen better.

Recognize Differences in Listening Difficulty

The second step to improving your listening is to *recognize differences in listening difficulty.* Listening is similar to reading in that you should listen differently depending on the purpose and degree of difficulty of the material. Yet many people "listen" about the same regardless of purpose or material. Listening intensity differs depending on whether you are listening primarily for enjoyment, for understanding, or for evaluation.

Much of our listening is for pleasure or enjoyment. Listening to music on the car radio is one example of this kind of listening. We are aware of the background sound—we find it soothing, relaxing, and generally pleasant. Much of our listening to conversation is for this purpose. For instance, when Tom and Paul talk about the game they saw on television, their listening is for pleasure, and the details of the conversation are likely to be soon forgotten. Unfortunately, many people approach all situations as if they were listening for pleasure. Yet how you listen should change qualitatively when you listen to understand or for evaluation.

Listening to understand is a more difficult challenge than listening for pleasure. For this kind of listening you need to develop greater intensity. Your classroom lectures provide a situation requiring this type of listening. Likewise, such informal situations as listening to directions (how to get to a restaurant), listening to instructions (how to shift into reverse in a foreign car), and listening to explanations (a recounting of the new dorm rules) also require listening to understand.

Most people approach all listening situations as though they were listening for pleasure. How should your listening style change when you are listening to understand?

But by far the most demanding challenge is listening to evaluate. Every day we are flooded with messages designed to influence our behavior. To function best in this context, we have to be able to recognize the facts, weigh them, separate them from emotional appeals, and determine the validity of the conclusions presented.

Critical listening takes time, effort, and energy; and to be frank, many of us are just not willing to work at it. Many Americans consider listening a passive venture; they have fallen into the habit of "watching" television or "listening" to the radio to relax. As a result of years of associating listening with relaxing, many have acquired or developed bad listening habits. Whereas listening for entertainment may be relaxing, listening for information or listening critically is work. You have to recognize when it is appropriate to "go into high gear" in your listening; and equally important, you have to know what it means to be in high gear! *p34, 252*

The remainder of the recommendations in this section are directed toward helping you in your efforts to understand and to evaluate. Later in this chapter we will consider criteria for listening critically to public speeches. Then, in the chapters on persuasive speaking, we will discuss tests of evidence and reasoning that are as important to listening to arguments as they are to constructing them.

Get Ready to Listen

The third step to improving your listening is to get yourself ready to listen. Listening efficiency increases when the listener follows the apparently elementary practice of really being ready to listen. Getting ready involves both physical and mental application.

What physical characteristics indicate that you are ready to work at listening? An outward sign is whether you look as if you are listening. Poor listeners often slouch in their chairs. Their eyes wander from place to place. They appear to be bored by what is going on. In contrast, good listeners sit upright—sometimes almost on the edge of their chairs. They rivet their eyes on the speaker. These physical signs of attention indicate alertness.

These recommendations may sound simplistic to you. But test them out for yourself. When I discuss listening in class, I precede short comprehension tests by saying, "For the next five minutes, I want you to listen as hard as you can. Then I'm going to give a test on what you heard." What happens when the class realizes it has an investment in what will take place? Students straighten up and turn their eyes to the front of the room; extraneous noises—coughing, clearing throats, rustling—drop to zero.

Getting ready to listen also means getting ready mentally. Mentally, you need to stop thinking about any of the thousands of miscellaneous thoughts that constantly pass through your mind; all your attention should be directed to what a person is saying. In effect, anyone who is talking with you is in competition with all the miscellaneous thoughts and feelings that you are having. Some of them may be more pleasant to tune into than what people are saying to you. Anticipation of an exciting evening; thoughts about a game, a test, or what's for dinner; and re-creating scenes from a memorable movie or television show may offer more attractive pleasures than listening to the speaker. Yet attention paid to such competing thoughts and feelings is one of the leading causes of poor listening.

A fourth step in improving your listening is to withhold evaluation. This recommendation means you should control both arbitrary judgments about a subject and emotional responses to content. It is a human reaction to listen attentively only to what we like or what we want to hear. Yet such an attitude is self-limiting and self-defeating. We listen to learn and to gather data for evaluation. Neither of these goals is possible if we refuse to listen to anything outside our immediate interests. For instance, if a classmate indicates that he or she will talk about the history of a union, you may say you are interested neither in history in general nor in unions in particular. If during the first sentence or two of the speech you find yourself saying, "I don't think I am going to be interested in this topic," you should remind yourself that judgment must follow, not precede, the presentation of information. Poor listeners make value judgments about the content after the first few words; good listeners suspend judgment of the value of the message until they have heard it. It is true that some speeches will not be very good. But you will not be able to make this judgment until the speaker has finished. Often you will find that even a poor speech will have a good idea or some good supporting details that you will want to remember.

You also need to control your emotional responses to the speaker's personality. We all wish that every speaker we had to listen to was physically appealing, dynamic, and exciting. The fact is that a number of speakers you hear will be dowdy and, at times, boring. Poor listeners let the way a speaker looks and sounds turn them off. Poor listeners make snap value judgments about quality of material on the basis of physical appearance. So at the beginning of a speech, you must tell yourself that you will hear the speaker out regardless of how the speaker looks or sounds.

In addition, you need to control your emotional responses to the words you hear. Are there any words or ideas that act as red flags for you? Does the mere utterance of these words cause you to lose any desire to listen attentively? For instance, do you have a tendency to react emotionally when people use any of these words?

racist	communist	gay
Jew	Arab	yuppie
abortion	AIDS	gun control
feminist	busing	welfare

Would any of these or similar words turn you off? Often poor listeners (and occasionally even good listeners) are given an emotional jolt when a speaker touches a nerve. At this point all you can do is to be wary. When the speaker trips the switch to your emotional reaction—let a warning light go on before you turn off. Instead of tuning out or getting ready to fight, work that much harder at being objective. Can you do it? If you can, you will improve your listening.

Since it is easier to pay attention to a speech if it is well presented, the principles in this book are directed to making speeches so clear and interesting that good and poor listeners alike will pay attention. Nevertheless, some of the speeches you hear, in or out of class, will be less than good. In such instances, you will have to work to make the most of the experience.

Listen for Ideas and Meaning

A fifth step to improving your listening is to listen for ideas and meaning. Some people mistakenly think that their listening is at its best when they can feed back the words or the details that were communicated. But good listening goes beyond that. Good listening means understanding the key ideas behind the words and details presented. Listening for key ideas is one of the easiest parts of listening to learn. The information we will discuss in Chapter 4, which deals with organizational patterns, will help you separate key ideas from details.

For now, keep in mind that most speeches will usually have two to five main points. Often a speaker will preview the main points in the introduction. Early in the speech the speaker may say something like, "Today I want to share with you the three causes of juvenile crime—poverty, permissiveness, and broken homes." At this point you know that the speech will have three points and you can look for them. If the speaker does not preview points, you must still listen for them.

As important as recognizing major and minor points is discerning the overall meaning, which requires a sensitivity to the message's verbal and nonverbal elements. For instance, when a person says, "Isn't it a beautiful day?" in a sarcastic tone when the rain is pouring down, we are likely to recognize the conflict between the words spoken and the tone of voice. Nonverbal signs such as sarcastic vocal tone, body action, and movement may tell us to disregard the normal meaning of the words. In addition to contradicting meaning, nonverbal cues may supplement or modify the meaning. When a person says, "I'm really angry," we measure the degree of anger by the nonverbal cues; when a person says, "I'm not sure how much we should give," we measure the extent of undecidedness by the nonverbal cues. Since a speaker's meaning sometimes is communicated unintentionally by nonverbal cues, we must be alert to all aspects of the message.

A good listener, therefore, absorbs all the speaker's meaning by being sensitive to voice tone, facial expression, and body action, as well as to the words themselves. Nonverbal cues may reveal a speaker's sincerity, depth of conviction, confidence, and true understanding and may have many subtle implications, regardless of the words the speaker uses.

The final step to improve your listening is to listen actively. Research on learning indicates that listeners learn better and faster and make sounder judgments about what they hear when they are mentally and physically active. Active listening involves you in the process of determining meaning. Too often people think of the listening experience as a passive activity in which what they remember is largely a matter of chance. In reality, good listening is hard work that requires concentration and willingness to mull over and at times verbalize what is said. Good listening requires using mental energy. If you really listen to an entire fifty-minute lecture, for instance, when the lecture is over you will feel tired because you will have put as much energy into listening as the lecturer put into talking. Since you can think faster than any speaker can talk, you will have time to use several active listening skills. Active listening includes repeating, questioning, paraphrasing, and notetaking.

Listen Actively

Repeating items of information helps you remember. For instance, when the speaker says, "The first major election reform bill was passed in England in 1832," the active listener might mentally repeat, "reform bill, England, 1832."

Good questioning helps you anticipate material. For instance, when a speaker says, "There are four steps to coding data," you will ask yourself, "What are the four steps?" If the speaker goes on to tell you the steps, asking the question will help you emphasize the steps. If the speaker doesn't give you the steps, asking the question focuses on information you need to get. After the speech is over you may have an opportunity to ask the question directly, or later you can look up the steps. Good questioning also helps you test the soundness of the material. For instance, when the speaker says, "Swimming is an activity that provides exercise for almost every muscle," active listeners might inwardly question the point, examining the supporting material offered.

Paraphrasing helps you check your understanding. A *paraphrase* is a statement of what the person's words meant to you. After a speaker has talked for a few minutes, you can say to yourself, "In other words, how the mixture is put together may be more important than the ingredients used." If this makes sense to you, then you can be confident that you have an understanding. If you cannot paraphrase, it is likely that something was missing from the explanation or you weren't listening carefully enough.

Using *mnemonic devices* will also help. A *mnemonic device* is any artificial technique used as a memory aid. Some of the most common rules for forming mnemonics are taking the first letters of items that you are trying to remember and forming a word. For example, if you were listening to a professor lecture on three types of speeches intended to entertain, to inform, and to persuade, a useful mnemonic for remembering the three purposes is PIE, standing for *p*ersuade, *i*nform, and *e*ntertain. When you are trying to remember some items in sequence, you can form a sentence with the words themselves or you can assign words using the first letters of the words in sequence to form some easy-to-remember statement. For instance, when you first studied music, you may have learned the notes of the scale in the following way: For the notes on the treble clef lines (E-G-B-D-F) you may have learned "every good boy does fine," and for the notes of the treble clef spaces (F-A-C-E) you may have remembered the word *face.*

Active listening can also mean taking notes. Whereas poor listeners fidget, doodle, or look about the room, good listeners often take notes on what the speaker is saying. Repeating, asking questions, and paraphrasing helps you take good notes. Most college students take notes in classes; yet the quality of their notes varies tremendously. Just sitting down with a pen or pencil and a piece of paper does not guarantee good notetaking. Likewise, leaving class with pages of writing is not evidence of good notetaking either.

What are good notes? Good notes are a brief outline of what the speaker has said including the overall idea, the main points of the message, and key developmental material. Good notes are not necessarily very long. In fact, many excellent lectures can be reduced to a short outline.

Suppose you were listening to a supervisor instruct candidates for a secretarial position about the duties of the job. The supervisor might say:

As prospective employees you should be aware of a few details. Typing and distributing mail are the most important duties of this job. Now about the typing. Some people may give you a lot, but it may not have anything to do with department work. You will want to be careful about spending time on private work. Some people will be real sticklers about details. Make sure that you check details carefully before you type. And of course, some will give you work at the last minute and expect you to finish it.

Mail comes twice a day—at 10 and 2. You will sort it and put it in the respective boxes. If there is any mail that doesn't belong here, bundle it and mark it for return to the main post office.

Now let me take a minute to talk about your breaks. You get ten minutes in the morning and afternoon (take your break at about 10:30 and 2:30—they're relatively quiet times). And of course, you get an hour for lunch. Although the time for lunch is flexible, you should probably leave for lunch by 12:15.

Notes

Typing and mail most important duties

1. Typing
   Be sure it relates to dept. work
   Check details
   Be wary of late work

2. Mail
   10 and 2
   Sort
   Bundle left over, return to post office

3. Breaks
   2—10:30 and 2:30 best
   Take lunch by 12:15

This short passage included a lot of specific detail. Yet the 193 words of explanation can be outlined in just 44 words. Since the speeches you hear will vary in detail, good notetaking may range from 10 percent to as high as 20 percent (the amount in our example). The point is not the number of words, but how accurately the notes reflect the sense of what the speaker said.

The better note taker you become, the better listener you will be.

The following are two separate analyses. Answer each question honestly. It is important for you to know what you do well and what you need to work on. For each of the analyses there are five questions. For

**EXERCISE 1
Evaluating
Your Listening**

each question score 5 for "almost always," 4 for "usually," 3 for "occasionally," 2 for "seldom," and 1 for "almost never." Write your score for each question in the "score" column. Then, add your scores.

Analysis A	Almost always	Usually	Occasionally	Seldom	Almost never	Score
I listen *differently* for enjoyment, understanding, evaluation.						
I consciously recognize the speaker's purpose.						
When people talk, I differentiate between their main points and supporting details.						
At various places in a speech, I paraphrase what the speaker has said to check my understanding.						
When I am listening for information or to evaluate, I take good notes of major points and supporting details.						

Analysis B	Almost always	Usually	Occasionally	Seldom	Almost never	Score
I stop listening when what a person is saying is not interesting to me.						
I pretend to listen to people when I am really thinking about other things.						

Analysis B (*cont.*)	Almost always	Usually	Occasionally	Seldom	Almost never	Score
When a person's way of speaking annoys me (such as muttering, stammering, or talking in a monotone), I stop listening carefully.						
When I perceive the subject matter as very difficult, I stop listening carefully.						
When people use words that I react to negatively, I stop listening and start preparing responses.						

Analysis A focuses on positive listening behaviors, and Analysis B focuses on negative listening behaviors. If your score for the first analysis is much higher than your score for the second (20 points or more to 10 points or less), your listening behaviors are positive and should yield good results. If your scores for the two analyses are very similar (say 15 points for each), you need to work on limiting negative behaviors and perfecting skills that will raise your level of positive behaviors. If your score for the *second* analysis is much higher than for the first (20 points or more to 10 points or less), you are likely to need a great deal of work on developing skills designed to improve your listening.

CRITICAL ANALYSIS OF SPEECHES

Improving general listening efficiency will enable you to gain more information from the speeches you hear in class. But evaluating speeches and determining the kinds of material that work with audiences require that you listen critically. To listen critically, you have to have sound standards to apply. The material in the remainder of this book is directed toward helping you understand the critical standards to apply in preparing your own speeches and in criticizing the work of others. In this section, let's look at the elements you must consider in order to listen critically to speeches and to form a sound evaluation of their effectiveness.

Public speeches are fair game. Perhaps more than any other form of communication, a speech is evaluated instantly by nearly everyone who hears it. In this section we want to preview the elements that should be considered in determining a speech's value. Our goal is not only to determine whether a speech was good or bad but also to determine *what* made the speech more or less effective in achieving its goal.

When is a speech a good one? On the surface, a speech is a good one when it is successful, when it (1) achieves its goal or (2) brings the audience significantly closer to that goal. If a speech motivates you to go see a particular movie or convinces you that Congress should pass handgun control laws or helps you understand how the pyramids were built, then the speech was a success. Yet sometimes a speech is measured as a success even when the goal is not achieved. If none of the members of the audience were planning to go see the particular movie, but after hearing the speech some were willing to consider going; or if most members of the audience were hostile to any form of gun control legislation, but now they are willing to weigh the arguments; or if the majority of the audience had no idea how the pyramids were built, but now they have some comprehension; then the speech has achieved some measure of success.

But success is not the only measure of a good speech. A good speech is also a responsible speech. Responsible speakers earn our trust. They proceed ethically. Many speeches by such people as Hitler, Joseph McCarthy, and other demagogues of history were successful, but that success was achieved in part through lying, distortion, and overuse of emotional appeals. Public speakers have legal and ethical responsibilities; if speeches do not meet these legal and ethical responsibilities, then they are not good ones.

Basic Speech Critique

The following questions are applicable to evaluation of all kinds of speeches. With each question I have included the page numbers where a complete discussion of each question occurs. When you have answered these questions, you will have a sound basis for evaluation of the specific speech and an awareness of the material necessary for giving an effective speech. Throughout the text we will focus on key points of this basic critique in order to help you develop specific criteria for particular types of speeches.

A speech includes organization, content, language, and delivery. As you listen to a speech you will answer the following questions (yes or no):

Content

_____ Was the goal (specific purpose) of the speech clear? (pages 48–51)

_____ Did the speaker have specific facts and opinions to support statements? (pages 58–61)

_____ Did the speaker offer a variety of kinds of supporting material? (pages 62–68)

_____ Did the speaker adapt the content to the audience's interests, knowledge, and attitudes? (pages 52–56)

_____ Did the speaker adapt the content to the occasion? (pages 56–58)

Organization

_____ Did the introduction gain attention, gain goodwill for the speaker, and lead into the speech? (pages 80–85)

_____ Were the main points clear statements? (pages 72–79)

_____ Did the main points prove or explain the specific goal of the speech? (pages 72–79)

_____ Did the conclusion tie the speech together? (pages 85–89)

Language

_____ Was the language clear? (pages 101–106)

_____ Was the language vivid? (pages 106–109)

_____ Was the language emphatic? (pages 109–112)

_____ Was the language appropriate to the audience? (pages 112–118)

Delivery

_____ Did the speaker sound enthusiastic? (page 122)

_____ Did the speaker look at the audience? (page 123)

_____ Was the delivery spontaneous? (pages 123–124)

_____ Did the speaker show sufficient vocal variety and emphasis? (pages 124–129)

_____ Was articulation satisfactory? (pages 129–130)

_____ Did the speaker have good posture? (pages 130–132)

_____ Did the speaker show sufficient poise? (pages 138–142)

Evaluate the speech as (check one) _____ excellent, _____ good, _____ average, _____ fair, _____ poor.

Use the information from your check sheet to support your evaluation.

ASSIGNMENT
Speaking and Listening

1. *Narrating an experience.* Prepare a two- to three-minute personal experience. Think about experiences that you have had that were humorous, suspenseful, or dramatic, and select one that you think your audience would enjoy hearing about.

   A narrative is a telling of events. The purpose of a narrative is to relate a sequence of events in chronological order. The primary goal of a narrative is to make a point in such an interesting way that the audience will remember the point because of the way it was presented.

   As you construct your narrative speech consider the following elements:

   a. Usually a narrative has a point to it, a climax that the details build up to. A joke has a punch line; a fable has a moral; a narrative has an ending that makes the story interesting.

   b. A narrative is developed with supporting details. A narrative speech can be lengthened or shortened depending on the number of and the development of supporting details. Supporting details give background, but most of all they build the story so that the point of the story has maximum effect.

   c. A narrative is often developed with suspense in mind. Part of the power of a narrative is to withhold the punch line until the end. If you can tease the audience, you will hold their attention. They will be trying to see whether they can anticipate what you have to say. Vocally, a slight pause before the punch line will heighten the effect.

   d. A narrative often includes dialogue. A story will be much more enjoyable to an audience if they can hear it unfold through dialogue.

e. A narrative is often humorous. Although not all narratives are funny, more often than not they will have elements of humor. If what happened can be made funny, the humor will hold attention.

How should you prepare your narrative? To build your narrative, select the experience you want to tell, gather the material necessary to help you make the point of the story, organize the material, and then practice telling the story a few times until the key ideas are firmly in mind. Don't try to memorize the story; if you have practiced it two or three times, you should be able to tell it reasonably well. (The next four chapters discuss these and other steps of complete speech preparation.)

2. *Listening to a narrative.* Have someone read the following narrative to you.[4] Listen to understand and to remember. You should certainly remember the climax or punch line and the specific supporting details that lead to the climax. After you have heard it, take the short quiz that follows. Which of the chapter's recommendations helped you the most with your listening?

A while back, I joined a local gym with the express purpose of taking up weight lifting in hopes that someday people would have difficulty in telling me and Arnold Schwarzenegger apart. One day, when I had returned to my locker after my usual bone-crushing workout, I noticed that my lock was through the handle of my locker, not through the hole at the bottom that locks the locker. "Dumbhead," I said to myself, "That's a sure way of ending up in trouble." And sure enough, when I opened the locker my worst fears were confirmed—my wallet was gone, my keys were gone, and my pants were gone. I was outraged. I couldn't even drive myself home. I went running out of the locker room and up to the clerk who worked at the desk. I started yelling at him, "Call the police—I've been robbed."

"What happened?" he asked.

"I've been robbed!" I repeated.

"Are you sure?" he asked.

"Of course I'm sure," I said, "I looked in my locker and my clothes are gone!"

"Okay," he said, "I'll call the police."

Since I knew it would take a while for the police to come, I thought that maybe if I went back to the scene of the crime I could find some evidence—perhaps the thief had dropped part of my clothing, or maybe a credit card had fallen from my wallet. So I approached the locker the second time and did a double take when I noticed that now the lock was through the hole at the bottom of the handle as it should have been. "Great," I said, "Now that everything is gone I remembered to put the lock back on right." So I unlocked the locker, opened the door—and found my pants, my wallet, and my keys. A slow red burn of embarrassment began to form. I had looked in the wrong locker—one that was one row behind.

What could I do? "No problem," I said to myself. "I'm a man, right? I can take it, right? I can swallow my pride, look directly at the clerk, and announce, 'I've made an error. I'm sorry you had to call the police. In fact, I'll even make the call myself and apologize directly to the police.'"

I took several firm strides back toward the desk, full of resolve and feeling very proud of my manly behavior. Then I stopped and said to myself, "Nah, I'll just go out the back door."

Answer the following statements T for true, F for false, or N for information not included:

_____ 1. The narrator was going to the gym for a weight-lifting workout.

_____ 2. The narrator took his lock with him by mistake to his workout.

_____ 3. When the narrator opened the locker door, the locker was entirely empty.

_____ 4. The narrator telephoned the police.

_____ 5. The desk clerk was female.

_____ 6. The narrator's actual locker was one row from the one he had looked into.

_____ 7. The lock was a combination lock.

_____ 8. When the narrator discovered his error, he was embarrassed.

_____ 9. The narrator phoned the police to apologize.

_____ 10. The punch line of the narrative is that the narrator found his clothes.

Answers: 1 T, 2 F, 3 N, 4 F, 5 F, 6 T, 7 N, 8 T, 9 F, 10 F

NOTES

1. Ralph Nichols and Leonard A. Stevens, *Are You Listening?* (New York: McGraw-Hill, 1957), 5–6.
2. Paul Rankin's original study, done more than fifty years ago, showed that people spend more time listening than they do in any other form of communication. Rankin, "The Measurement of the Ability to Understand Spoken Language," Ph.D. diss., University of Michigan, 1926, University Microfilm, 1952, Publ. No. 4352; cited by Nichols and Stevens, *Are You Listening?*, p. 6. A study by Verderber, Elder, and Weiler found that college students spend 50 percent of their communication time listening. Rudolph Verderber, Ann Elder, and Ernest Weiler, "An Analysis of Student Communication Habits" (unpublished study, University of Cincinnati, 1976).
3. Arthur S. Freese, *You and Your Hearing* (New York: Charles Scribner's, 1979), 67.
4. Delivered in Speech class, University of Cincinnati. Used with permission of Andy Gilgoff.

**Part One
SUGGESTED
READINGS**

Agel, Jerome B. *Test Your Word Power.* New York: Ballantine, 1984. This book is typical of many of the short and inexpensive vocabulary-building books on the market.

Arnold, Carroll C., and John Waite Bowers, eds. *Handbook of Rhetorical and Communication Theory.* Boston: Allyn & Bacon, 1984. This work is the most complete summary of current research on communication theory.

Berlo, David K. *The Process of Communication: An Introduction to Theory and Practice.* New York: Holt, Rinehart & Winston, 1960. Berlo's study is important because it was the first to consider communication as process.

Devito, Joseph A. *The Communication Handbook.* New York: Harper & Row, 1986. This dictionary of communication words and concepts is an invaluable addition to the library of any student of communication.

Floyd, James J. *Listening: A Practical Approach.* Glenview, Ill.: Scott, Foresman, 1985. This is a relatively short paperback (137 pp.).

Wolff, Florence I., Nadine C. Marsnik, William S. Tacey, and Ralph G. Nichols. *Perceptive Listening.* New York: Holt, Rinehart & Winston, 1983. In addition to its many exercises and listening tests, this book provides lengthy analyses of all kinds of listening.

FUNDAMENTAL PRINCIPLES

How do I get started? Where do I go for material? How do I put my speech together? Is rehearsal important? How do I cope with nervousness? These are the kinds of questions you need to have answered in order to learn to give the very best speeches. This four-chapter part explains and develops the steps you can follow to prepare and present your speeches. Part Two includes advice on selecting topics, writing specific purposes, analyzing audiences and occasions, finding material, organizing material, wording the speech, and delivering the speech.

THREE

SELECTING TOPICS AND FINDING MATERIAL

They say you cannot make a silk purse out of a sow's ear, and indeed, whether it is purses, buildings, or speeches, you can get a lot farther if you have good material to work with. By using a little common sense and by proceeding systematically, you will find that determining what to say is much easier than you might expect. Let us consider the essentials of good content: selecting your topic, writing your specific purpose and thesis statement, analyzing your audience, analyzing the occasion, and finding your material.

Although each of these topics is presented separately, they are not independent units. None of the steps can be completed without information gained from completing one of the other steps. For instance, "determining your specific purpose" may require insights from "finding your material" in order to phrase the purpose clearly. So even though I discuss each step separately, the steps do overlap; they are sometimes accomplished in one order, sometimes in another order, and sometimes nearly simultaneously.

PRINCIPLE I

Effective speaking begins with good content.

SELECTING YOUR TOPIC

When you are invited to speak, you are not likely to have to choose your own topic. A representative of the group asking you to speak usually tells you what the group wants you to talk about. For classroom speech assignments, however, topic selection is usually left to you. You use the same guidelines for finding a good topic for a classroom speech as for selecting topics for ordinary conversation. When you are conversing with your friends, you talk about *topics you know something about* and *topics that interest you.* For instance, if you have just seen a good movie or gone to a new restaurant or viewed a particularly good television show, you are likely to talk about the experience. Likewise, if you are concerned with the performance of a particular sports team or with the city council's position on a public issue or with the lack of progress in the development of a national energy policy, you are likely to talk about these concerns.

If you follow this advice for your classroom speech topics, you will be doing what most important speakers do. Just as Lee Iacocca talks about automobiles, Gloria Steinem about women, Jesse Jackson about black self-determination, Paul Samuelson about economics, and Billy Graham about God, for your speeches you will do well to talk about subjects that you know something about and that interest you.

Since your main areas of interest probably include your major (or prospective profession), your hobbies (or spare-time activities), or current events (or social issues), these are the areas you will consider as you seek a specific topic.

To generate a list of specific topics from these general categories, I suggest you use a form of brainstorming. *Brainstorming* is an uncritical, nonevaluative process of generating ideas, much like the old word-association process: To the words *rock music* you might associate "beat," "new wave," "punk," "electronic," or "amplifiers." When you start with a word or idea related to a subject you know about and are interested in, you can often list twenty, thirty, or even fifty other related words.

Start by dividing a sheet of paper into three columns. Label column 1 "Major" or "Vocation," label column 2 "Hobby" or "Activity," and label column 3 "Current Events" or "Social Issues." Work on one column at a time. If you begin with column 2, "Hobby," you might write "pocket billiards." Then you would jot down everything that comes to mind, such as "cue," "English," "games," "tables," "equipment." Work for at least five minutes on a column. Then begin a second column. Although you may not finish in one sitting, do not begin an evaluation until you have listed at least twenty items in each column.

When you believe your list under each column is complete, read the entries and check the three or four words or phrases that sound most compelling to you. Brainstorming allows you to take advantage of

Hobby: Computers

games	history	hardware	home units
software	CRTs	costs	chips
printers	technology	crime	memory
floppy disks	hard disks	terminals	languages
BASIC	FORTRAN	terminology	word processing
	capabilities	programming	graphics
list processing			

Figure 3.1. *Brainstorming.*

a basic commonsense principle: It is easier to select the correct answer to a multiple-choice question than it is to think of the answer to the same question without the choices. And it is easier to select a topic from a list than to come up with a fresh topic. Instead of asking yourself, "What should I talk about?" ask yourself, "What are the one, two, or three best topics that I have listed under each heading?" The computer buff whose brainstorming list is shown in Figure 3.1 will find it much easier to decide to talk about memory, computer crime, or chips from the twenty-four topics listed than to think of new choices.

If the words or phrases you select still seem too general, start a new brainstorming list with one of these topics. For instance, in a few additional minutes of brainstorming on the broad topic of "programming," that computer buff might list "writing," "goals," "debugging," "principles," "uses," "graphics," and "cost effectiveness," and have a preference for "programming graphics."

If you select two or three topics from each of the three columns of your brainstorming list (Exercise 1), you will have six to nine good topics, enough for all your speeches this term!

EXERCISE 1
Brainstorming

1. Fill in the blanks under the three headings (such as "art history" under vocation or major, "chess" under hobby or activity, and "water pollution" under current event or issue). Then brainstorm a list of twenty to forty words in each column:

	Vocation or Major	Hobby or Activity	Current Event or Issue
1.	_____	_____	_____
2.	_____	_____	_____
3.	_____	_____	_____
4.	_____	_____	_____
5.	_____	_____	_____
6.	_____	_____	_____

2. Check three topics in each column of each list that are most interesting or most important to you.

WRITING YOUR SPECIFIC PURPOSE AND THESIS STATEMENT

Each of the words you checked in the brainstorming exercise identifies a topic for your speech. Continue the preparation process by turning that topic into a specific purpose and writing a thesis statement.

Specific Purpose

Your *specific purpose* is a single statement that summarizes exactly what you want to do with the speech or what response you want from your audience as a result of the speech. The specific purpose may be stated as an infinitive phrase. The infinitive (to describe, to explain, or to prove) indicates the intent; the rest of the phrase states your goal. For instance, the statement "to explain the four steps of a four-stroke engine" is a specific purpose. It contains your intention (to explain) and the limits of the topic (the four steps of a four-stroke engine). Let's look at several other examples:

To show the importance of a good warm-up for athletes in the prevention of injuries

To describe characteristics of the five common kinds of coastlines

To persuade that states should raise their minimum drinking age to twenty-one

To explain the three basic forms of mystery stories

To motivate the audience to join Amnesty International

To give insight into the concept of Karma

Thesis Statement

Your specific purpose serves as a basis for your thesis statement. Whereas the specific purpose summarizes what you want to do with the speech or what response you want from your audience, the *thesis statement* is a sentence that outlines the specific elements that were forecast in the specific purpose. Although your specific purpose in a speech on diamonds—"to explain the four major criteria for evaluating a diamond"—clearly states what you want to do (explain the criteria), it does not tell what those criteria are. The thesis statement for such a speech would be "Diamonds are evaluated on the basis of carat (weight), color, clarity, and cut." Likewise, for the specific purpose, "to motivate the audience to donate money to United Appeal," a thesis statement would be "You should donate to United Appeal because it covers a wide variety of charities with one gift, it spends a very low percentage on overhead, and it allows you to designate your dollars to specific agencies if you so desire."

Relationship Among Elements

With any topic, a number of specific purposes are possible and a specific purpose may be explained with many different thesis statements. Let us illustrate this relationship among subject area (heading of brainstorming list), topic (word or phrase you have checked on your list), specific purpose, and thesis statement with two additional examples:

Subject Area: Computers

Topic: Essentials of computer hardware

Specific Purpose: To explain the three essentials of computer hardware

Thesis Statement: The three essentials of computer hardware are the central processing unit, memory, and input/output devices. (This topic is used as the basis for the sample outline at the end of Chapter 4. Turn to page 94 to see where the specific purpose and thesis statements appear on a complete outline.)

Subject Area: Euthanasia (current events/issues)

Topic: Legalization of euthanasia

Specific Purpose: To prove that overt euthanasia should be legalized

Thesis Statement: Euthanasia should be legalized because it relieves the pain and suffering of the terminally ill and because it is in keeping with legal precedent.

Steps for Writing Goal

Now let's consider a step-by-step procedure for writing the specific purpose and thesis statement.

1. *Keep writing until your tentative specific purpose is a complete statement.* Suppose that for the subject of dyslexia you selected the topic "recognizing symptoms of dyslexia in children." This does not yet qualify as a complete statement. Changing the wording to "recognizing four symptoms of dyslexia in children" limits what you will say to a specific number. "To explain ways of recognizing symptoms of dyslexia in children" is a completely stated specific purpose.

2. *Write out three or more different wordings of the specific purpose.* Even if you like your first statement, write at least two additional ones. You may find that the second, third, or fourth turns out to be the clearest statement.

3. *Do not write the specific purpose as a question or as an imperative.* "Can dyslexia symptoms be recognized?" is a good question for discussion, but it is not a good specific purpose because it does not show direction. "Dyslexia—living in a backward world" may be a clever title, but it, too, fails as a specific purpose for much the same reason: It does not give clear enough direction.

4. *Write the specific purpose so that it contains only one idea.* "To explain four symptoms of dyslexia in children and the need for mainstreaming dyslexics in the schools" includes two distinct ideas, either of which can be used—but not both. Make a decision. Do you want to talk about symptoms? Then the purpose "to explain four symptoms of dyslexia in children" is the better statement. Do you want to talk about dealing with dyslexics in the schools? Then the purpose "to prove the need for mainstreaming dyslexics in the schools" is the better statement.

5. *Precede the specific purpose with an infinitive or infinitive phrase that shows intent.* If you regard your idea as noncontroversial, universally accepted, or an expression of observation, then your intent is basically informative and will be shown with wordings such as "to explain," "to show," "to indicate," or "to have the audience understand." If, however, your idea is controversial, a statement of belief, or a call to action, then your intent is persuasive and that intent will be shown with statements such as "to convince," "to motivate," "to prove," or "to have the audience act."

6. *When you have sufficient information, write a thesis statement that explains the specific purpose.* You may not be able to complete this step until you have found material for your speech. For instance, you may know that you want "to explain the symptoms of dyslexia in children," but you may not yet have enough material to itemize the major symptoms. After you have studied the subject, you will be able to write a thesis statement like this one: "Dyslexics frequently reverse letters and words, have confusion between their left and right hands, have serious problems following instructions, and have difficulty remembering printed words or symbols."

Having a clearly stated specific purpose written at this stage of preparation will pay big dividends for you later. How? First, a clearly written specific purpose will help you limit your research. If you want "to explain the location of the world's greatest diamond mines," you can limit your reading to "locations," saving many hours of preparation time. Second, a clearly written specific purpose (explained with a clear thesis statement) will assist you in logically organizing your ideas. The main points of a speech grow directly from the purpose and will be forecast in the wording of the thesis statement. The main points for the specific purpose "to explain the location of the world's greatest diamond mines" will specify locations.

Classifications of Purpose

As you write a number of specific purpose statements, you may notice that almost all of them can be grouped under three major headings: speeches that are concerned with understanding information, speeches that involve belief or action, and speeches that entertain. Because speech is a complex act that may serve many purposes, these headings are useful only in showing that in any communicative act one overriding purpose is likely to predominate. For instance, Johnny Carson's opening monologue may give some information and may even contain some intended or unintended persuasive message, yet his major goal is to entertain. Your history professor's discussion of the events leading up to World War I may use humor to gain and hold attention, and the discussion of the events may have some persuasive overtones, yet the professor's primary goal is to explain those events in a way that will help the class understand them. Political candidates may amuse you with their anecdotes about life in politics and may give you some information about political issues, but their goal is to persuade you to vote for them.

Since one common way of assigning classroom speeches is by purpose and because methods of development differ according to purpose, the assignments discussed later in this book are made by purpose. Part Three deals with informative speeches and Part Four with persuasive speeches.

EXERCISE 2
Writing Specific Purposes

1. Write three well-worded specific purposes for a topic for which you indicated a preference on your brainstorming sheet (page 48). Which of the three best meets the first five tests of a specific purpose?

2. Write a complete thesis statement for the specific purpose that you believe best meets the tests.

ANALYZING YOUR AUDIENCE

Since you are planning to give your speech to a specific audience and to meet a specific occasion, you need to analyze your audience and the occasion very carefully before you go very far in speech preparation. *Audience analysis* is the study of audience knowledge, interests, and attitudes. You will use the results of this analysis to guide you in selecting supporting material and organizing and presenting the speech. For purposes of clarity, we will discuss audience and occasion separately; you will see, however, that an audience cannot be separated from the place, setting, and circumstances of the speech.

Gathering Data

Since you can't give a prospective audience a comprehensive examination, an aptitude test, or an opinion poll, you must get the information some other way. How can you gather data on an audience beforehand?

If you already know many of the listeners you can gather data from your previous observation and experience. For instance, a fraternal organization, a church group, or your speech class can be analyzed in this way.

If you don't know who the listeners will be, you can ask the chairperson or group contact person to provide information about them for you. If you just cannot get information, you will have to guess. Such things as the kind of people most likely to attend a speech, the location of the meeting place, and the sponsor of the speech may be useful. Moreover, immediately before you speak you will have a chance to observe the audience and talk with a few of its members.

What are you looking for in your audience analysis? Judgments (guesses) about audience knowledge, interest, and attitudes can be made by gathering the following data:

Age: What is the average age? What is the age range?

Sex: Is the audience all or predominantly male? female? Or is the sex of the group reasonably evenly balanced?

Occupation: Is everyone of one occupation such as nurses? bankers? drill press operators? Is everyone of a related occupation, such as professionals? educators? skilled laborers?

Income: Is average income high? low? intermediate? Is range of income narrow? large?

Race, religion, nationality: Is the audience primarily of one race, religion, or nationality? Or is the audience mixed?

Geographic uniqueness: Are the people from one state? city? region?

Group affiliation: Is the audience made up of members of one group such as a gardening club? professional organization? political group?

Processing Data

From your data you will determine how the members of the audience are alike and how they differ. The ways that they are alike or different will help you predict audience knowledge, interests, and attitudes.

The following three groups of questions give you a good working framework for such an analysis. As you gain experience, you may change wording or add other questions.

1. *What are my predictions of my listeners' interest in this topic?*

    Do my listeners already have an immediate interest? If not, can I relate my topic to their interest? It is the rare topic that will create an automatic interest, and some topics will require special creativity to make them interesting.

    What kinds of material are most likely to arouse or to maintain their interest? Audiences will be most receptive to material it finds interesting.

2. *What are my predictions of my listeners' knowledge of this topic?*

    Are my listeners likely to have enough information to allow them to understand my speech? For some subjects, special knowledge is necessary; for others, some basic level of information may be necessary before the speech will make sense (for example, an explanation of calculus requires understanding certain mathematical information).

    Will the speech provide new information to most of my listeners? As we have said, a speech that does not provide either new information or new insights will need to be reconsidered.

    What kinds of development and language will best meet their level of knowledge? Audiences will be most receptive to material that relates to that level.

3. *What are my predictions of my listeners' attitude toward this topic?*

    Will my listeners be sympathetic? apathetic? hostile? Knowing or at least attempting to determine audience attitude beforehand should help you determine procedure.

    Can I expect them to have any preconceived biases that will affect their listening, understanding, or emotional reactions?

If sympathetic, how can I present my material to take advantage of their favorable attitude?

If hostile, how can I present my material to lessen or at least not arouse their hostility?

Suppose, for instance, that you are scheduled to talk to a fifth grade class about the role of computers in business and industry. The members of the class have many things in common: (1) They are roughly the same age, (2) they go to the same school and have had similar educational experiences, and (3) they live in the same city, the same part of a city, or the same geographic area. Their total knowledge will be far more limited than that of an adult audience—especially their knowledge of the use of computers in general; their interests will be similar since they are all about the same age; their attitude about computers is likely to be open; and they are likely to be quite inquisitive. In your speech, then, if you talk about the uses of computers in an educational setting and about computers in relation to toys, games, and other objects within their experience, you will be adapting your speech directly to them.

Yet even when members of the audience are dissimilar, you can find similarities that you can adapt to. Suppose your speech on computers will be given to a local adult community organization. If that is the only information you have about the group, you could still make some good guesses about similarities: Because it is an adult organization, you can assume that most of the audience will be married and many will have homes and families; because it is a local community organization, members have a geographic bond. In addition, since they are adults, you can assume they have some knowledge about computers in general; their interests will relate in part to home, family, and neighborhood; their experience with computers will be varied—some will be very positive about what computers may be able to do for them; others will be fearful and will see the computer as an intrusion into their privacy. In your speech, then, you can allude to the influence of computers, talk about the effects of computer technology, and recognize the differing attitudes about computers.

1. Complete the following questions about your classroom audience:
   a. The age range is from _____ to _____. The average age is about _____ .

**EXERCISE 3
Analyzing Your
Audience**

b. There are _____ males and _____ females.

c. My estimate of the income level of the class is _____ below average, _____ average, _____ above average.

d. The class is basically _____ the same race or _____ a mixture of races.

e. The class is basically _____ urban or _____ rural.

2. Write your purpose sentence.

3. Based on this information, complete the following:
   a. The class's interest in the subject will be
   b. The class's knowledge of the subject will be
   c. The class's attitude toward the subject will be
   d. As a result, I will have to make sure that I

ANALYZING THE OCCASION

While you are analyzing your audience, you will also want to analyze the occasion and the effect it will have on both speech preparation and presentation. Your analysis should include the following five questions.

When will the speech be given? The question of *when* includes whether the speech is part of some special occasion, what time of day it occurs, and where it occurs on the program.

Some speeches commemorate a special occasion such as the Fourth of July, the anniversary of the founding of an organization, or Martin Luther King's birthday. In such cases, the occasion itself will affect the content of the speech.

The time of day the speech is presented provides a different set of problems. For instance, a speech given just before a meal presents a different problem from a speech given after a meal. Before a meal the audience may be anxious, short of patience, and hungry; an audience that hears you after a meal may be lethargic, mellow, and at times on the verge of sleep.

Equally important is where your speech occurs on the program. If you are the featured speaker you have an obvious advantage: You are the focal point of audience attention. In the classroom, yours is one of many speeches. Your place on the schedule may well affect how you are received.

In your classroom speech you will be guaranteed enough speaking time, but going first or last will still make a difference. For instance, if you go first, you may have to be prepared to meet the distraction of a few class members strolling in late; if you speak last, you must counter the tendency of the audience to be a bit weary from listening to several speeches in a row.

Where will the speech be given? The room in which you are scheduled to speak will have an effect on your presentation. If you are fortunate, your classroom will be large enough to seat the class comfortably; but classrooms vary in size, cleanliness, seating arrangements, and the like. You have to meet the demands of any situation.

Outside of the school setting you may encounter even greater variations. You should study any place in which you are scheduled to speak before you make final speech plans. If possible, visit the place and see it for yourself. Ask where you will be standing when you deliver your speech. In most instances you will have some kind of a speaking stand, but you can never count on it. You must be prepared to accept the existing situation.

What facilities are necessary to give the speech? For many speeches you will have no special needs. For some you may want a microphone, a chalkboard, an overhead projector, or slide projector and screen. If the person who has contacted you to speak has any control over the setting, make sure you explain what you need. But always have alternative plans in case what you asked for does not arrive.

What are the time limits for the speech? The amount of time you have to speak greatly affects the scope of your speech and how you develop the speech. Keep in mind that the time limits for your classroom speech are going to be quite short. Students often get overly ambitious about what they can accomplish in a short speech. "Three Major Causes of World War I" can be outlined and briefly discussed in five minutes; "A History of World War I" cannot. Although you want your topics to have depth, avoid trying to cover too broad an area.

What are the expectations for the speech? Every occasion provides some special expectations. For your classroom speeches one of the major expectations is meeting the assignment. Whether the assignment is made by purpose (to inform or to persuade), by type (expository or descriptive), or by subject (book analysis or current event), your specific purpose should reflect the nature of that assignment.

**EXERCISE 4
Analyzing the
Occasion**

1. Complete the following questions about your classroom occasion:
   a. When will the speech be given?
   b. Where will the speech be given?
   c. What facilities are necessary to give the speech?
   d. What are the time limits for the speech?
   e. What is the specific assignment?

2. Draw conclusions about the effect that the occasion will have on your speech. What is the most important factor you must take into account to be prepared to adapt to that occasion?

FINDING YOUR MATERIAL: WHERE TO LOOK

Much of your effectiveness as a speaker will depend on the quality of your material. To be sure you have the best material, you need to start with your own experiences and work outward to other sources.

Your Own Knowledge

If you look carefully at your own knowledge and experience, you will find that you already have a great deal of good material for your speeches. For instance, athletes have special knowledge about their sports, coin collectors about coins, detective-fiction buffs about mystery novels, do-it-yourself advocates about house and garden, musicians about music and instruments, farmers about animals or crops and equipment, and camp counselors about camping. For most of your speeches, then, you should be your first, if not your best, source of information. Your firsthand knowledge will contribute to unique, imaginative, and original development of your speeches. Even when you use other sources your knowledge and experience will still be an important part of your preparation.

You will want to try to verify the accuracy of key facts that you plan to use. Our minds play tricks on us, and you may find that some fact you remember is not really a fact at all. Still, verifying a fact is far easier than discovering new information.

Observation

After you have decided what you know about the topic, you can decide what you can learn by observing. Good, specific information on many topics can be gained from observation. For instance, if you plan to talk

Information for speeches can be found in many places, not just the library. Firsthand knowledge, observation, and interviews can provide unique material for outstanding speeches.

about how newspapers are printed, you can learn a lot about the operation by taking a tour of your local newspaper's printing plant and observing the process in action. Or if you plan to talk about the effectiveness of your city council, you can observe the council in action by attending a couple of meetings. Through observation you can get material that will add a personal dimension to your speech to make it more interesting.

Some people don't look for material this way because they are not very observant, but anyone can learn to be a better observer. Get in the habit of seeing, not just looking. Pay attention to everything around you. Mentally repeat important observations. And most important, take notes on what you see. Why are police officers better observers than most eyewitnesses? Because they have been trained to use their powers of observation. And they always take careful notes.

Interviewing

You can often get a great deal of valuable information from an interview. Ask yourself who are the people most likely to have the kind of information you need. For instance, for the speech on newspapers you should consider interviewing a reporter or one of the editors; for a speech on the city council you should consider interviewing a council member or the mayor. Will people take the time to talk with you? You will be surprised how cooperative people will be if you approach them correctly. When you have decided whom you want to interview, call well beforehand to make an appointment.

A good interview is a product of good questions. If you have written down exactly what you hope to find out, you will maximize the available time and you will not waste the time of people who are willing to talk with you. We will discuss interviewing in detail in Chapter 12.

A variation of the interview is the survey. A *survey* is a list of one or more questions that can be asked of a great number of people. For instance, if you want to know what students think of a particular course, the chances of the local football team, or how well the council is doing in governing the city, you can take a survey.

Sometimes a survey can be taken on one question. For instance, you could write:

> The College of Arts of Sciences is considering requiring all Arts and Sciences students to take the three-hour course, Fundamentals of Effective Speaking, for graduation. Please indicate your reaction to this proposal:
>
> _____ I agree
> _____ I disagree
> _____ No opinion

Of course, a survey can be considerably longer. The shorter the survey, the more likely you are to get a large number of responses.

In addition, you will want to make sure that you have polled a large enough group and that you have sampled different segments of the larger group before you attempt to draw any significant conclusions from your poll.

Reading

For many of your speeches, the best material will come from what you read. Effective speakers are also effective researchers. Whether your library is large or small, well equipped or poorly equipped, you have to know how to find what you need. To get started in library research you will want to use the card catalog to find available books, and the *Readers' Guide to Periodical Literature* and the *Magazine Index* to find available magazine articles. On pages 220–224, we discuss a more complete list of library sources.

The card catalog indexes all your library's holdings by author, title, and subject and guides you to the best books on your topic. Your library is likely to have at least one or two books on any subject you choose.

The *Readers' Guide to Periodical Literature* is a yearly index of articles in some 200 U.S. journals. Articles from such diverse magazines as the *Atlantic, Ebony, Business Week, New Yorker, Newsweek, Reader's Digest, Vital Speeches,* and *Yale Review* are indexed by topic. You can probably find listings for several up to one hundred or more articles in just one or two of the most recent volumes.

Your library may also have the *Magazine Index.* The *Magazine Index* is an index of nearly 350 magazines covering the past five years. The *Magazine Index* is on microfilm on a special machine that is usually located in the same area of the library as the *Readers' Guide.* Each month the editors feature a number of "Hot Topics" that are kept in a looseleaf binder by the microfilm machine.

Until you become skilled at research, you will want to consult frequently with your reference librarian, who can suggest various biographical sources, statistical sources, newspapers, government documents, and other materials the library holds that may provide material for your topic. Do not hesitate to ask the library staff for assistance. Helping patrons is one of their major professional responsibilities, and with very few exceptions, librarians are delighted to be of service.

EXERCISE 5
Listing Sources

For one of the three specific purposes you wrote for Exercise 2 (page 52), list three written sources that would provide information. (For the speech itself, don't forget to consider your personal knowledge, observation, and interviews or surveys.)

The reason for reviewing your own knowledge of a subject, and for observing, interviewing, surveying, and reading, is to find material that you might use in your speech to explain and support the points you make. Some of the material you find may be used as is. For instance, an example in the school paper of how a budget cut affects your school's academic program can be reported in the form you found it. Other material you find will be used in a different form. For instance, the height of a building, a statistic that you find in an almanac, may be used to create a comparison in your speech "The Changing Face of the City." In this section, we focus on material that you can find and use as is; in Chapter 12, we will discuss the creation of different forms of development or support using the same basic factual material. Most of the material you are looking for is factual information, which takes a variety of forms.

Eventually you will test your information to see (1) how well it supports, amplifies, or proves the points you wish to make and (2) how interesting the material will be to your audience. In your reading, you should look for examples, illustrations, anecdotes, narratives, statistics, quotable explanations and opinions, comparisons, definitions, descriptions, and visual aids.

Examples and Illustrations

Examples are single instances that show or prove a point. As you speak, your audience is going to be looking for examples. Suppose that in your speech you say, "Computers have made some colossal errors"; or "The University of Southern California has produced many of the NFL's best running backs"; or "American cars are beginning to rival the quality of foreign cars." In each case listeners are likely to say, "Give me an example."

For the statement, "American cars are beginning to rival the quality of foreign cars," you might say, "Ford Escorts and Plymouth Horizons have frequency-of-repair records that are coming much closer to Nissan and Toyota."

Examples are easy to find because the writer or speaker will often say "for example" or "in some instances" or other such words.

You should also watch for illustrations. *Illustrations* are more detailed examples. In his speech entitled "Of Mermaids and Magnificence," John R. Silber used Sam Houston as an example of a hero as outcast. He developed the Sam Houston example into the following illustration:

> Sam Houston is one type of the democratic hero: ambitious, large-spirited, driven by a personal code of honor, in touch with the people and with the land, a friend to the indigenous peoples, but a pioneer in promoting civilization in their territories. But it is surely worth remembering that Houston, honored as a genuine hero, died an outcast, despised by his fellow Texans for opposing Texas' secession from the Union. Houston and other heroes have found that doing the right thing is seldom popular and often fails to achieve success in any obvious sense. Indeed, having a clear recognition of this fact, the unpopularity of opposing the popular, is one of the traits that defines the hero—especially in a democracy.[1]

In your speech you will be able to use examples individually or in series. In the following passage, notice how Mario Cuomo uses a series of examples to support his point about the importance of family education:

> I learned to do all the basic things from my family before I ever went to school. . . . The real tough teaching jobs were left up to my mom and pop: things like tying my shoes, not playing with fire, learning my way to the potty, picking up my own toys and socks, not hitting my brother or sister, standing up to the bully down the block. In short, I learned to be a worker, a citizen, a neighbor, a friend, a husband and—I hope—a civilized human being—all under the tutelage of this marvelous university called the family— and all before I set foot in a school.[2]

Because examples help make ideas so clear and vivid, you should look for them and use them frequently.

Anecdotes are brief, often amusing stories; *narratives* are tales, accounts, personal experiences, or lengthier stories. Each presents material in story form. Do you remember the last time one of your professors said, "That reminds me of a story"? Probably more people listened to

Anecdotes and Narratives

the story than to any other part of the lecture. Because holding audience interest is so important in a speech and because audience attention is likely to be captured by a story, anecdotes and narratives are worth looking for, creating, and using. For a two-minute speech, you have little time to tell a detailed story, so one or two anecdotes or a very short narrative would be preferable. In longer speeches, however, including at least one longer anecdote or narrative will pay dividends in audience attention as well as in audience understanding.

The key to using stories is to make sure that the point of the story states or reinforces the point you make in your speech. In his speech about the importance of supervision, Joseph Toot made the point that good supervision is a lost art. To lay the groundwork for his point, he related the following story:

> I can perhaps best approach the theme of my remarks this evening by recalling to you the story of the construction foreman who was very big, very husky, and *very* tough. He invariably ruled his crew with an iron hand and enjoyed a fearsome reputation. One day, he lined up his new crew and announced to them—as was his custom—"The first thing I want you to know is that I can lick any man in my crew." At this point stepped forward one young fellow, obviously even bigger, huskier, and tougher than the foreman, who said in a quiet but self-assured voice, *"You can't lick me."* The foreman sized him up carefully, nodded his head in agreement, and replied, "You're right . . . you're *fired.*"[3]

Neither the anecdote nor the narrative need be humorous to be effective. In a speech entitled "The Soviet Threat," John Garwood made the point that the people of Russia are aware of the nature of their suppression and are willing to communicate their feelings to tourists. Near the beginning of his speech he narrated several experiences that illustrated the point. This final one in the series uses description, dialogue, and climax, which are important parts of developing a good narrative:

> One late afternoon after returning to Moscow from Novosibirsk, I was walking through Red Square on my way to Hotel Rossia when a man walked beside me and said, "Aren't you one of the Americans who visited Moscow University recently?"
> I said, "Yes, I was there."

He said, "When you get home will you tell your friends that we are not free to study, free to travel, free to read foreign journals, free to go from country to country, or place to place as you are." With this abrupt message, he disappeared in the crowd.[4]

Comparisons and Contrasts

Probably the very best ways of giving meaning to new ideas are through comparison and contrast. *Comparisons* show similarities; *contrasts* show differences. Although you can create comparisons very easily, you should still keep your eye open for comparisons in your research.

Comparisons may be literal or figurative. Literal comparisons show similarities of real things: "It costs about as much as a luxury automobile"; "It's about the size of a chestnut." Figurative comparisons express one thing in terms normally denoting another: "He's as fast as greased lightning"; "She's skinny as a pencil." Metaphors, figures of speech in which a word or phrase denotes one kind of object or idea used in place of another ("Advertising is the sparkplug that makes our system work"), and similes, figures of speech in which a thing or an idea is likened to another ("He walks like an elephant"), are both forms of comparisons.

Notice the way Stephen Joel Trachtenberg used metaphor when he said:

Yes, there are some risks . . . but they are risks worth taking. The benefits are worth the dangers. The eagle flying high always risks being shot at by some hare-brained human with a rifle. But eagles—and young eagles like you—still prefer the view from that risky height to what is available flying with the turkeys far, far below.[5]

Comparisons are also cast as contrasts that focus on differences. "Unlike last year when our entire attack was on the ground, this year we've really been passing" illustrates contrast. Or as John Diebold said, "It took Johannes Kepler, the 17th-century astronomer, four years to calculate the orbit of Mars. Today a computer can do it in four seconds."[6]

Because comparisons and contrasts talk about unknowns in terms of the familiar, they are excellent forms of explanation.

Statistics

Statistics are numerical facts. *Statistical* statements, such as "Seven out of every ten voted in the last election" or "The cost of living rose 13.5 percent in 1979," enable you to pack a great deal of information into a small package. When statistics are well used they can be most impressive; when they are poorly used, they may be boring and, in some instances, downright deceiving. How can you use statistics effectively?

1. *Make sure that the statistics are true.* Taking statistics from only the most reliable sources and double-checking any startling statistics with another source will help you avoid using faulty statistics.

2. *Make sure you know when your statistics were true.* In 1971 only 12 out of 435, or 2.8 percent, members of Congress were women. If you wanted to make a point about the number of women in Congress today, you would want the most recent figures.

3. *Use statistics comparatively whenever possible.* Notice how John Lawn uses comparisons of his statistics in the following passage:

   Drug users are 3-½ times as likely to be involved in a plant accident. Drug users are 5 times as likely to file a workers' compensation claim. Drug users receive 3 times the average level of sick benefits. Drug users function at 67% of their work potential.[7]

   In your comparisons, be careful not to present a misleading picture. For instance, if we say that during the past six months Company A doubled its sales while its nearest competitor, Company B, improved by only 40 percent, the implication would be misleading if we did not indicate the size of the base; Company B could have more sales, even though its improvement was only 40 percent.

4. *Do not overuse statistics.* Although statistics may be an excellent way of presenting a great deal of material quickly, be careful not to overuse them. A few pertinent numbers are far more effective than a battery of statistics. When you believe you must use many statistics, try preparing a visual aid, perhaps a chart, to help your audience visualize them.

Donald Baeder points out that whereas in the past chemicals were measured in parts per million, today they are measured in parts per billion or even parts per trillion. In the following passage, he goes on to say:

For those of you who have trouble imagining those proportions, let me give you two simple analogies.

One part per billion is the equivalent of one drop—one drop!—of vermouth in two 36,000 gallon tank cars of gin—and that would be a very dry martini even by San Francisco standards!

One part per trillion is the equivalent of one drop in two thousand tank cars.[8]

Visual Aids

A *visual aid* is a form of speech development that allows the audience to see as well as hear about the material. A speaker will rarely try to explain complicated material without using visual aids, such as charts, drawings, or models. In information exchange, visual aids are especially important in showing how things work, are made, are done, or are used. Some common visual aids and how to use them will be considered in Chapter 8.

Description

A *description* is a verbal picture or an account in words. We think of description as relating to concrete, specific things. Thus, we try to describe a room, a city, a park, a dog, or any other object, place, person, or thing with the goal of enabling the audience to hold a mental picture that corresponds to the actual thing. The elements of description will be discussed in Chapter 10.

Definition

A *definition* is a statement of what something is. Our entire language is built on the assumption that we, as a culture, share common meanings of words. Of course, most of us can define only a fraction of the words in the English language. For instance, a standard collegiate dictionary may have more than 100,000 entries, whereas first-year students may have vocabularies ranging from 10,000 to 30,000 words. Since many of the words we want to use may not be totally understood by our audience, we need to offer definitions when they are appropriate. And, of course, the nature of the definition will determine whether the audience really understands. The types of definitions, their uses and functions, will be discussed in detail in Chapter 11.

Quotable Explanations and Opinions

When you find an explanation or an opinion that seems to be just what you are looking for, you may quote it directly in your speech. Because we want to see *your* creative processes at work, we do not want to hear long quotations strung together representing your speech. Nevertheless, a well-selected quotation might be perfect in one or two key places. If you keep quotations relatively short and few in number, they can and should serve you well.

First, you should keep your eye open for famous quotations that will work well for you in your speech. Robert Albright, president of Johnson C. Smith University, used a Victor Hugo quotation to show that the time for excellence is now: "There is one thing stronger than all the armies in the world, and that is an idea whose time has come."[9]

Second, look for particularly clear, concise statements of ideas that will work well for you, regardless of their literary merit. In the following passage, notice how Willard Butcher helps add force to his point with a short quotation:

> I believe we have one critical task: *to go public.* We must take our message directly into American homes . . . to the people . . . to the ultimate deciders of our society's fate. We need nothing less than a major and sustained effort in the marketplace of ideas. As Judge Learned Hand noted, "Words are not only the keys to persuasion but the triggers of action."[10]

One last point—if you use a direct quotation, you should give credit to the source. The use of any quotation or close paraphrase that is not documented is plagiarism.

FINDING YOUR MATERIAL: HOW TO RECORD

In your research (including not only printed sources, but also personal knowledge, observation, and interviews), you will find specific materials that you will want to save to use in your speech. How should you record these materials? Since you will use only some of the material and can never be sure of the order in which you will use the material, you need to record the material so you can easily select and move it around. The *notecard method* is probably the best.

Record each item of information on a separate 3-by-5-inch or 4-by-6-inch card. Although it may seem easier to record materials from one source on a single sheet of paper (or to photocopy source material), sorting and arranging material is much easier when each item is recorded separately. On each card, indicate the source, the name of the author if one is given, and the page number from which it was

```
┌─────────────────────────────────────────────────┐
│                                                 │
│    Topic:  Women's pay--age contrasts           │
│                                                 │
│    "A Labor Department study shows that         │
│    women 45 or older make only 61% of what      │
│    men earn, but those under 20 make 92%."      │
│                                                 │
│                    "Battle of the Sexes,"       │
│                    Forbes, April 6, 1987, p.13  │
│                                                 │
└─────────────────────────────────────────────────┘
```

Figure 3.2. *Example of a notecard recording information.*

taken. Should you decide to quote directly or to reread the source material, you will know where it came from. Figure 3.2 illustrates a useful notecard form.

How many sources should you use? As a rule, you should never use fewer than three sources. One-source speeches often lead to plagiarism; furthermore, a one- or two-source speech just does not give you sufficient breadth of material. By selecting, combining, adding, cutting, and revising, you will develop an original approach to your topic.

In the next two chapters we will examine how to organize, develop, and adapt material to your audience.

From sources you identified in Exercise 5 (page 61), find one example of each of the following and write a notecard for each: example, illustration, comparison, statistics, and quotation. On your notecards, be sure to cite the title, source, date, and page number of the article.

**EXERCISE 6
Note Cards**

NOTES

1. John R. Silber, "Of Mermaids and Magnificence," *Vital Speeches,* July 15, 1986, 591.
2. Mario M. Cuomo, "The Family," *Vital Speeches,* February 15, 1980, 268.

3. Joseph F. Toot, Jr., "The Lost and Crucial Art," *Vital Speeches,* February 1, 1980, 236–237.
4. John D. Garwood, "The Soviet Threat," *Vital Speeches,* May 15, 1980, 459.
5. Stephen Joel Trachtenberg, "Five Ways in Which Thinking Is Dangerous," *Vital Speeches,* August 15, 1986, 653.
6. John Diebold, "The Impact of the Information Age on Science," *Vital Speeches,* February 1, 1986, 244.
7. John C. Lawn, "Drugs in America," *Vital Speeches,* March 15, 1986, 323.
8. Donald L. Baeder, "Chemical Wastes," *Vital Speeches,* June 1, 1980, 497.
9. Robert L. Albright, "New Visions, New Vistas," *Vital Speeches,* May 1, 1986, 434.
10. Willard C. Butcher, "Going Public for the Private Enterprise System," *Vital Speeches,* February 15, 1980, 266.

FOUR

ORGANIZING SPEECH MATERIAL

When you have enough material for a speech, you can begin to organize it in a usable form. A speech can be organized in many different ways. You want to find or create the way that makes the most sense and best achieves your goal.

From the beginning of the organizational process, you should work in outline form. Your goal is to develop a complete speech outline, which is a short, complete-sentence representation of the speech. The value of working with an outline is that you can test the logic, development, and overall strength of the structure of your speech before you begin to practice the wording or the delivery. In this chapter, we discuss the development of each part of the outline: the body, the introduction, and the conclusion. We conclude the chapter by examining a complete outline and discussing the tests you should make before practicing the speech.

PRINCIPLE II

Effective speaking involves organizing material so that it develops and heightens the speech's specific purpose.

PREPARING THE BODY OF THE SPEECH

You may assume that since the introduction is the first part of the speech the audience hears, you should outline it first. If you think about it, however, you will realize that it is very hard to work on an introduction until you have considered the material you will be introducing. Unless you have a very good idea of what will be in the speech, you should probably begin by outlining the body.

To organize the body, select and state the main points, determine the best order, and then work on outlining the material that explains or supports the main points.

Selecting and Stating Main Points

Main points are the key building blocks of your speech. If your audience remembers nothing else about the speech, you expect it to remember the main points. Since main points are so important, they should be carefully selected and worded.

If your specific purpose is well written, the main-point ideas will already be stated or suggested. For instance, what would be the main points for a speech that has the specific purpose, "to explain the four most important guidelines for planting roses"? Each main point would be one of the four guidelines. If the thesis statement is well written at this stage of preparation, selection and statement of main points are even easier. If the thesis statement is, "Roses should be planted in an area that receives morning sun, is close to a supply of water, contains well-drained soil, and is away from trees and shrubs," writing out the main points will be no problem whatsoever. In outline form, the main points would be written:

I. Roses should be planted in an area that receives four to six hours of morning sun.
II. Roses should be planted close to a supply of water.
III. Roses should be planted in an area with good, well-drained soil.
IV. Roses should be planted in an area away from other trees and shrubs.

When you are satisfied with the content of the main points, test their wording to make sure they are complete sentences that are specific, vivid, and parallel in structure. Main points are *specific* when their wording tells exactly what you mean. Main points are *vivid* when their wording arouses interest. Main points are *parallel* when their wording follows the same structural pattern, often using the same introductory words for each main point. To illustrate well-worded main points, let us examine three contrasting ways of stating the same main points.

Specific Purpose: To explain the insights our clothes give us into our society.

Thesis Statement: Our clothing gives us insight into the casual approach, youthful look, similarity in men's and women's roles, and lack of visual distinction between the rich and the poor.

Set 1	Set 2	Set 3
I. Casual	I. They are casual.	I. Our clothes indicate our casual look.
II. Youthful	II. They are youthful.	II. Our clothes indicate our emphasis on youthfulness.
III. Similarities	III. There is a similarity between men's and women's roles.	III. Our clothes indicate the similarity in men's and women's roles.
IV. Little distinction	IV. There is little distinction between the rich and the poor.	IV. Our clothes indicate the lack of visual distinction between the rich and the poor.

The labels in the first column indicate only the subject areas. Although the words *casual, youthful, similarities,* and *little distinction* relate to the purpose and indicate the subject areas of the thesis statement, how they are related is unknown. In the second set, the complete-sentence main points are clearer than the labels. Nevertheless, the use of *they* and *there* with the verb *to be* makes the statements vague.

Notice the significant improvement in the third set. Not only do the main points include each of the classifications, but also their wording explains the relationships of the categories to the purpose sentence. In addition, starting each with "Our clothes indicate" makes the main points parallel. If the audience remembers only the main points of set 3, they will know exactly what our clothes tell us about our society.

As you begin to phrase prospective main points, you may find your list growing to five, seven, or even ten points that seem to be main ideas. Since every main point must be developed in some detail, it is usually impractical to have more than two to five main points. If you have more than five, you need to rework your specific purpose to limit the number of points or you need to group similar ideas under a single heading.

Determining the Best Order

An audience is likely to understand and remember main points better if they follow some identifiable order. Time order, space order, topic order, and problem-solution order are four of the most common ways to order main points. On pages 259–262, we consider additional ways of ordering points that may be used for persuasive speeches.

Time order. *Time order* is an order that follows a chronological sequence of ideas or events. It tells the audience that there is a particular importance to the sequence as well as to the content of those main points. This kind of order often evolves when you are explaining how to do something, how to make something, how something works, or how something happened. For each of the following examples, notice how the order of the main points is as important to the speech's idea as the wording of the main points.

Specific Purpose: To explain the four simple steps involved in antiquing a table.

Thesis Statement: Antiquing a table can be accomplished by following four steps: cleaning the table, painting the base coat, applying the antique finish, and shellacking.

  I. Clean the table thoroughly.
 II. Paint the base coat right over the old surface.
III. Apply the antique finish with a stiff brush, sponge, or piece of textured material.
 IV. Apply two coats of shellac to harden the finish.

Specific Purpose: To explain the path followed by a Roman citizen as he progressed upward in government office.

Thesis Statement: As he progressed upward in government office, a Roman citizen followed the path of gaining military experience, serving as a quaester, serving as aedile, serving as praetor, and finally obtaining a consulship.

I. Before he was eligible for office, a young Roman needed ten years' military experience.
II. At age twenty-eight, he was eligible for the office of quaester.
III. The office of aedile, next in line, could be skipped.
IV. After serving as aedile, or quaester if he skipped aedile, a Roman could become a praetor.
V. At age forty-two, the Roman could obtain a consulship.

Space order. *Space order* is an order that follows a spatial relationship of main points and is likely to be used in descriptive, informative speeches. If your intent is to explain a scene, place, object, or person in terms of its parts, a space order will allow you to put emphasis on the description, function, or arrangement of those parts. Because we remember best when we see a logical pattern to the development, you should proceed from top to bottom, left to right, inside to outside, or any constant direction that the audience can follow visually. For each of the following examples, notice how the order proceeds spatially:

Specific Purpose: To describe the Student Union.

Thesis Statement: The game room is in the basement, dining rooms are on the first floor, and meeting rooms and offices are on the top three floors.

I. The basement contains the game room.
II. The first floor contains the various dining rooms.
III. The second, third, and fourth floors contain meeting rooms and offices.

Specific Purpose: To describe the three layers that make up the earth's atmosphere.

Thesis Statement: The earth's atmosphere comprises the troposphere, the stratosphere, and the ionosphere.

I. The troposphere is the inner layer of the atmosphere.
II. The stratosphere is the middle layer of the atmosphere.
III. The ionosphere is the succession of layers that constitute the outer regions of the atmosphere.

Topic order. *Topic order* is an arbitrary order of main points that develop the speech purpose. At your discretion, points may go from general to specific, least important to most important, or in some other logical order. If all the topics are of equal weight, their order is unimportant; if topics vary in weight and audience importance, how you order them may well influence whether your audience understands or accepts them. Although the relationship of the wording of the topics to the thesis statement is arbitrary, the following four examples illustrate some of the major possibilities.

In many informative speeches, the main points are written to spell out the topics that are stated in the thesis statement. The first example illustrates the identification of topics.

Specific Purpose: To explain the major roles of the presidency.

Thesis Statement: The president is chief of foreign relations, commander in chief of the armed forces, head of his party, and head of the executive branch.

   I. The president is chief of foreign relations.
  II. The president is commander in chief of the armed forces.
 III. The president is the head of his party.
 IV. The president is the head of the executive branch.

The second example illustrates writing main points as definitions of the topics stated in the thesis statement.

Specific Purpose: To indicate three elements of extrasensory perception.

Thesis Statement: Telepathy, clairvoyance, and precognition are three elements of extrasensory perception.

   I. Telepathy refers to the communication of an idea from one person to another without benefit of the normal senses.
  II. Clairvoyance refers to seeing events and objects that take place elsewhere.
 III. Precognition refers to the ability to know what is going to happen before it happens.

The third example illustrates writing each topic stated in the thesis statement as a cause.

Specific Purpose: To explain the major causes of juvenile crime.

Thesis Statement: The major causes of juvenile crime are poverty, lack of discipline, and broken homes.

   I. One major cause is poverty.
  II. A second major cause is lack of discipline.
 III. A third major cause is broken homes.

The fourth example illustrates writing each topic stated in the thesis statement as a reason. Although a statement-of-reasons order may be appropriate for an informative speech, it is more likely to be the organization for a persuasive speech.

Specific Purpose: To motivate the class to give to United Appeal.

Thesis Statement: The reasons for giving to United Appeal are that one agency covers many charities, you can determine where your money goes, and administrative costs are low.

   I. The United Appeal combines a wide variety of charities.
  II. You can determine who gets all or most of your money.
 III. Administrative costs are very low, so most money goes to the charities themselves.

As we will see in the chapter on persuasion, there are many variations of the topic-order method.

Problem-solution order. *Problem-solution order* is a kind of organization in which the main points are written to show that (1) there is a problem that requires a change in attitude or behavior (or both), (2) the solution you are presenting will solve the problem, and (3) the solution you are presenting is the best way to solve the problem. The problem-solution organization works best for a persuasive speech: You want to prove to the audience that a different solution is needed to remedy a major problem.

Specific Purpose: To convince the audience that a minimum annual cash income should be guaranteed to families with incomes below $7500.

Thesis Statement: A minimum annual cash income should be guaranteed to families with an income below $7500 because nearly 20 percent of the people in the United States live on incomes below this level, because such a guaranteed income would eliminate poverty, and because such an income is better than welfare.

I. Nearly 20 percent of the people in the United States are living on incomes below the poverty level of $7500.
II. A guaranteed cash income would eliminate the problem of poverty for these people.
III. A guaranteed cash income is a much better solution than the present welfare system.

Summary of Guidelines

Let's summarize the guidelines for stating the main points that we have just discussed. To serve as a visual example, let us reproduce the outline of the main points we discussed on page 73.

Specific Purpose: To explain the insights our clothes give us into our society.

Thesis Statement: Our clothing gives insight into the casual approach, youthful look, similarity in men's and women's roles, and lack of visual distinction between the rich and the poor.

I. Our clothes indicate our casual look.
II. Our clothes indicate our emphasis on youthfulness.
III. Our clothes indicate the similarity in men's and women's roles.
IV. Our clothes indicate the lack of visual distinction between the rich and the poor.

1. *State each main point as a complete sentence.* Notice each of the four main points is a complete sentence.

2. *State each main point in a way that develops the key words in the specific purpose.* Since the specific purpose speaks of "insights," then each main point is an insight; if the specific purpose speaks of the "steps" involved, then each main point should be a step. If you have written the thesis statement correctly, you will already have part of the wording for each main point.

3. *State each main point as specifically and as concisely as possible.* For example, saying "Our clothes indicate our emphasis on youth-

fulness" is more concise than saying "The clothes in our society indicate the emphasis most of us are likely to place on trying to look as youthful as we can."

4. *State main points in parallel language.* Because the first main point says "Our clothes indicate . . . ," each of the other main points should also begin "Our clothes indicate. . . ."

5. *Limit the number of main points to a maximum of five.* If you have more than five points, you are likely to find that two or more of the points can be placed under a broader heading. For guidelines on grouping main points, see page 189.

6. *Organize the main points so that they follow a time order, space order, topic order, or problem-solution order.* In this example, the main points follow a topic order.

Taken collectively, the main points outline the structure of your speech. Whether your audience understands, believes, or appreciates what you have to say will usually depend upon how you develop those main points.

In Chapter 3 you learned to look for examples, illustrations, statistics, comparisons, and quotations. Now you must select the most relevant of those materials and decide how you will use them to develop each of the main points.

Selecting and Outlining Supporting Material

1. *List supporting material.* First, write down each main point and under it state the information that you believe develops that main point. For example, for the first main point of a speech with the specific purpose "To explain the criteria for evaluating diamonds":

I. Carat is the weight of a diamond.
Recently standardized.
Used to be weighed against the seed of the carob.
Now the weight is a standard 200 milligrams.
Weight is also shown in points.
How much a diamond costs depends on its size.
But the price doesn't go up in even increments—it multiplies. A ½-carat diamond costs $1000; a 1-carat, $3000.
The reason involves the amount of rock that has to be mined.

2. *Outline the material.* Once you have listed the items of information that make the point, subordinate material to show the relationships between and among ideas. Use a consistent set of symbols and indent some ideas more than others to accomplish this organization. For example, organization of the statements about diamonds might evolve into the following outline:

I. Carat is the weight of a diamond.
   A. Diamond weight has only recently been standardized.
      1. Originally, merchants measured the weight of a diamond against a carob seed.
      2. Now the carat has been standardized as 200 milligrams.
   B. As diamond weights increase, costs multiply.
      1. A ½-carat stone will cost about $1000.
      2. A 1-carat stone will cost about $3000.

For each of the subpoints you should have various examples, illustrations, anecdotes, and other material to use in the speech itself. Put down enough material on paper so that you can test both the quality and the quantity of your material.

PREPARING THE INTRODUCTION

Now that the body of the speech is ready for practice, you can concentrate on ways of beginning your speech. Let's consider what you hope to accomplish in a speech introduction.

Goals of the Speech Introduction

A good introduction will (1) get initial attention, (2) create a bond of goodwill between you and your audience, and (3) lead into the content of your speech. Let us look at these goals separately.

Getting attention. Although your audience is captive (few will get up and leave), its physical presence does not guarantee that the members will listen. Many audiences are like the one you face in class: a group of people who, though they may not throw tomatoes, have little motivation for giving undivided attention. They hope they will like your speech, but if they do not, they can always daydream. So, the first goal is to create an opening that will win listeners' undivided attention. You may get attention by pounding on the stand, by shouting "Listen!" or by telling a joke, but the attention will be short-lived if it doesn't lead well into the body of the speech. The opening sentence (or more, depending on the length of the speech) *directs* attention to the body of the speech.

Creating a bond of goodwill.   If the audience has heard you before, it may be looking forward to hearing you again. On the other hand, members of the audience may not know you at all. Or they may even view you as a potential threat, as a person who will tell them things they do not want to hear, who will make them feel uncomfortable, or who will make them work. If they are going to invest time listening to you, they have to be assured that you are okay. To meet this second goal your opening must make the audience feel good about listening to you. Creating goodwill may be done with a separate statement, but in most speeches it is done through the sincerity of your voice and your apparent concern for the audience as people. Although the importance of creating goodwill is less in an informative speech, it is vital in a persuasive speech.

Leading into the content.   Third, the introduction must focus audience attention on the goal of the speech—usually you just tell your listeners what you are going to talk about. For instance, after your attention getter, you may say directly, "In this speech I'll show you the five steps in creating a gourmet's delight." In persuasive speeches, you may be less direct and keep the audience in suspense until their attention is firmly established. We will discuss indirect approaches when we consider alternate organizations in the persuasive speaking section.

Since a thesis statement as a forecast of your main points can be used to lead into the speech, it is written as the last point of your outline of the speech introduction (as you will see in the model outline on pages 94–95). If there is some strategic reason for *not* stating the thesis statement, write it on the outline, but put it in parentheses. This means that your speech has a thesis statement, but that you have a reason for not stating it in the introduction.

Typical Introductions

How you begin your speech is largely up to your imagination. The only way to be sure that your speech introduction is a winner is to try three to five different ones in practice and pick the one that seems best.

How long should the introduction be? Introductions by professional speakers vary widely in length. Yours should be long enough to put the audience in the frame of mind that will encourage them to hear you out—and, of course, the shorter the speech, the shorter the introduction.

The seven types of introductions included in this section will work for both short and long speeches.

Startling statement.   Especially in a short speech, the kind you will be giving in your first few assignments, you must get your listeners' attention and focus on the topic quickly. One excellent way to do this is to make a startling statement that will penetrate various competing thoughts and go directly to the listener's mind. The following two openings illustrate the attention-getting effect:

> If I came before you with a pistol pointed at you, you would be justifiably scared. But at least you would recognize the danger to your life. Yet every day we let people fire away at us with messages that are dangerous to our pocketbooks and our minds, and we seldom say a word. I'm talking about television advertisers.

> History reveals that twenty-two civilizations have risen and declined or disappeared during the life of human beings on this earth. Today I'd like to discuss with you why civilizations rise and fall.[1]

Question.   The direct question is another way to get your listeners thinking about your ideas. Like the startling statement, this opening is also adaptable to the short speech. The question has to have enough importance to be meaningful to the audience. Notice how a student began her speech on counterfeiting with a series of short questions:

> What would you do with this ten-dollar bill if I gave it to you? Take your friend to a movie? Treat yourself to a pizza and drinks? Well, if you did either of these things, you could get in big trouble—this bill is counterfeit!

Story.   Since nearly everyone enjoys a good story, it is a sure way to get audience attention. However, remember that a good opening must lead into the speech as well as get attention. If your story does both, you probably have an unbeatable opening. If it is not related to the subject, save it for another occasion. Since most good stories take time to tell, they are usually more appropriate for longer speeches. Still, you can occasionally find a short one that is just right for your speech. How do you like this one for the opening to a speech entitled "Making Money from Antiques"?

At a recent auction, bidding was particularly brisk on an old hand-blown whiskey bottle, and finally a collector on my left was the successful taker at $50. When the purchase was handed over to him, an aged but sharp-eyed farmer standing nearby leaned over and took a good look at the bottle. "My God," he gasped to his friend, "it's empty!" To that farmer an empty bottle wasn't worth much. But in today's world anything that's empty might be worth a fortune—if it's old enough. Today I want to talk with you about what might be lying around your basement or attic that's worth real money—a branch of antiques called "collectibles."

Personal reference. Since you want to build goodwill with your audience, a direct personal reference may be a particularly good opening. Of course, any good opening has an element of audience adaptation, but the personal reference is directed solely to that end. A personal-reference opening like this one on exercising may be suitable for any length of speech:

Say, were you panting when you got to the top of those four flights of stairs this morning? I'll bet there were a few of you who vowed you're never going to take a class on the top floor of this building again. But did you ever stop to think that maybe the problem isn't that this class is on the top floor of the building? It just might be that you are not getting enough exercise.

Quotation. A particularly vivid or thought-provoking quotation makes an excellent introduction for any length speech. Still, you need to use your imagination to develop the quotation so that it yields maximum benefits.

Notice how this speaker uses the quotation opening:

George Bernard Shaw once wrote, "The road to hell is paved with good intentions." Probably no statement better describes the start of our tort system in this country. With the best of intentions, the scales of a system designed to render justice have been tipped. The balance has moved so far toward the desire to compensate all injuries and all losses that the overall cost to society has become too high. We have reached a point where exposure to liability is becoming almost limitless and incalculable, making everyone—governments, businesses and individuals—a victim.[2]

Suspense. An extremely effective way of gaining attention is through suspense. If you can start your speech in a way that gets the audience to ask, "What is he leading up to?" you may well get it hooked for the entire speech. The suspense opening is especially valuable when the topic is one that the audience might not ordinarily be willing to listen to if started in a less dramatic way.

Consider the attention-getting value of the following:

It costs the United States $20 billion in *one* year. It has caused the loss of more jobs than a recession. It has caused the death of more than 35,000 Americans. No, I'm not talking about a war; but it is a problem just as deadly. The problem is alcoholism.

Compliment. It feels good to be complimented. We like to believe we are important. Although politicians often overdo the compliment, it is still a powerful opening when it is well used. Consider the following opening on the free economic system:

Thank you, Ladies and Gentlemen. I am honored to be speaking to such a fine group of concerned Americans. Your membership in the United States Industrial Council, and your presence at today's National Issues Seminar, affirm your belief in the central role played by millions of individual businesses in creating jobs, wealth and managerial skills for a world that desperately needs all three.[3]

Selecting Your Introduction

How do you know whether the introduction you have drafted meets the goals for your speech? You cannot tell unless you compare it with something. I suggest that you work on three or four different introductions, then pick the one you like best.

For instance, if you were giving a speech on juggling, you might prepare the following three introductions:

It takes physical skill, agility, and dexterity. It promotes an overall mind and body balance. It is meditation and it is relaxation. What am I talking about? The art of juggling. Today, I'd like to teach you how to juggle.

They called him the Lord of the Rings. Cool, confident, and graceful, Anthony Gados recently won the overall title in the thirty-ninth annual International Jugglers' Association competition with a score of 94.83 out of 100, which is five full points above the highest score ever achieved. He can juggle eight rings, nine balls, and almost anything else, and he makes an average of $1000 per show. Also, Anthony was scolded at the IJA for spitting milk at his brother. You see, Anthony is only thirteen years old, and he's the world's juggling genius. Today, I'd like to teach you what Anthony could do at the age of five, the three-ball cascade.

One night on the David Letterman show, I saw a man juggle a chili dog, a mug of beer, and a slinky. As I watched him, I said to myself, "Nancy, if this man can juggle a chili dog, a mug of beer, and a slinky, you can juggle three stupid beanbags." So, I started off with a mission—to teach myself how to juggle. And I did. Today, I'd like to teach you the basic steps in juggling.

Which introduction do you prefer?

Although each has been discussed individually, the various types of introductions may be used alone or in combination, depending on the time you have available and the attitude of your audience. The introduction is not going to make your speech an instant success, but an effective introduction will get an audience to look at you and listen to you. That is about as much as you have a right to ask of an audience during the first minute or two of your speech.

For the topic that you are planning to use for your first speech, prepare three separate introductions that would be appropriate for your classroom audience. Which is the best? Why?

**EXERCISE 7
Speech
Introductions**

PREPARING THE CONCLUSION

Shakespeare said, "All's well that ends well," and nothing could be truer of a good speech. The conclusion offers you one last chance to hit home with your point. Too many speakers either end their speeches so abruptly that the audience is startled or ramble on aimlessly until

A well-prepared and well-delivered conclusion will help the audience remember your message. Although the conclusion may only constitute 5 percent of the total speech, it deserves more than 5 percent of your preparation time.

they exhaust both the topic and the audience. A poor conclusion (or no conclusion at all) can destroy much of the impact of an otherwise very effective speech. Even the best conclusion cannot do much for a poor speech; but it can help heighten the effect of a good speech.

Goals of Conclusions

What is a conclusion supposed to do and how can you make your conclusion do that? A conclusion has two major goals: (1) wrapping up the speech in a way that reminds the audience of what you have said and (2) hitting home in such a way that the audience will remember your words or consider your appeal. Look at it this way: You may have talked for five minutes or fifty-five minutes, but when you get near the end you have only one last chance to put the focus where you want it. So, even though the conclusion will be a relatively short part of the speech, seldom more than 5 percent, it is worth the time to make it good.

The following are some of the most common types of conclusions.

Summary. By far the easiest way to end a speech is by summarizing its main points. Thus, the shortest appropriate ending for a speech on the warning signals of cancer would be, "So remember, if you experience a sudden weight loss, lack of energy, or blood in your urine or bowels, then you should see a doctor immediately." The virtue of such an ending is that it restates the main points, the ideas that are, after all, the key ideas of the speech.

Even when you summarize you may want to add something to give the summary greater impact. The following are several ways of adding to, or taking the place of, the summary.

Story. Storylike material works just as well for the speech conclusion as for the speech introduction. In his speech, "Profitable Banking in the 1980s," Edward Crutchfield ends with a personal experience showing that bankers must be ready to meet competition that can come from any direction:

> I played a little football once for Davidson—a small men's college about 20 miles north of Charlotte. One particularly memorable game for me was one in which I was blindsided on an off-tackle trap. Even though that was 17 years ago, I can still recall the sound of cracking bones ringing in my ears. Well, 17 years and 3 operations later my back is fine. But, I learned something important about competition that day. Don't always assume that your competition is straight in front of you. It's easy enough to be blindsided by a competitor who comes at you from a very different direction.[4]

Humor. You can use humor effectively in the beginning, middle, or end of a speech. Usually a humorous conclusion will leave an audience with a good impression of you. And if an audience feels good about you, they may well adopt your message.

The following conclusion of Ruth Bryant's speech on the application of economic principles illustrates the power of humor:

> There was a joke going around Moscow last year. It seems that in the big May Day parade, the final vehicle, following all of those

rockets and tanks, was a truck carrying three solemn-looking, middle-aged men. Chairman Brezhnev turned to one of his aides and asked what in the world those men were in the parade for.

"Those men are *economists*, Comrade," the aide replied. "Their destructive capability is enormous!"

Amen to that, and thank you for letting me get some of that destructive capability out of my system.[5]

Appeal.   The appeal is a common way of ending a persuasive speech. It describes the behavior you want the audience to follow after they have heard your arguments.

Notice how Reginald Jones uses figurative language to develop his direct appeal for restoration of technological leadership:

> Our economy, like Gulliver in Jonathan Swift's masterpiece, is a giant potential source of strength when freed to serve the nation. But thousands of Lilliputian disincentives and regulations—no one perhaps in itself disabling—are weakening the ability of the business community to serve.
>
> Let's untie Gulliver. The world community will be better served by a United States that has domestic and international vitality than by a weakened giant.[6]

Emotional impact.   Of all the conclusions possible, none is more impressive than one that drives home the most important point(s) with real emotional impact. Consider the powerful way General Douglas MacArthur finished his speech when he ended his military career:

> But I still remember the refrain of one of the most popular barrack ballads of that day, which proclaimed most proudly that—
> "Old soldiers never die; they just fade away."
> And like the old soldier of that ballad, I now close my military career and just fade away—an old soldier who tried to do his duty as God gave him the light to see that duty.
> Good-by.

Selecting a Conclusion

As with introductions, it is difficult to tell whether your conclusion is effective unless you have something to compare it with. I suggest that you work on several conclusions for your speech, then choose the best one.

If you were speaking on juggling, you might create the following conclusions:

So, the four steps of learning to juggle are to choose your weapons, get into position, practice your tosses, and begin the cascade.

And you can learn to juggle, too. Just follow my directions. Choose your weapons (start with something like a beanbag). Get into position. Practice your tosses. And finally, begin the cascade. Come on, you can all learn to do it—juggle!

So, if you will just learn to choose your weapons, get into position, practice your tosses, and begin the cascade, you can learn to juggle. And who knows, maybe one night you'll be on the David Letterman show.

For the topic you are planning to use for your first speech, prepare three different conclusions you could use.

EXERCISE 8 Speech Conclusions

WRITING A TITLE

For most of your classroom speeches, no title for your speech will be necessary, unless your professor requires one. You will be called upon to speak, you will walk to the front of the class, and you will begin. But in many real-life situations you will want a title. A title is probably necessary when you are going to be formally introduced, when the speech is publicized, and when the speech is going to be published. Especially when the group that invited you is trying to motivate people to attend the speech, a good title may play an important part in attracting an audience for the speech. A title should be brief, descriptive of the content, and, if possible, creative.

Three kinds of titles are the simple statement of subject, the question, and the creative title. For many speeches, the title may be a shortened version of the specific purpose. For instance, if your specific purpose is "to explain three major causes of juvenile crime," the title may be "The Causes of Juvenile Crime" or, even more simply, "Juvenile

Crime." Sometimes you can put the title in question form. Depending on what you planned to do in the speech on juvenile crime, you might title the speech "Can the Causes of Juvenile Crime Be Eliminated?" In some cases, however, you may want to create some catchy title to help the group that has engaged you build an audience. Under these circumstances, you may want to go through a brainstorming process to yield a title.

The following three groups of titles illustrate the three types we have mentioned:

Shortened Purpose

The Peace Movement

Women and Work

A Good Business Climate

Selling Safety

Office Automation

Domestic Manufacturing

The Housing Crisis

Question

Too Much of a Good Thing?

Do We Need a Department of Play?

Are Farmers on the Way Out?

What Is the Impact of Computers on Our Behavior?

Is Industrial Policy the Answer?

Creative

Teaching Old Dogs New Tricks (The Need for Adult Computer Literacy)

Promises to Keep (Broadcasting and the Public Interest)

The Tangled Web (How Environmental Climate Has Changed)

Freeze or Freedom (On the Limits of Morals and Worth of Politics)

Sense and Sensitivity (The Engineer and the Public Conscience)

The descriptive statement and the question give a clear idea of the topic, but they are not very eye- (or ear-) catching. Creative titles capture interest but do not give a clear idea of content unless they include the subtitles as indicated in parentheses.

Once you have your purpose written you can write a title. When you are trying to be creative, you may find a title right away or not until the last minute.

For the topic you are planning to use for your first speech, write three titles, a shortened purpose, a question, and a creative one. Which do you like the best?

EXERCISE 9
Titles

THE COMPLETE OUTLINE

Now that we have considered the various parts of an outline, let us put them together for a final look. A speech outline is a short, complete-sentence representation of the speech that is used to test the logic, organization, development, and overall strength of the structure before any practice begins.

Does a speaker really need to write an outline? Most of us do. Of course, there are some speakers who do not prepare outlines, who have learned through trial and error alternate means of planning speeches and testing structures that work for them. Some accomplish the entire process in their heads and never put a word on paper, but they are few indeed. As a beginner, you can save yourself a lot of trouble if you learn to outline ideas as suggested. Then you will *know* the speech has a solid, logical structure and that the speech really meets its intended objective.

Rules of Outlining

What rules should you use to guide your writing of the development of the speech? The following five rules will help you test your thinking and produce a better speech. In my years of working with beginning speakers, I have observed ample proof of the generalization that there is a direct relationship between the quality of the outline and the quality of the speech content.

1. *Use a standard set of symbols.* Main points are usually indicated by Roman numerals, major subdivisions by capital letters, minor subheads by Arabic numerals, and further subdivisions by lower-case letters. Although you can show a greater breakdown, you will rarely need to subdivide an outline further. Thus an outline for a speech with two main points might look like this:

    I.
     A.
       1.
       2.
     B.
    II.
     A.
     B.
       1.
         a.
         b.
       2.

2. *Use complete sentences for major headings and major subdivisions.* By using complete sentences you are able to see (1) whether each main point really develops the speech goal and (2) whether the wording really makes the point you want to make. Although a phrase or key-word outline is best when the outline is to be used as a speaker's notes, for the planning stage (the blueprint of the speech) complete sentences are best. Unless you write key ideas out in full, following the next two rules will be difficult.

3. *Each main point and major subdivision should contain a single idea.* This rule assures you that development will be relevant to the point. Let us examine a correct and an incorrect example of this rule.

Incorrect	**Correct**
I. The park is beautiful and easy to get to.	I. The park is beautiful.
	II. The park is easy to get to.

Developing the incorrect example will lead to confusion, for the development cannot relate to both ideas at once. If your outline follows the correct procedure, you will be confident that your supporting material is relevant to the main point and that the audience will see and understand the relationship.

4. *Minor points should relate to or support major points.* This principle is called *subordination.* Consider the following example:

I. Proper equipment is necessary for successful play.
   A. Good gym shoes are needed for maneuverability.
   B. Padded gloves will help protect your hands.
   C. A lively ball provides sufficient bounce.
   D. A good attitude doesn't hurt.

    Notice that the main point deals with equipment. A, B, and C (shoes, gloves, and ball) are related to the main point, but D, attitude, is not. It should appear somewhere else, if at all.

5. *Main points should be limited to a maximum of five.* A speech will usually contain from two to five main points. Regardless of the length of time available, audiences will have difficulty assimilating a speech with more than five points. When a speech seems to have more than five points, you usually can group points under headings in such a way that the number will be five or fewer. Audiences will remember two main points, with four divisions each, more easily than they will remember eight main points.

6. *The total words in the outline should equal no more than one-third to one-half of the total number of words to be used in the speech.* An outline is a skeleton of the speech and should be a representation of a speech—not a manuscript with letters and numbers. One way of testing the length of an outline is by computing the total number of words that you could speak during the time limit and then limiting your outline to one-third of that total. Since approximate figures are all that are needed, you can assume that your speaking rate is about average—160 words per minute. Thus, for a two- to three-minute speech, roughly 320 to 480 words, the outline should be limited to 110 to 160 words. The outline for an eight- to ten-minute speech, roughly 1200 to 1500 words, should be limited to 400 to 500 words.

    Now let us look at an example. The following outline illustrates the principles in practice. In the analysis I have tried to summarize and emphasize each of the various rules we have considered separately, as well as to make suggestions about some other facets of the outlining procedure.

Specific Purpose: To explain why Roquefort cheese is so unique.

Writing the specific purpose at the top of the page before the outline of the speech reminds the speaker of the goal. The speaker should refer to the specific purpose to test whether everything in the outline is relevant.

The heading *Introduction* sets this section apart as a separate unit. The introduction (1) gets attention, (2) gains goodwill, and (3) leads into the body.

Introduction

I. For millions of Americans the answer to the question, "What kind of dressing would you like on your salad?" is "Roquefort, please."

II. Yet very few of us realize how truly unique this delectable product is.

The thesis statement outlines the elements that were forecast in the specific purpose. In an informative speech, the thesis statement is likely to be presented as a forecast of the body of the speech; in a persuasive speech presentation of the thesis statement may be withheld if there is some strategic reason for so doing— if so, it should be written in parentheses.

Thesis Statement: The three distinct elements of Roquefort cheese are that it's trademarked, it's made from ewe's milk, and its distinct flavor comes from a mold grown only one place in the world.

The heading *Body* sets this section apart as a separate unit. Main point I reflects a topical relationship of main ideas. It is stated as a complete, substantive sentence. The main point could be developed in many ways. These two subdivisions, shown by consistent symbols (A and B) indicating the equal weight of the points, consider the origin and the restrictions.

Body

I. Roquefort cheese is trademarked.
   A. Cheesemakers still follow legislation of the Parliament of Toulouse that dates from 1666.
   B. All salad dressings claiming to be Roquefort must contain at least 15 percent legislated Roquefort.

Main point II continues the topical relationship. The sen-

II. Roquefort cheese is made exclusively from ewe's milk, instead of from cow's or goat's milk.

A. This particular type of sheep dates back to Neolithic times.
B. Ewe's milk is quite precious.
   1. It takes thirty ewes to produce the amount of milk that could be gotten from one cow.
   2. It takes 800,000 ewes to keep the cheesemakers in business.

III. Roquefort cheese is made from molds grown only in caves located in Roquefort-sur-Soulzon.
   A. The mold is grown in caves that were discovered four to six thousand years ago.
      1. The caves are 1-¼-miles long and 300 yards deep.
      2. The caves are made up of blocks that resemble sugar cubes.
   B. The specific mold, *Penicillium roquefortii,* grows in cracks and fissures of these caves.
   C. The mold is cultivated in bread, ground, and injected into the cheese to give the distinctive color and flavor.

Conclusion

I. We see then that Roquefort cheese is truly unique because it is trademarked, made from ewe's milk, and flavored with a mold grown in only one place in the world.
II. The next time you ask for Roquefort on your salad, you'll have a better appreciation of what you are getting.

Bibliography

"Cheese," *Encyclopedia Americana* 6 (1983): 354–358.

Lecler, René. "Hommage á Fromage," *Saturday Review* (June 24, 1972): 77.

Marquis, Vivienne, and Patricia Haskell. *The Cheese Book.* New York: Simon & Schuster, 1985.

Wernick, Robert. "From Ewe's Milk and a Bit of Mold: A Fromage Fit for a Charlemagne," *Smithsonian* (February 1983): 57–63.

tence is a complete, substantive statement paralleling the wording of main point I. Furthermore, notice that each of the main points considers one major idea. The degree of subordination is at the discretion of the speaker. After the first two stages of subordination, words and phrases may be used in place of complete sentences in further subdivisions.

Main point III continues the topical relationship, is parallel to the other two in phrasing, and is a complete, substantive sentence.

Throughout the outline, notice that each statement is an explanation, definition, or development of the statement to which it is subordinate.

The heading *Conclusion* sets this apart as a separate unit. The content of the conclusion is a form of summary tying the key ideas together. Although there are many types of conclusions, a summary is always acceptable for an informative speech.

In any speech where research was done, a bibliography of sources should be included.

**EXERCISE 10
The Complete
Outline**

Complete an outline for your first speech assignment. Test the outline to make sure that it conforms to the assignment. Title optional.

NOTES

1. Based on Howard E. Kershner, "Why Civilizations Rise and Fall," *Vital Speeches,* January 15, 1974, 216.
2. William M. McCormick, "The American Tort System," *Vital Speeches,* February 15, 1986, 267.
3. Based on Rafael D. Pagan, Jr., "A System That Works," *Vital Speeches,* July 15, 1980, 594.
4. Edward E. Crutchfield, Jr., "Profitable Banking in the 1980s," *Vital Speeches,* June 15, 1980, 537.
5. Ruth A. Bryant, "Inflation: The Seven Percent Solution," *Vital Speeches,* June 15, 1980, 522.
6. Reginald H. Jones, "The Export Imperative," *Vital Speeches,* November 1, 1980, 36.

FIVE

SPEECH WORDING

When you are ready to begin thinking about presenting your speech, the emphasis switches from what you plan to say to how you plan to say it. The next two chapters consider the question of how you get from the outline stage of preparation to presenting the speech.

If you were preparing a research paper, a newspaper article, or a magazine story, you would write out drafts of the work, criticize what you had written, and rewrite until you were satisfied. Drafting a speech in a similar way may help you. However, good writing and good speaking are not necessarily the same; good speech is not measured by the eye but by the ear. Instead of thinking of "writing out" a speech, think of "speaking it out"—think of building on your own conversational style. A tape recorder rather than a typewriter is the instrument you should use to record what you say. If you do not own a tape recorder and cannot borrow one, get friends or relatives to listen to various wordings and to share their reactions with you. Or, if you are self-conscious about practicing in front of an audience of friends or relatives, train your ear to really listen to what you say while you are practicing. You do this by trying different wordings of ideas each practice period. You will see that your mind will retain wordings that sound especially good to you and change awkward, hesitant, or otherwise ineffective wordings. Unless a speech is to be delivered from manuscript, the wording does not become final until it is actually presented to the audience.

PRINCIPLE III

Effective speaking is a product of clear, vivid, emphatic, and appropriate wording.

Written and oral language are not totally different, but if you compare tapes of what people say orally with sections of books and magazines, you are likely to find that oral language uses (1) a smaller vocabulary, (2) shorter words, (3) shorter sentences, (4) more personal words, (5) more repetition, (6) more contractions, and (7) more qualifiers—expressions like "I think," "it seems to me," "that is to say," and the like.

The steps of speech practice—including a discussion of how this practice is handled *without resulting in memorization*—will be discussed in Chapter 6. Here we will consider what criteria you can use to measure whether or not the words you are using in practice will result in an effective oral style. To put it another way, what wording can you use that will be instantly intelligible when heard by your specific audience? To help achieve an oral style adapted to the specific audience, you need to test your language for clarity, vividness, emphasis, and appropriateness.

Before we examine these criteria and show how you may meet them in your speeches, let us take a brief look at some aspects of language that affect your speech or writing.

YOUR LANGUAGE CARRIES MEANING

Many students think that once they have good material and have written a clear, logical outline, the speech will just fall into place. In short, people take wording for granted. But for many of us the wording itself becomes a major hurdle to effective speaking. For some the problem is grammar and syntax. Faulty sentence construction, use of double negatives, and disagreement between subject and verb are but three such problems that mark speakers as ignorant and detract from their speaking effectiveness. But effective speech wording goes far beyond grammatical correctness. The words you select and the way you use them affect the perception of the reality you are trying to communicate. Consider the following sentences:

The huge dog snarled menacingly as I entered his sight.

The collie barked joyfully as I came into view.

Both sentences narrate the event of a dog barking when it saw me. But the meanings a listener or a reader would get from the wording differ immensely.

In short, language is a controlling device. It is the means by which you control the perceptions that the audience gets from your speech. As a result, language is too important to leave to chance. If you are not in control of your wording, you lose the opportunity to communicate effectively.

Words and Meaning

First, we have to remind ourselves that language is symbolic. The words we use in our speeches represent ideas, objects, and feelings— they are not those ideas, objects, and feelings. The word *chair* is only a symbol for an object you sit on. The choice of words used to represent objects, ideas, and feelings is *arbitrary*—a matter of choice. Whether the word is *chair, sister,* or *predilectory,* we know that someone at some time had to use those letters (sounds) in that order for the first time. When enough people begin to use a given word to carry the same meaning, that word becomes a part of our language. Meanings for words are passed on from generation to generation. But in passing on meanings, people do not learn exactly the same meanings for words, nor do they learn exactly the same words. We must never assume, therefore, that another person will know what we are talking about just because we have used the "right" word.

Complications in Using Words

One of the major complications in the use of words is the knowledge that words carry both denotative and the connotative meanings for each of us.

Denotation. *Denotation* is the direct, explicit meaning or reference of a word; in short, denotation is the dictionary meaning. Knowing dictionary definitions is useful in communication, but even with a firm grasp of word denotations, you can still encounter problems. Let us examine a few.

One problem is multiple meanings. If we looked up the 500 most commonly used English words in any dictionary, we'd be likely to find more than 14,000 definitions. Some of these definitions would be similar, but some would be much different. Take the word *low* for instance. *Webster's New World Dictionary* offers twenty-six meanings for *low.* Number 1 is "of little height or elevation"; number 8 is "near the equator"; and number 16 is "mean; despicable; contemptible."[1] No matter how we look at these three definitions we have to admit that they are quite different.

A second problem is that meanings of words change with time. According to W. Nelson Francis, in the seven hundred years *nice* has been in the English language it "has been used at one time or another to mean the following: foolish, wanton, strange, lazy, coy, modest, fastidious, refined, precise, subtle, slender, critical, attentive, minute, accurate, dainty, appetizing, agreeable."[2] You can probably think of a word that has changed meanings during your lifetime. One example is the word *gay.* Although *gay* can still mean joyous, that meaning is becoming obsolete. If you describe another person as "gay," and you mean happy or joyous, you will probably be misunderstood; some will think you mean "homosexual."

A third problem is the influence of context. The position of a word in a sentence and the other words around it may change the denotation. When a young girl says, "Dad, you owe me a dime," the meaning is somewhat different from when she says, "Dad, I need a dime for the machine." In the first case, she is looking for two nickels, ten pennies, five pennies and a nickel, or a single ten-cent piece. In the second case, she is looking specifically for the small coin that we call a dime. Examples of influence of context abound. Think of the difference between "George plays a really *mean* drum" and "the way George talked to Sally was downright *mean.*"

Connotation. Whereas denotation refers to the most basic, explicit definition of a word, *connotation* refers to the suggestion of meaning apart from what it usually describes. Connotations often are a result of feelings that people have about the spoken word.

If a person has had any experience with the referent the word symbolizes, the person is likely to have some feelings about that word. Consider the word *home.* If home to you is a place filled with fun, love, understanding, warmth, and good feelings, it means something far different to you than it would if home were a place filled with fighting, bickering, punishment, confinement, and harsh rules.

Any word has potential feelings and values attached to it for the person using the word. As a speaker, then, you must take into account both the standard denotative meaning and the potential connotative meaning of the word to the specific person or persons in the audience. If in his speech Carl says, "Americans have very special feelings about dogs," Carl must understand that his sentence denotes a domesticated animal, a denotation that his audience is likely to share. But if he is planning to communicate ideas of warmth and happiness with his sentence he may not succeed since some members of his audience may not share this meaning—this connotation—of the word *dogs*.

If you know how others feel about the words they use, you can better understand and communicate with them. A congressional representative who is going to use words like *busing, schools,* and *taxes,* in a speech to her constituency must consider the connotations these words are likely to have for the audience. Then she must make a special effort to use the words in a way that will increase the likelihood of the audience getting the same meaning she intended.

Now that we have looked at language in general, let us discuss the four criteria we apply to the use of words in speeches. Our goal is to give guidelines you can apply to make your wording clearer, more vivid, more emphatic, and more appropriate.

SPEAKING CLEARLY

You want your speech to be clear. That is, you want your audience to have instant understanding of the words you use. Your speech will become clearer if you will learn to rely on precise, simple, and specific/concrete words and learn to eliminate unnecessary clutter.

Use Precise Words

Precise words are those that most accurately represent your ideas. Although you can never be completely sure that the word you select will create a meaning in the minds of your audience that is exactly the meaning you intended, the more precise your wording, the less likelihood of confusion.

Suppose you said in your speech, "Tom often *sprinted* for the bus each morning." Although you could not be completely sure that everyone in your audience had a mental image of Tom running as fast as possible for the bus, your chances are much better than if you had said, "Tom often *ambled* toward the bus each morning." Since *amble* means to "move at a slow, easy pace," few if any members of your audience would picture Tom running as fast as possible if you said "amble"!

In almost any situation we have choices of words, each one of which will change the audience's perception of what we mean. Suppose you want a more precise word than *said* in the sentence, "Tom said, 'That bus was never this early before.'" Notice the changes in the meaning of the sentence if you use *stated, averred, growled, indicated, intoned, suggested, shouted, purred,* or *complained.* To speak clearly, you have to know what words mean and how they relate to each other.

A good learning exercise is to play "synonyms." Think of a word, then list as many words as you can that mean about the same thing. When you have completed your list, refer to a book of synonyms, like *Roget's Thesaurus,* to see which words you have omitted. Then write what you think is the meaning of each word focusing on the shades of difference among the words. When you're done, look up each of the words, even those of which you are sure of the meaning. You will be surprised to find how many times the subtle meaning of even a familiar word escapes you. The goal of this exercise is not to get you to select the rarest word, but to encourage you to select the best word, the most precise word, to get across your idea.

As you practice the wording of your speeches, you must be constantly asking yourself, "What meaning do I want my audience to get?" Then check to see whether the words you are planning to use are the precise words for carrying those meanings.

To communicate more precisely, you may need to enlarge your vocabulary. The smaller your vocabulary, the less chance you have of communicating effectively. As a speaker you will have fewer choices from which to select the word that you want; as a listener you will be limited in your ability to understand the words used. You will recall that in Chapter 2 we encouraged you to enlarge your vocabulary by working through a basic vocabulary book and by making note of and later looking up words that people use in their conversations that you are not able to define precisely.

Although precise wording does not ensure effective communication (the person to whom you are speaking may not understand that word, or contextual factors may interfere), you are more likely to communicate effectively if your word choice is precise.

Use Simple Words

For some reason beginning public speakers get the idea that to be effective they must impress their audience with their splendid vocabularies. As a result of looking for precise words they go overboard and use words that appear pompous, affected, or stilted to the listener. Speaking precisely does not mean speaking obscurely. So when you have a choice, select the simplest, most familiar word. The following story illustrates the problem with pretentious, unfamiliar words:

> A plumber wrote to a government agency, saying that he found that hydrochloric acid quickly opened drain pipes but that he wasn't sure whether it was a good thing to use. A scientist at the agency replied, "The efficacy of hydrochloric acid is indisputable, but the corrosive residue is incompatible with metallic permanence."
>
> The plumber wrote back thanking him for the assurance that hydrochloric acid was all right. Disturbed by this turn of affairs, the scientist showed the letter to his boss, another scientist, who then wrote to the plumber: "We cannot assume responsibility for the production of toxic and noxious residue with hydrochloric acid and suggest you use an alternative procedure."
>
> The plumber wrote back that he agreed, hydrochloric acid worked fine. Greatly disturbed by this misunderstanding, the scientists took their problem to the top boss. He wrote to the plumber: "Don't use hydrochloric acid. It eats hell out of the pipes."

Of course, any number of words give public speakers difficulty. The following list gives a few examples. Why would you use

edifice instead of *building*

apparel instead of *clothing*

inter instead of *bury*

betrothal instead of *engagement*

commence instead of *begin*

eschew instead of *avoid*

nuptials instead of *wedding*

presage instead of *predict*

pulchritude instead of *beauty*

residence instead of *home*

vista instead of *view*

Use Specific/ Concrete Words

Specific/concrete words help clarify ideas. Such words call up a single image. People who don't discipline themselves to think sharply fill their speeches with words that are too general or too abstract to limit choices. General and abstract words allow the listener the choice of many possible images rather than a single intended image. The more choice you give a listener, the more likely that listener will have a different image from the one you intended.

Compare the following sentences. What's the difference in word selection?

He brought several *things* with him.
He brought *four bags of potato chips, a pound of ham, and a case of beer* with him.

She lives in a *really big house.*
She lives in a *fourteen-room Tudor mansion.*

The backyard has *several different trees.*
The backyard has *two large maples, an oak, and four small evergreens.*

She drives a honey of a *car.*
She drives an *'88 silver Corvette* that's a real honey.

People say that Morgan's a *fair* grader.
People say that Morgan uses *the same standards for grading all students.*

I just get really angry with people who *aren't honest* in class.
I just get really angry with people who *cheat on tests* in class.

What are the differences? In the first sentence of each pair, the italicized words and phrases are general and abstract; in the second sentence the italicized words and phrases are specific and concrete. Words like *things, trees,* and *car* are general—they communicate no definite visual image; in contrast, *four bags of potato chips, two large maples, an oak, and four small evergreens,* and *'88 silver Corvette* are specific—they limit what you can picture. *Fair* and *aren't honest* are abstract—they cover a variety of possible behaviors; *the same standards for all students* and *cheat on tests* are concrete—they reduce choice to a single specific behavior.

When you select a general or abstract word to carry your meaning, you are inviting confusion. A listener may take the time to ask you questions to help sharpen the meaning of your message, but it is more likely that he or she will be satisfied with his or her own meaning, whether or not it coincides with yours. On the other hand, if you select specific or concrete words to carry your meaning, a person will more likely share your meaning without having to question you.

You can test how specific and concrete your word selections are by recording portions of your practice speech. As you listen to the playback, write down words you believe are imprecise and general or abstract. Then try to think of words that would create a clearer mental picture. If your speech is not clear, it may be that your thinking is not clear. For practice, look around the room you are in and label various objects. Do you see a lamp? How about making that more specific? Perhaps it's a fluorescent table lamp or a Tiffany floor lamp. The more success you have in practice sessions in thinking clearly and using precise, specific language, the more success you will have in your speeches.

Eliminate Clutter

One of the greatest enemies of clarity in speech is verbal clutter. This clutter includes unnecessary repetition of words, repetitious modifiers, and most of all, such vocal interferences as "uh," "um," "well uh," "okay," and "you know." Not only does clutter crowd out meaning, it also drives your listeners up a wall. Although we tolerate such clutter in conversation, we are much less likely to accept it in public speeches. Clutter is particularly noticeable in early stages of rehearsal when people are still unsure of what they will say. Clutter is also noticeable when people are extremely nervous or under stress. Regardless of the cause, if your speech is cluttered, the following suggestions will help eliminate as much clutter as possible:

1. *Train yourself to hear your interferences.* Even people with a major problem are just not aware of the amount of clutter in their speech. You can train your ears in at least two ways.

   Tape-record yourself talking for several minutes about any subject—the game you saw yesterday, the course you plan to take next term, or anything else that comes to mind. Before you play it back, estimate the number of interferences or the amount of clutter you used. Then compare the actual amount of clutter with your estimate. As you train your ears, your estimates will be closer to the actual number.

   Have a close friend listen to you and raise a hand every time you say "uh," or "you know," or any other filler sound, any time you repeat for no reason, or use repetitious modifiers. You may find the experience traumatic or nerve-racking, but before long, you will begin to hear the problems before your friend identifies them.

2. *Practice to see how long you can go without using clutter.* If you can learn to practice without vocal clutter, you will do better in your speeches. Set up practice periods two or three times a week. The first few times work on talking for 15 to 30 seconds at a time without clutter. Soon you will find yourself talking for several minutes without verbal clutter.

   During practice sessions, your speaking may not appear to be natural. You will concentrate so heavily on speaking without clutter that meaning may suffer. Eventually, however, you will speak more naturally *and* listen for and eliminate clutter. As your speaking becomes less cluttered, create practice situations that may ordinarily lead to increases in clutter. If you lapse into vocal interferences when you are under pressure, mentally re-create situations where you are required to speak under pressure. Likewise, if interferences occur when you are speaking to people in authority, create practice situations where you are speaking to your parents, college professors, city officials, and so forth.

3. *Monitor public speaking.* You will be making real headway when you reduce clutter in actual speaking situations, but don't worry about trying too hard in speeches. Improvement in speeches should come naturally as a result of improvement in practice. Just as an athlete works on skills in practice but concentrates on the game in competition, so you should stress work in practice but concentrate on your ideas and on the audience when you are giving a speech. Nevertheless, if practice is successful, you will find yourself able to monitor even public speaking *without* conscious effort.

SPEAKING VIVIDLY

Clear language helps the audience see the meaning; vivid language paints meaning in living color. Speaking vividly will make your speeches more interesting. *Vivid* means full of life, vigorous, bright, and intense. If your language is vivid, your audience will picture your meanings in striking detail. Consider the following two sentences:

No one [salesperson] ever left the hotel to look for business.

Nobody, but nobody, ever left the palace, crossed the moat at Fifth Avenue, and went looking for business.[3]

The first sentence is clear; the second is vivid. Vividness gives language staying power, makes it memorable.

Vivid speech begins with vivid thought. You must have a striking mental picture before you can communicate one to your audience. If you cannot feel the bite of the wind and the sting of the nearly freezing rain, if you cannot hear the thick, juicy sirloin strip steaks sizzling on the grill, if you cannot feel the empty yet exhilarating feeling as the jet climbs from takeoff, you will not be able to describe these sensations vividly. The more imaginatively you can think about your ideas, the more likely you can state them vividly.

In addition to thinking imaginatively, vividness can also be achieved through a conscious effort to use figurative language. Authorities identify some thirty figures of speech in modern writing and speaking. I want to discuss just six that I believe you already may be familiar with and that you can use relatively easily. The first two are comparative, the next two involve sound patterns, and the final two are based on contradiction.

Use Comparative Figures

You can make your speaking more vivid through comparisons.

Perhaps the easiest form of comparison to create is the simile. A *simile* is a direct comparison of dissimilar things. Similes usually contain the words *like* and *as.* Many common cliches we use are similes. We may say, "He runs like a turtle" or "She's slow as molasses" to make a point about lack of speed; we say, "He swims like a rock" or "She's built like a pencil" to dramatize a negative description. The problem with cliches is that their overuse has destroyed the vividness they once possessed. Similes are vivid when the basis for the direct comparison is imaginative or different. Robert Schertz created a vivid simile about trucking when he said, "They also seem to regard trucks as monstrous boxcars that can eat highways for breakfast."[4] This simile provides a sharp image with a humorous touch. Likewise, David Kearns used a fresh simile when he talked about public school teachers who send their children to private schools. He said, "That's like sitting in a restaurant and watching the chef go next door to eat."[5]

Another common comparative figure is the metaphor. Metaphors are much like similes. Instead of a direct comparison using *like* or *as, metaphors* build a direct identification. Metaphors are such a common part of our language that we seldom think of them as special. For years the Pittsburgh Steeler line was known as the "Steel Curtain"; problem cars are called "lemons"; a woman may be "kittenish"; a man may be a "bull in a china shop"; a team's infield may be a "sieve."

Since metaphors can make your speaking more vivid, you should consider using them in your speeches. As with similes, try to avoid the trite or hackneyed. The following are some of the kinds of metaphors that will work for you in a speech:

> Human progress is a chain, and every generation forges a little piece of it.[6]

> An America that truly is a land of opportunity whose school system becomes an engine of mobility for the minority poor.[7]

> It is imperative that we weave our fabric of the future with durable thread.[8]

And my personal favorite:

> I can attest to the fact that this fair city must surely be the one place on earth where sound travels faster than light. Here is a circus of curved mirrors and distorted images of lights and shadows, of leaks and red herrings—where it daily becomes more difficult to separate fact from fiction.[9]

Create Vividness Through Sound Patterns

Vividness can also be built with sounds. Parallelism creates vividness through word sound patterns, alliteration through specific sound repetition. *Parallelism* is a balance in the structure of words, phrases, and sentences. The following statement develops parallelism through repetition of introductory words: "Today is the day we must think; today is the day we must weigh and consider; but perhaps most important, today is the day we must act!" This statement achieves parallelism through balance in structure: "Bill will get accepted to graduate school. Sally will get her job with the ad agency. Paul will get his commission. What will you get?" With a little thought you can build parallel statements.

Alliteration is repetition of sounds in words or in stressed syllables within words. "Her audience represented a chorus of culinary klutzes" shows alliteration through the repetition of the *k* sound at the start of the three key words. Such phrases as "forget your furry friends," "guard the grandeur," "sing a song of sadness," and "hit the heights" are all examples of alliteration.

Don't overdo either parallelism or alliteration. Each is vivid when used sparingly.

The final two figures we will consider—irony and paradox—depend on apparent contradiction for their effect.

Irony implies a situation that is contrary to expectations or a difference between what is stated and what is meant. Irony is especially effective for building vividness. Speaking of a math teacher who is audited by the IRS for errors in computation suggests irony. We wouldn't expect a math teacher to make that kind of error. Saying, "Here comes the club scholar" to a person who is having difficulties with grades is *sarcasm,* the form of irony that shows a difference between what is said and what is meant.

Paradox, an apparent contradiction, is similar to irony. Stephanie Bennet shows a paradox related to women in industry:

> If she displays typically feminine behaviors, she is rejected as incompetent; if she does not display typically feminine behaviors, she is rejected as inappropriate.[10]

Although there is irony in both clauses, the result is a paradox.

In this section we have considered only a few of the many ways you can increase the vividness in your speeches.

SPEAKING EMPHATICALLY

In a five hundred word speech, all five hundred words are not of equal importance. You neither expect nor necessarily want an audience to remember every word you say. Still, if you leave it up to the listeners to decide which words are most important, they may select the wrong ones. You are the speaker; you should know what you want to emphasize. How can you do it? Although you can emphasize with your voice and body, in this section we want to consider how you can emphasize with wording, by means of proportion, repetition, and transition.

Proportion

Proportion means spending more time on one idea than on another. For example, if in a ten-minute speech on three causes of juvenile crime, you were to spend five minutes on poverty and only two minutes each on broken homes and permissiveness, the audience is likely to perceive the poverty point as the most important because of the time spent on it.

Emphasizing a particular point creates proportion. If you want to improve the perception of the importance of a point, then you need to add examples or an illustration to build its strength. If the point really is important, you should have enough material to use to build it. Although proportioning is effective, it may be a little too subtle for some audiences.

Repetition

Repetition is another way to emphasize an idea. If you say, "There are five hundred steps, that's five hundred," the repetition will tell the audience *five hundred* has great importance and should, therefore, be remembered. Repetition is widely used because it is both easy and effective.

If you want the audience to remember your *exact words,* then you can repeat the words: "The number is 572638, that's 5,7,2,6,3,8,"; or "A ring-shaped coral island almost or completely surrounding a lagoon is called an atoll—the word is *atoll.*" If you want the audience to remember an idea but not necessarily the exact words, you may wish to restate it rather than repeat it. Whereas repetition is the exact use of the same words, *restatement* is echoing the same idea but in different words. For instance, you could say, "The population is 975,439—that's roughly one million people"; or "The test will consist of about four essay questions, that is, all the questions on the test will be the kind that require you to discuss in some detail."

Transition

Transition is a third way to emphasize. Transitions are the words, phrases, and sentences that show idea relationships. Transitions summarize, clarify, forecast, and, in almost every instance, emphasize. Of the three methods of emphasis discussed here, transition is perhaps the most effective, yet the least used.

Internal transition. Internal transitions show the relationships among ideas in a speech. Our language contains a number of words that show idea relationships. Although the following list is not complete, it indicates many of the common transition words and phrases that are appropriate in a speech.[11]

Transitions	Uses
also and likewise again in addition moreover	You will use these words to add material.
therefore and so so finally all in all on the whole in short	You will use these expressions to add up consequences, to summarize, or to show results.
but however yet on the other hand still although while no doubt	You will use these expressions to indicate changes in direction, concessions, or a return to a previous position.
because for	You will use these words to indicate reasons for a statement.
then since as	You will use these words to show causal or time relationships.
in other words in fact for example that is to say more specifically	You will use these expressions to explain, exemplify, or limit.

Because these expressions give oral clues to idea relationships, you should use them in your speeches.

External transition. *External transitions* call special attention to words and ideas. Use them to show or call attention to shifts in meaning, degree of emphasis, and movement from one idea to another. External transitions tell the audience exactly how it should respond.

First, external transitions act like a tour guide leading the audience through the speech. You use them because you do not want to take a chance that the audience might miss something important. Speakers make use of the following kinds of statements:

(At the start of a speech) This speech will have three major headings.

We'll start by showing the nature of the problem, then we'll consider some of the suggested solutions.

(After the first main point) Now that we see what the ingredients are, let's move on to the second step, stripping the surface.

Second, external transitions can announce the importance of a particular word or idea. You know which ideas are most important, most difficult to understand, or most significant. If you level with the audience and state that information, the audience will know how to react. For instance, you might say any of the following:

Now I come to the most important idea in the speech.

If you haven't remembered anything so far, make sure you remember this.

But maybe I should say this again, because it is so important.

Pay particular attention to this idea.

These examples represent only a few of the possible expressions that interrupt the flow of ideas and interject subjective keys, clues, and directions to stimulate audience memory or understanding.

SPEAKING APPROPRIATELY

Speaking appropriately is the final way of improving your speech language. *Appropriateness* means using language that adapts to the needs, interests, knowledge, and attitudes of the audience. Appropriate language cements the bond of trust between speaker and audience.

Language must be adapted to the audience. Margaret Thatcher would adopt a very different speaking style when speaking to a small group of supporters than when speaking before Parliament. Using language appropriate for the audience can create trust; inappropriate language can alienate listeners.

Let us see how you can adapt your language to your audience and avoid language that alienates it.

Audience adaptation is how you get the members of the audience to feel that your speech relates directly to them. The process begins when you examine the materials you are planning to use and continues with phrasing that the audience perceives as relating to their experience.

Adapt Your Language to Your Audience

In most situations, the more personal you can make your language the more appropriate it will be. Often by merely speaking in terms of "you," "us," "we," and "our," you will give the audience a verbal clue to your interest in them. Suppose you were talking about some intricacies of football. Instead of saying, "When *an individual* goes to a football

Use Personal Pronouns

game, *he* often wonders why defensive players change their position just before the ball is snapped," why not try, "When *you* go to a football game *you* may often wonder why players change their position just before the ball is snapped." Although this may seem to be a very small point, it may make the difference between audience attention and audience indifference.

Ask Audience Questions

Although public speaking is not direct conversation with your audience, you can create the impression of direct conversation by generating a sense of personal involvement through *audience questions.* For instance, if we take the same example we used above, we can make one more change in phrasing that would increase audience adaptation. Instead of leaving the statement as, "When you go to a football game, you may often wonder why players change their position just before the ball is snapped," why not try, "When you go to a football game, have you ever asked, 'I wonder why Kessel moved to the other side of the line before the snap?' or 'I wonder why Jones started to rush the passer and then all of a sudden stepped back'?"

Audience questions generate audience participation; once the audience starts participating, it becomes more involved in the content. One caution: Because direct audience questions—trying to get the audience to answer aloud—may disrupt your flow of thought (and sometimes bring unexpected answers), the rhetorical question that requires only a mental response is usually safer. Rhetorical questions encourage the same degree of involvement, but they are easier to handle than direct questions. Audience questions are good means of adaptation because they will work in any part of the speech.

To be effective with questions, the questions must sound sincere. Practice until you can ask questions naturally and sincerely.

Share Common Experiences

If you think your audience has had experiences like yours, share them in the speech. Talking about common experiences will allow your audience to identify more with you. For instance, if you were talking to a group of Boy Scouts, in order to drive home the point that important tasks are often accomplished through hours of hard work, you might say, "Remember the hours you put in working on your first merit badge? Remember wondering whether you'd ever get the darned thing finished? And do you remember how good it felt to know that the time you put in really paid off?" (Notice how this example incorporates common experience along with personal pronouns and audience questions to heighten the adaptation.) When members of an audience identify with you as a speaker, they will pay more attention to what you have to say.

You want the audience to identify with the common experience so that they will think about it. The following is another example of sharing common experience. Edward Reavey, a businessperson, is talking with businesspeople about a common experience:

> The deterioration of costly service is partly our fault. We experience the consumer's service problems every day. As business people we know that the same kind of treatment is being given to our customers. Still, we don't do much about it. We tolerate the terrible, when it comes to service.[12]

Build Hypothetical Situations

Although you cannot involve the audience directly with every topic, you can relate to them by speaking hypothetically. Suppose you wanted to show the audience how it could turn a cast-off table or chair into a fine piece of refinished furniture. You could start the speech by placing the audience in the following hypothetical situation:

> Many times we relegate our cast-off end tables, a desk, a record cabinet to the land of the lost—the storage room of our basement. We know the piece of furniture is worth saving, but we don't know why. That cast-off is probably a lot heavier and a lot more solid than most furniture being made today. So what are we going to do with it? Why not refinish it? Let's assume for this evening that you have just such a piece of furniture in your basement. Let's take it out of that storage room and go to work on it. Where do we start? Well, first of all, we have to gather the right materials to do the job.

Whether members of the audience actually have such pieces of furniture is unimportant. Because of the hypothetical situation, they can still involve themselves in the procedure. The hypothetical situation is another excellent way of involving an audience in your speech.

Personalize Examples

Suppose you are giving a speech on Japan. In reading the 1987 *World Almanac,* you draw the following conclusions about Japan: Japan is a small, densely populated nation. Her 120 million people are crowded into a land area of 145,000 square miles. The population density is 827 persons per square mile.

Although you have the essential statistics about population and area you will not want to present them in your speech in this form because the passage is not adapted to your audience.

Notice how the following revision would be more likely to get members of the audience to feel that the material is related to them:

> Japan is a small, densely populated nation. Her population is 120 million—only about half that of the United States. Yet the Japanese are crowded into a land area of only 145,000 square miles— roughly the same size as the state of California. Just think of the implications of having one-half the population of the United States living in California, where 23 million now live. In addition, Japan packs 827 persons into every square mile of land, whereas in the United States we average about 64 persons per square mile. Japan, then, is about thirteen times as crowded as the United States.

This revision includes an invented comparison of the unknown, Japan, with the familiar, the United States and California. Even though most Americans do not have the total land area of the United States (let alone California) on the tip of the tongue, they know that the United States covers a great deal of territory, and they have a mental picture of the size of California compared to the rest of the nation. It is through such detailed comparisons that the audience is able to visualize just how small and crowded Japan is.

Your speeches will be much more effective if you will recognize that how well material adapts to your audience is a major criterion for its use: (1) If you have choices of which material you will use, choose the material that better relates to the audience; (2) if the material lacks audience adaptation, use your imagination to adapt it to the audience.

Avoid Inappropriate Language

Appropriate language has the positive value of cementing the bond of trust between speaker and audience. If members of an audience like and trust you, they are likely to believe you. This bond of trust is built with appropriate language. The more hostile the audience is to your ideas, the more care you need to take to use language that will be accepted by that audience. Yet, under strain, you can sometimes lose your temper and say things you do not really mean or express your feelings in language that is unlikely to be accepted by strangers. If you do that, you may lose all that you have gained.

Effect of inappropriate language. You've heard children shout, "Sticks and stones may break my bones, but words will never hurt me." I think this rhyme is so popular among children because they know it is a lie, but they do not know what else to do. Whether we are willing to admit it or not, words do hurt—sometimes permanently. Think of the great personal damage done to individuals throughout history as a result of being called "hillbilly," "nigger," "wop," "yid." Think of the fights started by one person calling another's sister or girlfriend a "whore." Of course, we all know that it is not the words alone that are so powerful; it is the context of the words—the situation, the feelings about the participants, the time, the place, or the tone of voice. You may recall circumstances in which a friend called you a name or used a four-letter word to describe you and you did not even flinch; you may also recall other circumstances in which someone else called you something far less offensive and you became enraged.

The message to remember is that we must always be aware that our language may have accidental repercussions. When we do not understand the frame of reference of the audience, we may state our ideas in language that distorts the intended communication. Many times a single inappropriate sentence may be enough to ruin an entire speech. For instance, the speaker who says, "And we all know the problem originates downtown," may be referring to the city government. However, if the audience is composed of people who see downtown not as the seat of government but as the residential area of an ethnic or a social group, the sentence takes on an entirely different meaning. Being specific will help you avoid such problems; recognizing that some words communicate far more than their dictionary meanings will help even more.

We should also caution against using words for their shock value. Such language often backfires on the user. Arousing anger and hostility toward an issue often results in anger and hostility toward the speaker.

Avoiding inappropriate language requires a sensitivity to an audience's feelings. Some of the mistakes we make are a result of the innocent use of expressions that are perceived as sexist to women and racist to minorities. Although the speaker may be totally unaware of being offensive, the audience may take legitimate offense anyway.

Sexist and racist language. *Sexist* or *racist language* is any language that is perceived as negative and that occurs solely because of differences in sex, race, or national origin. Since women and minorities have traditionally been the object of such language, they are likely to be the most sensitive to its use.

The following are a few of the kinds of usage problems that you should avoid:

1. *Avoid using words that have built-in sexism such as policeman, postman, chairman.* Much more acceptable are such labels as police officer, mail carrier, and chairperson.

2. *Don't modify generic labels with the words* black *or* female, *such as* black doctor *or* female professor. For instance, people are likely to say such things as "Roberts is a highly respected black surgeon" and "Carson is a good female professor." In each case, the modifier takes away from the value of the praise. Thus, "Carson is a good female professor" means "Carson is a good professor for a woman, although compared to men she's nothing special."

3. *Do not use male pronouns when no sexual reference is intended.* Examine the following sentence: "A doctor is an important member of a community: He is respected; he is deferred to; and he stands as a role model." Grammatically, the sentence is correct, but women often find such usage offensive. Better would be: "Doctors are important members of their community: They are respected; they are deferred to; and they stand as role models." The change may seem small, but it may be the difference between persuading or failing to persuade an audience.

Using common stereotypic expressions, "Morgan acts like an old lady" and "That was really white of you, Smith," will be perceived as offensive.

Very few people escape all sexist and racist language. By monitoring your usage, however, you can guard against frustrating all communication by assuming that others will react to your language the same way you do, and you can guard against saying or doing things that offend others and perpetuate outdated sex roles and racial stereotypes.

1. *Webster's New World Dictionary,* 2d college ed. (Cleveland, Ohio: William Collins & World, 1978), 839.
2. W. Nelson Francis, *The English Language* (New York: W. W. Norton, 1965), 122.
3. James Lavenson, "Think Strawberries," *Vital Speeches,* March 15, 1974, 347.
4. Robert H. Schertz, "Deregulation: After the Airlines, Is Trucking Next?" *Vital Speeches,* November 1, 1977, 40.
5. David T. Kearns, "Economics and the Student, *Vital Speeches,* July 1, 1986, 566.
6. Gerry Sikorski, "Will and Vision," *Vital Speeches,* August 1, 1986, 615.
7. Julius W. Becton, Jr., "Emergency Management," *Vital Speeches,* September 15, 1986, 719.
8. Ronald W. Roskens, "Webs of Sand," *Vital Speeches,* February 1, 1986, 233.
9. James N. Sites, "Chemophobia," *Vital Speeches,* December 15, 1980, 154.
10. Stephanie M. Bennet, "The Re-Entry Woman," *Vital Speeches,* June 1, 1980, 497.
11. After Sheridan Baker, *The Complete Stylist* (New York: Thomas Y. Crowell, 1966), 73–74.
12. Edward Reavey, Jr., "The Critical Consumer Need," *Vital Speeches,* October 15, 1971, 25–26.

SIX

PRACTICING THE DELIVERY

When Demosthenes, the famous Athenian orator, was asked, "What is the single most important element of speaking?" he answered, "Delivery." Today that opinion is echoed by many people who say, "It's not what you say, but how you say it that counts."

Why do people place such emphasis on the importance of delivery? Primarily because delivery is the source of our contact with the speaker's mind. *Delivery* is the use of voice and body to communicate the speech's message; it is what we see and what we hear. Think of delivery as a window through which we see a speech: When it is cracked, clouded over, or dirty, it obscures the content, organization, and language of the speech; when it is clean, it allows us to appreciate every aspect of the speech more fully. Although delivery cannot improve the ideas of a speech, it can help to make the most of those ideas.

Many people believe in the myth that only those who were born with good voices or some other innate talent have any chance to develop a powerful delivery. The fact is that most of the characteristics of good delivery are more a matter of practice than the luck of genetics. In this chapter we focus on those elements of delivery that can be improved or perfected if you are willing to take the time to practice. Then we consider how to practice your speech and how to cope with nervousness. Now let's turn to the essentials of good delivery.

PRINCIPLE IV

Effective speaking requires good delivery.

121

WHAT TO PRACTICE: CHARACTERISTICS OF GOOD DELIVERY

In your speech practice, as well as in the speech itself, you should be using your voice, articulation, and bodily action to develop a *conversational quality,* a delivery that sounds like conversation to your audience. Although speech making and conversation are not entirely the same, by using the best characteristics of conversation in your public speaking, you give listeners the feeling that you are conversing with them.

Essentials of Conversational Quality

The three essentials of conversational quality are enthusiasm, eye contact, and spontaneity.

Enthusiasm.   A review of speech research shows that by far the single most important element of effective speaking is speaker enthusiasm. A speaker who looks and sounds enthusiastic will be listened to and that speaker's ideas will be remembered.

The source of enthusiasm is a real, sincere *desire to communicate.* If you really want to communicate, if you really care about your topic and your audience, your voice will show your enthusiasm, and your audience will listen.

Your ability to sound enthusiastic is likely to relate to whether you are an outgoing or a reserved person. If you are an outgoing person who displays feelings openly, you may find it easy to sound enthusiastic in your speech. If you are rather reserved, your audience may not be able to pick up the more subtle signs of your enthusiasm as readily. If you are less likely to show feelings, then you will have to work to intensify your feelings about what you are doing so that your emotions can be communicated. How can you do this?

First, make sure that your topic excites you. You cannot afford to select a topic about which your feelings are lukewarm at best. An outgoing person might be able to show enthusiasm about an uninspiring topic—a reserved person cannot. To be perceived as enthusiastic, you must be truly excited. Second, you must get involved in the material. Try to develop vivid mental pictures of what you are trying to say. Mental activity will lead to physical activity. Third, you need to remind yourself that your speech will truly benefit the audience. If you can convince yourself that your audience ought to listen, you will raise your level of enthusiasm.

Eye contact. Effective speakers look at their listeners while they talk. Listeners concentrate better on what is said when the speaker establishes good eye contact. In conversation and public speaking alike, we expect speakers to look at us while they are talking, and if they do not, our attention falters. You can maintain a certain amount of control over your listeners' attention simply through good eye contact.

In addition to holding attention, good eye contact also increases listeners' confidence in the speaker. Aren't you likely to be skeptical of people who do *not* look you in the eye when they speak with you? Aren't you likely to trust speakers who *do* look you in the eye when they talk? Good eye contact is perceived as a sign of speaker sincerity.

As you gain skill in speaking you will learn the third benefit of good eye contact, insight into the audience's reaction to what you are saying. Since communication is two-way, your audience is *speaking* to you at the same time you are speaking to them. In conversation this audience response is likely to be verbal; in public speaking, response is shown by various nonverbal cues. Audiences that are paying attention are likely to be virtually on the edges of their seats with their eyes on you. Audiences that are not paying attention are likely to be yawning, looking out the window, and slouching in their chairs. By monitoring audience behavior, you can determine what adjustments, additions, changes, and deletions you need to make in your plans. As you gain greater skill, you will be able to make more and better use of the information you get about an audience through eye contact.

What is good eye contact? It is, of course, physically impossible to look at your entire audience at once. Good eye contact involves looking at individuals and small groups in all parts of your audience throughout your speech. As long as you are looking at people and not at the ceiling, the floor, or out the window, everyone in the audience will perceive you as having good eye contact. But do not spend all of your time looking front and center. The people at the ends of aisles and those in the back of the room are every bit as important as those directly in front of you.

Spontaneity. *Spontaneity* means being responsive to your ideas and their meaning while you are speaking. Lack of spontaneity almost guarantees a lessening of audience attention to your speech. Yet many speakers deliver their speeches sounding like students reciting memory work in a literature class. They are struggling so hard to remember the words that they are not communicating any sense of meaning. The words sound memorized, not spontaneous. Although good actors can make lines they have memorized sound spontaneous, most public speakers cannot.

How can you make your outlined and practiced speech sound spontaneous? The answer lies in the difference between knowing ideas and memorizing words. If I asked you for directions to your house, you would be able to deliver them spontaneously because you know where you live and how to get there. But if I asked you to write those directions down on paper and memorize them word for word, your delivery would deteriorate. Your delivery of that information would probably sound very labored because the word-for-word language would not be a part of you—you would struggle as you tried hard to remember individual words instead of communicating ideas.

The secret of spontaneity in public speaking is to know the ideas for your speech as well as you know how to get home. You study your outline and *learn* the material you are going to present, but you do not try to memorize *how* you are going to present it. We will consider spontaneity more when we get to the mechanics of good speech practice.

Mechanics of Delivery

The essentials of conversational quality are communicated through effective use of voice, articulation, and bodily action.

Voice. Just as our words communicate, so does the sound of our voice. The meanings expressed by the way we sound (called *paralanguage*) may tell our audience what we intend and may contribute to the meanings of our words. However, *how* we sound may interfere with sharing meaning and may at times even contradict our words.

Our voice has all the capabilities of a musical instrument. How we use it makes the difference between success or failure. To begin our discussion, let us take a brief look at the speech process.

In order to speak, we force the air from our lungs up through the trachea and larynx by controlled relaxation of the diaphragm and contraction of abdominal and chest muscles (Figures 6.1 and 6.2). As we exhale, we bring our vocal folds (muscles in the opening to the larynx that help to keep food from getting into the lungs) together closely enough to vibrate the air as it passes through them. This vibration

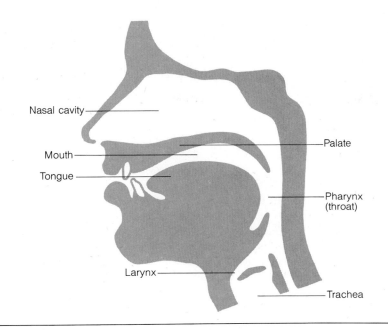

Nasal cavity

Mouth

Tongue

Palate

Pharynx
(throat)

Larynx

Trachea

Figure 6.1. *Section of the head area, showing the relationship of the nose, mouth, pharynx (throat), and larynx.*

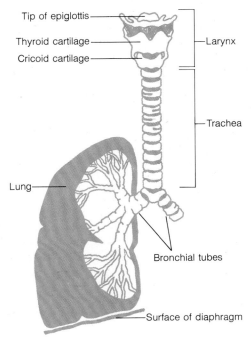

Tip of epiglottis

Thyroid cartilage

Cricoid cartilage

Larynx

Trachea

Lung

Bronchial tubes

Surface of diaphragm

Figure 6.2. *Section of the breathing apparatus, showing a lung, bronchial tubes, and trachea that lead to the cartilage area housing the larynx.*

(called *phonation*) produces a weak sound that is then built up or *resonated* as it travels through the pharynx (throat), mouth, and in some cases, the nasal cavity. This resonated sound is then shaped by the *articulators* (tongue, lips, palate, and teeth) to form the separate sounds of our language system. These individual sounds are then put together into words or distinguishable oral symbols. We call the sound that we produce *voice.*[1]

To improve our delivery we have to learn to get the major characteristics of voice (pitch, volume, rate, and quality) to work together to build a variety and expressiveness of voice that communicate our meaning.

Pitch is the highness or lowness of your voice. As we said, your voice is produced in the larynx by the vibration of your vocal folds. In order to feel this vibration, put your hand on your throat at the top of the Adam's apple and say "ah." Just as the change in pitch of a violin string is brought about by making it tighter or looser, so the pitch of your voice is changed by the tightening and loosening of the vocal folds.

The pitch that one uses most frequently is called the "key" of the voice. Although most people speak at a pitch that is about right for them, a very few have pitch problems. If you have questions about your pitch level, ask your professor about it. If you are one of the very few persons with a pitch problem, your professor can refer you to a speech therapist for corrective work. Since our normal pitch is satisfactory for most of us, the question is whether we are making the best use of our pitch range.

Volume is the loudness of the tone you make. When you exhale normally, the diaphragm relaxes, and air is expelled through the trachea. When you speak, you supplement the force of the expelled air on the vibrating vocal folds by contracting your abdominal muscles. This greater force behind the air you expel increases the volume of your tone.

To feel how these muscles work, place your hands on your sides with your fingers extended over your stomach. Say "ah" in a normal voice. Now say "ah" as loudly as you can. If you are making proper use of your muscles, you should feel the stomach contraction increase as you increase volume. If you feel little or no muscle contraction, you are probably trying to gain volume from the wrong source; and such a practice will often result in tiredness, harshness, and lack of sufficient volume to be heard in a large room.

Regardless of how large you are physically, you can increase the loudness of your voice. If you have trouble talking loudly enough to be heard in a large classroom, work on increasing loudness by increasing pressure on exhalation from the abdominal area.

Rate is the speed at which we talk. Although most of us talk between 140 and 180 words per minute, the best rate is highly individual. The test of rate of speed of speech is whether an audience can understand what you are saying. Usually even very fast talking is acceptable if words are well articulated and if there is sufficient vocal variety and emphasis.

Your instructor will tell you if he or she believes you talk too fast or too slowly. Before you can improve, you have to adjust your ear to a more appropriate rate of speed. One way to test your rate of speed is to read passages aloud to time yourself. First, time yourself to determine the exact number of words per minute you read. Then read the same passage again, this time making a conscious effort to decrease or increase the number of words per minute you read. At first, you may not be able to change the speed very dramatically. With practice you will see that you can read much faster or much slower when you want to. Moreover, you may find that a different rate of speed will sound strange to your ear. But if you practice daily, within a few weeks you should be able to accustom your ear to the change. When you can vary your reading rate, you will find that you will be able to vary your speaking rate as well. You will talk faster when the material is easy or when you are trying to create a mood of excitement. You will talk slower when the material is very difficult or when you are trying to create a somber mood.

Quality is the tone, timbre, or sound of your voice. The best vocal quality is a clear, pleasant-to-listen-to voice. Problems of quality are nasality (too much resonance in the nose on vowel sounds), breathiness (too much escaping air during phonation), harshness (too much tension in the throat and chest), and hoarseness (a raspy sound to the voice). If your voice seems to have too great a degree of one of these undesirable qualities, consult your professor. Although you can make some improvement on your own, improvement requires a great deal of work and rather extensive knowledge of vocal anatomy and physiology. Severe problems of vocal quality should be referred to a speech therapist.

It is through *vocal variety and expressiveness,* the contrasts in use of pitch, loudness, and rate, that help listeners understand your meaning. These variations give the voice the dimension that makes it easier or harder for an audience to pay attention and to understand. An expressive voice is not flawed by the two most common faults of speech melody: monotone and constant pattern.

A *monotonous voice* is one in which the pitch, volume, and rate remain constant, with no word, idea, or sentence differing from any other. Although very few people speak in a true monotone, many severely limit themselves by using only two or three pitch levels and relatively unchanging volume and rate. An actual or near monotone is likely to lull an audience to sleep. Without vocal clues to help them figure out the comparative importance of words and ideas, an audience will usually lose interest in what you are saying. To illustrate what proper vocal emphasis can do for meaning, let us work with the sentence, "I want to buy ice cream." First, say the sentence in such a way that the pitch, rate, and volume are held constant. Saying it this way represents a monotone. When you speak in such a monotone, the listener has to decide what meaning you intended. Second, say "buy" in a higher pitch, louder, and perhaps more slowly than the other words in the sentence. By stressing the one word, *buy,* you communicate the idea that you want to *buy* ice cream rather than make it or get it in some other way. Now say the sentence several more times, each time stressing a different word. With this one sentence, meaning can be changed significantly by changing only the vocal emphasis of the individual words *I, want, buy,* or *ice cream.* During an actual speech, you should give such vocal clues in almost every sentence to ensure audience interest and understanding.

The other common fault of vocal expressiveness is the *constant vocal pattern,* in which vocal variation is the same for every sentence regardless of meaning. This pattern is nearly as monotonous as a true monotone. A constant pattern is one in which every sentence ends with an upward pitch or in which the pitch goes up in the middle and down at the end of every phrase. Changes in pitch, volume, and rate will not help unless the changes are appropriate to the intended meaning. To cure a constant pattern you have to learn to correlate changes in voice with meaning.

If you talk in either a monotone or a constant pattern, you should set up a plan for improvement that you can practice every day. One such plan involves reading aloud. Select a passage and read it aloud to a friend. When you finish, ask your friend to tell you which words were higher in pitch, louder, or faster. When you find that you can read or speak in a way that your friend will recognize which words you were trying to emphasize, you will be showing improvement in using vocal variety to clarify meaning.

Articulation. *Articulation* is the shaping of speech sounds into recognizable oral symbols that go together to produce a word. Many speakers suffer from minor articulation problems of adding sound where none appears (ath*a*lete for athlete), leaving out a sound where one occurs (lib*a*ry for li*br*ary), transposing sounds (re*val*ent for re*lev*ant), and distorting sounds (tru*f* for tru*th*). Although some people have consistent articulation problems that require speech therapy (consistently substituting *th* for *s* in speech), most of us are guilty of carelessness that is easily corrected.

Articulation is often confused with pronunciation, the form and accent of various syllables of a word. In the word *statistics,* articulation refers to the shaping of the ten sounds (*s,t,a,t,i,s,t,i,k,s*); pronunciation refers to the grouping and accenting of the sounds (*sta-tis′-tiks*). If you are unsure of how to pronounce a word you are going to use in your speech, look it up in a dictionary.

Although true articulatory problems (distortion, omission, substitution, or addition of sounds) need to be corrected by a speech therapist, the kinds of articulatory problems shown by most college students can be improved during a single term. The two most common faults for most students are slurring sounds (running sounds and words together) and leaving off word endings. Spoken English will always contain some running together of sounds. For instance, everyone says "tha table" for "that table." It is just too difficult to make two *t* sounds in a row. But many of us carry slurring sounds and dropping word endings to excess. "Who ya gonna see" for "Who are you going to see" illustrates both these errors. If you have a mild case of "sluritis" caused by not taking the time to form sounds clearly, you can improve considerably by taking ten to fifteen minutes three days a week to read passages aloud, trying to *overaccentuate* each of the sounds. Some teachers advocate "chewing" your words; that is, making sure that you move your lips, jaw, and tongue very carefully for each sound you make. As with most other delivery problems, you must work conscientiously several days a week for months to bring about significant improvement.

Since constant mispronunciation labels a person as ignorant or

Word	Correct	Incorrect
arctic	arc'-tic	ar'-tic
athlete	ath'-lete	ath'-a-lete
family	fam'-a-ly	fam'-ly
February	Feb'-ru-ary	Feb'-yu-ary
get	get	git
larynx	ler'-inks	lar'-nix
library	ly'-brer-y	ly'-ber-y
particular	par-tik'-yu-ler	par-tik'-ler
picture	pic'-ture	pitch'-er
recognize	rek'-ig-nize	rek'-a-nize
relevant	rel'-e-vant	rev'-e-lant
theater	thee'-a-ter	thee-a'-ter
truth	truth	truf
with	with	wit or wid

Figure 6.3. *Problem words.*

careless or both, you will want to try to correct your mistakes. Figure 6.3 indicates many common problem words that students are likely to mispronounce or misarticulate in their speeches.

Bodily action. Bodily action serves many functions in speech. One of its functions is to stand for words—a nodding of the head means "yes," arms extended with palms down means "safe," thumbs down means disapproval. A second function is to supplement meaning—"The house is over there" (pointing), "It's about so big" (using hands to show the size), "You really make me mad" (stamping the foot). A third function of bodily action is to show our feelings—wide-open eyes for surprise, a scowl for anger, palms pressed against temples to express a mistake.

In normal conversation, bodily action often *defines* our meaning, and the same is true in public speaking. For instance, if, as you say "I am really sorry," you smile or chuckle, a person is not going to believe you. Now let's consider the principal variables of bodily action, namely, facial expression, gestures, and movement that affect our meaning.

Facial expression refers to the movement of the eyes and mouth. The eyes and mouth communicate far more than you might realize. You need only recall the icy stare, the warm smile, or the hostile scowl that you received from someone to understand the statement that the eyes (and the mouth as well) are the mirror of the mind. Your facial expression should be appropriate to what you are saying. Audiences will respond negatively to deadpan expressions and perpetual grins or scowls; they will respond positively to honest and sincere expressions that reflect your thoughts and feelings. Think actively about what you are saying, and your face will probably respond accordingly.

Gestures are the movement of hands, arms, and fingers. Gestures are usually descriptive or emphatic. When speakers say "about this high" or "nearly this round," we expect to see a gesture accompany the verbal descriptions. Likewise, when speakers say "We want you" or "Now is the time to act," we look for a pointing finger, pounding fist, or some other gesture that reinforces the point. If you gesture in conversation, you will usually gesture in speech. If you do not gesture in conversation, it is probably best not to force yourself to gesture in a speech. I suggest that you try to leave your hands free at all times to help you "do what comes naturally." If you clasp them behind you, grip the sides of the speaker's stand, or put your hands into your pockets, you will not be able to gesture even if you want to.

If you wonder what to do with your hands at the start of the speech so they do not seem conspicuous, you may either rest them on the speaker's stand partially clenched or hold them relaxed at your sides— perhaps with one arm slightly bent at the elbow. Once you begin the speech, forget about your hands—they will be free for appropriate gestures. If, however, you discover that you have folded your arms in front of you or clasped them behind you, put them back in one of the two original positions. After you have spoken a few times, your professor will suggest whether you need to be more responsive or somewhat restrained with your hands and arms.

Movement refers to motion of the entire body. Some speakers stand perfectly still throughout an entire speech. Others are constantly on the move. In general, it is probably better to remain in one place unless you have some reason for moving. However, a little movement adds action to the speech, so it may help you hold attention. Ideally, movement should help focus on transition, emphasize an idea, or call attention to a particular aspect of the speech. Avoid such unmotivated movement as bobbing and weaving, shifting from foot to foot, or pacing from one side of the room to the other. At the beginning of your speech, stand up straight and on both feet. If during the course of the speech you find yourself in some peculiar posture, return to the upright position standing on both feet.

With any bodily action, avoid mannerisms that distract the audience, like taking off or putting on glasses, smacking the tongue, licking the lips, or scratching the nose, hand, or arm. As a general rule, anything that calls attention to itself is bad, and anything that helps reinforce the idea is good.

Bodily action says the same kinds of things in a speech as it does in normal interpersonal or group communication. It is true that when you get in front of an audience you may tend to freeze up—that is, to limit your normal nonverbal action—and occasionally the speaking situation may bring out nervous mannerisms that are not so noticeable in your daily speaking. However, if you are thinking actively about what you are saying your bodily action will probably be appropriate. If you use either too much or too little bodily action, your instructor can give you some pointers for limiting or accenting your normal behavior. Although you may find minor errors, you should not be concerned unless your bodily action calls attention to itself—then you should determine ways of controlling or changing the behavior.

During practice sessions you may try various methods to monitor or alter your bodily action. If you have access to videotape, you will have an excellent means of monitoring your bodily action. You may want to practice in front of a mirror to see how you look to others when you speak. (Although some speakers swear by this method, others find it a traumatic experience.) Perhaps the best method is to get a willing listener to critique your bodily action and help you improve. Once you have identified the behavior you want to change, you can tell your helper what to look for. For instance, you might say, "Raise your hand every time I begin to rock back and forth." By getting specific feedback when the behavior occurs, you can make an immediate adjustment.

REHEARSAL: GUIDELINES FOR PRACTICE

Now that you understand what constitutes good delivery, you can begin to rehearse your speech.

How you practice will depend on the method of delivery you will be using. In this book we recommend developing the extemporaneous method. Although you may deliver speeches impromptu, from manuscript, or from memory, the extemporaneous method gives you by far the greatest flexibility.

Impromptu means speaking on the spur of the moment, without previous specific preparation. Although nearly all of our conversation is impromptu, most people prefer to prepare their thoughts well ahead of the time they face an audience. Regardless of how good you are at daily communication, you would be foolhardy to leave your preparation and analysis for formal speeches to chance. Audiences expect to hear a speech that was well thought out beforehand.

Manuscript speaking involves writing out the speech in full and then reading it aloud. The manuscript speech is a common and often misused mode of delivery. The advantage of a manuscript is that the wording can be planned very carefully. Although presidents and other heads of state have good reason to resort to the manuscript (even the slightest mistake in sentence construction could cause national upheaval), most speakers have little need to prepare a manuscript. Often their only excuse is the false sense of security that the written speech provides. The major disadvantages of the manuscript, as you can attest from your listening experience, are that manuscript speeches are not likely to be very spontaneous, very stimulating, or very interesting. Poor manuscript speaking results from a natural tendency to write a speech without any audience adaptation within it. Because of these difficulties, you should usually avoid manuscript speaking, except as a special assignment. Since learning to use a manuscript well can be important for formal or for sensitive occasions, we will talk about using manuscripts properly in Chapter 18 on speeches for special occasions.

A *memorized* speech is merely a manuscript committed to memory. In addition to the opportunity to polish the wording, memorization allows the speaker to look at the audience while speaking. Unfortunately for beginning speakers, memorization has the same disadvantages as the manuscript. Few individuals are able to memorize so well that their speech sounds spontaneous. Since a speech that sounds memorized adversely affects an audience, you should also avoid memorization for your first speech assignment.

Most speeches you will give, in and out of class, will be delivered extemporaneously. In ordinary conversation, extemporaneous is often used synonymously with impromptu. In a public speaking context, though, an *extemporaneous* speech is prepared and practiced, but the

Methods of Delivery

exact wording is determined at the time of utterance. Why should most of your speeches be given extemporaneously? Doing so gives more control to the speech than impromptu speaking, but it maintains the spontaneity. It allows far greater spontaneity and opportunity for audience adaptation than the full manuscript or memorized speech, but it is fully prepared. Most experienced speakers prefer the extemporaneous method for most of their speeches. And you will find that most of your assignments in this class will call for extemporaneous speaking. Now let's consider how a speech can be carefully prepared without being memorized.

Practicing the Speech

Inexperienced speakers often believe that preparation is complete once the outline has been finished. Nothing could be further from the truth. If you are scheduled to speak at 9:00 A.M. Monday and you have not finished the outline for the speech until 8:45 A.M. Monday, the

Rehearsal and thorough preparation are essential to a good speech. Rehearsal allows you to evaluate and hone your speech.

speech is not likely to be as good as it could have been had you allowed yourself sufficient practice time. Whatever the assignment, you should try to complete your outline at least two days before the speech is due. This will give you time to practice your speech. Practice gives you a chance to revise, evaluate, mull over, and consider all aspects of the speech.

A good rehearsal period involves going through the speech, analyzing what you say, and then going through the speech again.

First practice. You will want to use the following format for your rehearsal period.

1. *Read through your outline once or twice to get ideas set in your mind, and then put the outline out of sight.*

2. *Stand up and face your imaginary audience.* You want to make the practice as similar as possible to the speech situation. If you are practicing in your room, pretend that the chairs, lamps, books, and so forth in your view are people.

3. *Time the speech.* Write down the time that you begin.

4. *Give the speech.* Keep going until you have finished the ideas.

5. *Note the time you finish.* Compute the length of the speech for that first practice.

Analysis. Look at your outline again. Then begin the analysis. Consider such questions as Did you leave out any key ideas? Did you talk too long on any one point and not long enough on another? Did you really clarify each of your points? Did you try to adapt to your anticipated audience? Unless you are prepared to criticize yourself carefully, your practice will be of little value.

Second practice. Go through the entire process again. If you can get a friend or relative to listen to later practices, so much the better.

After you have completed one full rehearsal period consisting of two sessions of practices and criticism, put the speech away for a while. Although you may need to go through the speech three, four, or even ten times, there is no value in going through all the sessions consecutively. You may well find that a practice session right before you go to bed will be very helpful; while you are sleeping, your subconscious will continue to work on the speech. As a result, you are likely to find tremendous improvement in your mastery of the speech at the first practice session the next day.

How many times you practice depends on many things, including your experience, familiarity with the subject, and length of the speech. What you do not want to do is to practice the speech the same way each time until you have it memorized. An effective speaker needs to learn the difference between learning a speech and memorizing it. The former has to do with understanding ideas; the latter has to do with learning a series of words.

When people memorize, they repeat the speech until they have mastered the wording. Since emphasis is then on word order, any mistake requires backtracking or some other means of getting back to the proper word order. Unfortunately, this kind of practice does not make for mastery of content, it does not give additional insight into the topic, and it does not allow for audience adaptation during presentation. Another way speakers memorize is by saying the speech once extemporaneously and then repeating the same wording over and over again. The result is about the same in both instances.

When people stress learning ideas, instead of words, they practice their speech differently each time. Using principles of proper speech practice, the wording of the point concerning the amount of pure Roquefort that must be included before a salad dressing can be called "Roquefort" might evolve as follows:

First practice: All salad dressings claiming to be "Roquefort" must contain at least 15 percent of legislated Roquefort.

Second practice: How do you know what you're getting when you order Roquefort? According to law that dressing you order must contain at least 15 percent of legislated Roquefort.

Third practice: When you order Roquefort dressing you'll find that the taste varies from restaurant to restaurant. Still, according to law, you can be sure that what you are getting has at least 15 percent of the real thing—legislated Roquefort.

Notice that the same facts that were included in the outline are included in all three versions. These are the facts that you will attempt to include in every one of your practices. You should find that each practice gets a bit better and begins to sound more and more like a speech. For most speakers, at least three complete oral rehearsals are necessary. As you continue to practice, at some time you will reach that point of diminishing returns where additional practices do not help and may actually hurt. You have to learn how many times you must practice to cement the key ideas in your mind and to get the oral, conversational, spontaneous quality that is so important to good speaking without getting stale or beginning to memorize.

Should you use notes in practice or during the speech itself? If your professor allows the use of notes, the answer depends on what you mean by notes and how you plan to use them. My advice is to avoid using notes at all for the first short speech assignments. Then, when the assignments get longer, you will be more likely to use notes properly rather than as a crutch. Of course, there is no harm in experimenting with notes to see what effect they will have on your delivery. Figure 6.4 shows a typical set of notes made from the preparatory outline illustrated on pages 94–95.

Using Notes in the Speech

Figure 6.4. *Notes.*

```
ELEMENTS OF ROQUEFORT

Trademarked
    Toulouse 1666
    15% required

Ewe's milk
    Neolithic
    30 ewes to 1 cow
    800,000 ewes

Mold from caves
    Penicillium roquefortii
    in fissures
    injected
```

Appropriate notes are composed of key words or phrases that help trigger your memory. Notes will be most useful to you when they consist of the fewest possible words written in lettering large enough to be seen instantly at a distance. Many speakers condense their written preparatory outline into a brief word or phrase outline.

For a five- to ten-minute speech, a single 3-by-5-inch notecard should be enough. When your speech contains a particularly good quotation or a complicated set of statistics, you may want to write them out in detail on separate 3-by-5-inch cards.

During practice sessions you should use notes the way you plan to use them in the speech. Either put them on the speaker's stand or hold them in one hand and refer to them only when you have to. Speakers often find that making a notecard is so effective in helping cement ideas in their mind that during practice or later during the speech itself they do not need to use the notes at all.

EXERCISE 11
Rehearsal

Make a diary of your rehearsal program for your first speech. How many times did you practice? At what point did you feel you had a mastery of the substance? How long was each of your practice periods? Did you use notes?

WHAT TO DO ABOUT NERVOUSNESS

According to their study, R. H. Bruskin Associates found that when people were asked to pick items from a list of things that frightened them, 40.6 percent said they were frightened by speaking in public—more than anything else on the list, including heights, insects, flying, sickness, and death![2] Yet, you must learn to cope with nervousness because speaking is important. Through speaking we show others what we are thinking. Each of us has vital information to share: We may have the data needed to solve a problem; we may have a procedure that will save countless dollars; we may have insights that will influence the way people see an issue. Think of the tremendous loss to business and to governmental, educational, professional, and fraternal groups because fear prevents people from being heard!

Let's start with the assumption that you are indeed nervous—in fact, you are scared to death. Now what? Experience has proven that people (and this includes you) can learn to cope with these fears. Consider the following points:

1. *You are in good company.* Not only does 40 percent of the population regard public speaking as the thing they fear most, but many experienced speakers confess to nervousness when they speak. I can hear you now: "Don't give me that line—you can't tell me that [you fill in the blank with some person you know] is nervous when he [or she] speaks in public!" You doubt me? Ask the person. He or she will tell you. Even famous speakers like Abraham Lincoln and Franklin D. Roosevelt were nervous before speaking. The difference in nervousness among people is a matter of degree. Good speakers learn to channel their nervousness. The following statement may surprise you: I would be disappointed if you were not nervous. Why? Because you must be a little nervous to do your best. Of course I do not mean that you should be blind with fear, but a bit of nervousness gets the adrenalin flowing, and that brings you to speaking readiness.

2. *Despite nervousness, you can make it through a speech.* Very few persons are so bothered that they are literally unable to function. You may not enjoy the experience, but you can do it.

3. *Your listeners aren't nearly as likely to recognize your fear as you might think.* Inexperienced speakers find their fear increases because they think their audiences recognize their nervousness. This recognition makes the speaker more self-conscious, more nervous. The fact is that people, even speech instructors, will greatly underrate the amount of stage fright they believe a person has.[3] Once you realize that your audience doesn't really recognize the fear that you believe is so noticeable, you'll no longer experience the acceleration of nervousness.

4. *The more experience you get in speaking, the more able you become to cope with nervousness.* As you gain experience, you learn to think about the audience and the message and not about yourself. Moreover, you come to realize that audiences, your classmates more than any, are very supportive, especially in informative speech situations. After all, most people are in the audience because they want to hear you. As time passes, you will find that

having a group of people listening to *you alone* is a very satisfying experience.

Specific Behaviors

Now let's consider what you can do about your nervousness. Coping with nervousness begins during the preparation process and extends to the time you actually begin the speech.

The very best behavior for controlling nervousness is to pick a topic you know something about and that you are interested in. Public speakers cannot allow themselves to be content with a topic they don't care about. An unsatisfactory topic lays the groundwork for a psychological mindset that almost guarantees nervousness at the time of the speech. By the same token, having a topic that you know about and are truly interested in is the basis for a satisfying speech experience. In Chapter 3, we emphasized how to ensure that you had the best possible topic. Heed that advice and you will be well on the way to reducing nervousness.

Then give yourself enough time to prepare fully. If you back yourself into a corner where you must find material, organize it, write an outline, and practice the speech all in an hour or two, you will almost guarantee failure and destroy your confidence. On the other hand, if you will do a little work each day for a week before the assignment, you will experience considerably less pressure and will feel increased confidence.

The following timetable will work for most of the short speeches that you prepare for class.

Timetable

Days Before Speech	Task
7	Select topic; begin research
6	Continue research
5	Outline body of speech
4	Work on introduction and conclusion
3	Finish outline; find additional material if needed
2	First rehearsal session
1	Second rehearsal session
Due date	Give speech

Experience in preparing and the length and difficulty of the speech will affect your preparation schedule.

Giving yourself enough time to prepare fully includes sufficient time for practice. Follow the steps for effective speech practice. Your goal is to build habits that will take over and control your behavior during the speech itself. If our national love affair with big-time athletics has taught us anything, it is that careful preparation enables an athlete (or a speaker) to meet and overcome adversity. Among relatively equal opponents, the team that wins is the team that is mentally and physically prepared for the contest. When an athlete says, "I'm going into this competition as well prepared as I can possibly be," he or she is more likely to do well. In this regard, speech making is no different from athletics. If you assure yourself that you have carefully prepared and practiced your speech, you will do the kind of job that will make you proud.

During the preparation period you can also be psyching yourself up for the speech. If you have a good topic and are well prepared, your audience is going to profit from listening to you. That's right—even though this is only a class and not a professional speaking experience, the audience is going to be glad they have heard you. Now before you say, "Come on, who are you trying to kid!" think of speeches you have heard. When someone had really good ideas, didn't you listen? Of course you did. What you will find is that some of the speeches you hear in class are some of the best and most valuable speeches you are ever going to hear. Students learn to put time and effort into their speeches, and many of their speeches turn out to be quite good. If you work at it, your class will look forward to listening to you.

Perhaps the most important time for you is shortly before you give your speech. Research indicates that during the period just before you walk up to give your speech and the time when you have your initial contact with the audience, your fear is most likely to be at its greatest.[4]

When speeches are being scheduled, you may be able to control when you speak. Are you better off getting it over with, that is, being the first person to speak that day? If so, you can usually volunteer to go first. But regardless of when you speak, don't spend your time thinking about yourself or your speech. At the moment the class begins, you have done all you can to prepare yourself. This is the time to get your mind on something else. Try to listen to each of the speeches that comes before yours. Get involved with what each speaker is saying. Then when your turn comes, you will be as relaxed as possible.

As you walk to the speaker's stand, remind yourself that you have good ideas, that you are well prepared, and that your audience is going to want to hear what you have to say. Even if you make mistakes, the audience will profit from your speech.

When you reach the stand, pause a few seconds before you start. Take a deep breath; this pause may help get your breathing in order. Try to get movement into your speech during the first few sentences. Sometimes a few gestures or a step one way or another is enough to break some of the tension.

ASSIGNMENT
Diagnostic Speech

This first speech assignment gives you a chance to show how well you have learned the fundamentals of speech preparation and delivery. It will enable your instructor to show you which fundamentals you seem to have mastered and which you need to continue to work on as you learn other principles of informative and persuasive speech theory. In addition, this speech assignment offers you your first major opportunity to listen critically to speeches.

1. Prepare a three- to five-minute speech. The speech may be of any type. An outline is required. Criteria for evaluation will include essentials related to all four aspects of the speech: (1) *content* — whether the topic was well selected, whether the specific purpose was clear, and whether good material was used to develop and prove the points; (2) *organization* —whether the speech had a good opening, clearly stated main points, and a good conclusion; (3) *wording* —whether the language was clear, vivid, emphatic, and appropriate; and (4) *delivery* —whether voice and body were used to show enthusiasm and whether the speaker looked at the audience, showed spontaneity, and achieved vocal variety and emphasis.

2. For one or more of the speeches you *hear* during the first round, outline the speech as accurately as you can. As you are outlining the speech, answer the following questions yes or no:

Specific Purpose

_____ Was the specific purpose of the speech clear?

Content

_____ Did the speaker have specific facts and opinions to support statements?

_____ Did the speaker offer a variety of kinds of supporting material?

_____ Did the speaker adapt the content to the audience's interest, knowledge, and attitudes?

_____ Did the speaker adapt the content to the occasion?

Organization

_____ Did the introduction gain attention, gain goodwill for the speaker, and lead into the speech?

_____ Were the main points clear statements that proved or explained the specific goal of the speech?

_____ Did the conclusion tie the speech together?

Language

_____ Was the language clear?

_____ Was the language vivid?

_____ Was the language emphatic?

_____ Was the language appropriate to the audience?

_____ Did the speaker use transitions to emphasize or show relationships among ideas?

Delivery

_____ Did the speaker sound enthusiastic?

_____ Did the speaker look at the audience?

_____ Was the delivery spontaneous?

_____ Did the speaker show sufficient vocal variety and emphasis?

_____ Was articulation satisfactory?

_____ Did the speaker show sufficient poise?

_____ Did the speaker have good posture?

Evaluate the speech as (check one) _____ excellent, _____ good, _____ average, _____ fair, _____ poor.

Use the information from your check sheet to support your evaluation.

OUTLINE

Specific Purpose: To explain four major classifications of nursery rhymes.

Introduction

    I. "Hey diddle diddle, the cat and the fiddle, the cow jumped over the moon. The little dog laughed to see such sport, and the dish ran away with the spoon."
   II. Did you know that there are four major classifications of nursery rhymes?

Thesis Statement: The four classifications of nursery rhymes are ditties, teaching aids, historically based rhymes, and modern use rhymes.

Body

    I. Ditties are nursery rhymes with a prophetic purpose.
       A. A fortune-telling rhyme is told while counting the white spots on the fingernails.
       B. Just as in *Poor Richard's Almanack* by Benjamin Franklin, Mother Goose had her merry wise sayings.
       C. Traditionally, a rhyme on the topic of love fidelity is said while plucking the petals of a daisy.
   II. Some nursery rhymes were used as teaching aids.
       A. "Hickory Dickory Dock" is an example of onomatopoeia, an attempt to capture in words a specific sound.
       B. Song rhymes help children with their coordination.
          1. Historical background
          2. Children's usage
       C. Numbers in nursery rhymes obviously retain traces of the stages by which prehistoric people first learned to count.
  III. Many nursery rhymes have historical significance.
       A. Religious problems entered into nursery rhymes with "Jack Sprat."
       B. In England it is believed that some of these country rhymes may be relics of formulas the Druids used in choosing a human sacrifice for their pagan gods.
       C. Cannibalism is quite prevalent in nursery rhymes.
  IV. A modern classification of nursery rhymes is the parody.

A. The famous prayer "Now I lay me down . . . " was first published in 1737, but has now been parodied.

B. A joke has been created out of "Mary and Her Lamb."

Conclusion

I. Every song, ballad, hymn, carol, tale, singing game, dance tune, or dramatic dialogue that comes from an unwritten, unpublished word-of-mouth source contributes to the future culture of our nation.

II. Remember that with your next cute saying, teaching aid in the form of a rhyme, reference to history, or modern use of nursery rhymes, you may become the next Mother Goose.

Bibliography

Baring-Gould, William S., and Cecil Baring-Gould. *The Annotated Mother Goose.* New York: Clarkson A. Potter, 1962.

Bett, Henry. *Nursery Rhymes and Tales—Their Origins and History.* New York: Henry Holt, 1924.

Ker, John Bellenden. *An Essay on the Archaeology of Popular Phrases and Nursery Rhymes.* London: Longman, Rees, Orme, Brown, Green, 1837.

Mother Goose. *Mother Goose and the Nursery Rhymes.* London: Frederick Warne, 1895.

Read the following speech aloud at least once.[5] Examine it to see whether the specific purpose is clear; whether the material really develops the points; whether the speech has a good opening, clearly stated main points, and a good conclusion; and whether the language is clear, vivid, emphatic, and appropriate.

SPEECH: Classifications of Nursery Rhymes

"Hey diddle diddle, the cat and the fiddle, the cow jumped over the moon, the little dog laughed to see such sport and the dish ran away with the spoon." You recognize this as a nursery rhyme, and perhaps you always considered these nursery rhymes as types of nonsense poetry with little if any meaning. As we look at the four classi-

ANALYSIS

The speaker uses a common rhyme to capture our attention. From the beginning, the novelty of the topic and the development get and hold our attention. Notice the clever wording "There's more to nursery rhymes than meets the ear."

Throughout the speech, the speaker leads us through the organization. She begins the body of the speech by identifying the first classification. The next sentence gives us the three subdivisions of the major classification. The commendable part of this and all sections of the speech is the use of specific examples to illustrate the various types and subtypes.

Again the main point is clearly stated. She begins this section with an interesting look at a common rhyme. Once more, there is an excellent use of specifics to illustrate the point she is making. Although speech language should be informal, it should not be imprecise. Notice that the antecedent for "he" in "he's trying to show the ticking" is unclear. You should be careful to avoid these common grammatical errors. This section of the speech illustrates how information can sometimes be communicated in such an interesting way we are not even aware we have learned anything.

Again the speaker moves smoothly into the statement of the main point. As far as the

fications of nursery rhymes, I think that you'll see as I did that there's more to nursery rhymes than meets the ear.

One of the major classifications of nursery rhymes is ditties. Ditties are fortune-tellings, little wise sayings, or little poems on love fidelity, and they are the most popular form of nursery rhyme. There are various ways of telling your fortune through ditties. One is saying, "A gift, a ghost, a friend, a foe; letter to come and a journey to go." And while you say this little ditty, this fortune-telling, you count the little white spots on your fingernails. Or you can say, "Rich man, poor man, beggarman, thief, doctor, lawyer, merchant, chief," and count your buttons. Whichever button you end on is the type of guy you are going to marry. Another kind of ditty is the wise saying. Just as in *Poor Richard's Almanack* by Benjamin Franklin, Mother Goose had her own little sayings. She said, "A pullet in the pen is worth a hundred in the fen," which today we say as "A bird in the hand is worth two in the bush." Love fidelity, the third kind of ditty, can be proven while plucking the petals off a daisy. "Love her, hate her, this year, next year, sometime, never." But today's usage has brought it up to "Love me, love me not, love me, love me not."

Another classification of nursery rhymes is those used as teaching aids, such as the saying "Hickory dickory dock." This is the use of onomatopoeia, which is trying to develop a sound from the use of words. In this case, he's trying to show the ticking of a clock. "London Bridge," although it has some historical background, is used for teaching children coordination, such as running around the circle raising their hands up and jumping back down. Similarly, in the ancient times, man made up rhymes in order to make things easier for him to remember, such as in the saying, "One, two, buckle my shoe; three, four, close the door." And as time went on, he eventually found out that he could use the fingers and toes to count. This is where "This little piggy went to market and this little piggy stayed home" originated.

Also, did you know that nursery rhymes have historical background? The third classification of nursery rhymes are those of historical significance. In the Middle Ages, which is when most nursery rhymes were formed, the saying, "Jack Sprat could eat no fat, his wife could eat no lean; and so betwixt the two of them, they licked the platter clean," refers to the Catholic Church and the government of the old Roman Empire. This is when the Catholic Church was blessing tithes, and wiping the country clean. The government came in and collected the taxes; and between the two of them, the country had no wealth and no money. The Druids, in their relics of old formulas for selecting human sacrifices, used the "eeny, meeny, miny, moe." And cannibalism is quite prevalent in almost all the nursery rhymes. Such as in "Jack and the Beanstalk," the big giant eater, and "Fee, Fi, Foe, Fum, I smell the blood of an Englishman. Be he alive or be he dead, I'm going to use him to make my bread." This also came up again in Shakespeare with *King Lear* and *A Midsummer Night's Dream*. "Little Jack Horner" is about a man named Jack Horner, who was steward of the abbot of Glastonberry. And in 1542, he was sent by this abbot to King Henry VIII of England with a pie. And in this pie were documents which were the documents of the ownership of land around the Abbey of Glastonberry, in Somersetshire. And on his way to the king, he stuck in his thumb and pulled out a document to the ownership of Meld, which he kept to himself. And until this day, over in Somersetshire, the Manor of Meld belongs to the Horner family.

The fourth classification of the nursery rhyme is the modern use—parodies and jokes—such as in "Mary had a little lamb, its fleece was white as snow." Today the kids go around saying, "Mary had a little lamb and was the doctor ever surprised." Or else they tend to make parodies of these nursery rhymes. Such as the famous little prayer, "Now I lay me down to sleep. I pray the Lord my soul to keep. If I should die before I wake, I pray the Lord my soul to take." It was first published in 1737, so you can see the age of this prayer. But, nowadays, the children say in joke, "Now I lay me down to sleep with a bag of peanuts at my feet. If I should die before I wake, you'll know I died of a stomach ache."

So every song, ballad, hymn, carol, tale, dance rhythm, or any cute little saying that you might come up with may contribute to the future culture of our nation. So remember, the next time you start spouting wise sayings, using rhymes as a teaching aid, referring to our history, or when you start making jokes of the traditional nursery rhymes, who knows, you might be the next Mother Goose.

quality of information is concerned, this is probably the best section of the speech. Notice that she continues to use her examples and illustrations very well.

Of all the single examples in the speech, "Little Jack Horner" is probably the best.

Once more we are aware of the statement of a main point. The speaker returns to classifying and labeling information that, as an audience, we have in our possession. From the foregoing criticism you can see that the speech is a very clear, extremely interesting, informative speech.

This conclusion ties the speech together pretty well. The wording of the summary gives the conclusion a necessary lift. The speech is light but still informative. Through the excellent examples, the speaker gets and holds attention throughout the speech. This is a good example of an informative speech.

NOTES

1. If you are interested in a more detailed analysis of the anatomy and physiology of the process, ask your instructor to recommend one of the many excellent voice and articulation books on the market (see also Suggested Readings for Part Two).
2. "Fears," *Spectra,* Vol. 9 (December 1973), 4.
3. Theodore Clevenger, Jr., "A Synthesis of Experimental Research in Stage Fright," *Quarterly Journal of Speech* 45 (April 1959), 136.
4. Larry W. Carlile, Ralph R. Behnke, and James T. Kitchens, "A Psychological Pattern of Anxiety in Public Speaking," *Communication Quarterly* 25 (Fall 1977), 45.
5. Speech given in Fundamentals of Speech class, University of Cincinnati. Printed by permission of Susan Woistmann.

Adler, Ronald B. *Confidence in Communication.* New York: Holt, Rinehart & Winston, 1977. Although the focus of the book is on assertiveness training, Chapter 5, "Managing Communication Anxiety," presents a method for relaxation and desensitization that you may find useful for reducing tension.

Amato, Philip, and Donald Ecroyd. *Organizational Patterns and Strategies in Speech Communication.* Skokie, Ill.: National Textbook Company, 1975. This book focuses on speech organization.

Blankenship, Jane. *A Sense of Style.* Belmont, Calif.: Dickenson, 1968. Blankenship packs a great deal of valuable information about style into a short paperback volume.

Clevenger, Theodore, Jr. "A Synthesis of Experimental Research in Stage Fright," *Quarterly Journal of Speech* 45 (April 1959), 134–145. This article draws some eleven conclusions about stage fright that are still consistent with recent data.

Fisher, Hilda. *Improving Voice and Articulation,* 3d ed. Boston: Houghton Mifflin, 1981. Although there are many good books on voice and articulation, this has proved to be one of the best.

Gibson, James, and Michael Hanna. *Audience Analysis: A Programmed Approach to Receiver Behavior.* Englewood Cliffs, N.J.: Prentice-Hall, 1975. The programmed approach enables you to check your understanding of audience analysis systematically.

McCroskey, James C. "Oral Communication Apprehension: A Summary of Recent Theory and Research," *Human Communication Research* 4 (1977), 78. A companion article to the Clevenger article cited above.

Modisett, Noah F., and James G. Luter, Jr. *Speaking Clearly,* 2d ed. Minneapolis: Burgess, 1984 (paperback). Includes a number of excellent exercises for improving articulation.

Newman, Edwin. *Strictly Speaking: Will America Be the Death of English?* New York: Warner Books, 1975 (paperback). A highly readable and popular look at contemporary problems of English usage.

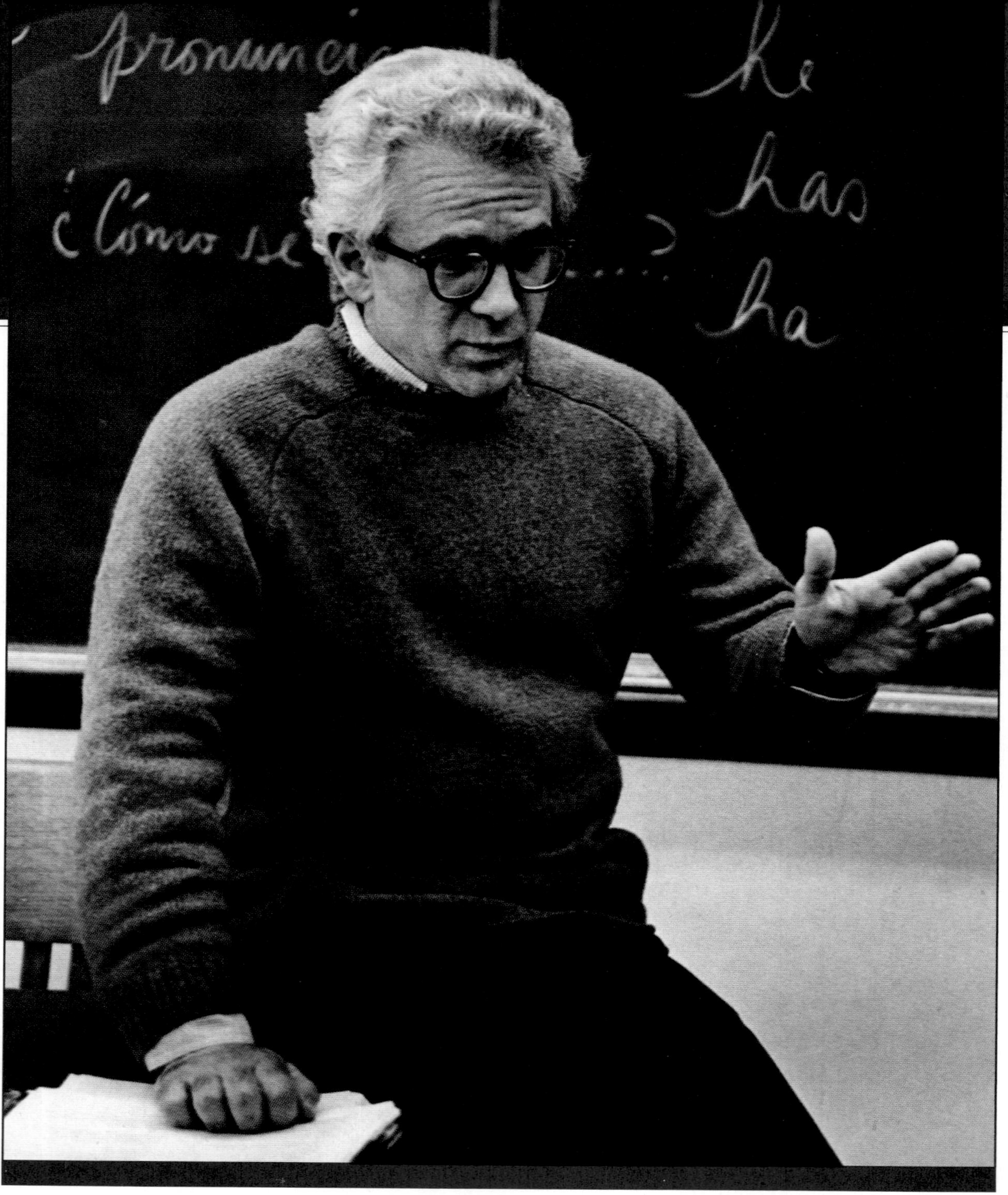
pronunci
¿Cómo se
he
has
ha

PART THREE

INFORMATIVE SPEAKING

A great amount of your public speaking will be informative. Although the material in this unit builds on the fundamentals presented in the last four chapters, the focus is on mastering the skills that are necessary for presenting information in ways that will be interesting, understandable, and memorable for your audience. After discussing principles of informative speaking, the unit continues with chapters on using visual aids, process explanation, description, definition, and using source material.

SEVEN

PREPARING INFORMATIVE SPEECHES

I t's difficult to make any good decision without adequate, accurate information. Unfortunately, our abilities to process and disseminate information have not improved as fast as our technology. As much as we talk, most of us are not nearly so good at informing as we could be. Yet learning to inform clearly and interestingly is not all that difficult. Whether your intention is to explain how a zipper is made, describe your new library, discuss Thor Heyerdahl's findings on the Ra expeditions, or explain how scientists are working to predict earthquakes, your ultimate purpose is to create understanding.

Chapters 8 through 12 consider different forms in which information can be presented. Here we focus on principles that are useful to your preparation of *any* informative speech.

GOALS OF INFORMATIVE SPEAKING

In this course you are likely to be asked to give one or more speeches in which your primary purpose is to inform. In these speeches you will want to follow principles that *help* your audience learn the material you present. How?

1. *Generate enough interest in the information to get the audience to listen.* Whether they should or not, people are quick to make value judgments about whether they will listen to the information you present. Thus, creating and maintaining audience interest in the information, especially early in the speech, is vital to your success in informing. If an audience isn't listening, they cannot learn. Your goal is to present information in ways that will arouse and maintain audience interest.

2. *Explain the information in ways that will enable the audience to understand it.* If an audience doesn't really understand the information, they are not going to remember it or be able to use it. Often people give verbal or nonverbal signs that they understand—they may say such things as "I see" and nod their heads—even when they *do not* really understand. Your goal is to explain information in ways that will not only increase their understanding of the information, but also explain it in ways that will enable them to use it.

3. *Discuss information in ways that will enable the audience to remember it.* The minute we hear information we begin forgetting some of it. Within a relatively short time we may lose anywhere from one-third to all of what we heard. Your goal is to present information in ways that will increase audience retention even over a long period of time.

The remainder of this chapter focuses on principles you can use to achieve these goals in your speeches.

SELECTING TOPICS AND SPECIFIC PURPOSES

PRINCIPLE 1

Audiences are more likely to listen to information they perceive as new.

Some topics have far more information potential than others. As a result, you want to make sure that the topics you select from your brainstorming list for your informative speeches will meet the test of newness. After you select a topic you must then shape a specific purpose that will have the potential to provide *new* information without being over the audience's head.

Since people are much more likely to listen carefully to material that is new than to material they think they already know, you want to make sure that you do not underestimate the knowledge level of your

audience. Think of the number of times that your listening interest dropped when someone began giving you information that you already knew.

What should you do if you find out that your classmates already know most of the basic information your topic suggests? Even if you select a topic with which most of your audience is familiar, you can write a specific purpose that uncovers new angles, new applications, or new perspectives. For instance, if you are considering a speech about football, talking about "how to play football" would be an unwise choice, since most people are probably familiar with basic

When preparing an informative speech, it is important not to overestimate or underestimate your audience's knowledge of the topic. You want to convey information your audience will find compelling and relevant, but you don't want to overwhelm them.

information about the sport. Instead, you may wish to speak on zone defenses or the differences between pass and run blocking, topics that are likely to provide new information even to those who think they have a pretty good grasp of football basics. The point is not to change the topic, but to keep reworking the specific purpose until you have uncovered an aspect of the topic that will be new to most of the audience. Again, when it comes to speech material, the tests of "newness" are whether the information adds to audience knowledge or gives new insights to information the audience already possesses.

It is equally dangerous for you to overestimate an audience's specific knowledge of your topic. Although your audience is likely to consist of some extremely intelligent and very able students, even intelligent people do not necessarily have a great amount of specific information about even those subjects with which they are familiar. Recently a young woman in class mentioned Adolph Hitler in her speech on ethics of leadership. She was very surprised when many of the people in class gave her very vague looks.

To test the general information level of one class of college students, the question "Who was Adolph Hitler?" was asked of more than one hundred students in a speech class at the University of Cincinnati. Although *most* students knew that Hitler was the ruler of Nazi Germany before and during World War II and that he was responsible for the oppression of Jews that led to the killing of 6 million Jews in Germany and occupied nations during the war, several of them mistakenly referred to him as "the leader of the Communist Party in Germany during the 1940s," "the ruler of Russia," and "a Jew who wanted to rule the world." On this same test of general information, the number of correct answers varied widely. Whereas 85 percent knew the name of the governor of Ohio, less than 50 percent could name both senators. Nearly 60 percent knew that Hank Aaron held the record for the most home runs in the lifetime of major leagues, yet less than 40 percent knew the name of the composer the Broadway hit "Amadeus" portrayed and less than 25 percent knew the author of *Moby Dick*.

But how do you know what is new to your audience of college students? How can you be sure of the information level of your audience? To find out, you may want to circulate a questionnaire containing questions about key information related to your topic, or you may want to interview two or three classmates a few days before your speech. But even if you don't have access to accurate data about class knowledge, you can still make some good guesses by assuming that most of your audience has roughly the same level of information you have. For instance, if you didn't know much of the specific information for your speech before you did your research, you can assume that most of your classmates will not be familiar with that information either.

If you aren't sure whether your audience knows some important information, in your speech you can "review" the facts, a language strategy that will be accepted by most people and will not insult their intelligence. For instance, the young woman referring to Hitler might have said in her speech:

> When we think of mass oppression in the twentieth century many of us are likely to think of Adolph Hitler. We recall from our history courses that Hitler was the leader of Nazi Germany who was directly responsible for the policies that resulted in the killing of more than 6 million Jews in Germany and occupied nations during World War II.

A short statement like this guarantees that the audience will have the necessary information to enable them to understand the point she was trying to make.

In most of your speeches, then, you will want to make sure that you take time to give the details about information you regard as key to the audience's understanding of your topic.

How well you have considered the knowledge level of your audience will be shown through your specific purpose. How you word your specific purpose will change the nature and emphasis of the speech. Let's review guidelines for writing an effective informative specific purpose:

1. *Write a tentative specific purpose that states the particular elements you wish to cover in the speech.*

2. *Write several potential wordings of the goal.* Your first wording may be right on target. Your first wording, however, is likely to be more general or broader than what you can cover in the time limits. Write at least two more and choose the statement that is the clearest and most specific. For instance, for a speech on hypnosis, you might write the following three: "To explain what doctors use hypnosis for"; "to explain the uses and techniques of hypnosis"; "to explain three medical uses of hypnosis." Although the three are

quite similar, the third one is the best. And you would probably choose it for the speech.

3. *Check to make sure the specific purpose contains only one idea.* "To explain the uses and techniques of hypnosis," the second purpose mentioned above, contains two ideas, either of which might be suitable for an informative speech.

4. *Check the infinitive or infinitive phrase to make sure that the intent of the speech is informative.* Although "to explain" is different from "to show," "to explain," "to show," "to describe," and "to define" are all suitable for informative speeches.

5. *Finally, check to make sure that the purpose you select neither underestimates nor overestimates current audience knowledge.* For instance, at any school where preregistration has been installed for years, the specific purpose "to explain the steps of preregistration" would underestimate audience knowledge; on the other hand, in a class with freshmen students from a variety of majors, the specific purpose "to explain engineering applications of vector analysis" would overestimate audience knowledge.

CHOOSING THE BEST ORGANIZATION

PRINCIPLE 2

Audiences are more likely to remember information that is emphasized.

One way of emphasizing information in a speech is to organize the information so that main points emphasize key ideas. Although good organization does not necessarily influence the *total* amount of information remembered, good organization does help you control which information the audience will remember.

The three types of organization of main points that are used most often for informative speeches are time order, space order, and topic order. Review how each of the orders serves a different function (Chapter 4).

In a time-order organization, each of the main points follows a chronological order. If you wished to explain the steps in conducting a readability test the main points would be

I. Find average sentence length.
II. Count the number of difficult words per hundred.

III. Add the average sentence length and number of difficult words per hundred.
IV. Multiply by 0.4.

If you organize your speech by time order, you will be putting emphasis on *steps* that you want the audience to remember. Demonstration and process speeches are usually organized by time order.

In a space-order organization, each of the main points follows a visual pattern from left to right, up to down, East to West, and so on. If you wished to describe the contents of a file cabinet, the main points would be

I. The top drawer contains folders for department majors.
II. The middle drawer contains forms for department business.
III. The bottom drawer contains dittos of material used by department faculty.

If you organize your speech by space order, you will be putting emphasis on spatial relationships that you want the audience to remember. Descriptive speeches are likely to follow a space order.

In a topic-order organization, each of the main points is a separate topic that is a logical subdivision of the specific purpose. If you wished to explain the criteria for selecting a course, the main points would be

I. Select courses that supplement your major fields.
II. Select courses that will make you more marketable.
III. Select courses that give you breadth of knowledge.

If you organize your speech by topic order, you will be putting emphasis on the topics that you want the audience to remember. Expository speeches, reports, and other explanatory speeches are usually organized by topic order.

In addition to your speech's having a clear organization on paper, an audience must be aware of the *presence* of that good organization. The first way of highlighting the presence of organization is through transitions. If you use good, clear transitions to preview points and to move from point to point, you will give your speech emphasis. If you get in the habit of using such preview phrases as "In my speech I will cover three goals, the first is . . . , the second is . . . , and the third is . . . ," you will often have more success getting an audience to remember main ideas than a speaker who does not. Likewise, you can focus audience thinking by using such directional transition statements between points as "Now we come to the second key point" or "Here's where we move from the third stage of development and go to the fourth."

Repetition is another way of highlighting main points and key items of information. The learning potential from repetition is unquestioned by those studying the memory process. For instance, when you meet someone for the first time, you will be more likely to remember the person's name if you repeat it a few times immediately after being introduced; when you are trying to learn a new definition, a formula for a compound, or a few lines of poetry, you will master them only after you have repeated them often enough to remember. We all know that some of the most effective, as well as the most irritating, television commercials are based on the simple device of repetition. As a student of public speaking, you should know when and how to repeat. Unfortunately, for inexperienced speakers the words that are most often repeated are *uh, well, now,* and *you know.* The artful speaker repeats main points and a few of the key items of information in the speech.

Sometimes you will want to repeat the words or ideas just as you said them: "The tallest building in the world is the Sears Tower in Chicago—that's the Sears Tower in Chicago." Other times you may want the audience to remember the idea, but not necessarily the specific words. So instead of repeating the words, you will restate the idea. Whereas repetition is the exact use of the same words, *restatement* is saying the idea again but in different words. For instance, you might say, "The Sears Tower is 1454 feet high—that's roughly 1500 feet!"

EMPHASIZING THE RELEVANCE OF YOUR INFORMATION

PRINCIPLE 3

Audiences are more likely to listen to information they perceive as relevant.

Rather than acting like a sponge to absorb every bit of information that comes our way, most of us act more like filters. We listen only to that information we perceive as relevant. *Relevance* is the personal value people see in information. It refers to how much information relates to audience needs and interests. Relevance might be called the "need to know" principle.

Vital information, information that is seen as truly a matter of life or death, is the ultimate in relevance. For instance, police cadets are likely to see information explaining what they should do when they are attacked as vital. Similarly, students may perceive information that is necessary to their passing a test as vital. If you can show the audience that your speech information is vital to their well being, they are more likely to listen.

In your speeches you must ask yourself whether the material you are planning to present is really important to the class. If so, you will want to emphasize that in the speech. Some topics and some information are highly relevant on their own. People look for information that affects them personally. For example, on the day of an important baseball game, a class picnic, or some other outdoor activity, any information you can present about the weather for that day will be perceived as relevant.

Developing relevance is more of a challenge when your information seems far removed from audience experience. Still, you can usually build some relevance if you will think creatively and take the time to work at it. A speech on Japan can focus on the importance of Japanese manufacturing to our economy; a speech on the Egyptian pyramids can be related to our interest in building techniques. Audience relevance can be shown for *any* topic. It is up to you to find what your audience needs to know and how your information meets those needs.

Although relevance is important throughout the speech, you should be sure to emphasize it in your speech introduction. For instance, suppose you were giving a speech to show the class the steps in computing readability levels. As class members listen to such a speech they are sure to ask, "Why should I listen to a speech on readability?" The following opening shows the relevance of readability levels to college students:

Have any of your textbooks just given you fits? Have you found yourself saying, "I just can't seem to understand this stuff"? Most of us have. Although we may have a gut reaction that the book's at fault, we are equally likely to blame our own lack of concentration. Yet, many times your gut reaction is correct. How can you tell whether the book is at fault? Perhaps the best way is by taking a few minutes to determine the readability level of the text. Today, I'm going to show you how you can quickly and easily test the readability level of any of your textbooks.

DEVELOPING INFORMATION CREATIVELY

PRINCIPLE 4

Audiences are more likely to show interest in and remember information that is presented creatively.

Since the purpose of an informative speech involves engaging your audience in learning, you want to do what you can to make your ideas interesting. By thinking creatively you can add originality to your speeches that will build and maintain interest. Before we offer methods of being creative, let us consider the nature of creativity.

The Nature of Creativity

In his book, John Haefele defines creativity as "the ability to make *new* combinations."[1] A creative speech is new; it is not copied, imitated, or reproduced. In short, your speech must be a product of, but not entirely different from, the sources you used. You find material, you put it in a usable form, then you inject your own insights, your own personality into the speech—insights and personality are the foundation of creativity.

Some people believe that creativity is possible only for a gifted person. Actually, we all have the potential for thinking creatively; some of us just have not given ourselves a chance to try.

First, you must have enough information to give you a broad base from which to work. You cannot be creative if you do not know much about the topic. Thomas Edison once said, "Genius is 1 percent inspiration and 99 percent perspiration." What this means is that you have to do your homework on the topic. The more you know, the more likely you are to approach the topic creatively.

Second, and equally important, give yourself enough time for the creative process to work. Once you think you are prepared (say, when you have completed your outline), you need time, perhaps two or three days, for your mind to reflect upon the material. You may find that the morning after a few uninspiring practices you suddenly have two or three fresh ideas for lines of development. While you were sleeping, your mind was still going over the material. When you awoke, the product of unconscious or subconscious thought reached your consciousness. Had there been no intervening time between those unrewarding practice sessions and the actual speech delivery, your mind would not have had the time to work through the material. So, we can be creative simply by giving our minds time to process the material we have.

Third, practice different ways of expressing important ideas. Beginning speakers are often so pleased that they have found a way of expressing an idea that they are likely to be content with the first thought that comes to mind. Suppose for your speech on computers, you thought you would begin the speech, "Years ago even the simplest computer had to be housed in a large room; today you can hold a functioning computer in your hand. Let's examine some of the advances that have led to computer miniaturization." Now, there is probably nothing wrong with that opening, but is it the best you could do? There is no way for you to know until you have tried other ways. A way to find different expressions of an idea is to brainstorm. Start your speech in two, three, or even five different ways. Although some of the ways you start will be similar, trying new ways will stretch your mind, and chances are good that one or two of the ways will be far superior and much more imaginative than any of the others.

Another way to show creativity is by trying different lines of development using the same material. For the speech you can then select the line of development you like best or that is most informative. With any given set of facts, you can develop by example, illustration, story, comparison or contrast, or a combination of these. For instance, let us say that you are to give a speech about England. You learn that London is a city of 7 million people, it rests roughly at the fifty-first parallel, its average temperature in the summer is in the mid-sixties and in the winter mid-forties, and it is the leading city in a nation of some fifty thousand square miles. With only these four facts about London, you could still be creative. You could develop a comparative line by comparing each of these with a familiar spot in the United States. You could develop a generalization line by making a statement using each of the facts as an example. Or you could develop an illustration or story line by taking one of the facts and developing a hypothetical situation. The potential is limited only by your willingness to work with the available material.

Fourth, you must be prepared for creative inspiration whenever it comes. Have you ever noticed how ideas come to you while you are washing dishes or shining your shoes or watching television or waiting at a stop light? Also, have you noticed that when you try to recall those ideas later they may have slipped away? Many speakers, writers, and composers carry a pencil and paper with them at all times, and when an idea comes, they make a note of it. Not all of these inspirations are flashes of creative genius, but some of them are good, or at least worth exploring. If you do not make note of your ideas, you will never know whether they were good.

Finally, by definition, creativity suggests occasional failure. You may work for two hours on a line of development that seems remarkably creative only to discover that it is inappropriate, wrong, or just plain ridiculous. If so, you have to be willing to forget the whole thing and start again. Creativity involves risk. When it pays off, it pays off in "A" speeches, audience applause, and regard for your work. But when it misfires, you must be willing to chalk it up to experience and start again.

Creativity in Speeches

Now let us consider speech methods that listeners perceive as creative.

Invent an association. One creative way of using materials is to invent associations of ideas. *Association* is the tendency of one thought to recall another similar thought. That means when one word, idea, or event reminds you of another, you are associating. When you walk into a room of people, you seek out the familiar faces. Likewise, when you are confronted with information that you do not readily understand, your ear listens for certain familiar notes that will put the new information into perspective. By associating new, difficult information with the familiar, a speaker can, through vivid comparisons, take advantage of this tendency of the audience.

For instance, if you were trying to show your audience how a television picture tube works, you could build an association between the unknown of the television tube and audience knowledge. The metaphor "a television picture tube is a gun shooting beams of light" would be an excellent association between the known and the unknown. The image of a shooting gun is a familiar one. A gun shooting beams of light is easy to visualize. If you made the association striking enough, every time your audience thought of a television picture tube, they would associate it with a gun shooting beams of light. If you can establish one or more associations during your speech, you are helping to ensure audience retention of key ideas.

Express ideas with emotional impact. A second creative way of using materials is to express ideas with *emotional impact.* Think back over your life and recall what stands out most vividly about the past. What you probably recall most readily are happenings, events, experiences, or accidents that had a highly emotional impact. Was it the day you got to drive the family car for the first time? Or the time you fell off the ladder reaching a little too far when you were painting? Or your first kiss? A good speaker can create this kind of impact through vivid anecdotes, illustrations, and examples. The more vivid you make your development, the more powerful the emotional impact will be. Too much repetition can become boring, but audiences seldom tire of those kinds of development that have emotional impact.

Some speakers achieve emotional impact through startling statements. Startling statements give an audience an emotional jolt. If your professor wears a new sport coat, it may get your attention; if your professor comes to class wearing a toga, a bearskin, or a loin cloth, it would be startling.

The startling is often accomplished through action. Blowing up a balloon and letting it sail around the room to illustrate propulsion would be startling. Taking off one's outer clothes in class to reveal a gym suit underneath would be startling. Sometimes, however, what you do may be so startling that the audience never recovers. So be careful. Although startling actions may get momentary attention, they can disrupt a speech if they are too overpowering.

Use humor. A third creative way of using materials is to express ideas humorously. You do not have to be riotously funny or sprinkle your speech with jokes. In fact, both are likely to hurt the audience's attention to your information more than they will help. To be most effective, relate humor to the topic. If you discover an amusing way of developing some point in your speech, your audience will listen. For instance, here is how one speaker heightened audience interest in his speech on hotel management:

> Frankly, I think the hotel business has been one of the most backward in the world. There's been very little change in the attitude of room clerks in the 2000 years since Joseph arrived in Bethlehem and was told they'd lost his reservation.[2]

If trying to be funny makes you self-conscious, then do not force humor into your speech. But if you think humor is one of your strengths, then make the most of it.

Use visual aids. A fourth creative way of using materials is to present them visually. You are more likely to make your point if you can show it as well as talk about it. Visual aids simplify and emphasize information as well as hold interest. They appeal to two senses at the same time: We listen to the explanation and we see the substance of the explanation. This double sensory impact helps cement the ideas in our mind. Finding, creating, and using visual aids are so important to speaking that Chapter 8 is devoted entirely to visual aids.

ASSIGNMENT
Informative
Speech

1. Prepare a four- to six-minute informative speech. An outline is required. Criteria for evaluation will include means of ensuring interest, understanding, and retention of information. Grading will focus on newness of information, organization and emphasis of information, relevance of information, and creativity.

2. Write a critique of one or more of the informative speeches you hear in class. Outline the speech. As you are outlining it, answer the following questions yes or no:

Specific Purpose

_____ Was the specific purpose clear?

_____ Was the specific purpose written with the knowledge level of this audience in mind?

Content

_____ Did the speaker have information that was new to the audience?

_____ Did the speaker develop the relevance of the information?

_____ Did the speaker develop ideas creatively by associating, giving emotional impact, making ideas startling, presenting material humorously, or using visual aids?

_____ Did the speaker use any special strategies to help you remember the main points and other key information in the speech?

Organization

_____ Did the speech follow a time order? space order? or topic order?

_____ Was the order appropriate for the intent of this speech?

_____ Did the introduction gain attention, gain goodwill for the speaker, and lead into the speech?

_____ Did the conclusion tie the speech together?

Language

_____ Was the language clear? _____ vivid? _____ emphatic? _____ appropriate?

Delivery

_____ Was the speech well delivered?

Evaluate the speech as (check one) _____ excellent, _____ good, _____ average, _____ fair, _____ poor.

Use the information from your check sheet to support your evaluation.

OUTLINE: INFORMATIVE SPEECH (4–6 minutes)

Specific Purpose: To explain the four stages Truman Capote went through as a writer.

Introduction

I. He was a high school dropout who spent much of his life hopelessly dependent on drugs and alcohol.
II. Yet he was one of the literary giants of the century.

Thesis Statement: The four stages of Truman Capote's writing career were learning his craft, experiencing major successes, becoming a reportorial novelist, and feeling the frustrations of unfulfilled promise.

Body

I. In the first stage of his life Capote learned his craft.
   A. Writing was his companion in his early years.
      1. His parents divorced and abandoned him when he was four.
      2. He was shifted about from one relative to another.
   B. He played with pens and paper like other young people practiced violin or piano.
      1. He wrote for four to five hours per day.

    2. He wrote adventure stories, comedy skits, and murder mysteries.

    3. He kept daily entries in his journal.

  C. Capote started writing seriously when he was eight years old.

  D. He was a published writer by age seventeen.

    1. He published stories in several magazines.

    2. Writing such stories occupied his time until he was twenty-three.

II. In the second stage of his life Capote blossomed as a novelist.

  A. His first novel, *Other Voices Other Rooms,* was published in 1948.

  B. This ten-year period was marked by the sharpening of his skills.

    1. He worked to conquer a variety of techniques.

    2. He experimented with a variety of types including short stories, essays, film scripts, and factual reportage.

  C. He had many successes, including *The Grass Harp, The Muses Are Heard,* and *A Christmas Memory.*

  D. This stage reached its culmination with *Breakfast at Tiffany's.*

III. In the third stage Capote began a literary sojourn over virgin terrain that ultimately produced his most famous work.

  A. Capote helped establish a new literary form—the nonfiction novel.

  B. He began work on *In Cold Blood.*

    1. It took him six years to complete the work.

    2. It was his most far-reaching experiment in reportage.

IV. In the final stage of his career Capote was frustrated with unfulfilled promise.

  A. These years were marked by a creative crisis.

    1. He began rereading his work looking for clues to a new beginning.

    2. He found what he believed was a new approach to writing.

  B. These years were marked by personal crisis.

    1. He began to drink heavily.

    2. He mixed drink with drugs.

  C. The years achieved nothing.

    1. His *Music for Chameleons* was a failure.

    2. *Answered Prayers* was never finished.

Conclusion

  I. Capote created a new form of fiction.

  II. But Capote died a virtual recluse.

Bibliography

Book Review Digest (1948, 1958, 1965).

Garson, Helen. *Truman Capote,* New York: Frederick Ungar, 1980.

Grobel, Laurence. *Conversations with Capote,* New York: New American Library, 1985.

Kroll, Jack. "Truman Capote 1924–1984." *Newsweek* (September 3, 1984): 69.

Reed, Kenneth T. *Truman Capote,* Boston: Twayne Publishers, 1981.

Read the following speech at least once aloud.[3] Examine it to see whether the speaker made the information relevant, whether the information would be new to a college audience, and whether the information was developed creatively.

SPEECH: Truman Capote: The Four Stages of His Career

ANALYSIS

He was abandoned by his own parents, he never learned to recite the alphabet, he dropped out of high school at the age of seventeen, he was hopelessly dependent on alcohol and drugs through much of his life. And he died alone in 1984, with no wife, no children. He also happened to be one of the literary giants of this century. His name? Truman Capote.

Notice the creative use of startling negative statements to build suspense in the introduction of the speech.

In order to give you some insight into the man and his writing, I want to talk about how his writing developed through four distinct stages.

The speaker promises us four main points, each of which say something about a stage in Capote's writing career.

In the first stage of his life, Capote developed his craft. As I mentioned, he was abandoned by his parents when he was only four years old when they were divorced. During those formative years when he was bandied about from relative to relative, he retreated to something he was comfortable with—reading and writing—his two greatest loves. He proved to be a true child prodigy. At the age of six he read *Robinson Crusoe* in its entirety. By the age of eight he was already writing seriously. Capote played with pens and paper like other young people practiced violin or piano. He wrote for four

Here the speaker shows us both Capote's motivation for writing and his dedication to the development of his craft.

"I liken this work to that of a young piano player" is an excellent comparison that helps us better understand the importance of his journal writing.

Notice the clear statement of the second point that emphasizes the significant aspect of that stage.

Good use of Capote's own words to help make a point.

Here and in other parts of the speech we see excerpts from reviews to give support to generalizations about the quality of Capote's writing.

Another good quote and an interesting tag point about the Hollywood film.

Here the speaker uses two sentences to establish the move to the third stage of Capote's writing career and the point he wishes to make about that stage.

Since this work is Capote's crowning achievement, the speaker is wise to spend so much time explaining the nature of the work. A good

to five hours a day during this stage of his development. This was a fun period for him as he dabbled in the writing of adventure stories, murder mysteries, and even some comedy skits. But probably the most significant writing was his devotion to journal entries. I liken this work to that of a young piano player who does the scales over and over again. Not a very beautiful exercise, but important if you're going to move on to the next stage. His work came to fruition when he published his first story at the age of seventeen. By the time he was twenty-three, he had articles in many of the most popular magazines of the day, including *New Yorker, Atlantic Monthly, Harpers,* and *Mademoiselle.*

In the second stage of his life, Capote blossomed as a writer. Capote was launched into the second stage of his writing with the publication of his first novel, *Other Voices, Other Rooms,* a book about the abnormal maturing of a thirteen-year-old boy. "When a book or study comes to me," he wrote, "it seems to come in its entirety." And so it did with this book. It was critically acclaimed and a best-seller. The *New York Herald* review said, "It is not only a work of unusual beauty, but a work of unusual intelligence." This ten-year stage was a very productive one for him—perhaps his most productive. He completed *The Grass Harp, A Christmas Memory, The Muses Are Heard,* and probably one of his most famous works, *Breakfast at Tiffany's,* a short novel concerning an irrepressible young New Yorker named Holly Golightly, that later became a film that starred Audrey Hepburn in the title role. On its publication Coleman Rosenberger of the *Tribune* wrote, "*Breakfast at Tiffany's* is new evidence of Truman Capote's virtuosity, his marvelous inventiveness of incident and character, his humor, his expertise of style." He wrote at this stage that he finally found the difference between good writing and bad writing. By this time in his life, he had become a star.

In 1959, Capote entered the third stage of his career. In this stage he began a literary sojourn over virgin terrain that ultimately produced his most famous work, *In Cold Blood.* This was truly a landmark book for it contributed largely to the establishment of a new literary form called the nonfiction novel. The nonfiction novel reads like any other novel except that the entire novel is factual. *In Cold Blood* took him six long years to write. It's about a multiple murder that took place in Kansas. Capote moved to Kansas to get a better feeling for the atmosphere and the environment of the time. He talked to the men who committed the murders and he watched their execution. It was a far-reaching, comprehensive work that the critics agreed was a masterpiece of reporting. *The New York Times Review of Books* said, "This is the best documentary account of American crime ever written." Now Capote announced that he had discovered the difference between good writing and true art.

At the height of his career, Capote's work moved into its final stage, the frustration of unfulfilled promise. These years were marked by a creative crisis for Capote, for during this stage he became very critical of all he had accomplished before. He downplayed what he had done and announced that he would form a new style—a new approach to writing. But the book that he worked on for years that was supposed to represent that approach, *Answered Prayers,* was never finished. These years were also marked by the virtual destruction of the person. His heavy drinking and drug abuse became a major part of his life, which caused or accompanied general bad health including pleurisy and cancer.

Even with this anticlimactic period of unfulfilled promise, Capote has left us a legacy of fifteen books and countless short stories, journalistic pieces, and magazine articles. He may have been a clown, a buffoon, a self-caricature in his later life. But anyone who has been moved by *Breakfast at Tiffany's* and has been riveted to his chair as he raced through *In Cold Blood* can never doubt the genius.

example of emphasis by proportion.

In the explanation we *see* the time and energy that Capote devoted to the preparation of this book.

This fourth point encapsulates the frustration of Capote's career.

Although a four- to six-minute speech cannot explain a complete career, the speaker has given us clear statements that we are likely to remember. Moreover, enough of Capote's works are mentioned and enough critical commentary included to help us understand why so many people praise his creative genius.

A good conclusion. Although the speaker doesn't summarize, he does capture the essence of Capote's writing career.

This is a good example of an informative speech.

NOTES

1. John W. Haefele, *Creativity and Innovation* (New York: Reinhold, 1962), 6.
2. James Lavenson, "Think Strawberries," *Vital Speeches,* March 15, 1974, 346.
3. Delivered in Speech class, University of Cincinnati. Printed by permission of Terry Loftus.

EIGHT

VISUAL AIDS

The visual aid is a unique form of speech development. Whereas speech, being primarily verbal, appeals to the ear, visual aids appeal to the eye. Whether a picture is worth a thousand words or not, research has shown that people learn considerably more when ideas appeal to both the eye and the ear than when they appeal to the ear alone.[1]

Although visual aids may be used in any kind of speech, they are vital to informative speeches that explain or demonstrate a process. Let us consider first the various kinds of visual aids and, second, how they can be used effectively.

KINDS OF VISUAL AIDS

The most common kinds of visual aids are you the speaker; objects; models; the chalkboard; pictures, drawings, and sketches; charts; and films, slides, and projections.

You the Speaker

For many speeches, *you* may be your best visual aid. For instance, through descriptive gestures you can show the size of a soccer ball, the height of a tennis net, and the shape of a lake; through your posture and movement, you can show the correct stance for skiing, a butterfly

Visual aids are vital to informative speeches because they help explain or demonstrate processes. There are many kinds of visual aids, such as models, drawings, charts, and slides. Here, the object itself—a soccer ball—is being used as a visual aid.

swimming stroke, and methods of artificial respiration; and through your own attire, you can illustrate the native dress of a foreign country; the proper outfit for a mountain climber, a cave explorer, or a scuba diver; or the uniform of a firefighter, a police officer, or a soldier.

Objects

When your speech involves objects, the objects themselves may make good visual aids, especially if they are large enough to be seen and small enough to carry around with you. A vase, a soccer ball, a braided rug, or a sword is the kind of object that can be seen by the audience and manipulated by the speaker.

When an object is too large to bring to the speech or too small to be seen, a model will usually prove a worthwhile substitute. A *model* is a representation used to show the construction of an object or to serve as a copy. If you were to talk about a turbine engine, a suspension bridge, an Egyptian pyramid, or the structure of an atom, a model might well be the best visual aid. Working models are especially eye-catching.

Models

As a means of visually portraying simple information, the chalkboard, a staple in every college classroom, is unbeatable. Unfortunately, the chalkboard is also easy to misuse and to overuse. Students and teachers often err by writing too much material while they are talking, which often results in material that is either illegible or is at least partly obscured by their body while they are writing. In addition, speakers tend to spend too much time talking to the board instead of to the audience.

Chalkboard

People are likely to use the chalkboard in an impromptu fashion because it happens to be available. Yet good visual aids require considerable preplanning to achieve their greatest value. Keep in mind that anything that can be done with a chalkboard can be done better with a pre-prepared visual aid that can be used when needed.

If you still want to use the chalkboard, either put the material on the board before you begin, or use the board for only a few seconds at a time. If you plan to draw your visual aid on the board before you begin, get to class a little early so that you can complete your drawing before the class begins. You may then want to cover what you have done in some way. It is not fair to your classmates to use several minutes of class time completing your visual aid. If you plan to draw or to write while you are talking, practice doing that as carefully as you practice the rest of your speech. If you are right-handed, stand to the right of what you are drawing. Try to face at least part of the audience while you work. Although it may seem awkward at first, your effort will allow your audience to see what you are doing while you are doing it.

Pictures, drawings, and sketches are popular types of visual aids. Pictures are popular because they are readily available. When you select a picture, make sure that the central features you wish to emphasize stand out. Colored pictures are usually better than black and white. Above all, however, you must make sure that they are large

Pictures, Drawings, and Sketches

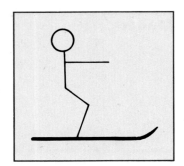

Figure 8.1. *A sample drawing.*

enough to be seen. The all-too-common apology, "I know you can't see this picture but . . ." is of little help to the audience.

Drawings are popular because they are easy to accomplish. If you can use a compass, a straightedge, and a measure, you can draw or sketch well enough for speech purposes. For instance, if you are making the point that water skiers must hold their arms straight, with their back straight and knees bent slightly, a stick figure (see Figure 8.1) will illustrate the point every bit as well as an elaborate, lifelike drawing. Stick figures may not be as aesthetically pleasing as professional drawings, but they work just as well. In fact, elaborate, detailed drawings are not worth the time and effort and may actually obscure the point you wish to make.

The major problems with drawing visual aids are size, color, and neatness. For some reason, people tend to make drawings and lettering far too small to be seen easily by everyone in the audience. Before you complete your visual aid, move as far away from it as the farthest student in class. If you can read the lettering and see the details, it is large enough; if not, you should begin again. Color selection may also cause some problem. Black or red on white are always good contrasts. Chartreuse on pink and other such combinations just cannot be seen very well. Finally, make sure that the visual aid is neat. There's no excuse for showing a tattered piece of smudged paper as a visual aid.

Figure 8.2. *A sample word chart.*

Computer Essentials

1. Central Processing Unit
2. Memory
3. Input/Output

A chart is a graphic representation of material that compresses a great deal of information into a usable, easily interpreted form. The word chart is a frequently used visual aid. For a speech on the parts of a computer, the speaker might make a word chart printing the items shown in Figure 8.2. To make the points more eye-catching, the speaker may use a picture or a sketch to portray each word visually.

The chart is also used to show organization, chains of command, or steps of a process. The chart in Figure 8.3 illustrates the organization of a student union board. Charts of this kind lend themselves well to what is called the striptease method of showing. The speaker prints the words on a large piece of cardboard, covers each word or phrase with pieces of cardboard or paper mounted with small pieces of cellophane tape, and then removes the cover to expose that portion of the chart as he or she comes to each point.

Maps are valuable charts indicating key elements of a territory. Maps allow you to focus on physical details such as mountains, rivers, and valleys; or on the location of cities, states, nations, parks, and monuments; or on automobile, train, boat, and airplane routes. You can make a map that includes only the details you wish to show. Whether you make your own map or not, the features you wish to emphasize should be easy to see. The weather map in Figure 8.4 is a good example of a map that focuses on selected details.

If your speech contains numbers, you may want to show them with some kind of a graph. The three most common types are the line

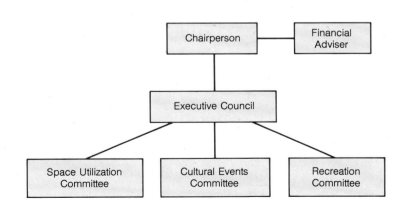

Figure 8.3. *A sample organizational chart.*

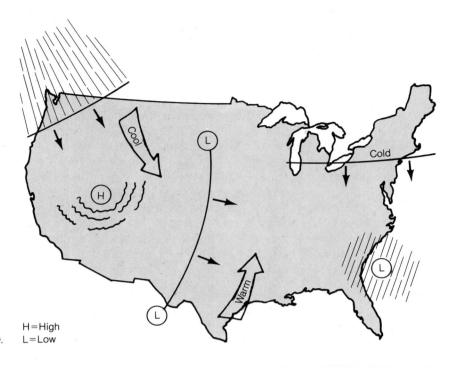

Figure 8.4. *A sample map.*

H = High
L = Low

graph, the bar graph, and the pie graph. If you were giving a speech on the population of the United States, you could use the *line graph* in Figure 8.5 to show population increase, in millions, from 1800 to 1980. If you were giving a speech on gold, you could use the *bar graph* in Figure 8.6 to show comparative holdings of the International Monetary Fund (IMF) and of world governments in gold (1985). In any speech where you want to show distribution of a whole, such as employment in Greater Cincinnati by industry category in 1986, a *pie graph* like the one in Figure 8.7 could be used.

To get the most out of your charts, however, you should be prepared to make extensive interpretations. Since charts do not speak for themselves, you should know how to read, test, and interpret them before you use them in speeches. Just as with drawings, the chart itself and any lettering should be large enough to be seen and the colors should be contrasting.

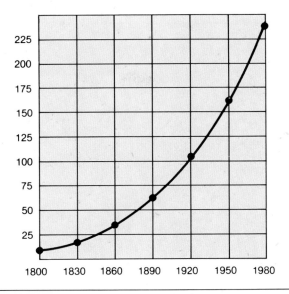

Figure 8.5. *A sample line graph showing population increase from 1800–1980 (in millions).*

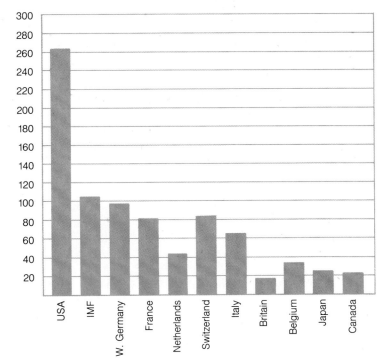

Figure 8.6. *Comparative holdings of gold in 1985 by world governments that are IMF members (in millions of fine troy ounces). (Source: 1987 World Almanac.)*

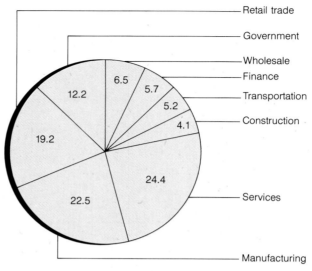

Figure 8.7. *Breakdown of Greater Cincinnati employment, by industry category, in percent. (Source: Ohio Bureau of Employment Services, September 1986.)*

Retail trade
Government
Wholesale
Finance
Transportation
Construction
Services
Manufacturing

6.5 5.7
12.2 5.2
19.2 4.1
24.4
22.5

Total 99.8% due to rounding.

Films, Slides, and Projections

In a classroom presentation, you will seldom have the opportunity to use films, slides, or projections. The scheduling of projectors, the need for darkened classrooms, and the tendency for these visual aids to dominate the speaker combine to outweigh the possible advantages of their use. Nevertheless, slides, opaque projections, and overhead projections can make even a classroom speech more exciting.

Slides are mounted transparencies that can be projected individually. In a speech, you use slides much the same way you do pictures. For instance, for a speech on scenic attractions in London, a speaker might have one or more slides of the Tower of London, the British Museum, Buckingham Palace, and the Houses of Parliament. You could show the slides and talk about each of them as long as necessary.

An *opaque projector* is a machine that enables you to project directly from a book, a newspaper, or a typed page. It is especially useful for materials that would be too small to show otherwise.

An *overhead projector* is a machine that uses special transparencies. The advantage of the overhead is that the room need not be darkened and you can write, trace, or draw on the transparency while you are talking. Overheads are especially useful for showing how formulas work, for illustrating various computations, or for analyzing outlines, prose, or poetry. Many of the kinds of things teachers use a chalkboard for can be done better with an overhead projector.

With each type of projection, you need to practice using the visual aid as often as you practice the speech itself. Notice that it takes longer to prepare mechanically projected visual aids than charts or sketches. If possible, use a partner to run the machinery for you while you are speaking. Make sure that each picture really relates to, supplements, or reinforces what you are saying.

USING VISUAL AIDS

As with any other speech skill, you must practice using visual aids to get the most from them. The following are some useful guidelines for you to consider in your practice:

1. *Show visual aids only when you are talking about them.* You are competing with visual aids for attention. When you are using a visual aid to make a point, you expect the audience's attention to be directed to it. But if your visual aids are still in view when you are talking about something else, the audience will be inclined to continue to look at them. So, when the visual aid is not contributing to the point you are making, keep it out of sight.

2. *Talk about the visual aid while you are showing it.* Although a picture may be worth a thousand words, you know what you want your audience to see in the picture. You should tell your audience what to look for; you should explain the various parts; and you should interpret figures, symbols, and percentages.

3. *Show visual aids so that everyone in the audience can see them.* If you hold the visual aid, hold it away from your body and point it toward the various parts of the audience. If you place your visual aid on a chalkboard or easel or mount it in some way, stand to one side and point with the arm nearest the visual aid. If it is necessary to roll or fold the visual aid, bring some transparent tape to mount it to the chalkboard or wall so that it does not roll or wrinkle.

4. *Talk to your audience, not to your visual aid.* You may need to look at the visual aid occasionally, but you want to maintain eye contact with your audience as much as possible to see how they are reacting to your visual material. When speakers become too engrossed in their visual aids, they tend to lose audience contact entirely.

5. *Don't overdo the use of visual aids.* You can reach a point of diminishing returns with them. If one is good, two may be better; if two are good, three may be better. But somewhere along the line, you will reach a point where one more visual aid is too many. Visual aids are a form of emphasis, but attempts to emphasize too many things result in no emphasis at all. Decide where visual aids would be of most value. A visual aid is an *aid* and not a substitute for good speechmaking.

6. *Pass objects around the class at your own risk.* People look at, read, handle, and think about whatever they hold in their hands; and while they are so occupied, they may not be listening to you. Moreover, when something is being passed around, the people who are not in possession often spend their time looking for the objects, wondering why people are taking so long, and fearing that perhaps they will be forgotten. If you are going to pass things out, have enough for everyone. Then keep control of audience attention by telling them what they should be looking at and when they should be listening to you. Anytime you actually put something in your listeners' hands, you are taking a gamble—make a conscious decision whether it is worth the risk.

ASSIGNMENT
Informative Speech Using Visual Aids

1. Prepare a three- to six-minute informative speech in which visual aids are the major kind of supporting material. An outline is required. Criteria for evaluation will include selection and use of visual aids. For an example of a speech using visual aids, refer to the sample speech on juggling on pages 195–198 of Chapter 9.

2. Write a critique of one or more of the speeches you hear in class. Outline the speech. As you are outlining it, answer the following questions about the visual aids yes or no. (To assist you in a complete analysis of the speech, you may also want to answer the list of questions on pages 166–167 in Chapter 7, which deals specifically with informative speeches):

Visual Aids

_____ Did the speaker select and construct useful visual aids?

_____ Were the visual aids and any printing or drawing large enough to be seen clearly by everyone in the audience?

_____ Did the speaker explain the visual aids?

_____ Did the speaker show the visual aids so that everyone could see them?

_____ Did the speaker talk to the audience and not to the visual aid?

_____ Did the speaker overdo the number of visual aids?

_____ If the speaker passed objects around to the audience, was he or she still able to keep audience attention on the speech?

NOTE

1. Bernadette M. Gadzella and Deborah A. Whitehead, "Effects of Auditory and Visual Modalities in Recall of Words," _Perceptual and Motor Skills_ 40 (February 1975), 260.

NINE

EXPLAINING PROCESSES

Much of our daily exchange of information involves explaining processes: telling how to do something, how to make something, or how something works. We give instructions to a friend on how to get more power on a forehand table-tennis shot; we share ideas with our neighbor on how to make homemade fettucine; and we talk with an employee of the water works on how the new water-purification system operates.

Your explanation is a success when an audience understands the process well enough to apply it. The more complicated the process, the more care you need to take with your explanation. Although an explanation of a process is often considered one of the easiest types of informative speeches to give, because it deals with specific, concrete procedures, you still need to consider the essentials carefully.

In this chapter we consider the five major issues of topic selection, speaker expertise, organization of steps, visualization through demonstration, and presentation.

TOPIC SELECTION

Chances are that the brainstorming lists you compiled earlier contain several ideas that relate to processes. Because topics of this kind are so abundant, you may be tempted to make your selection too hastily.

Before you decide on a topic you need to ask the following questions:

1. Will the topic provide much new information for the audience?
2. Is the topic specific enough to be covered in the time limits?

Let's consider a popular type of topic, "how to bowl" (or how to play tennis, baseball, basketball, or any other popular sport). The topic would appear to be a good one for you, especially if you are a very good bowler. But when we ask these two important questions, we see that the topic fails on both. First, because nearly all college students have bowled at some time and because many bowl frequently, "how to bowl" is unlikely to provide much new information for most of the class. Second, the topic is so broad that you are unlikely to be able to provide much depth within the time limits.

Then what are the alternatives with these kinds of popular topics? If bowling is your hobby, your brainstorming sheet should contain such items as "spare bowling," "scoring," "automatic pin setters," "select-ing a grip," "reading alleys," and "getting more pin action," any of which would be better than "how to bowl."

For a speech in which you explain a process, you should reject such general topics as "how to bake cookies," "how clocks work," and "how to play tennis," in favor of more informative and more specific topics such as "judging baked goods," "how a cuckoo clock works," or "developing power in your tennis strokes."

The following are some of the specific topics that students have found suitable for their speeches.

How to Do It	How to Make It	How It Works
racing start	spinach soufflé	football zone defense
racquetball kill shot	fishing flies	helicopter
hanging wallboard	paper figures	television picture tube
macramé	bird feeders	automatic teller
mulching roses	wood carvings	video disc
grading meat	home swimming pool	photocopier
tuning a car		

Audiences are much more likely to concentrate on the explanation of a process when they perceive the speaker as being an expert on that subject. The extent of your expertise on any topic is shown by your knowledge and experience with the process. This element of expertise on a topic explains why we listen to Julia Child tell us how to make chicken cacciatore, Dwight Gooden tell us how to pitch a curve, and

Your audience will be more receptive to your explanation of how champagne is made if they are convinced of your knowledge and expertise on the subject.

Neil Armstrong tell us how a moon rover works. And your audience will listen to you if you convince them of your knowledge and experience of the process you are explaining.

Suppose you wanted to give a speech on making a spinach soufflé. You can't tell another person how to make a soufflé unless you yourself know the process. To get the information for a speech on how to make a soufflé, you would usually turn to a good recipe. If you had a really good recipe, could you just read the recipe to them? No. Why? Because to explain the process well, you also have to have experience with the process. People who cook know that the first time they try to follow a recipe from a book they run the risk of at least partial failure, even when the recipe is said to be "kitchen tested." But to really guarantee your audience success with a recipe, you the speaker have to have had experience using it. This combination of knowledge and experience explains why Julia Child can turn a recipe into a gourmet's delight while she is explaining it to her audience.

Let's see why experience is so necessary. A recipe includes ingredients, quantities needed, and a way to proceed. The success of the dish depends on the *execution* of that recipe. Only our knowledge and experience tell us whether two eggs are even better than one, whether an additional few minutes letting the sauce sit is beneficial or disastrous, or whether the soufflé will taste even better if one of the suggested ingredients is omitted or substituted. If you are experienced, you will have tried many variations. Then, during the speech you can speak from that experience; and you will be able to guide your listeners by explaining whether alternate procedures will work equally well or whether such procedures might be ill-suited for this recipe.

ORGANIZATION OF STEPS

All but the simplest processes require many explanatory steps. In Chapter 4, in our discussion of outlining, we talked about limiting main points to no more than five, yet the process you plan to explain may seem to have nine, eleven, or even fifteen steps. Of course, you cannot leave any of them out. What you will need to do is redefine the steps in a way that will result in five steps or fewer. To do this, group the steps into units that can be easily understood and recalled. A principle of learning states: It is easier to remember and comprehend information that is presented in units than information presented as a series of independent items. Although you should not sacrifice accuracy for listening ease, you should use this principle whenever possible.

If you have more than five steps, group them so that the end product is fewer than five. Audiences will remember three points, each with three or four subdivisions, better than they will remember ten points. For instance grouping would be done as follows for a speech on woodworking.

A	**B**
1. Gather the materials.	1. Plan the job.
2. Draw the pattern.	A. Gather materials.
3. Trace the pattern on wood.	B. Draw a pattern.
4. Cut out the pattern so the tracing line can still be seen.	C. Trace the pattern on wood.
5. File to the pattern line.	2. Cut out the pattern.
6. Sandpaper edge and surface.	A. Saw so the tracing line can be seen.
7. Paint the object.	B. File to the pattern line.
8. Sand lightly.	C. Sandpaper edge and surface.
9. Apply a second coat of paint.	3. Finish the object.
10. Varnish.	A. Paint.
	B. Sand lightly.
	C. Apply a second coat of paint.
	D. Varnish.

Although both sets of directions are essentially the same, the redefinition of steps in *B* would enable an audience to visualize the process as having just three steps instead of ten. As a result, most people would remember the second set of directions much more easily than the first. If the process you plan to explain seems to have more than five steps, you will probably be able to work out a similar grouping. The "plan–do–finish" organization shown in *B* is a common type of grouping for explaining how to make something. A little thought on the best way of grouping similar steps will pay dividends in audience understanding and recall.

This example also illustrates the *time-order* organization that is used for most process speeches. Each point is a step in the process that must be completed before the next step can be taken. Because a process requires a step-by-step procedure, time order is the preferable organization form. Occasionally, however, you will find your material falling into a *topic order*. In such cases, the subdivisions of each topic will usually be discussed in a time order. For instance, you might want to show that there are three ways of making spares in bowling. Your main points would be the three ways—spot bowling, line bowling, and sight bowling; then each of the methods would be explained in terms of the steps involved.

Specific Purpose: To explain three ways of bowling for spares.

Thesis Statement: The three ways of bowling for spares are spot bowling, line bowling, and sight bowling.

   I. One way of spare bowling is spot bowling.
  II. A second way is line bowling.
 III. A third way is sight bowling.

If you used this topic organization for your speech on spare bowling, each of the three main points would then be explained in a time order.

VISUALIZATION THROUGH DEMONSTRATION

In impromptu explanations in conversation, you can help your audience visualize a process through word pictures. When you have time to prepare, however, you will probably want to make use of visual aids (see Chapter 8), and you may well want to give a demonstration.

Complete Demonstration

In a *complete demonstration* you actually show the entire process while you are talking about it. If you decide to demonstrate the process you will want to practice the demonstration many times until you can do it smoothly and easily. A demonstration calls for you to have all the necessary materials or ingredients, enough time to complete the entire process, and a means of doing the demonstration so that everyone in the audience can see what you are doing easily enough to follow along.

You may discover that demonstrating carries several potential problems. One problem with a demonstration is completing it professionally. Under the pressure of speaking before an audience, demonstrating even an apparently easy process can become quite difficult. Control of the material will be much more difficult in front of an audience than at home. Have you ever tried to thread a needle with twenty-five people watching you?

A second problem involves time. Demonstrations often take longer than planned. In practice you may be able to complete the demonstration in three minutes. But when you give that same demonstration in front of a class it might take five to six minutes. Why? Because you will be conscious of the class's attention. You will sense when the class is not understanding, and you will tend to slow down or develop the explanation more fully than you did during practice.

As a result of these problems, you may want to select an alternative method of presenting the process.

Modified Demonstration

A *modified demonstration* is one in which you complete the demonstration in various stages at home and do only part of the actual work in front of the audience. The modified demonstration is an excellent alternative to a complete demonstration, especially for a relatively complicated process.

For instance, suppose you decide to demonstrate the basic principles of flower arranging. Perhaps you had worked part-time for a florist and had learned how floral displays are made. To do the modified demonstration you would have (1) all of the materials necessary to complete the demonstration, (2) a mock-up of the basic floral triangle that florists use as a starting point for their arrangements, and (3) a completed example of one particular floral display.

In the first part of the speech, you would talk about all the materials you need and you would show them to the audience. Then you would begin the demonstration by beginning to make the basic floral triangle that florists use for their arrangements. For a minute or so you might actually use the materials you brought to start the process. But rather than trying to get everything together perfectly in the short time available, you could draw from a bag or some concealed place the partially completed arrangement that illustrates the floral triangle. At this stage, you would begin adding flowers to the basic triangle as if you were planning to complete a specific arrangement. Then from another bag you could draw the completed arrangement that illustrates one of the possible effects you were discussing.

Although this demonstration is modified, it is probably better than trying to complete an entire demonstration within a short time limit.

PRESENTATION

You can improve the presentation of your process if you keep the following pointers in mind.

Choose Material Carefully

The effectiveness of your explanation may depend on the nature and the number of materials, parts, equipment, or ingredients you select. You need to separate the essentials from the accessories. A bowler needs a ball and bowling shoes. Wrist bands, thumb straps, finger grips, and fancy shirts are all accessories that may not be worth mentioning. For some speeches, you will want to bring all the materials for display; for other speeches, a list of materials may do.

Speak Slowly and Repeat Key Ideas

Throughout your demonstration, speak slowly and repeat key ideas often. When you explain a process, it is important that an audience have time for the details to sink in. Do not rush. Especially during the visualization steps, you want the audience to have a chance to think about the steps. Give the audience sufficient time to absorb your words and your visual aids. It is a good idea to repeat key ideas to make sure the audience has command of the material.

Work for Audience Participation

If you can develop some audience participation (we learn best by doing), you may be even more successful. For instance, in a speech on origami, Japanese paper folding, you may want to give your audience paper so that each person can go through a simple process with you. You could explain the principles, then you could pass out paper and have the audience participate in making a figure; finally, through other visual aids, you could show how these principles are used in more elaborate projects. Actual participation will increase interest and ensure recall.

1. Prepare a three- to six-minute speech in which you show how something is made, how something is done, or how something works. An outline is required. Grading will focus on quality of topic; selection, construction, and use of visual aids; and skill in organization and presentation.

2. Write a critique of one or more of the process speeches you hear in class. Outline the speech. As you are outlining it, answer the following questions yes or no:

Specific Purpose

_____ Was the specific purpose clear?

_____ Was the specific purpose appropriate for this assignment?

Content

_____ Did the speaker select and/or construct useful visual aids?

_____ Were the visual aids and any printing or drawing large enough to be seen clearly by everyone in class?

_____ Did the visual aids illustrate key aspects of the process?

_____ Did the speaker show his/her expertise with the process?

_____ Did the speaker use any special strategies to help you remember the main points and other key information in the process?

Organization

_____ Did the introduction gain attention, gain goodwill for the speaker, and lead into the speech?

_____ Did the speech follow a time order?

_____ If not, was the order appropriate for a process explanation?

_____ Was the number of steps limited to five?

_____ Did the conclusion tie the speech together?

Language

_____ Was the language clear? _____ vivid? _____ emphatic? _____ appropriate?

Delivery

_____ Was the speech well delivered?

Evaluate the speech as (check one) ___ excellent, ___ good, ___ average, ___ fair, ___ poor.

Use the information from your check sheet to support your evaluation.

OUTLINE: PROCESS SPEECH (3–6 MINUTES)

Specific Purpose: To show the class how to juggle.

Introduction

I. Watching a juggler on the David Letterman show motivated me to learn how to juggle.
II. Today, I want to show you the basics for learning the cascade, the basis for all advanced forms of juggling.

Thesis Statement: Learning to juggle involves choosing your weapon, getting into position, practicing basic tossing, and going for the cascade.

Body

I. Choose your weapon.
   A. The three types of objects for juggling are the ball, the club, and the ring.
   B. The ball is the easiest.
      1. You won't fight the rotation of a club.
      2. You won't fight the spin of a ring.
   C. Select a ball that is small, heavy, and nonbouncing.
II. Get into position.
   A. Plant your feet.
   B. Position your arms.
      1. Keep your elbows at 90 degrees.
      2. Keep your forearms straight.
   C. Keep your eye contact in front of you.
      1. Focus high.
      2. Don't follow the ball.
III. Practice basic tossing.
   A. Start tossing with one ball.
      1. Get a consistent height.
      2. Keep a consistent distance from your body.

3. Practice with each hand.
4. Toss the ball back and forth.
   B. Add a second ball.
      1. Toss up and down with both hands.
      2. Toss from one hand to the other.
   C. Add the third ball.
      1. Hold it in the hand you favor.
      2. Hold it while you toss the other two.
IV. Go for the cascade.
   A. Prepare physically.
      1. Relax your muscles.
      2. Breathe deeply.
   B. Prepare mentally.
      1. Concentrate.
      2. Think in slow motion.
   C. Toss the balls in the cascade.

Conclusion

I. I learned to juggle in about three weeks.
II. You can, too, if you will choose your weapon, get into position, practice your tosses, and begin the cascade.

Study this speech in terms of the informative value of the topic, apparent knowledge and experience of the speaker, clarity of the steps, and visualization of the process.[1] Read the speech through aloud at least once. After you have read and analyzed the speech, turn to the analysis in the other column.

SPEECH: Juggling

One night on the David Letterman show, I saw a man juggle a chili dog, a mug of beer, and a slinky. As I watched him, I said to myself, "Nancy, if this man can juggle a chili dog, a mug of beer, and a slinky, you can certainly juggle three stupid beanbags. So I set off with a mission—to teach myself how to juggle. And I did. Today, I would like to teach you the four basic steps in juggling.

ANALYSIS

Notice how the opening captures audience interest and develops the speaker's expertise. I like the use of dialogue to help make the point.

The speech has four main points, and each of the points is clearly stated.

I like the reference to "weapon" and her clever explanation of why she used such a designation.

A good explanation of the types of "weapons" and a good justification for beginning with the ball-type.

In this section we see why this speech is an excellent example of demonstration. Here and throughout the speech, the speaker uses herself and her beanbags as the primary visual aids.

"Unlike a Ping-Pong ball" is a good use of specific contrast.

Good explanation of why to use a nonbouncing ball-type object. In this section the speaker continues to show creativity of development.

Like the first main point, the second main point is clearly stated.

As a result of her method throughout this section, the audience was led to concentrate on her *demonstration* of the directions.

Here and in several other places the speaker uses humor to add to the effectiveness of her explanation. Through vivid description and precise word choice she is able to maintain a light touch—we enjoy listening to her explanations.

The first step is to choose your weapon. I call it a weapon because it can be just that when you're learning. You will see that it can fly out of control and break something or injure your dog. The three kinds of weapons a juggler will use are a ball-type, like these beanbags; a ring-type, like a Frisbee with a whole cut out; and a club-type, like an umbrella or a bowling pin. I suggest you begin with a ball-type. You have enough to worry about with three bags moving in front of your face to not have to worry about the spin of a ring or the rotation of a club [she juggled three beanbags as she completed this sentence]. When choosing your ball-type, make sure it is small enough to fit easily in the palm of your hand so you can catch it. It should be heavy enough so it will go in the air where you want it to and land firmly, unlike a Ping-Pong ball that goes where it wants to. Finally, get something that won't bounce. [She dropped a beanbag.] When you're starting to juggle you'll find that 90 percent of your time will be spent picking up. It's easier to pick up something that's landed at your feet than to chase a tennis ball across the room. For these three reasons, beanbags are ideal for learning.

The second step is to get into the proper position. Just as a batter needs to be in a certain stance to hit effectively, a juggler has to get into position to juggle. Start by planting your feet. This will give you balance and instill in your mind not to walk. Beginning jugglers have this nasty tendency to chase after the balls like this [she moved forward as she juggled]. Plant your feet. You cannot get control if you're running all over the room. Next, position your arms. You want your arms at your side with a 90-degree bend to your elbow and with your forearms straight, like this. Finally, you want your eyes focused high. You want your eyes focused where the *path* of the ball will go. If you let yourself follow the ball with your eyes, by the time you have three balls going, you're going to look like one of those little dogs in the back of people's cars with their heads bobbing back and forth as they go down the street.

The third step is to practice your tosses individually with each hand. Now this part can be a little monotonous, as you'll see. But practicing tosses is important to develop skill with each hand. Start with ball number one. Just toss it up and down like this until you get a consistent height and consistent distance from your body. Then do it with your other hand. Okay, now begin to toss the bag from hand to hand. Now look at this diagram.

The third point is clearly stated.

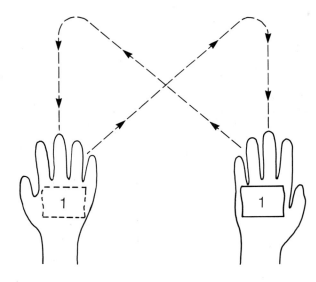

This is the only place in the speech where she uses a visual aid other than herself and her beanbags.

When you throw ball one, you want to aim at the point of the bow tie. You want to throw to that point and not to the middle. You want to throw it so that it reaches a high point here and then drops into your other hand. Now take ball two. Go back to tossing up and down until you get to the point where you can do it evenly, and then begin tossing from hand to hand again. Again, aim for that point. Now you're ready to add ball three. But don't juggle it. Hold it in your hand. Get the feel for it. And again just toss it from hand to hand like this. [She tossed the beanbag from hand to hand as she held the other bags, one in each hand.]

When you can feel it moving smoothly, you are ready to juggle. But there's something about releasing this third ball that will strike terror into the hearts of the bravest of us. I don't know why; it just does. Take a deep breath, relax your muscles, and concentrate: Think of these beanbags moving in front of your eyes as I do it. Think

The way she goes through the demonstration, the audience gets a real sense of involvement.

This section is another example of the addition of personal touches that add to the informative value of the speech.

in slow motion. I know that while I'm doing this [she juggled the beanbags as she talked], to you guys it looks like these balls are going pretty fast, but they're not—in my mind they're moving slowly because I know I have enough time when I release the third ball to catch the first one.

Now, you're ready for the fourth step—to begin the cascade. Don't panic. Go for one turn. A turn is when all three balls change positions in your hands. When you've done it once, then do it again. Eventually you will be able to continue—that's juggling.

Good conclusion. It lets the audience know what to expect and it summarizes the main points.

This is an excellent example of a process speech.

Now you may be asking yourself, Is it as easy as it looks? Yes, if you practice. It took me about three weeks till I could get to the point where I could keep the cascade going. And you can learn to do it too. Just follow my directions. Choose your weapons (start with something like these beanbags). Get into position. Practice your tosses. And finally, begin the cascade. Come on, you can all learn to do it—just juggle.

NOTE

1. Delivered in Speech class, University of Cincinnati. Printed by permission of Nancy Grant.

TEN

DESCRIPTIVE SPEECHES

"**W**hat does it look like?" "How do the parts fit together?" Questions like these are answered by describing. At least some of the informative communicating we do every day is descriptive. But like any of the skills of information exchange, description must be carefully worded to be effective.

A descriptive speech assignment provides an excellent opportunity for mastering this important language skill. Since the goal of description is to give an accurate, vivid, informative picture, we first look at the essentials of description. Then we consider the preparation of the descriptive speech, including topic selection, organization, and language suggestions.

ESSENTIALS OF DESCRIPTION

I was led into a family room so large that people at the far end seemed constructed on a smaller scale than I. The feature of the room was a huge flagstone fireplace that was a good 10 feet wide and at least 12 feet high. The opening was the size of a normal picture window. The fireplace comfortably held logs that were a full 3 feet long. As I stood before it, I got a sense of what a fireplace must have been like in a medieval castle.

Can you *see* the fireplace? Can you picture its immensity? Speech is descriptive when it provides word pictures that allow the audience to mentally picture what you are talking about.

How do you describe accurately and vividly? Effective description requires at least two skills: (1) observing and (2) communicating the observation. I cannot overemphasize the point that description is a product of alert observation. Since effective description reflects firsthand observation, you must first know what to look for, then you must create ways of reporting the essentials that will be accurate and vivid. You must be conscious of size, shape, weight, color, composition, age and condition, and the relationship among various parts.

Size

How large is the object? Size is described subjectively by "large" and "small" and objectively by dimensions. But description is more likely to be meaningful if it is compared. For instance, "The book, 6-by-6-by-3 inches thick, is the same length and width as your textbook, but more than twice as thick" is more descriptive than either of the following: "The book is a large one" or "The book is 9 inches by 6 inches by 3 inches."

Shape

What is its spatial form? Shape is described in terms of common geometric forms. "Round," "triangular," "oblong," "spherical," "conical," "cylindrical," and "rectangular" are all descriptive. A complex object is best described as a series of simple shapes. Since most objects do not conform to perfect shapes, you can usually get by with approximations and with comparisons to familiar objects. "The lake is round," "The lot is pie-shaped," and "The car looks like a rectangular box" all give reasonably accurate impressions. Shape is further clarified by such adjectives as "jagged," "smooth," and "indented."

Weight

How heavy is it? Weight is described subjectively as "heavy" or "light" and objectively by "pounds" and "ounces." As with size, descriptions of weight are clarified by comparisons. Thus, "The suitcase weighed about 70 pounds; that's about twice the weight of a normally packed suitcase" is descriptive.

What color is it? Color, an obvious necessity of description, is difficult to describe accurately. Although most people can visualize black and white, the primary colors (red, yellow, and blue), and their complements (green, purple, and orange), very few objects are these exact colors. Perhaps the best way to describe a color is to couple it with a common referent. For instance, "lime green," "lemon yellow," "brick red," "green as a grape," "banana yellow," and "sky blue" give rather accurate approximations.

Color

What is it made of? The composition of an object helps us visualize it. A ball of aluminum does not look the same as a ball of yarn. A pile of rocks gives a different impression than does a pile of straw. A brick building looks different from a steel, wood, or glass building. Sometimes you refer to what the object *seems* like rather than what it is. An object can appear metallic even if it is not made of metal. Spun glass can have a woolly texture. Nylon can be soft and smooth as in stockings or hard and sharp as in toothbrush bristles.

Composition

How old is it? What condition is it in? Whether an object is new or old can make a difference in its appearance. Since age by itself may not be descriptive, an object is often discussed in terms of condition. Condition is difficult to describe objectively, but it can be very important to an accurate description. The value of coins, for instance, varies tremendously depending on whether they are uncirculated or their condition is good or only fair. A 1917 Lincoln penny in fair condition may be worth 2 cents, whereas an uncirculated 1960 penny may be worth 10 cents. Books become ragged and tattered, buildings become run down and dilapidated, land is subject to erosion. Age and condition together often prove valuable in developing informative descriptions.

Age and Condition

How does it all fit together? If the object you want to describe is complex, its parts must be fitted into their proper relationship before a mental picture emerges. Remember the story of the blind men who described an elephant in terms of what each felt? The one who felt the trunk said the elephant was like a snake, the one who felt a leg said the elephant was like a tree, and the one who felt the body said the elephant was like a wall. Not only must we visualize size, shape, weight,

Relationship Among Parts

color, composition, age, and condition, but we must also understand how the parts fit together.

Since the ultimate test of description is whether it enables the audience to visualize, you should include too much detail rather than not enough. Moreover, if some particular aspect is discussed in two or three different ways, everyone might get the mental image, whereas a single description might make the image vivid to only a few. Begin your practice sessions with more material than you could possibly get into the time limits for your speech. As you gain a mastery of the material in practice, you can begin to delete until the speech is a workable length. Keep in mind, however, that with the descriptive speech, perhaps more than with any other, you will have to resist the desire to memorize.

PREPARING DESCRIPTIVE SPEECHES

Descriptive speech preparation follows the same steps as any other speech. We focus on some special aspects of those steps in this section.

Topic Selection

The goal of the descriptive speech is to give an accurate, vivid, informative description of an object, a structure, or a place. Although animals and people may seem like obvious subjects, the tendency to describe them in subjective rather than objective terms makes them less suitable for informative description.

The procedure for selecting a topic is to look at your original brainstorming lists to see whether they include any subjects that would be appropriate for description. If not, you can continue the brainstorming process with objects, structures, and places in mind. For instance, if your hobby is camping, you might list "turtleback campers," "camp site," "kerosene lantern," "tent trailer," "tent," "sleeping bag," and other items associated with camping. If your major interest is medieval history, you might list "moat," "castle," "jousting spear," "coat of mail," or "crossbow."

Evaluate your topic using the principal test of an informative speech: It must have the potential for providing new information for the audience. Your description of the object, structure, or place should give an accurate, vivid, verbal, informative picture of the topic.

The following are examples of topics that are appropriate for description:

Structures	Places	Objects
Cape Hatteras Lighthouse	Grand Tetons	corkscrew
Washington Monument	Natural Bridge	rattan chair
Golden Gate Bridge	Grand Canyon	racing ice skate
Superdome	Mammoth Cave	fisherman's seine

Organization

Most descriptive speeches are organized by space order. A description of a jet-powered racing car might go from back to front, front to back, outside to inside, or inside to outside. A description of a painting might go from foreground to background, background to foreground, left to right, or top to bottom.

Although space-order organization will be used most often, a topic order with space-order subdivisions will be appropriate when you are describing a class of objects. For instance, in a description of your campus, you might want to speak on the topics of its buildings, pathways, and wooded park areas. Or in a description of Yellowstone Park, you might talk about Old Faithful and Fountain Paint Pot as the two main topics. You would then develop each of these topics with a space-order arrangement of details.

An advantage of space-order organization is that it simplifies your decision about main points. Once you decide whether to go from left to right, top to bottom, or inside to outside, every key feature that the eye encounters becomes either a main point or an important subdivision of a main point.

Language

A descriptive speech is especially useful as a language exercise. A descriptive speech could be given with visual aids that show the object, structure, or place. But a descriptive speech is a language exercise that requires you to create *mental* pictures through clear, vivid, emphatic, appropriate language. Through comparative language, including simile and metaphor, you will be helping the audience to mentally *see* what you are talking about.

Test your wording to ensure that the language is informative, not poetic. Avoid florid description, emotive words, and excessive adjectives and adverbs as in "The Golden Gate Bridge silhouetted against the azure blue sky gives an awesome impression of majestic glory." A descriptive speech should not sound like a page from a poor literary magazine. By emphasizing information, not beauty, function not poetry, you should be able to make the speech clear, vivid, emphatic, and appropriate without being affected or artificial.

Practicing Description

Now let us see how description can be developed. As you work with your speech, revise the language from general to specific. For practice, begin with the following sentence:

Tom was a writer; at all times several pencils were on his desk.

The sentence labels Tom as a writer, and it begins to describe some of the tools of his work. Now let's revise the sentence to make it more descriptive. Try to give a better mental picture:

Tom was a writer; at all times at least five pencils adorned his desk.

"Five" is more descriptive than "several" because it is more specific; "adorned" is more descriptive than "on" because it carries a better mental picture. The following are two additional tries that create totally different pictures of the pencils on Tom's desk:

Tom was a writer; at all times at least five finely sharpened pencils lined the side of his desk, side by side in perfect order from longest to shortest.

Tom was a writer; five stubby pencils, all badly in need of sharpening and all well chewed, were scattered about his desk.

These examples just begin to show the different pictures that can be created depending on how you use the details you have observed.

Earlier you were cautioned about not memorizing a speech. Since you can describe any part of your topic in unlimited ways, keep the essentials in mind during each practice and use slightly different wordings each time to express your descriptions. By making minor changes each time, you will avoid memorization.

1. Prepare a two- to four-minute description. Write an outline. Grading will focus on quality of topic and clarity and vividness of the description.

2. Write a critique of one or more of the descriptive speeches you heard in class. Outline the speech. As you are outlining it, answer the following questions yes or no:

Specific Purpose

_____ Was the specific purpose clear?

_____ Was the specific purpose appropriate for description?

Content

_____ Did the speaker show good observation of the structure, place, or object he/she describes?

_____ Did the speaker select the necessary elements to make the description complete? ____ size? ____ shape? ____ weight? ____ color? ____ composition? ____ age and condition? ____ relationship among parts?

_____ Did the speaker use any special strategies to help you remember the main points and other key information in the description?

Language

_____ Was the language clear?

_____ Was the language vivid enough for you to "see" what was described?

_____ Was the language emphatic?

_____ Was the language appropriate to the audience?

Delivery

_____ Was the speech well delivered?

Evaluate the speech as (check one) ____ excellent, ____ good, ____ average, ____ fair, ____ poor.

Use the information from your check sheet to support your evaluation.

OUTLINE: DESCRIPTIVE SPEECH

Specific Purpose: To describe the exterior of the Cape Hatteras Lighthouse.

Introduction

I. How many of you have been to America's tallest lighthouse?
II. I recently visited the Cape Hatteras Lighthouse, the tallest in the United States.

Thesis Statement: The Cape Hatteras Lighthouse, located along the Outer Banks of North Carolina, has a 193-foot body and a 15-foot top that I will describe.

Body

I. The lighthouse is located along the Outer Banks of North Carolina.
   A. It stands on the beach.
   B. It stands in stark contrast to its surroundings.
II. The major portion of the lighthouse consists of its body.
   A. It is 193 feet tall.
      1. This would be the same as twenty stories.
      2. The interior has approximately four hundred steps.
   B. The body is shaped like a cylinder, with the base wider in the diameter than the top.
   C. The walls are made of brick.
   D. Black and white stripes spiral the sides of the body.
   E. There are three windows on both the north and south sides.
   F. It was built in 1870.
III. The top of the lighthouse sits on a fenced platform in which the actual light is enclosed.
   A. The height from the top of the body to the tip of the lighthouse is 15 feet.
   B. The platform's base is shaped like a half cone, with the base of the cone fitting on top of the main portion.
   C. The platform and the tip of the lighthouse are made of black steel.
   D. The section containing the light is made of clear glass.

Conclusion

I. Although the Cape Hatteras Lighthouse is only 208 feet tall, it really looks taller against its background.

II. America's tallest lighthouse is a major scenic attraction of Cape Hatteras.

___

As you read this speech analyze the descriptions of size, shape, weight, color, composition, age, condition, and relationship among parts.[1] Which descriptions are clear? Which are vivid? Which need more or better development? After you have read the speech aloud at least once, read the analysis in the other column.

SPEECH: The Cape Hatteras Lighthouse

I'm sure that some of you may have been atop the tallest building in this city or that country. But have any of you been up the tallest lighthouse? I've had a chance to visit the Cape Hatteras Lighthouse, the tallest lighthouse in America, and tonight I'd like to describe it to you.

The lighthouse is located along the Outer Banks of North Carolina. It stands on the beach in stark contrast to its surroundings. The lighthouse stands over 200 feet tall. Now, many of you may not think 200 feet is very much, but it is for a lighthouse, especially when it doesn't contain an elevator, and you try to climb the four hundred steps that comprise the twenty flights of stairs. When you stop to think of it, that's the equivalent of a twenty-story building!

Now, 193 feet of this structure is the body. The body is a somewhat cylindrical figure with the base wider than the top; the base is about 50 feet wide and the top is about 15 feet wide. The outside walls are made of brick, which seems to last pretty well since the lighthouse was built in 1870 right after the Civil War, some 110 years ago. Still this is relatively young for a lighthouse; most famous lighthouses date from the sixteenth or seventeenth centuries. The body of the lighthouse is painted black and white stripes all the way up; the stripes are about 10 feet wide, and they spiral their way up the entire body.

On top of this main structure is a 24-foot-wide steel platform, which contains the glass structure that has the light inside it. This platform has a half-cone shaped body with the bottom of the cone fitting exactly on the top of the base of the main structure. Inside a

ANALYSIS

The speaker begins by trying to develop common ground with the audience. The question is used to heighten audience attention.

This sentence locates the lighthouse.

In this section the speaker does a good job of giving meaning to "200 feet."

In this context, "somewhat cylindrical" is descriptive. The specific dimensions add to the overall picture. Mention of the age of the lighthouse gives a little more feel for its condition. The 10-foot-wide stripes "spiral their way up the entire body" is quite descriptive. Use of geometric form helps sharpen the description.

I particularly like the phrasing "an upside-down cone."

The conclusion emphasizes the overall picture. Although the speech is not especially creative, it does present a clear, descriptive picture. I believe an audience can *see* the lighthouse as the speaker finishes.

fenced area is the solid glass-paned structure that contains the light. On top of the glass structure is a top with a pointed roof that's like an upside-down cone. Now, the tip of this roof and the steel platform are all black. And the glass is clear so the light can be seen from all directions.

Although the Cape Hatteras Lighthouse is only 208 feet tall, it really looks taller against its background. The black and white stripes make it stand out against the blue background of the ocean and sky whether it's day or night. America's tallest lighthouse is a major scenic attraction of Cape Hatteras.

NOTE

1.   Delivered in Speech class, University of Cincinnati. Printed by permission of Karen Zimmer.

ELEVEN

SPEECHES OF DEFINITION

Since we cannot solve problems, or learn, or even think without meaningful definitions, the ability to define clearly and vividly is essential for the effective communicator. Ever since Plato first attacked the Sophists for their inability to define and classify, rhetoricians have seen definition as a primary tool of effective speaking. In fact, Richard Weaver, representing the view of many modern scholars, has named definition as the most valuable of all lines of development.[1]

In this chapter we first look at the most common ways words are, or can be, defined. Then we look at preparation of a speech of definition.

HOW WORDS ARE DEFINED

Although they differ in type, both of the following are examples of definition in speeches that show how the speaker is going to use the word:

Let's talk for a moment about humanity. By humanity, I really mean "people skills"—our ability to work with each other.[2]

And I know something about humility. For example, I was born in Nebraska, and my apologies to any of you here today who were

This park ranger is classifying and differentiating between two types of shells. This is one of the most common methods of definition. Think of the many times each day you use classification and differentiation.

born in Nebraska, but many Californians feel that Nebraskans are virtually brain-dead. It came home to me the other day when I saw a bumper sticker that read: "Committing suicide in Nebraska is redundant."[3]

How can you define words you will use in your speeches? The following are the five most common methods of defining. In your speech, they can be used separately or in combination. The ultimate test of the effectiveness of a definition in a speech is whether the audience can understand the meaning and can use the word appropriately.

Classification and Differentiation

When you define by *classification,* you give the boundaries of the particular word and focus on the single feature that gives the word a different meaning from similar words. For instance, a clarinet is a woodwind instrument. This statement defines *clarinet* by class. The definition is completed by saying it is a single-reed instrument consisting of a long tube made of wood, metal, or plastic that flares out at the end and contains holes and keys for playing. Each of the additional details helps to define by stating aspects of the clarinet that *differentiate* it from some or all other woodwind instruments.

Let us look at another example of classification and differentiation. A mansard is a roof (classification). The mansard has two slopes on each of the four sides; the lower slopes are steeper than the upper (description and differentiation).

Most dictionary definitions are of the classification-differentiation variety. The success of definition by classification is tested by the specificity of the differentiating details.

Synonym and Antonym

Synonym and antonym may be the most popular means of defining. Both enable the speaker to indicate approximate, if not exact, meaning in a single sentence; moreover, because they are analogous to comparison and contrast they are often vivid as well as clear. *Synonyms* are words that have the same or nearly the same meanings; *antonyms* are words that have opposite meanings. Defining by synonym is defining by comparison. For instance, synonyms for *sure* are "certain," "confident," and "positive." An antonym is "doubtful." Some synonyms for *prolix* are "long," "wordy," or "of tedious length." Its antonyms are "short" and "concise." Synonyms are not duplicates for the word being defined, but they do give a good idea of what the word means. Synonyms and antonyms are often the shortest, quickest, and easiest ways to clarify the meaning of a new word. Thus, we might define *compute* as "to calculate"; *ebullient* as "bubbling" or "boiling"; *pacific* as "appeasing" or "conciliatory"; and *sagacious* as "keenly perceptive," "shrewd," or "wise." Of course, the synonym or antonym must be familiar to the audience or its use defeats its purpose.

Use and Function

Another way to define is to explain the *use or function* of the object a particular word represents. Thus when you say, "A *plane* is a hand-powered tool that is used to smooth the edges of boards," or "A *scythe* is a piece of steel shaped in a half circle with a handle attached that is used to cut weeds or high grass," you are defining tools by indicating their use. Since the use or function of an object may be more important than its classification, this is often an excellent method of definition.

Etymology and Historical Example

Etymology is the derivation or historical account of a particular word. Since words change over time, origin may reveal very little about modern meaning. In some instances, however, the history of a word reveals additional insight that will help the audience remember the meaning a little better.

Take the word *tantalize,* for instance. *Tantalize* means "to tease" (definition by synonym). Does it mean exactly the same? If so, why use it? Definition by etymology or historical example may give a more complete meaning that will help a person remember the meaning and use it appropriately. In the case of the word *tantalize,* the following explanation adds considerable insight. Tantalus, the mythical king of Phrygia, was the son of Zeus. Tantalus committed the crime of revealing the gods' secrets to mere mortals. For his punishment he was condemned to stand up to his chin in water that constantly receded as he stooped to drink and to be surrounded by branches of assorted fruit that eluded his grasp whenever he reached for them. Thus, for eternity Tantalus was *tantalized* by food and drink that were shown to him but were forever withheld.

In this and similar circumstances, etymology and historical example can give excellent assistance in defining a word. Like any illustration, anecdote, or story, etymology and historical example increase the vividness of the explanation. The best source of word derivation is the *Oxford English Dictionary.*

Examples and Comparisons

Regardless of the way you define, you are likely to have to supplement your definitions with examples and/or comparisons to make them truly understandable. This is especially true when you are defining abstract words. Consider the word *just* in the following sentence: "You are being just in your dealings with another when you deal honorably and fairly." Although you have defined by synonym, listeners may still be unsure of the meaning. If you add, "If Paul and Mary do the same amount of work and we reward them by giving them an equal amount of money, our dealings will be just; if, on the other hand, we give Paul more money because he's a man, our dealings will be unjust." In this case, you are clarifying the definition with both an example and a comparison.

For some words a single example or comparison will be enough. For other words or in communicating with certain audiences, you may need several examples and comparisons.

In most instances, definitions are short and to the point. Occasionally, however, for purposes of information or clarification you may feel a need to present an extended definition. A speech of definition gives excellent practice in informative definition.

Topics

The best topics for extended definition are general or abstract words, words that give you leeway in definition and allow for creative development. On your brainstorming lists look for words like the following:

expressionism	rhetoric	logic
existentialism	epicurean	acculturation
status	fossil	extrasensory perception
epistemology	word processing	humanities

Organizing the Extended Definition

The organization of a speech of definition is likely to follow the organization of a dictionary definition. For instance, *Webster's Third New International Dictionary* defines *jazz* as "American music characterized by improvisation, syncopated rhythms, contrapuntal ensemble playing, and special melodic features peculiar to the individual interpretation of the player." This definition suggests four topics ("improvisation," "syncopation," "ensemble," and "special melodies") that could be used as a basis for a topic order for the speech. Assuming that you understand each of these topics, you might organize your speech as follows:

Specific Purpose: To explain the four major characteristics of jazz

I. Jazz is characterized by improvisation.
II. Jazz is characterized by syncopated rhythms.
III. Jazz is characterized by contrapuntal ensemble playing.
IV. Jazz is characterized by special melodic features peculiar to the individual interpretation of the player.

The key to the effectiveness of the speech would be how well you explain each of the topics. Your selection and use of examples, illustrations, comparisons, personal experiences, and observations will give the speech original, distinctive flavor.

Sometimes a dictionary gives you a starting point for an organization, but you have to create the topics. Suppose you wish to define or clarify the concept of "a responsible citizen." A dictionary will indicate that *responsible* means "accountable" and *citizen* means a "legal inhabitant who enjoys certain freedoms and privileges," but putting these two together does not really tell what a "responsible citizen" is. As you think about citizenship in relation to responsibilities, however, you might begin to list such topics as "social," "civic," and "financial." This thinking would lead you to the definition: "A responsible citizen is one who meets his or her social, civic, and financial obligations." The topical outline that evolves from such a definition would look like this:

Specific Purpose: To define "responsible citizen."

Thesis Statement: A responsible citizen is one who meets his or her social, civic, and financial obligations.

  I. A responsible citizen meets his or her social responsibilities.
 II. A responsible citizen meets his or her civic responsibilities.
III. A responsible citizen meets his or her financial responsibilities.

ASSIGNMENT
Definition Speech

1. Prepare a two- to four-minute definition. An outline is required. Grading will focus on clarity of the definition, organization, and quality of the developmental material.

2. Write a critique of one or more of the definition speeches you hear in class. Outline the speech. As you are outlining it, answer the following questions yes or no:

Specific Purpose

_____ Was the specific purpose clear?

_____ Was the specific purpose appropriate for definition?

Content

_____ Did the speaker select a method of definition, or combination, that truly clarified the word or concept? _____ classification? _____ synonym? _____ use or function? _____ etymology?

_____ Did the speaker use examples to develop the definition?

_____ Did the speaker show his/her expertise with the definition?

_____ Did the speaker use any special strategies to help you remember key aspects of the definition?

Organization

_____ Did the speech follow a topic order?

_____ If not, was the order appropriate for a definition?

Language

_____ Was the language clear? _____ vivid? _____ emphatic? _____ appropriate?

Delivery

_____ Was the speech well delivered?

Evaluate the speech as (check one) _____ excellent, _____ good, _____ average, _____ fair, _____ poor.

Use the information from your check sheet to support your evaluation.

OUTLINE: SPEECH OF DEFINITION (2–4 MINUTES)

Notice the clear statement of purpose and clear elucidation of the three main points, ensuring a clearly organized speech. Also notice that each main point is an essential part of the definition. This 160-word outline is within the recommended limits for a two- to four-minute speech.

Specific Purpose: To discuss the three major points in the definition of the word "fossil."

Introduction

  I. Haven't we all at some time picked up an object and thought it was a fossil?
  II. The common concept of a fossil is not clear.

Thesis Statement: A fossil must be the remains of a plant or animal, the remains must be preserved in rock by natural means, and the remains must be old.

Body

I. A fossil must be the remains of a plant or animal.
   A. This rules out all objects that never lived.
   B. This aspect of the definition would still seem to include recently living animals and plants.
II. The remains must be preserved in rock by natural means.
   A. Imprints are not natural means.
   B. Chemical replacement is the chief natural means.
III. The remains must be old.
   A. Our usual definitions of old aren't very useful.
   B. A fossil implies a degree of antiquity older than historic times.

Conclusion

I. Thus, a fossil can be described as the remains of a plant or animal, preserved in rock by natural means, and having a degree of antiquity older than historic times.

Study the following speech in terms of organization, clarity of definition, and means of developing the aspects of the definition.[4] Before you attempt to evaluate, read the speech aloud at least once. After you have read and analyzed the speech, turn to the detailed analysis.

ANALYSIS

The speaker begins with a question that states a reasonable assumption. With his allusion to the professors as fossils, the speaker got the laugh he wanted without detracting from the subject matter. Well-used humor that grows from the content will usually contribute to a speech.

This first main point is clearly stated. Enumeration is a satisfactory transitional device, for it lets the audience know

SPEECH: A Definition of Fossils

Haven't we all at some time picked up an object of some sort and wondered whether it was a fossil? Perhaps you found an old arrowhead or a petrified cow's horn and thought it was a fossil. Then you've got some people who like to refer to teachers or professors as fossils. So as you can see there is a great diversity as to what people commonly think fossils are. But there are three basic qualities that all fossils must possess.

First, a fossil must be preserved remains of a plant or animal. Well, this right away eliminates things that never have lived, such as Indian arrowheads, pretty stones, or crystals. Some people think these things are fossils but they aren't. What about the animals that die in the woods and their bones are left lying around? Aren't they preserved? Well, to a certain extent they are; but this example I think we'll find will be eliminated by the next part of the definition, which is that the fossil must be preserved by natural means.

Well, now, you can go and stick your foot or drop a leaf in some concrete and get a nice print. Fine. You can put your hand in some mud and make a nice imprint and watch it fill over. And, sure, maybe after the concrete or the mud hardens you might think you have a fossil, but you don't because it wasn't preserved by natural means. Now, what is natural means in relation to fossils? Well, specifically it's chemical replacement. I can draw a rough contrast to chemical replacement by what happens to this class after it leaves out. Now, I call it student replacement. As soon as the bell rings, some of us are kinda slow, we take our time getting our books together, and some of us get out very quickly. Well, as we go out, other students come in and take our places—gradually the whole class is replaced. And if I were standing up here, I would see the exact same arrangement of chairs, but the composition would be different. There'd be different people; their clothes would be different colors. So we have the same exact shapes, but we have a different composition. And this is what happens with fossils when they're replaced. The animals die or fall into the sea. The compounds within the shell are very unstable. So we have another compound that comes in and replaces them. And one by one we get a completely new object in the same shape but different composition.

Now the last criterion, one that's sort of a new point in geology, is how old is the fossil. Well, they have to be extremely old. I once

what point is being considered. Throughout this section and the rest of the speech, the speaker tends to overuse "well." Extraneous words of this kind seldom serve any useful purpose. In the speaker's favor, notice that throughout most of the speech his word choice is specific and concrete.

Notice that even though the second main point was introduced at the end of the first section, some of the emphasis is lost. Perhaps part of the problem is the abandonment of the enumeration. Speakers, especially beginners, tend to begin series with such statements as "the first. . . ." The device is self-defeating, however, if "one" is never followed by "two," "three," and "four." He might well have introduced the second part by saying, "The second characteristic of a fossil is that it must be preserved in rock by natural means." "Now, what is natural means . . ." represents a very good use of the rhetorical question. Well-phrased and well-presented questions interspersed throughout the speech encourage the audience to think along with the speaker. His explanation of chemical replacement is a very interesting invented comparison. It represents excellent use of originality and audience adaptation.

This transition and statement of the third main point are quite good. Notice, however, that the speaker has given up his enumeration. The story about the difference between zoology and geology is a good one. Although something may well stop "stinking" within a few months, the story adds another touch of humor to the speech. The final two sentences in this section are rather weak. It would have been better for the speaker to state his material more authoritatively.

heard a little story that says if it stinks, it belongs to zoology; if it doesn't, it belongs to the study of fossils. Well, most geologists will concede that a fossil must have a degree of antiquity older than historic time, and this will roughly go back to, say, 7000 B.C. or something like this. Scientists are not quite sure when.

A good summary. At the end of the speech, however, the "thank you" is unnecessary. If the speech was good, the audience will be appreciative anyway; if the speech was not good, the "thank you" has no real effect on the quality of the speech. Despite some questionable word selection and a few grammatical lapses, this is a worthy model for a speech of definition.

So, grouping all these things together, we can say that a fossil is the remains of a plant or animal, preserved by natural means in rock, and possessing a degree of antiquity older than historic times. Thank you.

NOTES

1. Richard Weaver, "Language Is Sermonic," in James L. Golden et al., eds., *The Rhetoric of Western Thought,* 3d ed. (Kendall Hunt, 1983).
2. Vince Kontny, "Business and Education, A Crucial Connection," *Vital Speeches,* May 1, 1986, 438.
3. Ibid.
4. Delivered in Speech class, University of Cincinnati. Printed by permission of Frank Ettensohn.

TWELVE

EXPOSITORY SPEECHES: USING RESOURCE MATERIAL

Throughout history people have sought answers to questions about the world around them. Unanswered questions stimulate research; research yields facts; and facts, when properly ordered and developed, yield understanding. Oral communication of the understanding of these questions is often made through reports, lectures, or the label we use in this chapter, expository speeches.

For effectiveness, meaningful expository speaking requires a creative use of source material beyond the experience of the speaker. In this chapter, we consider means of going beyond your own knowledge and then reporting that information in your speech. We will look at topics, library sources, interviewing, using source material, and avoiding pitfalls.

EXPOSITORY SPEECH TOPICS

Almost any topic on your brainstorming list can be used for an expository speech, but some will be better candidates than others. The test is whether preparation for the speech requires extensive research. If the answer is yes, it is probably a good candidate for this assignment.

The following lists, which are grouped under four broad categories of types of expository speeches, give examples of topics that make good expository topics:

Political, Economic, and Social Issues

air pollution solutions	effects of marijuana	cable television
cancer research	women's rights	effects of TV on children
urban renewal	solar power	school financing methods

Historical Events and Forces

pyramids	origin of gunpowder	Circus Maximus
one-room schools	Roman roads	pirates
castles	chivalry	Napoleonic wars
Stonehenge	witches	The Inquisition

Theories, Principles, and Laws

binomial theorem	magnetism	Archimedes' Law
condensation	binary number system	light refraction
relativity	X rays	harmonics
multiplier effect	supply and demand	

Critical Appraisals

Picasso	Van Gogh	jazz
new wave	Rembrandt	science fiction

LIBRARY SOURCES

In Chapter 3, we discussed the card catalog, the *Readers' Guide to Periodical Literature,* and the *Magazine Index* in locating books and articles to use for your speeches. In this section, we review these and look at other library sources that are basic to speech research, and we discuss a strategy for using each type of source material most advantageously.

Books

Books are especially good sources for major topics on which large amounts of material are available. Whether your library is large or small, well equipped or poorly equipped, it is likely to have at least one or two books on any subject you choose, but you must know how to find what you need. The card catalog indexes the library's holdings by title, author, and subject.

Good researchers often have to be creative to uncover all the books their library holds on a particular topic. Suppose you were researching the topic "unemployment." Whether you find anything or not under that heading, with a few minutes of creative thinking you should be able to come up with such additional headings as "employment," "national programs for unemployment," "state programs for unemployment," "poverty," "public works," "economics," "welfare," and other related headings. Many of your library's books will often be listed under these related headings.

Periodicals and Magazines

Periodicals are publications that appear at fixed periods: weekly, biweekly, monthly, quarterly, or yearly. Material you get from weekly, biweekly, and monthly magazines is more current than what you find in books. Of course, some magazines are more accurate, more complete, and more useful than others. Since you must know where and how to find articles before you can evaluate them, you should know and use several indexes: *Readers' Guide to Periodical Literature, Magazine Index, Education Index, Humanities Index,* and *Social Sciences Index.*

The *Readers' Guide to Periodical Literature,* an index of some 200 popular magazines and journals, is an excellent source for topics covered in popular magazines.

The *Magazine Index,* an index of nearly 350 magazines covering the past five years, is an excellent source of recent magazine articles. Instead of being in book form, the *Magazine Index* is on microfilm on a special machine usually located in the same area of the library as the *Readers' Guide.* A special aspect of the *Magazine Index* is that each month the editors feature a number of "Hot Topics," which are located in a looseleaf binder near the microfilm machine.

The *Education Index,* a cumulative subject index to a selected list of some 200 educational periodicals, proceedings, and yearbooks, will lead you to material directly or indirectly related to the field of education. You can find articles on such topics as school administration, adult education, intelligence, morale, tests and scales, and competency testing.

The *Social Sciences Index* and *Humanities Index* are each guides to more than 250 periodicals. These indexes have been published separately since 1974, when the *Social Sciences and Humanities Index* was divided in two. In contrast to the *Readers' Guide,* which indexes popular magazines, these indexes cover scholarly journals. The *Social Sciences Index* includes such journals as *American Journal of Sociology, Economist,* and *Psychological Review;* the *Humanities Index* includes such journals as *Modern Language Quarterly, Philosophical Review,* and *Quarterly Journal of Speech.*

To be a good researcher you have to know when a periodical index is likely to be the best source. First, a magazine may be your best source when the focus of the topic you are considering is less than two years old. Since it usually takes one to three years for current topics to appear in books and encyclopedias, it may be a waste of time to search the card catalog or encyclopedias for information. Occasionally a book is rushed into print within six months of an event, but such speed is rare (and the worth of such a hastily prepared work is questionable). Second, a magazine is probably your best source when the topic is so limited in scope that it is unlikely to provide enough material for a book or when you are looking for a very specific aspect of that particular topic. Third, a magazine may be your best source when you are looking for contemporary reactions to events at the time they actually occurred.

If you decide on using magazine indexes you have to know how to proceed in order to find the material you need. Indexes are published yearly for years before the current edition and in monthly and quarterly supplements for the current year. In order to find appropriate articles about your topic, you need to determine when the event occurred or during what years the topic was actively discussed. For example, if you are preparing a speech on what it was like to be a television writer during the McCarthy era, it would be a waste of time to begin your research with indexes of the 1980s. Rather, you should begin your research in 1953, the height of the McCarthy era, and work forward and backward from there until the supply of articles dries up. If you are preparing a speech on the effects of the Arab oil embargo of the early 1970s, you would begin with 1973.

Encyclopedias are books or series of books that promise to cover all subjects from A to Z. For such subjects as animals, countries, art, and other broad headings, you are likely to find important, basic information about the subject. Not only do encyclopedias give you an excellent overview of many subjects, but they also include bibliographies. As a result, an encyclopedia may be a good starting point for some broad subjects. But because the material is very general, covering only what is called "common knowledge," you should never limit your research to an encyclopedia.

Although an encyclopedia may be a good starting point, relatively few of the articles are very detailed, because they cannot possibly cover every topic completely. In addition, unless you consult an encyclopedia that was published that year, material is anywhere from one to five years out of date. Most libraries have a recent edition of *Encyclopaedia Britannica, Encyclopedia Americana,* or *World Book Encyclopedia.*

Encyclopedias

Statistical sources are books devoted to presenting statistical information on a wide variety of subjects. When you need facts and details, such as statistics about population, records, continents, heads of state, weather, or similar subjects, you should refer to one of the many single-volume sources that report such data. Two of the most popular sources in this category are the *World Almanac and Book of Facts* and the *Statistical Abstract.*

Statistical Sources

Biographical sources provide accounts of people's lives. When you need biographical details, from thumbnail sketches to reasonably complete essays, you can turn to one of the many available biographical sources. In addition to full-length books and encyclopedia entries, you should use such books as *Who's Who* (British subjects) and *Who's Who in America* (short sketches of U.S. citizens) or *Dictionary of National Biography* and *Dictionary of American Biography* (rather complete essays about prominent British subjects and U.S. citizens, respectively).

Biographical sources are excellent sources of information and personal details about people you plan to mention in your speech.

Biographical Sources

Despite the relatively poor quality of reporting in many of our daily newspapers, newspaper articles can still be good sources of facts and

Newspapers

interpretations of contemporary problems. Your library probably holds indexes of your nearest major daily and the *New York Times.*

You should approach newspaper research much the same way as you approach magazine research. Use newspapers to provide information on subjects that were current at a particular time.

Since library holdings vary so much, you should consult your reference librarian for details of other bibliographies, indexes, and special resources that your library may have.

INTERVIEWING

Although you are likely to go to written sources first for speech material, you should not overlook the potential of the interview. As newspaper reporters can attest, one or two good interviews can provide excellent, usable material for many speech topics.

Because good interviews do not "just happen," let us look at the principles that govern good interviewing for information. Interviewing involves defining the purpose of the interview, selecting the best person to interview, planning carefully, writing questions, conducting the interview itself, and interpreting the results.

Defining the Purpose of the Interview

Too often interviewers go into an information interview without a clear purpose for the interview. Your purpose is clear when you can write it in one complete sentence. Without such a clear purpose, your list of questions all too likely will have no direction. As a result, you will come out with information that does not fit well together. Suppose you are thinking about getting information about the food service in your dormitory. The following are possible specific purposes for your interview:

1. To get a personal sketch of the person responsible for meal planning

2. To determine the major elements a dietitian must take into account in order to plan dormitory meals

3. To determine how a dietitian can run a cost-effective program that provides good nutrition at a reasonable price

Somewhere on campus or in the larger community, there are people who have or who can get the information you want. How do you find out whom you should interview? Suppose you are going to be discussing a question related to food service in your dormitory. One of the employees can tell you who is in charge of the dining hall. Or you could phone your student center and inquire about who is in charge of food service. When you've decided whom you should interview, make an appointment. You cannot walk into an office and expect the prospective interviewee to drop everything on the spur of the moment.

Before going into the interview, get information on the topic. If, for instance, you are going to interview the dietitian who determines the menus and orders the food, you should already know something about the job of dietitian and something about the problems involved in ordering and preparing institutional food. Interviewees are more likely to talk with you if you appear informed; moreover, familiarity with the subject will enable you to ask better questions. If for some reason you

Selecting the Best Person

Interviewing is one of the best ways to find interesting material for speech topics. Good interviews don't just happen: you must select the best person to interview, and you must ask the right questions.

go into an interview uninformed, then at least approach the interviewee with enthusiasm and apparent interest in the job.

You should also be forthright in your reasons for scheduling the interview. Whether your interview is for a class project, a newspaper article on campus food, or some other reason, say so.

Planning Carefully

Good interviewing results from careful planning. A good plan begins with good questions. Write down all the questions you can think of, revise them until you have worded them clearly and concisely, and put them in the order that seems most appropriate. Your questions should be a mix of open and closed questions and should be neutral rather than leading. Moreover, you should be alert to the need for follow-up questions.

Open and closed questions. *Open questions* are broad based. They range from those with virtually no restrictions like, "Will you tell me about yourself?" to those that give some direction like, "Will you tell me about your preparation for this job?" *Closed questions* are those that can be answered yes or no or with only a few words, such as, "Have you had a course in marketing?" to "How many restaurants have you worked in?" Open questions encourage the person to talk; closed questions enable the interviewer to get much information in a short time.

Which type of question is superior? The answer depends on what kinds of material you are looking for and how much time you have for the interview. An opinion poll interviewer who wants specific responses to specific questions relies mostly or entirely on closed questions; a person primarily interested in the thoughts and feelings of another person may ask all open questions. In an information-getting interview for a speech, you will want enough closed questions to get the specifics you need and enough open questions to stimulate people to include anecdotes, illustrations, and personal views.

Neutral and leading questions. *Neutral questions* are those in which the person is free to give an answer without direction from the interviewer; *leading questions* are those in which the interviewer suggests the answer expected or desired. A neutral question would be, "How do you like your new job?" A leading question would be, "You don't like the new job, do you?" In the majority of interviewing situations, leading questions are inappropriate. They try to force the person in one direction and make the person defensive.

Primary and follow-up questions. *Primary questions* are planned ahead of time; *follow-up questions* relate to the answers you get to the primary questions. Some follow-up questions encourage the person to continue ("And then?" "Is there more?"); some probe into what the person has said ("What does 'frequently' mean?" "What were you thinking at the time?"); and some plumb the feelings of the person ("How did it feel to get the prize?" "Were you worried when you didn't find her?").

Your effectiveness with follow-up questions may well depend on your skill in asking them. Since probing follow-up questions can alienate the interviewee (especially when the questions are seen as threatening), in-depth probes work best after you have gained the confidence of the person and when the questions are asked in a positive climate.

When you list your questions leave enough space between them to fill in the answers as completely as possible. It is just as important to leave enough space for answers to the follow-up questions you decide to ask. Some interviewers try to play the entire interview by ear. However, even the most skilled interviewer needs some preplanned questions to ensure covering important areas. The order and type of questions depend somewhat upon what you are hoping to achieve in the interview.

Writing Questions

Introduction of the interview. In the opening stages you should, of course, start by thanking the person for taking time to talk with you. During the opening, try to develop good rapport between you and your respondent. Start by asking some questions that can be answered easily and will show your respect for the person you are interviewing. For instance, in an interview with the head dietitian you might start with such questions as, "How did you get interested in nutrition?" or "I imagine working out menus can be a very challenging job in these times of high food costs—is that so?" When the person nods or says "yes," you can then ask about some of the biggest challenges he or she faces. Your goal is to get the interviewee to feel at ease and to talk freely. Since the most important consideration at this initial stage is to create a climate for positive communication, keep the questions easy to answer, nonthreatening, and encouraging.

Body of the interview.   The body of the interview includes the major questions you have prepared. A good plan is to group questions so that the easy-to-answer questions come first and the hard-hitting questions that require careful thinking come later. For instance, the question, "What do you do to try to resolve student complaints?" should be near the end of the interview. You may not ask all the questions you planned to, but you don't want to end the interview until you have the important information you intended to get.

Conclusion of the interview.   As you draw to the end of your planned questions, again thank the person for taking time to talk with you. If you are going to publish the substance of the interview, it is a courtesy to offer to let the person see a draft of your reporting of the interview before it goes into print. If a person does wish to see what you are planning to write, get a draft to that person well before deadline to give the person the opportunity to read it and to give you the opportunity to deal with any suggestions. Although this practice is not followed by many interviewers, it helps to build and maintain your credibility.

Figure 12.1 gives you an idea of the method of setting up a question schedule for an interview.

Conducting the Interview

The best plan in the world will not result in a good interview unless you practice good interpersonal communication skills in conducting the interview. Let us focus on a few of the particularly important elements of good interviewing.

Be courteous and listen carefully.   Your job is not to debate or to give your opinion, but to get information from someone who has it. Whether or not you like the person and whether or not you agree with the person, you must respect his or her opinions. After all, you are the one who asked for the interview.

Put into practice your best listening skills.   If the person has given a rather long answer to a question, you should paraphrase what he or she has said to make sure your interpretation is correct. A *paraphrase* is a statement of your understanding of what the person has said. For instance, after the dietitian answered the question on interest in nutrition, you might paraphrase by saying, "So, if I understand you correctly, you are saying your interest in dietetics came largely by

Background
What kinds of background and training do
you need for the job?
How did you get interested in nutrition?
Have you worked as a dietitian for long?
Have you held any other food-related
positions?

Responsibilities
What are the responsibilities of your job
besides meal planning?
How far in advance do you plan meals?
What factors do you take into account when
you are planning the meals for a given
period?
Do you have a free hand or are constraints
placed upon you?

Procedures
Is there any set ratio for the number of
times you put a given item on the menu?
Do you take individual differences into
account?
How do you determine whether or not you
will give choices for the entree?
How do you try to answer student
complaints?
How do your prices compare with meals at a
commercial cafeteria?

Figure 12.1. *Interview questions for a school dietitian.*

accident." If your impression is correct, the person will let you know.
If you have misunderstood, it gives the person a chance to correct your
misimpression.

Keep the interview moving. You do not want to rush the person; but when the allotted time is ending, you should call attention to that fact and be prepared to conclude.

Be aware of your nonverbal impression. How you look and act may well determine whether or not the person will warm up to you and give you the kind of information you want. Consider your appearance. You want to be dressed appropriately for the occasion. Since you are taking the person's time, you should show an interest in the person and in what he or she has to say.

Interpreting the Results

The interview serves no useful purpose until you do something with the material, but you should not do anything with it until you have reviewed it carefully. Especially if you took notes, it is important to carefully write complete answers while the information is still fresh in your mind. After you have processed the material from the interview, you may want to show the interviewee a copy of the data you are going to use. You do not want to be guilty of misquoting your source.

You may also find it necessary to check out the facts you have been given. If what the person told you differs from material you have from other sources, you should double-check its accuracy.

The most difficult part is interpreting and drawing inferences from the material. Facts by themselves are not nearly so important as the conclusions that may be drawn from those facts. Carefully think through your analysis of the material before you present the substance in a speech or for publication.

USING SOURCE MATERIAL

As you find material, you will have to test its quality, decide how to cite the sources, and develop it creatively.

Testing Quality

The first test of the quality of your information is whether you have enough. Since finding most of the material on any subject could take a team of researchers weeks or more, for a class assignment we expect the speech to be comprehensive "within reason."

Do you have enough sources? To meet the test of having enough sources, you should have at least four different authoritative sources of information. Look into eight or ten different sources and then focus your efforts on the best four.

Do you have the right information? If you research properly, you will have more material on hand than you can read completely. But to know whether the material you have includes the information you need, you should develop an evaluation system that will enable you to review the greatest amount of information in the shortest period of time.

A skill that helps you with this is skimming. *Skimming* is the process of checking the source for certain predetermined characteristics. For instance, if you are evaluating a magazine article, spend a minute or two finding out what it covers. Does it really present information on the part of the topic you are exploring? Does it contain any documented statistics, examples, or quotable opinions? Is the author qualified to draw valid conclusions? If you are evaluating a book, read the table of contents carefully, look at the index, and skip-read pertinent chapters asking the same questions you would for a magazine article. During this skimming period, you will decide which sources should be read in full, which should be read in part, and which should be abandoned. Minutes spent in evaluation will save you hours of useless reading.

A second test of the quality of your information is whether the material you plan to use is accurate and objective. Determining accuracy can be a long and tedious job. In most instances, accuracy can be reasonably assured by checking the fact against the original source, if one is given, or against another article or book on the same subject. Although checking accuracy may seem a waste of time, you will be surprised at the difference in "facts" reported in two or more sources. If at least two sources say about the same thing, you can be a little more confident. Objectivity is tested much the same way. If two or more sources give different slants on the material, then you will know that what is being discussed is a matter of opinion. Only after you have examined many sources are you in a position to make an objective value judgment.

Citing Sources

A special problem of a research speech is how to cite source material. In speeches, as in any communication in which you are using ideas that are not your own, you should attempt to work the source of your

"According to an article about Margaret Thatcher in last week's Time magazine . . ."

"In the latest Gallup poll cited in last week's issue of Newsweek . . ."

"But in order to get a complete picture we have to look at the statistics. According to the Statistical Abstract, the level of production for the Common Market rose from . . ."

Figure 12.2. *Appropriate source citations.*

material into the context of the speech. Such efforts to include sources not only will help the audience evaluate the content but also will add to your credibility as a speaker. In a written report, ideas taken from other sources are designated by footnotes; in a speech these notations must be included within the context of your statement of the material. In addition, since a speech using sources is supposed to reflect a depth of research, citing the various sources of information will give concrete evidence of your research. Your citation need not be a complete representation of all the bibliographical information. Figure 12.2 gives examples of several appropriate source citations.

Although you do not want to clutter your speech with bibliographical citations, you do want to make sure that you have properly reflected the sources of your key information. If you practice these and similar short citations, you will find that they will soon come naturally.

Developing Creativity

In our discussion of the principles of informative speaking we discussed creativity in terms of finding new combinations for information. The greatest value of the creative process in expository speaking is helping you work out alternative methods of presenting factual material. From a body of factual material, an infinite number of lines of

City	Temperature						Precipitation	
	January		Yearly					
	Max.	Min.	High	Low	Extremes		July	Annual
Cincinnati	41	26	96	2	109	−17	3.3	39
Chicago	32	12	93	−6	103	−39	3.4	33
Denver	42	15	100	−5	105	−30	1.5	14
Los Angeles	65	47	88	39	110	28	T	14
Miami	76	58	96	44	100	28	6.8	59
Minneapolis	22	2	96	−21	108	−34	3.5	24
New Orleans	64	45	98	23	102	7	6.7	59
New York	40	17	97	11	106	−15	3.7	42
Phoenix	64	35	114	27	118	16	T	7
Portland, Me.	32	12	93	−6	103	−39	3.9	42
St. Louis	40	24	97	2	115	−23	3.3	35
San Francisco	55	42	86	33	106	20	T	18
Seattle	44	33	91	15	99	0	.6	38

Table 12.1. *Climatic Data*

development are possible. By using a creative process you can discover the available lines of development and select the one that will work best for you in the speech. To illustrate the inventive process, let us suppose you are planning to give a speech on climate in the United States and in your research you come across the data in Table 12.1.

In the following section, we want to show that (1) one set of data can suggest *several* lines of development on one topic and (2) the same point can be made in different ways.

1. *One set of data can suggest several lines of development.* Before you read the following material, study Table 12.1. What conclusions can you draw from it? If you are thinking creatively, you can draw the following conclusions:
   a. Yearly high temperatures in U.S. cities vary far less than yearly low temperatures.
   b. It hardly ever rains on the West Coast in the summer.
   c. In most of the major cities cited, July, a month thought to be hot and dry, produces more than the average one-twelfth of the precipitation that you might expect for the year.

Thus, this one table will produce at least three conclusions that suggest three different lines of development for a single speech on climate.

2. *The same point can be made in different ways.* Let's consider the statement, "Yearly high temperatures in U.S. cities vary far less than yearly low temperatures."
   a. Statistical development: Of the thirteen cities selected, ten (77%) had yearly highs between 90° and 100°; three (23%) had yearly lows above freezing; six (46%) had yearly lows between zero and 32°; and four (31%) had low temperatures below zero.
   b. Comparative development: Cincinnati, Miami, Minneapolis, New York, and St. Louis, cities at different latitudes, all had yearly high temperatures of 96° or 97°; in contrast, the lowest temperature for Miami was 44°, and the lowest temperatures for Cincinnati, Minneapolis, New York, and St. Louis were 2°, −21°, 11°, and 2°, respectively.
   c. Can you find another way of making the same point?

AVOIDING PITFALLS IN REPORTING

As you practice your expository speeches watch for two problems: using jargon and confusing theory for fact.

Using Jargon

Reports of complex material often get bogged down in jargon. *Jargon* is language that is known to people in a field, but is unknown to those outside that field. Many engineers, mathematicians, economists, and behavioral scientists have trouble talking with people outside their profession because they cannot get past the jargon. Good reporters are able to bridge the gap between specialists and the common person. You must understand your subject and be able to discuss it in language people can understand. Thus, a person discussing classical rhetoric would substitute synonyms for the terms *ethos, logos,* and *pathos.* A speaker explaining economics would find more common words than *microeconomics* and *macroeconomic tendencies,* and a speaker discussing heart disease would find synonyms for such terms as *myocardial infarction* and *myofibril contractile elements.*

Whether your speech is about history, economics, sociology, or any other subject, you must avoid misleading an audience by confusing theories with facts. People hypothesize about many things in this world. From these hypotheses they formulate theories. Be sure that you know whether the supporting material you offer is theory or fact. The formula πr^2 will give the area of a circle, pure water boils at 212 degrees Fahrenheit at sea level, and gravity can be measured. Relativity, evolution, and multiplier effects are theories that may or may not be valid. If you keep this differentiation in mind, you can avoid confusing yourself and your audience.

Confusing Theory for Fact

1. Prepare a four- to seven-minute expository speech. An outline and a bibliography are required. Grading will focus on quality of topic, quality of the content, use of source material, and creativity in development. The speech should be informative and interesting. A question period of one to three minutes will follow (optional).

2. Write a critique of one or more of the expository speeches you hear in class. Outline the speech. As you are outlining it, answer the following questions yes or no:

ASSIGNMENT Expository Speech

Specific Purpose

_____ Was the specific purpose clear?

_____ Was the specific purpose appropriate for exposition?

Content

_____ Did the speaker show his/her expertise with the material?

_____ Did the speaker appear to have enough sources of information?

_____ Did the speaker cite sources adequately?

_____ Did the speech have enough high-quality information?

_____ Did the speaker show creativity in making the information interesting?

_____ Did the speaker use any special strategies to help you remember the main points and other key information in the speech?

Organization

_____ Did the introduction gain attention, gain goodwill of the speaker, and lead into the speech?

_____ Were the main points clear statements?

_____ Was the order appropriate for an expository speech?

_____ Did the conclusion tie the speech together?

Language

_____ Was the language clear? _____ vivid? _____ emphatic? _____ appropriate?

_____ Did the speaker use transitions to emphasize or show relationships among ideas?

Delivery

_____ Was the speech well delivered?

Evaluate the speech as (check one) _____ excellent, _____ good, _____ average, _____ fair, _____ poor.

Use the information from your check sheet to support your evaluation.

OUTLINE: EXPOSITORY SPEECH (4–7 MINUTES)

Specific Purpose: To explain the nature, causes, symptoms, and treatments of dyslexia.

Introduction

  I. Try to read the following sentence (visual aid).
 II. Dyslexia can be a frustrating disorder.

Thesis Statement: Dyslexia is a disorder that affects large numbers of people, has at least three potential causes, is characterized by any combination of six major symptoms, and is treated through drugs and education.

Body

  I. Dyslexia is a disorder that affects large numbers of children.
    A. Dyslexia is "a serious difficulty with reading that cannot be attributed to other causes."

B. Dyslexia affects more than 10 percent of the population.
   1. More than 25 million people suffer from it.
   2. It affects four times as many boys as girls.
II. Dyslexia has several potential causes.
   A. Dyslexia may be caused by abnormalities in areas of the left hemisphere of the brain.
   B. Dyslexia may begin during fetal development due to abnormal levels of a male hormone.
   C. Dyslexia may be caused by malfunctions in the inner ear.
III. Dyslexia is characterized by six symptoms that can occur in different combinations.
   A. Reading skills of dyslexics are far behind those of peers without any apparent explanation.
   B. Letters, words, and numbers are frequently reversed.
   C. There is confusion between left and right with lack of preference.
   D. Speech reversals occur well past infancy.
   E. There is difficulty in learning and remembering printed words or symbols.
   F. There are problems with organizing and managing simple tasks.
IV. Dyslexia is treated with drugs and education.
   A. Drugs have shown both long-term and short-term effects.
   B. The greatest amount of emphasis has been on education.
      1. Dyslexics improve by tracing letters in the air and on paper.
      2. Dyslexics improve by repeating familiar sounds.
      3. Dyslexics improve by repeating words.
      4. Dyslexics learn through phonic analysis.

Conclusion

I. We have seen the nature of, the causes of, the symptoms of, and the treatment for dyslexics.
II. If Albert Einstein was able to contribute, others can.

Bibliography

Daugherty, Jimi. "Dyslexics: Learning to Cope with a Different View," *News Record* (February 24, 1984).

"Dealing with Dyslexia," *Newsweek* (March 22, 1982): 55–56.

"Details on Dyslexia," *Consumer Research Magazine* (August 1985): 38.

"Facts about Dyslexia," *Child Today* (November/December 1985): 23–27.

Kaercher, D. "Diagnosing and Treating Dyslexia," *Better Homes and Gardens* (August 1984): 119–120.

Levinson, Harold. *Smart but Feeling Dumb.* New York: Warner Books, 1985.

Read the following speech aloud at least once.[1] Examine the speech to see how well the topic has been limited, how substantial the research is, how well bibliographical citations have been introduced, and how creatively the information has been developed.

ANALYSIS

SPEECH: Dyslexia

I'd like to ask you all to read this for a moment [speaker shows a visual aid].

Imagine for a moment just how frustrating it would be ot have everything you reab look as jumbled as this sentence. [handwritten reversed text visual aid]

As a result of this very good opening, the audience experiences first-hand the frustration of the dyslexic.

The speaker clarifies the four areas that she will cover in the speech.

Here the speaker begins the first main point. Although we get a good idea of where we

You probably found this effort a frustrating experience. What it said was, "Imagine for a moment just how frustrating it would be to have everything you read look as jumbled and foreign as this sentence." Yet, this is how people with dyslexia are likely to perceive what they read [refers again to visual aid]. Today, I'd like to help you understand the nature of dyslexia, its probable causes, its major symptoms, and its treatments.

Dyslexia is defined as "a serious difficulty with reading that cannot be attributed to other causes." According to Dr. Kaiser of the Office of Veterans Affairs and Handicapped Services here on the

University of Cincinnati campus, about one in every ten Americans is affected by this problem. Roughly, that's more than 25 million Americans. Moreover, the disability occurs in four times as many boys as girls, and it affects adults as well as children. Many dyslexics are frustrated people living in a topsy-turvy world where nothing seems to go right. According to Earl Chambers, a Cincinnati graduate of a couple of years ago who is a dyslexic, "It's the not knowing that frustrates you," he says. "When facing a time-testing situation, for example, a dyslexic might panic at the thought of having to read and answer fifty questions and not ever have time to finish the test." Mary Lou Danefield, coordinator of disability programs in the Minnesota schools, says, "Dyslexia can be combated— but first it must be understood." Dyslexia is the most challenging of the learning disabilities that have been discovered in recent years. The point is that many children who in the past have been diagnosed as retarded and who are treated as untrainable may well be dyslexics who can be helped to lead a relatively normal life.

Although researchers have been studying dyslexia seriously for the past thirty years, the primary causes are still a mystery. Nevertheless, researchers have focused their studies on several potential causes. According to an article in the March 22, 1982, issue of *Newsweek,* researchers at the Beth Israel Hospital in Boston are in search of clues to the biological roots of dyslexia. Some researchers have found abnormalities in the left hemisphere of the brain associated with language development. Other researchers hypothesize that the disorders may result from damage to the left side of the brain during fetal development, perhaps due to abnormal levels of a male hormone. These researchers point to the fact that there is an increased rate of left-handedness among dyslexics. Some recent research has suggested that dyslexia is linked to a defect on the fifteenth chromosome. From a different angle, Dr. Harold Levinson, in his book *Smart but Feeling Dumb,* chronicles his efforts to validate the hypothesis that brain dysfunction comes from inner ear problems. Researchers are hoping that by eventually pinpointing causes, they will discover means of prevention.

Whatever the causes of dyslexia, researchers are in agreement about the major symptoms. While a trained psychologist is the best judge of when dyslexia occurs, he is likely to look especially for these six symptoms or combination thereof.

are in the speech, the speaker needs to state the first point more specifically.

Notice that throughout the speech the speaker uses a great deal of specific material. Some of her material came from interviews (specifically the material about the size of the problem) and some from written sources.

Good use of a quotation. I like the way she personalizes the material in this section.

Notice that the speaker gives short, but satisfactory, citations of the sources of supporting material.

Good transition to causes, the second main point of the speech.

Here is more good documentation of supporting material.

This section includes a reasonably good explanation of the potential causes.

Once again, we see a good transition statement leading us to the third topic of the speech, major symptoms.

Notice how each of the symptoms is listed and explained. In most cases the speaker gives one or two short examples to help us understand the symptom. An excellent job of covering the six symptoms in a relatively short section.

Part of the reason why this is a good expository speech is that high-quality information is well organized. Moreover, even in this relatively short speech, she includes enough supporting material to help us understand.

Again we see a good transition to the fourth topic, treatment.

This quotation puts the importance of continuous treatment into perspective.

A clear statement of the specifics of treatment, drugs, and education.

Good job of comparing the value of treatments. She shows that although there have been some successes with drugs, the greater success has been with education.

One symptom is exhibition of reading skills that are far behind those of peers *without any apparent explanation.* We're aware that many retarded children have reading difficulties—but we're talking about otherwise normal people.

A second is the frequent reversal of letters or numbers in both reading and writing—*God* for *dog* or *was* for *saw,* for example.

A third is confusion between left and right and the lack of preference for using one hand over the other. By the age of six, most children develop a hand preference—dyslexics may not.

A fourth symptom is reversal in speech well past infancy. For example saying *aminal* instead of *animal.*

A fifth is serious difficulty in learning or remembering any kind of printed words or symbols. When confronted with the number 537, for instance, the dyslexic may not recognize it and, if he or she can recognize it, may quickly forget it.

A sixth problem is organizing simple patterns—a difficulty in following simple instructions. A dyslexic might not be able to respond correctly to "Walk to the first stop light, turn right, and go to the third house."

Now that we have looked at the nature, suspected causes, and symptoms, let's move on to the treatment of dyslexia. According to Dr. C. Keith Conners of the Children's Hospital National Medical Center, and reported in *Newsweek,* dyslexia is like alcoholism: "It is never really cured." But, nearly every dyslexic can achieve a sixth-grade reading level, and dyslexics have finished college and gone on to graduate school.

Dyslexia is being treated by drugs and by education. Some researchers who are trying to deal with root causes are experimenting with drug therapy. For instance, Dr. Levinson is working with antihistamines to deal with what he believes are inner ear problems. Another treatment of dyslexia is with a drug called piracetam, which resembles a brain chemical. It has proved somewhat effective in treatment by aiding transmission between two hemispheres of the brain. But to date the best treatment for dyslexia is education. Dyslexics can be helped to improve their condition by professionals who work on a one-to-one basis to help them do activities like tracing letters in the air or on paper until they become familiar with the letters. Another educational method is the use of spelling. By learning and repeating a letter time and time again, dyslexics become familiar with the way that letter is pronounced. The third form of treatment is through the use of phonics. They are taught to sound out letters rather than to memorize whole words.

By learning more about dyslexia—by understanding the causes, symptoms, and treatment—we can better understand this disorder that affects so many people. If Albert Einstein, Woodrow Wilson, and Nelson Rockefeller, who were dyslexics, were able to deal with their problems, we should certainly be able to hope for the best.

Good short summary.

Excellent final point. It leaves the speech on an upturn.

NOTE

1. Delivered in Speech class, University of Cincinnati. Printed by permission of Kelley Kane.

**Part Three
SUGGESTED
READINGS**

Biagi, Shirley. *Interviews That Work: A Practical Guide for Journalists.* Belmont, Calif.: Wadsworth, 1986. An excellent short work that focuses on information interviewing.

Guth, Hans P. *Words and Ideas,* 5th ed. Belmont, Calif.: Wadsworth, 1980. Although this is a book on writing, chapters on observation, personal experience, definition, tone and style, and the research report present material that can be adapted to the study of informative speaking.

Jacobsen, David, Paul Eggen, Donald Kauchak, and Carole Dulaney. *Methods for Teaching: A Skills Approach,* 2d ed. Columbus, Ohio: Charles E. Merrill, 1985. A good section on expository and discovery teaching, which focuses on principles of learning.

Lowman, Joseph. *Mastering the Techniques of Teaching.* San Francisco: Jossey-Bass, 1984. In Chapter 5, "Selecting and Organizing Material for Class Presentation," Lowman presents principles of learning, research support for the principles, and value of visual aids.

Petrie, Charles. "Informative Speaking: A Summary and Bibliography of Related Research," *Speech Monographs* 30 (June 1963), 79–91. This twenty-five-year-old summary is still a useful source.

Rubin, Rebecca B., Alan M. Rubin, and Linda J. Piele. *Communication Research: Strategies and Sources.* Belmont, Calif.: Wadsworth, 1986. A comprehensive analysis of research sources.

PERSUASIVE SPEAKING

Perhaps some of your most important speeches will be those given to persuade. Your study of persuasion presupposes an understanding of fundamentals and informative principles. After the presentation of principles of persuasion, the unit considers the skills of reasoning, motivating, and critical evaluation.

THIRTEEN

PRINCIPLES OF PERSUASIVE SPEAKING

Have you ever imagined yourself giving such a stirring speech that you help the nation avoid war, or you push through legislation that guarantees that poverty will be abolished, or you get a date with that person you have had an eye on for six weeks? Although everything works superbly in our fantasies, our real-life attempts at changing attitudes or modifying behavior are not always so successful. Let's face it: Speaking persuasively is perhaps the most demanding of speech challenges. Moreover, there is no formula for success—no set of rules to guarantee effectiveness. Even the highest-paid speech consultants can only promise to suggest speech strategies they believe have a high probability of success. So although we cannot provide a sure-fire formula for success, we can identify the variables of persuasion that lead to success.

In this opening chapter of the persuasive speaking unit, I want to suggest the modifications and extensions of informative speech preparation that must be made to increase your chances of persuading. In Chapters 14, 15, and 16, we will discuss in detail the skills of reasoning, motivating, and critical thinking and will introduce speech assignments giving you an opportunity to put those skills into practice.

For now, we will deal with the elusive answer to the question What makes a speech persuasive? A persuasive speech is one that is intended to reinforce a belief, change a belief, or move an audience to action. Your speech will be more persuasive (1) if your proposition, a persuasive specific purpose, is clear, reasonable, and supportable; (2) if you build the body of the speech with good reasons and evidence; (3) if you organize the speech according to expected audience reaction; (4) if you motivate your audience through emotional appeal; (5) if you build your credibility and use it effectively; and (6) if you deliver your speech convincingly.

WRITE A PERSUASIVE SPEECH PROPOSITION

PRINCIPLE 1

You are more likely to persuade an audience when your proposition is clear, reasonable, and supportable.

Although any random statement may influence another person's actions (merely saying, "I see the new Penney's store opened in Western Woods" may "persuade" another person to go to Penney's for some clothing need), the successful persuader does not leave the effect of the message to chance. A well-worded proposition (persuasive specific purpose) states what you want your audience to believe or to do.

Wording Propositions

Let's consider guidelines for writing a proposition.

1. *Write a tentative proposition that states your specific intent.* For an anti-lottery speech you might try "to prove that state lotteries should be outlawed."

2. *Write several potential wordings of the proposition.* Your first wording may be on target, but it may be more general or abstract than necessary; write at least two more and choose the statement that is the clearest and most specific.

3. *Write the goal so that it contains only one idea.* "To prove that state lotteries and abortion should be outlawed" contains two ideas, either of which might be suitable for a persuasive speech.

4. *Include an infinitive or infinitive phrase that shows your persuasive intent.* You will want to use such infinitives as "to persuade," "to motivate," "to prove," or "to petition."

5. *Consider rewording the proposition if it appears to call for a total change in audience attitude.* Expecting a complete shift in attitude or behavior as a result of one speech is unrealistic. William Brigance, one of the great speech teachers of this century, used to speak of "planting the seeds of persuasion." If you present a

modest proposal seeking a slight change in attitude, you may be able to get an audience to consider the value of your message. Later, when the idea begins to grow, you can ask for greater change. For instance, if your audience believes that taxes are too high, you are unlikely to make them believe otherwise. However, you may be able to influence them to see that taxes are not really as high as they originally thought or not as high as other goods and services. Because your classroom speaking allows only one effort, you are going to have to make the most of it.

6. *Consider rewording the proposition if the action you advocate seems impractical.* When an audience perceives what you want them to do is impractical, they are likely to ignore your appeal regardless of its merits. For instance, if your goal is to persuade the class to write a letter to their representative in Congress to protest a cut in revenue sharing, the act of writing a letter may seem impractical to many class members. If, on the other hand, you change the request to writing a short message on a postcard *and* you give your audience pre-addressed postcards, they are more likely to dash off a few lines if they agree with the merits of your appeal.

   Does this mean you should never ask an audience to do something that may seem impractical? No; but you must recognize that the greater the demand you place on your audience, the more prepared you must be to meet resistance.

After you have written several persuasive propositions you will note that they can be grouped by similarities in intent and subject matter. Since persuasive speeches are often assigned in one of two ways, by intent (or general purpose) or by subject matter, it is useful to understand the distinctions of these classifications. Let's look at each.

Kinds of Persuasive Propositions

Classification by general purpose.   Propositions that are classified by general purpose may be phrased in one of three ways: (1) to *reinforce a belief* held by an audience, (2) to *change a belief* held by an audience, or (3) to *move the audience to act*.

1. *Speeches to reinforce a belief* (often called *inspirational* speeches) are usually based on such universally held social beliefs and values as patriotism, moral–ethical guidelines, and justice. In

such speeches, the speaker will try to strengthen a prevailing attitude. The following are typical propositions designed to reinforce a belief:

To stress that America is the land of opportunity

To reinforce the idea that we have a responsibility to vote

To reinforce the concept that we have freedom of worship

2. *Speeches to change or alter a belief* clearly state the belief or attitude that is to be supported. Although some classmates may favor the propositions before the speech is given, a speech intending to change or alter a belief seeks a change from majority opinion or from current practice. For instance, since Americans may deduct house-payment interest on their federal income tax forms and since most Americans believe that such a deduction is worthwhile, a speech supporting the proposition "to prove that deduction of house-payment interest on federal income tax should be abolished" would seek to change majority opinion. The change of belief may provide a springboard for action, but the focus of the speech is on a logical position in favor of the proposition. The following are typical propositions designed to change a belief:

To prove that capital punishment should be abolished

To persuade the audience that Kentucky should establish a state lottery

To support the proposition that the Bluebirds are the best team on the circuit

To prove that Social Security taxes should be lowered

3. *Speeches to get action* are designed to motivate the audience to take the action stated in the proposition. The audience may or may not already believe in the logic of the proposition. But the speaker wants more than intellectual agreement; he or she wants the audience to act. The following are typical propositions designed to get action:

To motivate the audience to buy Easter Seals

To persuade the audience to eat at the Manor Restaurant

To motivate the audience to buy Wheat Puffs

To persuade the audience to write to their representative in Congress to support the Powell bill

To motivate the audience to see the school's production of "A Chorus Line"

Classification by subject matter.   The subject matter of a persuasive speech proposition may (1) establish a fact (past, present, or future); (2) evaluate a person, place, thing, or action; or (3) propose a policy.

1. *Propositions establishing a fact* attempt to prove that something is true. Not only are propositions of fact a mainstay in courts of law, but also they are common to other contexts as well. The following are typical propositions of fact:

   To prove that Jones is guilty of murder in the first degree

   To persuade the audience that SAT tests are discriminatory

   To prove that Larson is guilty of shoplifting

   To convince the audience that Parsons is guilty of robbery

   To prove that the greenhouse effect is a reality

2. *Propositions of evaluation* are those that attempt to prove that a person, place, thing, or action is good or bad. The following are typical propositions of evaluation:

   To prove that Jones is the best quarterback in the league

   To persuade the audience that small schools are better for most students than large schools

   To prove that accounting is the best course to take to prepare a person for a career in business

3. *Propositions of policy* present a proposed action. Propositions of policy are most likely to be heard in legislative settings where lawmakers give speeches in favor of or opposed to suggested legislation. Propositions of policy are easy to identify for they are likely to include the word "should." The following are typical propositions of policy:

To establish that work on nuclear power plants should be halted

To persuade the class that budgets for women's athletics should be increased

To prove that the United States should raise income taxes

To persuade the class that the United States should establish mandatory, periodic drug tests for all air traffic controllers

Notice that both sets of propositions meet the same tests of propositions for persuasive speeches. Despite their differences in emphasis, a list of propositions can be grouped in either way. For instance, "to prove that Parsons is guilty of robbery" may be listed as either a proposition designed to change the audience's belief or a proposition of fact; "to motivate the audience to go to the school's production of 'A Chorus Line'" may be listed as a proposition to get action or a proposition of policy. Whether your professor assigns speeches by purpose or by content, the advice in the remainder of this chapter will help you prepare a speech giving you the best possible chances for success.

EXERCISE 1
Writing
Propositions

1. Write a persuasive proposition. Rewrite it two or three times with slightly different wordings. Which one would be the best wording for your classroom audience? Why?

2. Is the proposition one to reinforce a belief, change a belief, or move the audience to action?

3. Is the proposition one of fact, evaluation, or policy?

BUILD THE BODY WITH GOOD REASONS AND EVIDENCE

PRINCIPLE 2

You are more likely to persuade an audience when you give them logical reasons and good evidence.

The main points of a persuasive speech are usually stated as reasons, statements that tell *why* a proposition is justified. Human beings take pride in being rational. We seldom do anything without some real or imagined reason. One way of reasoning with your audience is to provide good, well-supported reasons in support of your proposition.

Reasons are statements that answer the question Why? How do you get a list of reasons to consider? You can identify some good reasons by just taking a little time to think about the subject for the speech. For instance, suppose you wanted to persuade your friends to increase their level of exercise. You might begin by asking yourself, "Why should my friends increase their level of exercise?" You might then think of the following three reasons: (1) to help them control their weight, (2) to help them strengthen their cardiovascular system, and (3) to help them feel better. For most of your speeches, however, you will need to supplement your own thoughts with reasons you discover by observing, interviewing, and reading. Find as many reasons as you can through research and then choose the best.

For instance, for a speech in support of the proposition, "The United States should overhaul the welfare system," you might think of or find at least six reasons:

I. The welfare system costs too much.
II. The welfare system is inequitable.
III. The welfare system does not help those who need help most.
IV. The welfare system has been grossly abused.
V. The welfare system does not encourage seeking work.
VI. The welfare system does not encourage self-support.

Once you've compiled a list of possible reasons, select the best ones (probably no more than three or four) on the basis of how well they prove the proposition, whether they can be supported, and how much impact they are likely to have on the audience.

1. *Choose the reasons that best prove the proposition.* Sometimes statements look like reasons, but don't supply much proof. For instance, "The welfare system is supported by socialists" may sound like a reason for overhauling it, but it doesn't really offer much proof that the system needs overhauling.

2. *Choose reasons that can be supported.* Some reasons that sound impressive cannot be supported with facts. A reason that cannot be supported should not be used in the speech. For instance, the fourth reason above, "The welfare system has been grossly abused," sounds like a good one; but if you cannot find facts to support it, you should not use it in your speech. You'll be surprised how many reasons mentioned in various sources have to be dropped from consideration for a speech because they can't be supported.

3. *Choose reasons that will have an impact on the intended audience.* Suppose that in support of the proposition "Eat at the Sternwheeler," you have a great deal of factual evidence to support the reason, "The seafood is excellent." Even though you have a good reason and good support, it would be a poor reason to use in the speech *if the majority of the audience did not like seafood!*

Although you cannot always be sure about the potential impact of a reason, you can make a reasonably good estimate of its possible impact based on your general audience analysis. For instance, on the topic of eating out, a college audience is likely to weigh price much more than an audience of business executives.

Finding Evidence to Support Your Reasons

Reasons are only generalizations. Although some are self-explanatory and occasionally even persuasive without further support, most require development before people will either accept or act upon them. You should look for two major kinds of evidence: fact and expert opinion.

Facts. The best support for any reason are facts, verifiable statements. That metal is heavier than air, that World War II ended in 1945, and that Oakland won the World Series in 1972, 1973, and 1974 are all facts. If you say, "It's really hot today—it's up in the nineties" and the thermometer registers 94 degrees, your support (temperature in the nineties) is factual.

Expert opinions. Statements from people who have a good reputation for knowledge on the subject are *expert opinions.* Although factual support is best, there are times when facts are not available or they are inconclusive. In these situations, you will have to further support your conclusions with opinion. The quality of opinion as evidence depends on whether the source, the person giving the opinion, is an expert or not. If Tom Roth, your gasoline station attendant, says there probably is life on other planets, his statement would not be evidence—the opinion is not expert; his expertise lies in other areas. If on the other hand, Nancy Marshall, an esteemed space biologist, says there is a likelihood of life on other planets, her opinion is evidence—it is expert. Of course, opinions are most trustworthy when they are accompanied by factual data. If Bill Campbell, an automotive engineer, says that a low-cost electric car is feasible, his opinion is valuable since automotive engineering is his area of expertise. If accompanying his opinion, he shows us the advances in technology that are leading to a low-cost battery of medium size that can run for more than two hundred hours without being recharged, his opinion is worth even more.

Let's illustrate evidence by supporting a proposition with fact and opinion.

Specific Purpose: To persuade the class to shop at Schappenhouper's food stores. Why?

Reason: Because the prices are lower.

Evidence by Fact

If we look at prices at four major markets for five basic foods—eggs, chopped meat, lettuce, potatoes, and milk—we find the prices are lower on average as Schappenhouper's. Beginning with eggs, whereas prices at Schappenhouper's are 53 cents a dozen, at store A they are 56 cents, at B they are 61 cents, and at C they are 57 cents. Next let's look at chopped meat . . . , and so on.

Evidence by Expert Opinion

Mrs. Goody, our fraternity cook who comparison shops every week, says, "I shop at Schappenhouper's because prices are lower for comparable foods."

We will analyze reasoning in more depth and discuss speeches using reasoning as the primary means of development in Chapter 14.

EXERCISE 2
Selecting Reasons

1. Write a proposition you could use for your first persuasive speech.

2. Write at least six reasons in support of that proposition.
    I.
    II.
    III.
    IV.
    V.
    VI.

3. Mark the three or four reasons you believe are best.

4. For reason I, find one fact and one opinion that you could use in support.

ORGANIZE ACCORDING TO EXPECTED AUDIENCE REACTION

PRINCIPLE 3

You are more likely to persuade an audience when you organize your material according to expected audience reaction.

Although the nature of your material and your own inclination may affect your organization, the most important guideline is expected audience reaction. As a result, the specific organization you select will depend on whether your audience favors your proposition and to what degree. Every textbook on persuasion discusses the importance of identifying audience attitude toward a topic.

Attitudes

An *attitude* is a predisposition for or against people, places, or things. For instance, in reference to the concept of physical fitness, a person may be predisposed to favor good physical fitness. As a result, that person would have a positive attitude toward physical fitness.

Students of persuasion realize that when people express attitudes there is a difference between their opinions and their behavior. An *opinion* is a verbal expression of an attitude. Saying, "I think physical fitness is important" is an opinion reflecting a favorable attitude about physical fitness. A *behavior,* on the other hand, is an action related to or resulting from an attitude. As a result of their attitudes, people behave in certain ways. For instance, people who believe in the value of physical fitness may work out at least three times a week in order to stay in good physical condition. Working out is the behavior that results from the attitude.

In summary, a person may have a favorable *attitude* toward physical fitness. In conversation, the person will give the *opinion* that good physical conditioning is, in fact, important. Then, as a result of this attitude the person works out at least three times a week.

Classifying Audience Reaction

Since much of your success depends on the kind of audience you face, you must find out your audience's attitude toward your proposition. Audience attitudes are expressed by opinions. These opinions may be distributed along a continuum from hostile to highly in favor (see Figure 13.1). Even though any given audience may have one or a few individuals' opinions at nearly every point of the distribution, audience opinion will tend to cluster at a particular point on the continuum. The

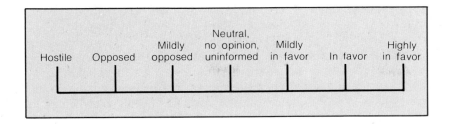

Figure 13.1. *An opinion continuum.*

point at which audience opinions cluster represents the general audience attitude on that proposition.

Except for polling the audience, there is no way of being sure of your assessment. However, by examining the data in the way described in Chapter 3, you will be able to make reasonably accurate estimates. For instance, skilled workers are likely to look at minimum wage proposals differently from business executives; men will look at women's rights issues differently from women; Protestants are likely to look at property tax levies for schools differently from Catholics. The more data you have about your audience and the more experience you have in analyzing audiences, the better are your chances of judging their attitudes relatively accurately. A precise differentiation of opinion is seldom necessary.

As a result of a sample of audience response or a good guess based on insight into audience behavior, you can place your audience in one of the following classifications: *no opinion*—either no information or no interest; *in favor*—already holding a particular belief; *opposed*—holding an opposite point of view. These classifications may overlap. Since you will, however, have neither the time nor the opportunity to present a line of development that will adapt to all possible attitudes within the audience, you should assess the prevailing attitude and knowledge and work from there.

No opinion.   An audience that has no opinion is either uninformed or apathetic. If they are uninformed, you should give them enough information to help them understand the subject before you launch into reasons for asking them to believe or do what you want. Suppose you wanted "to persuade the class to support a move to ungraded primary schools." Probably only a few members of your class will know what an ungraded primary school is. Even those who know the definition may not know enough about it to form an opinion. In the early part of the speech, then, you would explain what an ungraded primary school is and how it works.

Since the class is unlikely to have biases against the topic, you can approach the audience directly. If you can show enough good reasons, you will have a good chance of persuading them. Still, you will have to be very careful about how much time you spend on the informative part of the speech. If you have only five minutes to speak and it takes that long to define an ungraded primary school and show how it works, you won't have any time for presenting reasons and evidence.

If the audience is apathetic, all of your effort can be directed to breaking them out of their apathy. Although an apathetic audience may be difficult to motivate, you will have nearly the entire speech time to create interest and commitment. Suppose you wanted "to persuade the class to attend the production of 'Fiddler on the Roof.'" If the audience is apathetic, you can spend your entire time generating excitement about the production.

In favor. If your audience is in favor, you can devote most of your time to bringing them to a specific action. Although this sounds like an ideal situation, it carries with it many hazards. When an audience is already in favor, they are seldom interested in a rehash of familiar material and reasons. If you make a mistake in your approach, you can actually turn the audience against the proposal.

Many times people are in favor of doing *something,* but they are not in agreement on *what* to do. Your job is to provide a specific course of action they can rally around. When you believe your audience is on your side, try to crystallize their attitudes, recommit them to a particular direction, or suggest a specific course of action that will serve as a rallying point. Suppose you were thinking about giving a speech on the need for increased parking space for students. If students had been talking about this for a long time, they would not be interested in hearing a general call for more parking. On the other hand, if you could focus the speech on the need for an underground garage or a new system for determining priority, you would be giving a solution to a commonly agreed-on problem. The presentation of a well-thought-out specific solution would increase the likelihood of audience action.

Opposed. An audience that is opposed will range in attitude from slightly negative to thoroughly hostile. If an audience is slightly negative, you can approach them rather directly with your plan, hoping that the weight of your argument will swing them to your side. Suppose you wished "to convince the class that the United States is spending too much money for space exploration." Although most people are likely to have an opinion and as many as half may be against the proposal, you can proceed with a rather straightforward presentation of reasons. Such a speech may convince those who are only slightly negative and will not alienate those who may already agree with you.

If they are hostile, you will usually have to approach the topic indirectly—working hard to develop common ground—and perhaps be content with planting the seeds of persuasion and not expecting much at the moment. Suppose you wanted "to persuade the class that the federal government should guarantee a minimum annual income to all citizens." Since there is an excellent chance that most of the audience will be negative to hostile, you aren't likely to get very far with a straightforward approach. To get this kind of an audience even to listen requires a great deal of motivation. Two of the indirect approaches mentioned in the next section will give you a chance to at least hold their attention. Next week, next month, or even next year, some of the audience may come to your way of thinking, but do not expect too much to happen on the basis of one speech.

Methods of Organization

The following organizational methods may be useful as is or they may suggest an organization that you believe will work for your audience given the material with which you have to work. To illustrate persuasive organizational patterns, I will use the same proposition and the same (or similar) arguments. With some topics and some material, one form is likely to be best—the forms are not entirely interchangeable. Nevertheless, by using essentially the same arguments, you can contrast the forms and, I believe, understand their use better.

Statement-of-reasons method. When you believe your listeners have no opinion on the subject, are apathetic, or are perhaps only mildly in favor or opposed, the straightforward topical statement of reasons may be your best organization. With this pattern, each reason is presented as a complete statement justification for the proposition:

Specific Purpose: To persuade the audience to vote in favor of the school tax levy on the November ballot.

I. Income will enable the schools to restore vital school programs.
II. Income will enable the schools to give teachers the raises they need to keep up with the cost of living.
III. The actual cost to each member of the community will be very small.

You will notice that although reasons are the main points for each of the following types of organization, the reasons are worded and organized differently to meet the goals of each of the particular patterns.

Problem-solution method. The problem-solution pattern of reason provides a framework for clarifying the nature of the problem and for illustrating why the new proposal is the best one. There are usually three reasons in a problem-solution speech: (1) that there is a problem that requires action; (2) that the proposal will solve the problem; and (3) that the proposal is the best solution to the problem. This pattern may be best for an audience that has no opinion or is mildly pro or con. Let's see how a problem-solution organization would look for the school tax levy proposition:

Specific Purpose: To persuade the audience to vote in favor of the school tax levy on the November ballot.

I. The shortage of money is resulting in serious problems for public education.
II. The proposed increase is large enough to solve those problems.
III. For now, a tax levy is the best method of solving the schools' problems.

Comparative-advantages method. The comparative-advantages pattern focuses on the superiority of your newly proposed course of action. With this pattern, you are not trying to solve a grave problem as much as you are suggesting a better alternative. You will notice that the comparative-advantages pattern looks much like the statement of reasons pattern. The primary difference is that in this pattern, each reason states one specific advantage of the proposition over current policy. This pattern can work for any audience attitude except hostility. A comparative-advantages approach to the school tax levy proposition would look like this:

Specific Purpose: To persuade the audience to vote in favor of the school tax levy on the November ballot.

I. Income from a tax levy will enable schools to raise the standards of their programs.
II. Income from a tax levy will enable schools to hire better teachers.
III. Income from a tax levy will enable schools to better the educational environment.

Criteria-satisfaction method. When you are dealing with audiences that are opposed to your ideas, you need an organizational pattern that will not aggravate their hostility. The criteria-satisfaction pattern is one of two patterns that are particularly effective with hostile audiences. The pattern focuses on developing a yes-response before you introduce the proposition and reasons. A criteria-satisfaction organization for the school tax levy proposition would look like this:

Specific Purpose: To persuade the audience to vote in favor of the school tax levy on the November ballot.

I. We all want good schools.
A. Good schools have programs that prepare our youth to function in society.
B. Good schools are those with the best teachers available.
II. Passage of the school tax levy will guarantee good schools.
A. Passage will enable us to increase the quality of vital programs.
B. Passage will enable us to hire and keep the best teachers.

Negative method. The negative pattern, the other method that is particularly effective for hostile audiences, focuses on the shortcomings of all of the potential solutions to a problem except the one offered in the proposition. For instance, for the problem of potential sources of funds for schools, money could come from reducing services, from the federal government, from the state government, or from increased property taxes. To persuade a hostile audience to vote for a tax levy, you might use the following organizational pattern:

Specific Purpose: To persuade the audience to vote in favor of the school tax levy on the November ballot.

I. Saving money by reducing services and programs will not help the schools.
II. The federal government will not increase its help to the schools.
III. The state government will not increase its help to the schools.
IV. All we have left is to pass the tax levy.

MOTIVATE THROUGH EMOTIONAL APPEAL

PRINCIPLE 4

You are more likely to persuade an audience when your language motivates them.

Through your reasoning you may be able to convince the audience that your ideas are sound. Yet an audience's intellectual agreement may not be enough to affect their behavior. For instance, people may *believe* that giving to the Cancer Fund is a good idea, but they may not have given. Motivation is the prod that pokes or nudges people from passivity to action.

You motivate people through your wording of key ideas. What you strive for is the creation of emotional appeal through language. Keep in mind, however, that the effect of the use of emotional language in persuasive communication is still not entirely understood: Research results have been inconclusive and at times contradictory.[1]

Emotional Appeals Supplement Logic

Good speech development seems to be logical–emotional. So instead of looking for additional material that will arouse an emotion, you should look for good, logical reasons that *if properly phrased and developed* will arouse emotions.

Suppose you are trying to get your audience to support a more humane treatment of the elderly. One of your reasons might be, "The elderly are often alienated from society." If you have material to support that reason, you can then ask yourself, "How can I phrase the material in a way that will motivate the audience to actually *feel* the impact of that material?" You could say:

> Currently the elderly are alienated from society. A high percentage live in nursing homes, live on small fixed incomes, and exist out of the mainstream of society.

This states the facts, but provides little motivation. Contrast the following statement of the same material:

Currently the elderly are alienated from the society that they worked their entire lives to support. What happens to the elderly in America? They become the forgotten segment of society. They are often relegated to "old people's homes" so that they can live out their lives and die without being a bother to their sons and daughters. Because they must exist on relatively small fixed incomes, they are confined to a life that for many means separation from the very society they helped create.

With just the addition of an audience question and some restatement of the point, the same material takes on considerably more emotional strength.

Perhaps your greatest opportunities for emotional appeal occur in the introduction and conclusion to your speech. Betsy Burke's speech on euthanasia illustrates an excellent use of emotional appeal in both her introduction and her conclusion. She began her speech as follows:[2]

Focus Emotional Appeals in Introduction and Conclusion

Let's pretend for a moment. Suppose that on the upper right-hand corner of your desk there is a button. You have the power, by pushing that button, to quickly and painlessly end the life of one you love: your brother or father. This loved one has terminal cancer and will be confined to a hospital for his remaining days. Would you push the button now? His condition worsens. He is in constant pain and he is hooked up to a life-support machine. He first requests, but as the pain increases he pleads, for you to help. Now would you push that button? Each day you watch him deteriorate until he reaches a point where he cannot talk, he cannot see, he cannot hear—he is only alive by that machine. Now would you push that button?

After giving reasons for changing our laws on euthanasia, she ended her speech as follows:

I ask again, how long could you take walking into that hospital room and looking at your brother or father in a coma, knowing he would rather be allowed to die a natural death than to be kept alive in such a degrading manner? I've crossed that doorstep—I've gone into that hospital room, and let me tell you, it's hell. I think it's time we reconsider our laws concerning euthanasia. Don't you?

Regardless of your beliefs about euthanasia, I think you will agree with me that you would be inclined to feel the sadness.

Describe Your Feelings and Your Images

To develop effective emotional appeals, you have to practice describing your feelings and your mental images. If you are involved enough in a topic to give a persuasive speech, then it is likely that you have some strong feelings about the people, conditions, or situations that relate to that topic. What are they? Are your feelings ones of sadness? happiness? guilt? anger? caring? grief? If you feel sadness, anger, and grief about the elderly, you may well see pictures of nursing homes, the elderly huddled together in wheelchairs in front of their TVs with blank looks on their faces.

Then, once you have an image, practice describing it and your feelings about it. Your first practices are likely to be clumsy—maybe even laughable. But as you work with your descriptions, you will find yourself speaking more and more vividly and with more genuine feeling.

Throughout the speech you must avoid pedantic and dry statements of fact. For instance, you may decide to use the statement, "One out of every eight children suffers some birth defect." As impressive as that statement seems, you will realize far more emotional involvement with a short case history or one specific example. People do not see or feel statistics.

When it is time to outline, make sure that every main point and major subdivision is stated with an emotional appeal in mind. "The atmosphere is good" does not build an appeal nearly as well as, "The warm lighting and soft music enhance your dining pleasure."

A speech that has an emotional wallop is going to motivate the audience.

BUILD YOUR CREDIBILITY

PRINCIPLE 5

You are more likely to persuade an audience when it likes, trusts, and has confidence in you.

Have you ever noticed when people are debating a major issue that some people's ideas seem to carry more weight than others regardless of the quality of their information? People are often swayed by something about the speakers themselves. The Greeks had a word for this concept; they called it *ethos*. But whether we call it ethos, image, charisma, or the word I prefer—*credibility*—the effect is the same:

PART FOUR / PERSUASIVE SPEAKING

Almost all studies confirm that speaker credibility has a major effect on audience belief and attitude.[3]

Why are people so willing to rely on the opinion of others? Since it is impossible to know all there is to know about everything (and even if it were possible, few of us would be willing to spend the time and effort), we seek shortcuts in our decision making. We rely on the judgment of others. We ask ourselves why take the time to learn about the new highway proposal, or all the restaurants in town, or all the candidates' records when someone we trust tells us how to behave? Is our reliance based solely on blind faith? No; the presence (or our perception of the presence) of certain qualities will make that person a *high-credibility* source for us.

Characteristics of Credibility

Although speech experts differ in their listings of the characteristics of credibility, most include competence, intention, character, and personality.

Competence. Your qualifications or capability are a major aspect of your competence—what we might call your track record. What is your level of competence for your speech? Do you have good material from reliable sources? Are you sure of your facts and figures? If you have a history of giving good advice, being a clear thinker, supporting ideas with good evidence, doing careful planning, and so forth, your audience is likely to see you as competent.

Think of how you are attracted by a competent professor. Although all professors are supposed to know what they are talking about, some are more convincing than others. Professors demonstrate their competence by having information that proves accurate and by presenting more detail—an example, a story, or a list of additional reading material—when a student asks questions. But not all professors maintain high credibility with their students. When a professor constantly corrects what he or she said earlier or gives "facts" that turn out to be far different from what other sources verify, a student's faith in that professor drops considerably.

Intention. This second characteristic refers to a person's apparent motives. When salespeople say, "This coat is perfect for you," you may question their intentions because you know that they are trying to sell you the garments they help you try on. On the other hand, if a bystander looks over at you and exclaims, "Wow, you really look good in that coat!" you are likely to accept the statement as true because the by-stander has no reason to make such a statement if it were not true. The more positively you view the intentions of the person, the more credible his or her words will seem to you.

What are your intentions in your speech? Are you presenting a proposition that is in the best interests of the audience? Then show them your good intentions.

Character. A speaker's character comprises his or her mental and ethical traits. We are more likely to trust and believe in a person whom we perceive as honest, industrious, trustworthy, dependable, strong, and steadfast. We will often overlook what are otherwise regarded as shortcomings if a person shows character.

Will your audience perceive you as honest, industrious, and trustworthy?

Personality. The final characteristic, personality, is the total of a person's behavioral and emotional tendencies. In short, it is the impression a person makes on us. Sometimes we have a strong gut reaction about a person based solely on a first impression. Based on such aspects as enthusiasm, friendliness, warmth, a ready smile, and caring or lack of it, we take a natural liking or disliking to a person.

Are you enthusiastic about your subject? Will your audience perceive you as friendly, warm, and caring?

Demonstrating Credibility

Credibility is not something that you can gain overnight or turn off or on at your whim. Nevertheless, you can avoid damaging your credibility and perhaps even strengthen it somewhat during a speech or a series of speeches. You will probably see the cumulative effect of credibility during this term. As your class proceeds from speech to speech, some speakers will grow in stature in your mind and others will diminish. Below we discuss six aspects of credibility that you can develop.

Be ready to speak on time. Developing credibility begins with your attitude toward the schedule. Being ready to speak on time shows the class that you are willing to assume responsibility. This is but one sign of good speech character.

Show complete preparation.   You can demonstrate competence by letting the audience know that you have experienced what you are talking about or that you have made an exhaustive study. In a speech on police public relations, for instance, you might say, "I had read about police public relations, but I wanted to see for myself, so I spent several days talking with police officers, watching how they worked, and riding around in squad cars." Or to show the amount of work you have done you might say, "I had intended to read a few articles to prepare for this speech, but once I began, I became fascinated with the subject."

Emphasize your interest in the audience.   You can show your good intentions by emphasizing the benefits to be gained from your ideas. Remember, you are speaking for the benefit of the audience. You want your audience to understand that you really care about them and what happens to them. For instance, a speaker might show fairness by saying, "It would be easy for me to say we could get by without new taxes; such a move might get me elected, but I just don't see any way out of new taxes."

Look and sound enthusiastic.   If you have a positive attitude about your topic, your audience is likely to become enthusiastic as well. If an audience suspects that you do not really care, they are certainly not going to.

Evaluate others' speeches thoughtfully.   If you can explain why a speech was a good one, the class will develop a respect for your understanding of speech principles. Then they are more likely to respect your ideas when you present your speech.

Behave ethically.   What are ethics? *Ethics* are the standards of moral conduct that determine our behavior. Ethics include both how we ourselves act and how we expect others to act. How we treat those who fail to meet our standards says a great deal about the importance we give to ethics. Although ethical codes are personal, society has a code of ethics that operates on at least the verbal level within that society.

Especially when we believe strongly in the righteousness of our cause, we are faced with the temptation of bowing to the belief that the end justifies the means—or to put it bluntly—that we can do *anything* to achieve our goals. We are all well aware of people who have ridden roughshod over society's moral or ethical principles.

In Chapter 1, we outlined the major ethical responsibilities of the speaker. In this section we want to look at specific behaviors that affect your persuasive speaking.

How you handle ethical questions says a great deal about you as a person. What is your code of ethics? The following five guidelines reflect the standards of hundreds of students that I have seen in my classes during the past few years. I believe that these five make an excellent starting point for a set of personal ethical standards.

1. *Lying is unethical.* Of all the attitudes about ethics, this is the one most universally held. When people know they are being lied to, they will usually reject the speaker's ideas; if they find out later, they often look for ways to punish the speaker who lied to them.

2. *Name-calling is unethical.* Again, there seems to be an almost universal agreement on this guideline. Even though many people name-call in their interpersonal communication, they say they regard name-calling by public speakers to be unethical.

3. *Grossly exaggerating or distorting facts is unethical.* Although some people seem willing to accept a little exaggeration as a normal product of human nature, when the exaggeration is defined as "gross" or "distorted," most people consider the exaggeration the same as lying. Because the line between some exaggeration and gross exaggeration or distortion is often difficult to distinguish, many people see *any* exaggeration as unethical.

4. *Condemning people or ideas without divulging the source of the information is unethical.* Where ideas originate is often as important as the ideas themselves. Although a statement may be true regardless of whether a source is given, people want more than the speaker's word when a statement is damning. If you are going to discuss the wrongdoing of a person or the stupidity of an idea by relying on the words or ideas of others, you must be prepared to share the sources of those words or ideas.

5. *Suppression of key information is unethical.* If you have material to support your views, you should present it; if you have a motive that affects your view, you should divulge it. An audience has a right to this information. Its members have the right to make a choice, but they must have the information in order to exercise that right.

These are but starting points in the construction of your ethical standard. Effective speaking should be ethical speaking.

DELIVER YOUR SPEECH CONVINCINGLY

Effective delivery for persuasive speeches is no different from effective delivery for any speech. But because delivery is so important, it is worth a moment to focus on one key aspect of delivery that is especially relevant to persuasion: The effective persuader shows conviction about the subject. Some people show conviction through considerable animation. Others show it through a quiet intensity. However it is shown, though, your conviction must be perceived by the audience.

PRINCIPLE 6

You are more likely to persuade an audience if your delivery is convincing.

Jesse Jackson is one of the most dynamic public speakers today. He uses a dramatic, animated speaking style to deliver his message.

If the audience does not perceive you as convinced, the audience is not likely to be convinced. If you really do have a strong conviction about the subject, there is a good chance that your voice and your bodily action will show it.

ASSIGNMENT
Persuasive Speech

The following assignment is appropriate for several situations: (1) as an assignment for a persuasive speech when time permits only a single persuasive speech assignment for the term; (2) as a diagnostic persuasive speech assignment that precedes one or more of the skills assignments that follow; or (3) as a final assignment for the persuasive speech unit to be given after students have practiced with one or more of the following chapter assignments.

1. Prepare a four- to seven-minute persuasive speech on a topic designed to change a belief or to bring your audience to action. An outline is required. Grading will focus on clarity of purpose, soundness of reasons and evidence, organization, motivation, and credibility.

2. For one or more of the speeches you hear during the first round, write a speech analysis. Outline the speech as accurately as you can. As you are outlining the speech, answer the following questions yes or no:

Proposition (Specific Purpose)

_____ Was the proposition clear?

_____ Was the proposition adapted to this audience's interests, knowledge, and attitudes?

Content

_____ Did the speaker present sound reasons?

_____ Did the speaker have specific facts and opinions to support these reasons?

_____ Did the speaker use emotional appeal to supplement the logic of the speech?

_____ Did the speaker build his or her credibility?

_____ Was the speaker ethical in handling the material?

Organization

_____ Did the introduction gain attention, gain goodwill for the speaker, and lead into the speech?

_____ Were the main points (reasons) clearly stated?

_____ Did the conclusion tie the speech together?

Language

_____ Was the language clear? _____ vivid? _____ emphatic? _____ appropriate?

Delivery

_____ Was the delivery convincing?

Evaluate the speech as (check one) _____ excellent, _____ good, _____ average, _____ fair, _____ poor.

Use the information from your check sheet to support your evaluation.

OUTLINE: PERSUASIVE SPEECH (4–7 MINUTES)

Proposition (Specific Purpose): To persuade the audience that parents should limit the time their children spend viewing television.

Introduction

I. Television is America's most frequent baby-sitter.
II. Children watch television an average of more than twenty-five hours per week.
III. Excessive television viewing can be very harmful to children.

Thesis Statement: Parents should limit the time their children spend viewing television because heavy television viewing desensitizes children to violence and increases violent tendencies in children.

Body

I. Heavy television viewing leads to major problems for children.
   A. Heavy television viewing desensitizes children to violence.
      1. By age fifteen the average child has seen more than thirteen thousand televised murders.

2. Some of the most violent television programs are children's cartoons.
3. Too often, children watch, but they don't feel anything.
   B. Heavy television viewing encourages aggressive traits in children.
   1. Children learn that a violent character is successful.
   2. Children translate violent tendencies into action.
II. The problem can be solved by limiting the number of hours children watch television.
   A. Many voluntary programs of limiting viewing have been tried.
   B. Children show many improvements even after short periods of time.
   1. Children are more calm and relaxed.
   2. Children play less violently.
III. Limiting the number of hours of television viewing is a good solution.
   A. It does not require formation of regulatory commissions.
   B. It does not involve any programming censorship.

Conclusion

I. Television viewing leads to desensitization toward violence and aggressive tendencies in children.
II. Television, America's most popular baby-sitter, must be controlled.

Bibliography

Friedrich, L. K., and Stein, A. H. "Television Content and Young Children's Behavior," in J. P. Murray, E. A. Rubenstein, and G. A. Comstock, eds., *Television and Social Behavior,* vol. 2. Washington, D.C.: U.S. Government Printing Office, 1972.

Hickey, Neil. "Does Television Violence Affect Our Society? Yes." *TV Guide* (June 14, 1975).

Kiester, Edwin, Jr. "Here's What TV Is Doing to Us." *TV Guide* (December 17, 1977).

Safran, Claire. "Tonight's Assignment: No TV!" *TV Guide* (April 7, 1979).

"What Television Is Doing to Children." *Newsweek* (February 21, 1977).

Read the following speech aloud. Then, analyze it on the basis of organization, reasoning and evidence, motivation, and speaker credibility. After you have read and analyzed the speech refer to the analysis in the other column.[4]

SPEECH: Television and Children

Do you have a little brother or sister? A niece or nephew? A preschool-age neighbor? Do you know who is their most frequent baby-sitter? If these children are like the average child in the United States, their most frequent and favorite baby-sitter is likely to be a television set! This baby-sitter can take children to faraway places, make them laugh, and teach them many things. Unfortunately some of the things that television teaches are very harmful and need to be stopped.

According to current Nielsen reports, children watch television an average of over twenty-five hours per week. Many children watch television for longer periods of time than they spend in school. They watch television for longer periods of time than they spend with their family or playing with their friends.

Today I want to discuss with you the potential harms of this heavy television viewing to children and how those harms can be controlled.

Let me start by clarifying the problem: Heavy television viewing leads to two major problems for children. The first problem is that heavy television viewing desensitizes children to violence. It does this by exposing children to so much violence that the concept of violence is no longer meaningful. By the time children who watch an average of twenty-five hours of television a week reach the age of fifteen it is estimated that they will have witnessed more than thirteen thousand televised killings! The sad part is that some of the most violent shows are children's programs. Especially cartoons. The average cartoon hour has six times the amount of violence than that which occurs in the average adult drama series. In one of her syndicated columns, Erma Bombeck wrote, "During a single evening, I once saw 12 people shot to death, two people tortured (one a child), one dumped in a swimming pool, two cars explode with people in

ANALYSIS

The speaker opens with three questions. The reference to the role of television as a baby-sitter adds to the attractiveness of the opening. She gives credit to some positive effects of television; then she lays the groundwork for the problem.

The speaker continues her opening by clearly documenting exactly how much time the average child watches television.

This statement leads the speaker into the body of the speech. Her wording tells us that she will follow a problem-solution pattern.

Here she stresses the point that heavy television viewing leads to two major problems. She then clearly states the first problem: that heavy television viewing desensitizes children to violence.

She supports her statement with statistics and a quotation. Although these statistics are quite dramatic, she needs to document her source. The emphasis placed on the fact that children's cartoons are even worse than regular programming helps make the point even stronger. The Bombeck quote is a very powerful one. In addition to supporting the reasoning, it adds a strong emotional appeal.

The second problem, that heavy television viewing encourages aggressive traits in children, is also clearly stated.

This is another excellent bit of information, but again the speaker needs to give us specific documentation for the source of this study.

The speaker gives us partial documentation for this study. But, she needs to tell us when the study was done.

This point is developed with a detailed example of a study, a quotation from a psychologist, and the conclusion of both the original surgeon general's report and the follow-up study.

This final sentence is a good strong wrap-up to this reason.

Here the speaker moves from the problem to the solution. The solution to the problem is clearly stated.

them, and a man who crawled three blocks with a knife in his stomach. And you know something? I didn't feel shock or horror. I didn't feel excitement or repugnance. The truth is, I didn't feel anything." Children watch television, they see what is happening, but far too often they don't feel anything.

The second problem is that heavy television viewing encourages aggressive traits in children. Children learn from television that a violent character is successful. And they use that violent behavior as a role model. A study was done in which children were shown two different television shows. In these shows the heroes accomplished the same goals but one used violent means and the other one used nonviolent means. What did the study show? The children rated the hero who used the violent means as more successful, as more wonderful—the hero they would want to model themselves after.

In addition, studies have shown that children translate these violent tendencies into action. Friedrich and Stein did a study where three different groups of preschool children were shown three different kinds of programs. One group saw a violent television program, one group saw an educational television program, and one group saw what was basically a neutral program. The children were shown these three kinds of television programs for just a half hour three times a week, for a month. It was found that the children who had seen the violent television programs for just those three half-hour episodes for the one-month period actually played more violently and more aggressively with their playmates than those children who had seen either type of the other two programs. Dr. Robert Liebert, a psychologist at the State University of New York, said, "The amount of TV violence a child viewed at age 9 was the single most important determinant of how aggressive he was at age 19." Both the original 1973 surgeon general's report on television violence and children and the 1983 follow-up study confirm that television violence encourages aggressive behavior in children.

So our problem: Television violence has a harmful effect on children's behavior by desensitizing them and by teaching them violent aggressive actions.

But there is a solution to this problem and the solution is basically an easy one. Parents need to limit the number of hours that their children spend watching television. By reducing the total number of hours children watch, we can reduce both the desensitization and the aggressive behavior. This is a simple solution that every family can accomplish. We don't have to create another regulatory commission; we don't have to censor television programmers. All we have to do is to limit the amount of hours that our children spend watching television.

Does such a simple solution work? Yes. A 1979 issue of *TV Guide* reported that at the Horace Mann School for Nursery Years in New York families had begun a voluntary program of limiting the television viewing of their children. After just three weeks, there was a dramatic change at school. In addition to many other benefits such as being more creative in play, all the children were calmer and much more relaxed. Children were no longer recreating the violent behavior in their play that they had earlier.

So we have seen that excessive television viewing on the part of small children leads to desensitization toward violence and aggressive tendencies. Television may be America's most popular baby-sitter. But for the good of our children, it must be controlled.

Here the speaker shows that the solution does not require any legislation or any infringement on programmers' rights. Although this was the third point on her outline, mentioning the point here is all right.

Although the support for how well the solution works is a little skimpy, it is well documented. We would like to see more evidence that such a plan does work. Still, at least the speaker did try to give some support for the effectiveness of the plan.

The summary conclusion is satisfactory. Notice how the speaker returns to the theme developed in the opening of the speech.

Throughout the speech, the speaker blends logical information and emotional appeal quite well. Although she has enough evidence to support the statement of the problem, she needs more specific documentation of sources. In all, a good persuasive speech following a problem-solution pattern.

NOTES

1. See Ronald L. Appelbaum and Karl W. Anatol, *Strategies for Persuasive Communication* (Columbus, Ohio: Charles E. Merrill, 1974), 102–103, for a summary of conflicting research studies.
2. Speech on euthanasia delivered in Persuasive Speaking, University of Cincinnati. Portions reprinted by permission of Betsy R. Burke.
3. Kenneth E. Andersen and Theodore Clevenger, Jr., "A Summary of Experimental Research in Ethos." *Speech Monographs* 30 (1963), 59–78.
4. Delivered in Speech class, University of Cincinnati. Printed by permission of Mary Heintz.

FOURTEEN

REASONING WITH AUDIENCES: SPEECHES OF CONVICTION

When Lyndon Johnson was president, he often began talks with colleagues by saying, "Let's reason together." In public speaking, *reasoning* with an audience means presenting arguments and evidence in support of a proposition. Many times when you face an audience, especially if you regard the audience's attitude as neutral, apathetic, or only slightly negative, you may find that reasoning with them is the best procedure.

In this chapter we discuss elements of reasoning and preparing a speech to convince.

REASONING DEFINED

Reasoning is the process of drawing inferences from facts or proving propositions with reasons and facts. So, we can reason to arrive at a logical conclusion, and we can reason to prove the validity of our position to others. Let us consider the relationship between drawing inferences and forming arguments.

Drawing Inferences

Suppose you notice that your car is "missing" at slow speeds and stalling at lights, that your gas mileage is lower than normal, and that your car isn't as peppy as it should be. What do these facts mean? If you know anything about cars, you will probably infer that your car needs a tune-up.

Forming an Argument

Further suppose that to get the money for a tune-up for your car you have to convince your wife, husband, father, mother, or whoever is in charge of the purse strings, that the car does in fact need a tune-up. You will use the same material you used to draw the inference to form the arguments you will use to convince that other person. You start with the conclusion, "The car needs a tune-up." Then you present your observations as four reasons in support of that proposition: (1) The car is "missing" at slow speeds; (2) it is stalling at lights; (3) it is getting lower than normal gas mileage; and (4) it is not nearly as peppy as usual. In your presentation, you would elaborate the reasons with appropriate details.

THE REASONING PROCESS

Whether you draw inferences from facts or whether you plan to present arguments with supporting facts, you need a method of studying the reasoning process. A good way of doing this is to identify the essentials of the argument and put them down on paper.

Essentials of Reasoning

Reasoning is a product of three essentials: data, a conclusion, and a warrant for the conclusion.

Data. *Data* are the evidence, assumptions, or assertions that provide the basis for a conclusion. In the car example we used to define reasoning, the data are "missing at slow speeds," "stalling at lights," "lower than normal gas mileage," and "lack of pep."

Conclusion. The *conclusion* is the inference drawn or the inference to be proven. In our example, the conclusion is, "The car needs a tune-up."

Warrant. A *warrant* is a statement that explains the relationship between the data and the conclusion. It is a verbal statement of the reasoning involved. It shows how the conclusion follows from the data that have been presented. Warrants are usually implied rather than stated. But in order to test the soundness of the reasoning, a warrant must actually be stated. One way of stating the warrant for our car example is to say that missing at slow speeds, stalling at lights, lower gas mileage, and lack of pep are all *signs* or *indications* that the car needs a tune-up. The warrant, then, indicates how you arrived at the conclusion from the data supplied.

Diagraming reasoning. To get a visual picture of the reasoning, you can use the diagrammatic method developed by Stephen Toulmin.[1] Let's see how this looks. Using *(D)* for data, stated or observed; *(C)* for conclusion; *(W)* for warrant; and an arrow to show the direction of the reasoning, our example could be written as follows:

(D) Engine misses at slow speeds.
   Car stalls at lights.   *(C)* The car
   Gas mileage is lower than usual.   needs a
   Car lacks pep.   tune-up.

   (W) (These occurrences are major signs
         of the need for a tune-up.)

The warrant is written in parentheses because it is implied rather than actually stated.

The conclusion you draw becomes the proposition (or specific purpose) for your speech, and the data become the reasons and support. The car tune-up speech would be outlined as follows:

Proposition: To convince the audience that the car needs a tune-up.

I. The engine misses at slow speeds.
II. The car stalls at lights.
III. Gas mileage is lower than usual.
IV. The car lacks pep.

Turning Reasoning into a Speech Outline

FORMS OF REASONING: TYPES OF WARRANTS

After you have written a number of warrants, you will see that they fall into one of several groups, each having certain clearly defined characteristics. In this section we look at several of the most common rants or forms of reasoning and group them under their traditional headings of inductive or deductive.

Inductive reasoning means working from specifics to some conclusion. In inductive reasoning you discover what is true or what was true in the past, and then you predict that something is true or will be true in the future. The conclusions of inductive arguments are tested on the basis of probability. That is, we predict that the conclusion will be true most of the time. The higher the probability (the closer to 100 percent), the better the argument. Four common forms of inductive reasoning are generalization, analogy, causation, and sign.

Deductive reasoning is a form that moves from premises to conclusions. If the premises are true, then the conclusion is not just probable, as in an inductive argument, but *certain*.

Generalization Warrant

In reasoning by generalization we draw a conclusion based on a series of examples or cases. Suppose that Paula Larson is running for senior class president, and we plan to argue that Paula will win the election. If we found several related items of information, we could use them as the basis for a generalization. For instance, in examining Paula's record as a campaigner, we discover that she was successful in her campaign for treasurer of her high school junior class, for chairperson of her youth group at church, and for president of her sorority. From these three examples of Paula as a candidate for office, we generalize that she will be successful in future campaigns, of which president of the senior class is one. We predict that what was true in several instances is true (or will be true) in all instances (or at least in the instance we are considering).

Let us look at other examples of reasoning by generalization:

Instances: Dan Snider, an Alpha, is editor of the school paper; Paul Dreiser, an Alpha, is president of the Intrafraternity Council; Ken Stewart, an Alpha, is student body president.

Generalization conclusion: Alpha fraternity is an organization of campus leaders.

Instances: Al is a liberal and he votes Democrat; Marge is a liberal and she votes Democrat; Dean is a liberal and he votes Democrat.

Generalization conclusion: Liberals vote Democrat.

Now let us return to the reasoning of the generalization on Paula Larson for president. In diagram form, the argument would look like this:

(D) Paula was successful in her campaign for treasurer of her junior class, in her campaign for chairperson of her church youth group, and in her campaign for president of her sorority. $\longrightarrow$ *(C)* Paula will be elected president of the senior class.

(W) (What is true in representative campaigns will be true in this campaign.)

Now suppose we wished to prepare a speech predicting Paula's victory. A speech outline using instances as reasons would look like this:

Proposition: Paula Larson will be elected president of the senior class. (Conclusion)

I. Paula has run successful campaigns in the past.
   A. Paula was successful in her campaign for treasurer of her high school junior class.
   B. Paula was successful in her campaign for chairperson of her church youth group.
   C. Paula was successful in her campaign for president of her sorority.

Analogy Warrant

An *analogy* is a comparative generalization. In reasoning by analogy, what is true of something with one set of circumstances will be true of something else with similar circumstances. Suppose that in trying to predict Paula Larson's success in her candidacy for president we compare her circumstances with Heather Nelson's who was elected president two years ago. As we compare the two we find several similarities: Both are very bright, both have a great deal of drive, and both have track records of successful campaigns. Reasoning by analogy, we argue that since Paula is similar to Heather in so many ways and since Heather was elected, Paula too will be elected senior class president.

Let's look at other examples of reasoning by analogy:

Comparable example: The affirmative action program at Carson Limited has increased levels of employment and promotions of women and members of racial minorities.

Analogy conclusion: (Since our company is similar to Carson Limited in so many ways), an affirmative action program will result in increased levels of employment and promotions of women and members of racial minorities here.

Comparable example: New York is making money from off-track betting.

Analogy conclusion: Ohio (similar to New York in so many ways) would make money from off-track betting.

Now let us return to reasoning by analogy that Paula will be elected president. In diagram form, the argument looks like this:

(D) Heather who is bright, has a great deal of drive, and has a track record of successful campaigns was elected two years ago. }——→ *(C)* Paula will be elected president of the senior class.

(W) (Because Paula is similar to Heather in brightness, drive, and track record.)

Now suppose we want to prepare a speech predicting Paula's victory using analogy. A speech outline using this argument would look like this:

Proposition: Paula Larson will be elected president of the senior class.

I. Paula has the same characteristics as Heather Nelson who was elected two years ago.
   A. Paula and Heather are both bright.
   B. Paula and Heather both have a great deal of drive.
   C. Paula and Heather both have track records of successful campaigns.

Causation is a form of reasoning that proves a conclusion on the basis of a special connection between the data and the conclusion. When we say that a causal relationship exists, we mean that one or more circumstances cited always (or at least usually) produce a predictable effect or set of effects. In analyzing Paula's campaign for election, you might discover that Paula has campaigned intelligently and has won the endorsements of key campus organizations. If these two items can be seen as causes for victory, then you can argue that Paula will win the election.

Other examples of causal reasoning are the following:

Causal factors: Clark is intelligent, has studied hard, and has a good attitude.

Causal conclusion: (Since intelligence, study, and good attitude are causes of passing grades), Clark will pass the course.

Causal factors: Moose Gordon is back in the lineup at offensive tackle, and Speedy Marshall is fully recovered from his leg injury.

Causal conclusion: (Since the two key players on the team are back at full strength), Stellar University will win the big football game.

Now let us diagram the Paula-will-be-elected argument to test the reasoning involved.

(D) Paula has campaigned intelligently and has won the endorsements of key campus organizations. ⟶ *(C)* Paula will be elected president.

(W) (Intelligent campaigning and key endorsements are causes of, or result in, winning elections.)

Now suppose we want to prepare a speech predicting Paula's victory using causal reasoning. A speech outline using this argument would look like this:

Proposition: Paula Larson will be elected senior class president.

I. Paula has engaged in the procedures that result in victory.
   A. Paula has campaigned intelligently.
   B. Paula has key endorsements.

Sign

Sign is a form of reasoning that proves a conclusion on the basis of a connection between the symptoms and the conclusion. Signs are indicators. When certain events, characteristics, or situations always or usually accompany something, we say that these events, characteristics, or situations are *signs*. For instance, leaves turning brown and falling are signs of autumn. A fever, nausea, and blotchy skin are signs of an allergic reaction. Signs are often confused with causes; but signs are indicators, not causes. A fever is a sign of sickness. It occurs when a person is sick, but it does not cause the sickness. If in analyzing Paula's campaign, you notice that Paula has more campaign posters than all other candidates combined and a great number of students from all segments of the campus are wearing Paula for President buttons, you may argue that these are indicators or signs that Paula may win the election.

The following are other examples of sign reasoning:

Signs: New car sales are skyrocketing. Housing starts are up.

Sign conclusion: (Since car sales and housing starts are signs of a recovery), the recession is over.

Signs: Tom has bleary eyes and a runny nose.

Sign conclusion: (Since bleary eyes and a runny nose are signs of a cold), Tom has a cold.

Now let us return to the Paula-will-win-the-election argument. In diagram form, the argument looks like this:

(D) Paula has more campaign posters than all other candidates combined.
Students from all segments of campus are wearing her campaign buttons. ⟶ *(C)* Paula will win the election.

(W) (Numbers of campaign posters and buttons are signs of an election victory.)

Now suppose we want to prepare a speech predicting Paula's

victory using sign reasoning. A speech outline using this argument would look like this:

Proposition: Paula Larson will win the election for student body president.

I. The key signs of an election victory are present in Paula's campaign.
   A. Paula has more campaign posters than all other candidates combined.
   B. Students from all segments of the campus are wearing her campaign buttons.

A speech may be the product of one or many forms of inductive reasoning. The following is an example of an outline in support of the prediction of Paula's victory that uses all the forms we have discussed. In preparing your speech you might select the arguments from among the four listed that you think would be most persuasive to your audience.

Using Warrants in Combination

Proposition: Paula Larson will win the election for student body president.

I. Paula has run successful campaigns in the past.
   A. Paula was successful in her campaign for treasurer of her high school class.
   B. Paula was successful in her campaign for chairperson of her church youth group.
   C. Paula was successful in her campaign for president of her sorority.
II. Paula has the same characteristics as Heather who won two years ago.
   A. Both are intelligent.
   B. Both have drive.
   C. Both have good track records in campaigns.
III. Paula has engaged in procedures that result in campaign victory.
   A. Paula has campaigned intelligently.
   B. Paula has key endorsements.
IV. Paula's campaign has the key signs of an election victory.
   A. Paula has more campaign posters than all other candidates combined.
   B. Students from all segments of the campus are wearing her campaign buttons.

Deduction

As we have mentioned, *deduction* is a form of reasoning that is used in moving from statements that are true to a related statement that must be true. A deductive warrant may be stated: "If two related premises are true, then a conclusion based on those two premises must be true." Suppose that you missed hearing the results of the student election but you hear Paula giving a victory speech to the student body. You might reason as follows: Only winners give victory speeches, Paula is giving a victory speech, so Paula must have won the election.

Now let us diagram the deductive argument about Paula's victory to test the reasoning.

(D) A person must win to give a victory speech. Paula is giving a victory speech. ⟶ *(C)* Paula must have won the election.

(W) (If it is true that a person must win to give a victory speech and that Paula is giving a victory speech, then it is certain that Paula won the election.)

The following are other examples of deductive reasoning:

Premise: Ever since the University of Cincinnati became a state university, UC has raised its tuition each year that state funding has not kept pace with inflation.

Premise: State funding was not increased at all for next year although rate of inflation was 4 percent.

Deductive conclusion: The University of Cincinnati will raise its tuition next year.

Premise: Every time the total rainfall up river is more than three inches in a week Old Coney is flooded a few days later.

Premise: The rainfall up river during the last four days was a staggering five inches.

Deductive conclusion: Within the next few days Old Coney will be flooded.

As you study your resources, try to draw conclusions from the data.

When the time comes to prepare the speech, you can use the product of your reasoning to form arguments.

Next we consider the process of preparing a speech in which the emphasis is on reasoning with the audience.

PREPARING A SPEECH OF CONVICTION

You can practice reasoning by preparing and presenting a speech of conviction. A *speech of conviction,* or a *speech of reasons* as it is sometimes called, is one in which you support your proposition with clear reasons and good support for the reasons. Your goal is to convince your audience that they should believe what you tell them.

To be effective, persuasive speakers must present speeches with clear reasons that are well-supported.

Many times in real-life situations reasoning with audiences is your best strategy for winning their support. Under these circumstances, the speech-of-conviction model is the one you will follow. Although you will try to develop your credibility and your audience may have an emotional reaction to your arguments, your emphasis will be on clear, well-supported reasons.

Topic and Specific Purpose

You can, of course, give a speech of conviction on any topic. Moreover, the proposition (specific purpose) of the speech can be one to inspire, to change a belief, or to move to action. (Or if assignment of topic is made by content, the proposition may be one of fact, evaluation, or policy.) The emphasis in the assignment at the end of this chapter is not on the *type* of proposition, but on the *means of supporting* the proposition.

Main Points and Support

You will recall from our discussion of reasoning in Chapter 13 that when you reason with an audience your main points will be reasons, statements answering the question Why? placed after the proposition. From your own experience and knowledge, observation, interviews, and reading, you may discover any number of reasons that you could use in the speech.

After you have a list of reasons, select the best ones based on the following:

1. Choose the reasons that best prove the proposition.

2. Choose reasons that can be supported.

3. Choose reasons that will have an impact on the intended audience.

4. Choose reasons for which you have sufficient facts and expert opinions to satisfy audience questions.

Suppose that you selected the proposition, "to prove that the United States should determine the president by direct election." After conducting the tests listed above, you might arrive at the following three reasons to use in your speech:

I. Direct election of the president is fair.

II. Direct election of the president is certain.

III. Direct election of the president is a popular plan.

After you have stated good reasons, or sometimes as you are looking for good reasons, you should amass the best possible material to support those reasons. From sources that you have read, from interviews you have conducted, from observation, or from your own experience, you want to collect examples, illustrations, statistics, quotations, and personal observations that really give support to each of the reasons. Moreover, you want to clearly document each piece of data so that you can present at least a portion of that documentation in the speech.

The next step in your preparation is to write a complete outline, including an introduction, a conclusion, and a bibliography. Test the structure of your speech with an outline. If the outline meets the tests discussed on pages 91–93, you know that the proposition is clear, the reasons (main points) prove the proposition, and each reason is supported. The following is a slightly abbreviated outline of a speech advocating direct election of the president:

Writing a Logical Outline

Proposition: To prove that the United States should determine the president by direct election.

Introduction

I. In several instances we have barely avoided the electoral catastrophe of having the president selected by the House of Representatives.

II. Direct election offers the best alternative to the Electoral College.

Thesis Statement: Direct election should be adopted because it is fair, because it is certain, and because it is popular.

Body

I. Direct election of the president is fair.
   A. It follows the one-person, one-vote policy laid down by the Supreme Court.
   B. It allows each vote to count equally, regardless of where it is cast.

C. It eliminates the possibility of the election of a candidate who receives a fewer number of popular votes.
II. Direct election of the president is certain.
  A. The identity of the new president would be public knowledge as soon as the votes were counted.
  B. The election of the president would not be subject to political maneuvers.
III. Direct election of the president is popular.
  A. A recent Gallup Poll showed that the majority favors direct election.
  B. Many political leaders have voiced their approval of the plan.

Conclusion

I. The time to anticipate possible catastrophe is now.
II. Support direct election of the president.

Bibliography

Berns, Walter, ed. *After the People Vote: Steps in Choosing the President.* Washington, D.C.: American Enterprise Institute, 1983.

Longley, Lawrence D., and Alan G. Brown. *The Politics of Electoral College Reform.* New Haven: Yale University Press, 1972.

Matthews, Donald R., ed. *Perspectives on Presidential Selection.* Washington, D.C.: Brookings, 1973.

Polsby, Nelson W., and Aaron Wildavsky. *Presidential Elections: Strategies of American Electoral Politics,* 5th ed. New York: Scribner's, 1980.

Who Should Elect the President? Washington, D.C.: League of Women Voters, Publication 345, 1969.

When you examine this outline you will see that

1. The proposition is clear.

2. The thesis statement is clear.

3. The body has three good reasons.

4. Each reason is supported. (It is assumed that each of the A, B, C statements has evidence.)

5. There is a bibliography.

1. Prepare a three- to six-minute speech to convince. An outline is required. The speech should have a short introduction that leads into the proposition. By the end of the speech (probably by the end of the introduction), the audience should be aware of the proposition. The major portion of the speech should be on the statement and the development of two to five *good reasons.* Development should prove the truth of the reasons through facts and/or expert opinion and should indicate the relevance of the reasons to the audience. A brief conclusion should summarize the reasons or in some way re-emphasize the importance of the proposition. Grading will focus on quality of topic, clarity and quality of reasons, quality of evidence, and delivery.

2. Write a critique of one or more of the speeches of conviction you hear in class. Outline the speech. As you are outlining it, answer the following questions yes or no:

Proposition (Specific Purpose)

_____ Was the proposition clear?

_____ Was the proposition adapted to the audience's interests, knowledge, and attitudes?

Content

_____ Did each reason answer why the proposition should be believed?

_____ Was each reason important to the consideration of the proposition?

_____ Was each reason related to audience needs and interests?

_____ Was each reason supported with evidence?

_____ Were good examples presented?

_____ Was expert opinion presented?

_____ Was evidence well documented?

Organization

_____ Did the introduction gain attention, gain goodwill for the speaker, and lead into the speech?

_____ Were the reasons clearly stated?

_____ Did the speaker use any special strategies to help you remember the reasons and their support?

Language

_____ Was the language clear? _____ vivid? _____ emphatic? _____ appropriate?

Delivery

_____ Was the delivery convincing?

Evaluate the speech as (check one) _____ excellent, _____ good, _____ average, _____ fair, _____ poor.

Use the information from your check sheet to support your evaluation.

OUTLINE: SPEECH OF CONVICTION (3–6 MINUTES)

Specific Purpose: To convince the audience that they should learn to speak Spanish.

Introduction

  I. What if you found yourself all alone in a foreign country, incapable of communicating with those around you, only to learn that the country was the United States?
 II. Such a scenario is not that far from reality, for Spanish is the second most popular spoken language in the United States.

Thesis Statement: You should learn to speak Spanish because it will benefit you personally, economically, and practically.

Body

  I. Learning to speak Spanish will benefit you personally.
   A. You will be able to learn a great deal about Spanish culture.
   B. You will appreciate the beauty of the language.
   C. You will have fun.
 II. Learning to speak Spanish will benefit you economically.
   A. You will be qualified for one of the many jobs available to those who speak Spanish.
    1. Translators are needed in many areas.
    2. Companies are expanding into Spanish-speaking countries.
   B. You will be less likely to be taken advantage of by Spanish-speaking merchants.

III. Learning to speak Spanish will benefit you practically.
   A. You will be better prepared for the future.
      1. The Spanish-speaking population is growing at a phenomenal rate.
      2. By the year 2000 there will be 30 to 35 million Spanish-speaking people in the United States.
   B. You will be better able to communicate with your own neighbors.
      1. Western cities have significant Hispanic populations.
      2. Major cities in other parts of the country have growing Hispanic populations.

Conclusion

 I. Spanish is the language of the future.
 II. Wake up to reality—learn Spanish while you're still ahead of the game.

Bibliography

Arcienga, Thomas A. "Bilingual Education in the 1980's" *Educational Digest* (September 1982): 8–10.

"Florida's Latin Boom." *Newsweek* (November 11, 1985): 55–56.

Kiddle, M. E., and B. Wegmann, *Perspectivas.* New York: Holt, Rinehart & Winston, 1978.

"Language War in Florida." *Newsweek* (June 30, 1986).

As you analyze this speech of conviction, judge whether each of the reasons is clearly stated in the speech and whether the developmental material supports the reasons clearly, completely, and interestingly.[2] After you have made your own analysis, study the analysis given here.

SPEECH: Learn to Speak Spanish

ANALYSIS

What if you suddenly found yourself all alone in a foreign country incapable of communicating with those around you? Then what if

Creation of this hypothetical situation helps the speaker

get the audience interested by developing curiosity about the intent of the speech.

Here the speaker tells us that she will try to convince the audience by presenting three major benefits. Her goal is to present three reasons (benefits) that we will find logically compelling enough to convince us that we should learn Spanish. If the audience is convinced of the logic of the development, then they may not only give intellectual agreement to the proposition, but they may also be moved to action. For the speech to work, the audience will have to see the reasons as compelling, and they will have to believe that the reasons have been supported strongly enough to be believed. Notice that the first point is clearly stated. Also notice that each of the points are adapted to the audience. The speaker puts the emphasis on "you."

Much of the strength of the proof is through the speaker's own experience. She relies on her experience to carry much of the weight of the support for the first two points in the speech. Although her authority comes through rather strongly, we could use some documented evidence to support a few of the assertions, most notably, "as language experts say." Nevertheless, I like her use of examples to give support to her points.

The speaker's second benefit is clearly stated. Here, partic-

you found that this foreign country was your own United States? This may sound like an episode from the "Twilight Zone," but it's really not that far from reality, for Spanish is the second most popular spoken language in the United States.

I'd like to convince you why you should start to learn to speak Spanish now. You will benefit from learning to speak Spanish in at least three major ways.

First of all, learning to speak Spanish will benefit you personally. Spanish is educational. You can learn a great deal about the second most dominant culture in the Western hemisphere. If you check our library or the library downtown, you'll find a large section of books written in Spanish about the Spanish culture. And I think that's a very educational experience. Moreover, you will find yourself developing a much greater appreciation of the beauty of the language. According to the authors of *Perspectivas,* a Spanish language book, Spanish poetry is some of the most beautiful poetry you'll ever read. One of my favorites is *Noches Serena,* translated *Night of Stars.* Although it's true that this poem has been translated into English, there's an old saying, "Tradutori, traditori," meaning "the translator is a traitor." As language experts say, you just cannot translate Spanish into English effectively—especially poetry.

On a personal level, learning Spanish will be just plain fun. It's fun to be one of those people who can communicate with someone on your left side when the person on your right side doesn't understand what you are saying. It's also fun because it makes the foreigner in the United States feel very much at home. And I've had a couple of friends who felt really impressed that I went out of my way to learn their language. It made them feel very comfortable, and it was just kind of a neat feeling for me as well.

Secondly, learning to speak Spanish can benefit you economically. There's an increasing demand for Spanish fluency in the

United States today. And translators are needed in literally every area of society—in government, in law, in education, in medicine—you name it, there's a need for it. When I worked at the Cleveland Clinic a couple of years ago, people came in from all over the continent for care at its world-renowned cardiology department. And since so many of the people who came through spoke only Spanish, there was a tremendous need for Spanish translators. One of the jobs of the translator was to make the person feel at home outside of their country, but to do that you had to speak Spanish.

In addition, United States companies are expanding into Spanish-speaking countries and there's a need for workers who know the language. And I understand that for those who are willing to learn Spanish, or who speak it already, the pay package is very good. Also, if you do decide to travel to any Spanish-speaking countries—Spain for its art or culture, Mexico or Peru with their historic monuments, or Central America for its beautiful, sunny beaches—the Spanish people will be less inclined to take advantage of you. They are not going to be able to say, "Hay un americano muy estúpido—no problema, no problema," but the "no problema" will benefit *you* because you can speak Spanish.

Finally, learning to speak Spanish will benefit you practically. By the year 2000 it is estimated that there will be 30 to 35 million Spanish-speaking people in the United States. Right now, all across the United States, and I don't just mean Florida or California, I mean major cities all across the United States, there is a significant population of Spanish-speaking people, so you might need this language just to communicate with your very own neighbor.

Spanish is clearly the language of the future. There is no longer a simple choice to learn that language; there is an urgency brought on by the dramatic growth of this language in our country. So whether you sign up for a course here at the university, take a community education class, or study on your own, wake up to reality and learn to speak Spanish while you still have the advantage.

---

ularly, we see the speaker using her own experience to provide support for her point. I think this section shows that a person's direct experience can often carry more support for a reason than a quotation or factual statement from a random source.

"I understand that" is weak. Here is one of the places where documented source material is necessary.

Good use of a hypothetical example to help make the point.

A very interesting and rather persuasive section. Her use of Spanish adds to her personal credibility and gives added weight to the example.

Final point is clearly stated. Good use of statistics. I would still like to hear the source for these statistics.

A very good conclusion.

All this speech lacks to make it superior is more documentation for key points. The reasons are clear, and taken as a group they provide strong support for the need to learn Spanish. Moreover, the use of personal experience and examples give plenty of support for the reasons. By the end of the speech, the majority of the class did believe that there were benefits to learning Spanish.

NOTES

1. Stephen Toulmin, *The Uses of Argument* (Cambridge: Cambridge University Press, 1958).
2. Delivered in Speech class, University of Cincinnati. Printed by permission of Mary Jo Cranley.

FIFTEEN

MOTIVATING AUDIENCES: SPEECHES TO ACTUATE

Reasoning provides a solid logical base for persuasion and a sound rationale for change of audience attitude. But what if sound reasoning is not enough to bring action? What else can you do to increase the audience's chances of doing what you recommend? The catalyst for firing the imagination, causing commitment, and bringing to action is the psychological aspect of persuasion called *motivation.*

In this chapter we consider three psychological approaches that will help you determine your overall strategy; then we consider a specific speech assignment, the speech to actuate, to help you put what you have learned into practice.

STRATEGIES

Through the years many individuals have set forth rhetorical and psychological theories of motivation. Although the following three theories are not the only ones available—nor are they necessarily the only ones that work—they do help explain why people behave as they do.

What is likely to bring an audience to action? We can summarize the strategies involved as follows:

1. People are more likely to act when the proposition presents a favorable cost-reward ratio.

2. People are more likely to act when the proposition creates dissonance.

3. People are more likely to act when the proposition satisfies a strong unmet need.

Now let us examine the theories behind these statements.

Cost-Reward

People are more likely to act when they see that the suggested proposition presents a favorable cost-reward ratio. John Thibaut and Harold Kelley explain social interactions in terms of rewards received and costs incurred by each member of an interaction.[1] *Rewards* are the benefits received from a behavior. Rewards can be economic gain, good feelings, prestige, or any other positive outcome. *Costs* are units of expenditure. They can be perceived in terms of time, energy, money, or any negative outcome of an interaction.

According to Thibaut and Kelley, each of us seeks situations in which our behavior will yield us rewards in excess of the costs; or, conversely, each of us will continue our present behavior unless we can be shown that either lower costs or higher rewards will come from changing a particular behavior. Let's consider an example. Suppose you are asking your audience to give money to a charity. The money you are asking them to give is a negative outcome—a cost; however, giving money can be shown to be rewarding. That is, members of the audience may feel civic-minded, responsible, or helpful as a result of giving. If in the speech you can show that those rewards outweigh the cost, then you can increase the likelihood of the audience's giving.

Strategies growing from this theory are easy for most people to understand because the theory is so easily supported by common-sense observations. What makes this theory work for you is your ability to understand the cost-reward ratios in relation to the specific topic operating within your particular audience. Suppose that you are, in fact, trying to motivate the audience to give money to a charity. Assuming that this audience has nothing against this particular charity and assuming they agree that giving to this charity has merit, how do you proceed? You could ask each person to give 10 cents. Since the cost is very low, you are unlikely to meet much resistance, and you will probably get a high percentage of donations; but you will not be making much money for that charity. What if you decide to ask for a donation of $10 from each person? Since $10 is likely to represent a lot of money to members of a college audience, they must be shown that

$10 really is not that much money (a difficult point to make for any audience); or they must be shown that the reward for giving $10 is worth the $10 gift. For most of your audience, talking about how good giving makes a person feel will not be enough. You will have to show them some very tangible rewards.

In general, people look at calls for action on the basis of a cost-reward ratio—the higher the cost, the greater the reward. Thus, the higher the perceived cost, the harder you will have to work to achieve your goal. In summary, you must achieve one of the following:

1. You must show that the time, energy, or money investment is small.

2. You must show that the benefits in good feelings, prestige, economic gain, or other possible rewards are high.

In your speech, then, you are looking at ways to minimize cost and maximize gain. The speech at the end of this chapter is an excellent example of this strategy.

Cognitive Dissonance

People are more likely to act when the suggested proposition creates dissonance. A second theory from which your persuasive strategies may be drawn is the theory of cognitive dissonance. *Cognitive dissonance* is an inconsistency that occurs between two or more cognitive elements. A *cognition* is a thought or a piece of knowledge about some situation, person, or behavior. For example, if you worked hard to save $35 for a gift for your friend, the amount you saved would be one cognitive element. If you proceeded to spend $75 for the gift, the amount you actually spent would be a second cognitive element. The inconsistency between money available and money spent would create a discomfort. This discomfort is what Leon Festinger, the originator of this theory, calls cognitive dissonance.[2]

Festinger holds that whenever you get yourself in one of these states of discomfort (and some of us may find ourselves in this state quite often), you have a great desire to *reduce the discomfort.* The greater the degree of discomfort experienced, the greater the desire to reduce it.

What determines the degree of discomfort? According to Festinger the amount of dissonance you are likely to feel depends on at least two factors.

The first factor is the number of elements in each cognition. You are likely to experience less dissonance if there are only two conflicting cognitions than if there are several. For instance, high pay for a job combined with low prestige for that job may create cognitive dissonance, but the degree will be relatively low because only two cognitions are in competition. On the other hand, if higher pay and a better location are in competition with low prestige, little chance for advancement, and less desirable duties, the degree of dissonance will be considerably greater.

The second factor in determining the degree of discomfort is the importance of the entire issue. For instance, a person usually experiences less dissonance after making a decision to buy a certain pair of shoes than after making a decision to buy a new car.

When a person experiences dissonance, what can he or she do to relieve it? Festinger suggests four methods of reducing or relieving dissonance:

1. *A person may change his or her attitude toward the decision.* If you bought your friend a present that cost more than you had planned to pay, you can reduce the dissonance by telling yourself that your friend is worth every penny you spent.

2. *A person can change his or her behavior.* If you smoke excessively and the smoking is hurting your relationship with a friend, you can stop smoking.

3. *A person can change the environment in which the dissonance occurs.* If you are an actor of only average ability, but wish to have major parts in school plays, you can go to a smaller school where it is more likely that you can get better parts.

4. *A person may add new cognitive elements.* If you have paid too much for your friend's gift, you might tell yourself that you can cut expenses by avoiding evening snacks for a month.

Now that you can see what cognitive dissonance is, you may be asking what it has to do with developing a persuasive strategy. As a speaker, you have opportunities to create dissonance in the mind of each person in the audience and then to provide the means of relieving the dissonance you have created.

Consider a situation in which you wish to motivate the audience to stop buying cigarettes and liquor from people who obtain their merchandise from out of state. People may buy these products because they are cheaper; people may know that the reason they are cheaper is because the taxes for those products are lower in another state, and these savings are being passed along to them. How can you create dissonance in the minds of these people? You may develop a line of argument linking trafficking in out-of-state cigarettes and liquor with organized crime. Most people believe that supporting organized crime is wrong. If you can show your audience that what looks like a small savings to them mounts up to really big business for "smugglers," you may well create dissonance between the cognition of saving money and the cognition of supporting organized crime. Although members of your audience may choose to repress a perception of the information you cite, or bury that dissonance, or devalue the issue (three common ways of rationalizing), if you can make the point strongly enough, at least some may feel compelled to do something to relieve that dissonance by not buying the products under the circumstances you describe. In summary:

1. People look for ways to relieve dissonance when confronted with conflicting cognitions.

2. You can create dissonance by presenting conflicting cognitions.

3. Your speech proposition can be perceived as a way of relieving the dissonance you have created.

Basic Needs

Abraham Maslow's hierarchy of needs theory is a third theory from which persuasive strategies may be developed. Persuasion is more likely to occur when the proposition satisfies a strong unmet need in members of the audience. If people are hungry, their main concern is to obtain food. Thus, if you are able to identify audience needs, you have a good start for planning your persuasive strategy.

Maslow divides basic human needs into five categories:[3]

1. Physiological needs

2. Safety needs

3. Belongingness and love needs

4. Esteem needs

5. Self-actualization needs

Notice that he places these needs in a hierarchy: one set of needs must be met or satisfied before the next set of needs emerges. The physiological needs for food, drink, and life-sustaining temperature are the most basic; they must be satisfied before the body is able to consider any of its other needs. The next level consists of safety needs—security, simple self-preservation, and the like; they emerge after the basic needs have been met, and they hold a paramount place until they, too, have been met. The third level includes the belongingness or love needs: the need to identify with friends, loved ones, and family. In a world of increasing mobility and breakdown of the traditional family, it is becoming more and more difficult for individuals to satisfy this need. Nonetheless, once the belongingness needs have been met, the esteem needs predominate: the quest for material goods, recognition, and power or influence. Maslow calls the final level the self-actualizing need; this involves developing one's self to meet its potential. When all other needs have been met, this need is the one that drives people to their creative heights and urges them to do "what they need to do to fulfill themselves as human beings."

What is the value of this analysis to you as a speaker? First, it provides a framework for and suggests the kinds of needs you may appeal to in your speeches. Second, it allows you to understand why a line of development will work on one audience and fail with another. For instance, if your audience has great physiological needs (if they are hungry), an appeal to the satisfaction of good workmanship, no matter how well done, is unlikely to impress them. Third, and perhaps most crucial, when your proposition conflicts with an operating need, you will have to be prepared with a strong alternative in the same category or in a higher-level category. For instance, if your proposition is going to cost money (if it is going to take money in the form of taxes), you will have to show how the proposal satisfies some other comparable need.

Let us try to make this discussion more specific by looking at some of the traditional motives for action. These motives are not the only ones; we present them to suggest the kind of analysis you should be doing. You have selected a proposition and have determined reasons for its acceptance. Now try to relate those reasons to basic needs and discover where you may be getting into difficulty by coming into conflict with other motives or other needs.

Wealth. The desire for wealth, the acquisition of money and material goods, is a motive that grows out of an esteem need. For example, those who have little money can perhaps be motivated to buy a Ford Escort, a Chevette, or a Dodge Omni primarily because they get such good gas mileage and are so economical to operate. Those who have a great deal of money can perhaps be motivated to buy a Rolls-Royce or a Cadillac because they are prestigious. Does your proposition affect wealth or material goods in any way? If its effect is positive, you may want to stress it. If your plan calls for giving up money, you will need to be prepared to cope with an audience's natural resistance. You will have to involve another motive from the same category (esteem) or from a higher category to override the loss of any money the audience will have to give up.

Power.　Another esteem need is power. For many people, personal worth is dependent upon their power over their own destiny, the exercise of power over others, and the recognition and prestige that comes from such recognition of power. If your proposition allows a person, group, or community to exercise power, it may be worth emphasizing. On the other hand, if your speech takes power away from part or all of the audience, you will need to provide strong compensation to motivate them.

Conformity.　Conformity is a major source of motivation for nearly everyone. Conformity grows out of a need for belongingness. People often behave in a given way because a friend, a neighbor, an acquaintance, or a person in the same age bracket behaves that way. Although some people will be more likely to do something if they can be the first one to do it or if it makes them appear distinctive, most people feel more secure when they are acting in ways that conform with others of their kind. The old saying that there is strength in numbers certainly applies to conformity. If you can show that many people similar to the members of your audience favor your plan, that argument may well provide motivation.

Pleasure.　When you are given a choice of actions, you often pick the one that gives you the greatest pleasure, enjoyment, or happiness. On at least one level, pleasure is a self-actualizing need; however, it also operates as an esteem need. If your speech relates to something that is novel, promises excitement, is fun to do, or offers a challenge, you can probably motivate your audience on that basis.

These are only four possible motives for action growing out of basic audience needs. Sex appeal, responsibility, justice, and many others operate within each of us. If you discover that you are not relating your material to basic audience needs, you probably need to revise your procedure.

However, knowing which needs an audience has and appealing to those needs are two different things. To maximize your effectiveness you must understand how to trigger these needs.

What happens when your proposition does not meet a specific audience need? Either you can change the wording of your proposition so that it is in tune with audience needs, or you can work to create or uncover an audience need that the proposition will meet. For instance, if you are giving a speech intended to motivate the audience to go to dinner at Le Parisien (a very expensive restaurant), your proposition may meet a need to eat out occasionally, but it is in opposition to most people's need to eat for a reasonable price. For this speech to be effective, you will either have to change the proposition to recommend a more modest restaurant (The River Captain, for instance) or you must arouse some needs that would be met by going to Le Parisien.

In planning strategy in terms of basic needs, you must find out

1. What needs does the audience have at this time?

2. Can the proposition be written to satisfy those needs, and if so, how?

3. If the proposition does not meet those needs, how can you change the wording to activate unexpressed and perhaps unrealized needs?

PREPARING A SPEECH TO ACTUATE

Practice with motivation may be best accomplished with a speech-to-actuate assignment, a speech calling for the speaker to bring the audience to action.

Preparing a speech to actuate requires you to think creatively about your overall plan and about the specific means you can use to implement the plan. This preparation will involve (1) phrasing the proposition (specific purpose) in a way that gives you the best opportunity to achieve success, (2) finding reasons and evidence in support, (3) analyzing your audience's attitude toward the subject matter to determine where you will have common ground and where you will have to work to meet objections to the action you call for, (4) writing an outline that is organized to take into account what you have learned from your audience analysis, (5) developing language that will motivate, (6) placing special emphasis on the introduction and conclusion, and (7) practicing the delivery.

Phrase the Topic and Proposition

Like the topic for a speech to convince, the topic for a speech to actuate can be on any subject. Since the goal of a speech to actuate is to bring your audience to action, you will want to state the proposition in a way that gives you an opportunity to succeed. You will not be able to achieve action on a speech topic that the entire audience opposes. You can get action by starting with a premise on which the majority of the audience agrees. For instance, suppose you wanted to give a speech on the proposition "to persuade the class to test-drive a small, front-wheel-drive American car." This proposition has a chance to succeed. It is clearly written. It is specific, but it still allows the audience some choice. You could try the proposition "to persuade the class to buy a small front-wheel-drive American car"; but by asking them to test drive rather than buy, you are likely to increase your chances for success.

Find Reasons

At this point your preparation for a speech to actuate is the same as for a speech to convince. Since all persuasive speeches depend on finding reasons, this will be your second step. For your speech on test driving front-wheel-drive American cars you may have uncovered the following reasons you could use:

1. Front-wheel-drive cars handle very well.

2. Small, front-wheel-drive American cars get good mileage.

3. Front-wheel-drive American cars are generally safer than foreign front-wheel-drive cars.

4. Small, front-wheel-drive cars cost less than larger cars.

5. Front-wheel-drive cars now come with all major options.

6. The quality of American front-wheel-drive cars is improving.

Let us further suppose that you have been able to find good evidence to support each of these six reasons.

Analyze Your Audience

The key to your success with this speech will depend on your understanding of the audience's attitude toward American cars generally and front-wheel-drive cars specifically. To start with, you would work with the basic questions asked on pages 54–55.

1. Will my listeners be sympathetic, apathetic, or hostile?

2. Can I expect them to have any preconceived biases that will affect their listening, understanding, or emotional reactions?

3. If they are sympathetic, how can I present my material so that it will take advantage of their favorable attitude?

4. If they are hostile, how can I present my material in a way that will at least not increase their hostility?

The answers to question 2 are likely to provide much of the insight you need for this speech.

For instance, with the front-wheel-drive car proposition, you probably will discover that the audience has a favorable attitude toward buying American products in general. (Few people are opposed to American-made products in general.) And the audience is likely to favor purchasing a small, front-wheel-drive car, since during the past decade Americans have been buying more and more small, front-wheel-drive cars.

The problem is that although the audience is likely to have a favorable attitude toward small, American-made, front-wheel-drive cars in principle, Americans have still been buying far more foreign-made, front-wheel-drive cars.

The question then becomes What is keeping people from purchasing small, front-wheel-drive American cars? At least three factors seem to be involved: gas mileage, quality of workmanship, and habitual buying practices. Let us consider each of these negative reactions in order to determine a strategy for dealing with them. The following process illustrates the kind of thinking you need to be doing.

1. *The American car doesn't get comparable gas mileage.* This has been true, but the difference is narrowing. Moreover, since American cars begin with a lower base price, the small amount of gasoline saved with the highest-mileage foreign cars will not offset the original price difference.

2. *The American small car is not quality made.* Again, this appears to have been very true in the past, but evidence is accumulating that American small-car workmanship is improving, resulting in a car with a record comparable to the imports on such important indexes as frequency of repair and buyer satisfaction.

3. *Americans are out of the habit of looking for a small, front-wheel-drive, American-made car.* This seems to be especially true and is probably the area you will have to work on the hardest. Yet, if you are able to show the great improvements in American-made cars, you may be able to meet this problem.

The next step is to write an outline that is organized to take into account what you have learned from your audience analysis. Let us look at a tentative (and shortened) outline of the body of a speech that takes this audience analysis into consideration and that you can construct on the front-wheel-drive car example.

Outline the Speech

Body

I. American car manufacturers are producing small, front-wheel-drive cars that are truly competitive with foreign imports.
   A. The small, front-wheel-drive American car gets comparable mileage to most foreign small cars.
   B. The small, front-wheel-drive American car is often safer to drive.
   C. The small, front-wheel-drive American car is much less expensive, even in those instances where miles per gallon is not as good.

II. Manufacturers are putting quality back into the American car.
   A. Frequency-of-repair records are much better.
   B. Workmanship is much improved.
   C. Buyer satisfaction is much higher.

Select two reasons on the basis of what appear to be the major audience motivators: (1) truly competitive and (2) high quality. The first point lays the groundwork for the competitive factors, that is, gas mileage is comparable. Furthermore, it introduces two additional factors that have high-motivation possibilities: (1) safety and (2) lower initial cost. The second reason hits the quality point head on. Since Americans are out of the habit of buying American, you should select points to try to jolt the audience into giving the American car another look and to show that when a person does buy American, satisfaction is high.

How you develop each of the points will be vital to the success of the speech. You will have to think of how to make the points that will get and hold audience attention.

The following are three language strategies you may consider using.

Create a common ground.   In a persuasive speech you are trying to establish the feeling that both you and the audience are operating from the same value system and sharing many of the same experiences. In short, you are in this together. The response you seek from the audi-

Creating a common ground is central to motivating an audience. Corazon Aquino was able to inspire a revolution because she understood the mood of the people and was able to show that she shared with them a common set of values, beliefs, and attitudes.

ence is, "We agree" or "We have so much in common, on so many various points, that we can reach agreement on a single point of difference." In trying to get support for their latest programs politicians often try to show audiences that they have the same background; the same set of values, beliefs, and attitudes; the same overall way of looking at things so that a point of difference does not represent a difference in philosophy.

Develop yes-responses. Psychologists have found that when people get in the habit of saying yes, they are likely to continue saying yes. If you can phrase questions that establish areas of agreement early in your speech, the audience will be more likely to listen to you and, perhaps, to agree with your proposition. The criteria-satisfaction method of organization is built on the yes-response. For instance, if you asked, "Do you like to have a good time? to get your money's worth? to put your money into a worthy cause? to support your community if you will profit from the support?" and then asked, "Will you support Playhouse-in-the-Park?" you would be using the yes-response method.

Suggest agreements. Suggestion involves planting an idea in the listener's mind without developing the idea. It is stated in such a way that its acceptance is sought without analysis or consideration.

Speakers often use suggestion through directives. Such expressions as, "I think we will all agree," "As we all know," and "Now we come to a most important consideration" are forms of suggestion that will help you direct audience thinking.

You will need to place special emphasis on the introduction and the conclusion. One way of starting the speech that is honest, yet thought provoking, follows:

Emphasize the Introduction and Conclusion

> Our indignation with American auto companies that have been trying to sell us shoddy merchandise has forced many of us to turn to foreign cars. For several years now, the cry "Buy American" has been totally ignored. In fact, many of us are so in the habit of looking to the foreign car we don't even consider the American-made product. Are you thinking of buying a new car soon? If so, take another look at American-made—especially at the small, front-wheel-drive American car. I think you will be pleasantly surprised.

Likewise, you could conclude the speech on a similar note:

We Americans want quality, and we'll look anywhere until we find it. The time has come to look again at a place we've neglected— right here at home. When you start looking for that new car, go to the American-manufactured car first. I think you'll buy one!

Practice the Delivery

Practice the delivery of your speech until it adds to the force of motivation you are trying to develop.

ASSIGNMENT
Speech to Actuate

1. Prepare a four- to seven-minute persuasive speech on a topic designed to bring your audience to action. An outline is required. In addition to clarity of purpose and soundness of reasons, grading will focus on your credibility, your ability to satisfy audience needs, and your ability to phrase your ideas in a way that will motivate.

2. Write a critique of one or more of the speeches to actuate that you hear in class. Outline the speech. As you are outlining it, answer the following questions yes or no:

Proposition (Specific Purpose)

_____ Did the proposition call for a specific audience action?

_____ Was the proposition adapted to the audience's interests, knowledge, and attitudes?

Content

_____ Did the speaker use cost-reward motivation?

_____ Did the speaker use cognitive-dissonance motivation?

_____ Did the speaker use basic-needs motivation?

_____ Were good reasons presented?

_____ Was good evidence used in support?

_____ Did the speaker build his/her credibility?

_____ Did the speaker analyze the audience correctly?

_____ Did the speech create common ground?

_____ Did the speaker develop yes-responses?

_____ Did the speaker suggest agreements?

Organization

_____ Did the introduction motivate?

_____ Did the speech follow an organization that related to audience attitudes?

_____ Did the speaker use any special strategies to help you remember the main points and other key information?

Language

_____ Was the language clear? ____ vivid? ____ emphatic? ____ appropriate?

Delivery

_____ Was the delivery motivating?

Evaluate the speech as (check one) ____ excellent, ____ good, ____ average, ____ fair, ____ poor.

Use the information from your check sheet to support your evaluation.

OUTLINE: SPEECH TO ACTUATE (4–7 MINUTES)

Proposition (Specific Purpose): To persuade listeners to donate their eyes to an eye bank.

Introduction

I. Close your eyes and imagine living in a world of darkness.
II. Millions live in this world.

Thesis Statement: People should donate their eyes to an eye bank because corneas are necessary for sight, because corneas can be transplanted, and because donors know that through a donation a part of them lives on and they can be as useful to humanity in death as in life.

Body

I. The windows through which we see the world are the corneas.
   A. They are tough, dime-sized, transparent tissues.
   B. Normally they are clear.
   C. When they are distorted, they blot out the light.
II. Those with injured corneas have the hope of normal sight through a cornea transplant.
   A. The operation works miracles, but it cannot work without donors.
   B. If eyes are transplanted within seventy-two hours after the death of the donor, the operation can be 100 percent successful.
   C. The operation has turned tragedy into joy.
III. There are many reasons for donating.
   A. The donor knows a part of him goes on living.
   B. The donor knows he can be as useful to humanity in death as in life.
IV. I hope you will consider becoming a donor.
   A. Leaving your desire in your will is not enough—the operation must come within seventy-two hours of death.
   B. Get forms and details from a Cincinnati eye bank.
   C. Then, when you die, someone who needs the chance can see.

Conclusion

I. Close your eyes again—now open them.
II. Won't you give someone else the chance to open theirs?

Read this speech aloud at least once and analyze the use of motivation.[4] What motives is the speaker appealing to? After you have analyzed the speech, read the analysis given here.

ANALYSIS

Much of the strength of this speech is a result of the speaker's ability to involve members of the audience personally and get them to feel what she is saying. This open-

SPEECH: Open Your Eyes

Would all of you close your eyes for just a minute. Close them very tightly so that all the light is blocked out. Imagine what it would be like to always live in a world of total darkness such as you are experiencing right now, though only for a moment. Never to see the flaming colors of the sunset, or the crisp green of the world after the rain—never to see the faces of those you love. Now open your eyes, look all around you, look at all of the things that you couldn't have seen if you couldn't have opened your eyes.

The bright world we awake to each morning is brought to us through two dime-sized pieces of tough, transparent, semielastic tissue; these are the corneas, and it is their function to allow light to enter the lens and the retina. Normally, they are so clear that we don't even know they are there; however, when they are scratched or scarred either by accident or by disease, they tend to blur or blot out the light. Imagine peering through a rain-slashed window pane or trying to see while swimming under water. This is the way the victims of corneal damage often describe their vision.

"To see the world through another man's eyes." These words are Shakespeare's, yet today it can literally be true. Thanks to the research by medical workers throughout the world, the operation known as a corneal transplant or a corneal graft has become a reality, giving thousands of people the opportunity to see. No other generation has held such a profound legacy in its possession. Yet, the universal ignorance of this subject of cornea donation is appalling. The operation itself is really quite simple; it involves the corneas of the donor being transplanted into the eyes of a recipient. And if this operation takes place within seventy-two hours after the death of the donor, it can be 100 percent effective.

No one who has seen the human tragedy caused solely by corneal disease can doubt the need or the urgency. Take the case of a young woman living in New Jersey who lost her sight to corneal disease. She gave birth to a baby and two years ago, thanks to a corneal transplant, she saw her three-year-old baby girl for the first

ing is a striking example of audience involvement. She does not just tell the audience what it would be like—she has them experience the feeling. The speaker very successfully lays the emotional groundwork for total audience reception of her words.

Here the speaker begins the body of her speech by telling us about the role of the cornea. Notice throughout the speech the excellent word choice, such as "The bright world we awake to each morning is brought to us through. . . ." Here again she does not just tell us what it is like but asks us to imagine for ourselves what it would be like. The "rain-slashed window pane" is an especially vivid image.

The speaker continues in a very informative way. After asserting that corneal transplants work, she focuses on the two key points that she wants the audience to work with—the operation works, but it must be done within seventy-two hours. Notice that there is still no apparent direct persuasion. Her method is one of making information available in a way that will lead the audience itself to thinking about what effects the information might have on them personally.

In this segment of the speech, she launches into emotional high gear. Still, her approach remains somewhat indirect. Although we stress the importance of directness in language in this speech, the use of "no one" repeatedly throughout the examples is done by design. Although a more direct method might be effective, in this case the indirectness works quite well. The real effectiveness of the section is a result of the parallel structure and repetition of key phrases: "no one who has seen . . . human tragedy . . . great joy . . . can doubt the need or the urgency." As this portion of the speech was delivered, the listeners were deeply touched by both the examples themselves and their own thoughts about the examples. Also note how the examples themselves are ordered. The first two represent a personal effect; the final one a universal effect.

At this point in the speech the audience should be sympathetic with the problem and encouraged by the hope of corneal transplants. Now the speaker must deal with the listener's possible reaction of "that may be a good idea for someone else, but why me?" It is in this section that she offers reasons for our acting. If the speech has a weakness, it may be here. I would have liked a little further development of the reasons or perhaps the statement of an additional reason. Here she brings the audience from "Good idea—I'll do something someday" to "I'd better act now." She reminds them of the critical time period and tells them how they can proceed to make the donation. In this

time. And no one who had seen this woman's human tragedy caused solely by corneal disease nor her great joy at the restoration of her sight can doubt the need or the urgency. Or take the case of the five-year-old boy in California who was playing by a bonfire when a bottle in the fire exploded, flinging bits of glass, which lacerated his corneas. His damaged corneas were replaced with healthy ones in an emergency operation, and no one who had seen this little boy's human tragedy caused solely by corneal laceration nor the great joy to his young life of receiving his sight back again can doubt the need or the urgency. Or take the case of Dr. Beldon H. Scribbner of the University of Washington School of Medicine. Dr. Scribbner's eyesight was damaged by a corneal disease that twisted the normally sphere-shaped corneas into cones. A corneal transplant gave Dr. Scribbner twenty-twenty corrective vision and allowed him to continue work on his invention—the artificial kidney machine. And no one who has seen this man's human tragedy caused solely by corneal disease, nor the great joy brought not only to Dr. Scribbner but to the thousands of people his machine has helped save, can doubt the need or the urgency.

There are many philosophies behind such a gift. One of them was summed up by a minister and his wife who lost their daughter in infancy. They said, "We feel that a part of her goes on living." Or take the case of the young woman who was dying of cancer. She donated her eyes and did so with this explanation: "I want to be useful; being useful brings purpose and meaning into my life." Surely if being useful is important there are few better ways than to donate your eyes to someone who lives after you. But no matter which philosophy you do adopt, I hope each of you will consider donating your eyes to another who will live after you and who otherwise would have to survive in the abyss of darkness. It will do you no good to leave your eyes in your regular will if you have one; for as I mentioned earlier, there is a seventy-two-hour critical period. If you wish to donate your eyes, I would suggest you contact Cincinnati Eye Bank for Sight Restoration at 861-3716. They will send you the appropriate donor forms to fill out, which should be witnessed by two of your closest friends or by your next of kin so that they will know your wishes. Then, when you die and no longer have need for your sight someone who desperately wants the chance to see will be able to.

Will all of you close your eyes again for just a moment? Close them very tightly, so that all the light is blocked out. And once more imagine what it would be like to live always in a world of total darkness such as you are experiencing right now, never seeing the flaming colors of a sunset, or the crisp green of the world after a rain—never seeing the faces of those you love. Now open your eyes. . . . Won't you give someone else the chance to open theirs?

section it might be worth a sentence to stress that the donation costs nothing but a little time.

Here the speaker brings the audience full circle. Although she could have used different images, the repetition of those that began the speech takes the emphasis off the images themselves and places it in what the audience can do about those who are in these circumstances. The last line of the speech is simple, but in the context of the entire speech it is direct and quite moving. This is a superior example of a speech to actuate.

NOTES

1. John W. Thibaut and Harold H. Kelley, *The Social Psychology of Groups* (New York: Wiley, 1959).
2. Leon Festinger, *A Theory of Cognitive Dissonance* (Evanston, Ill.: Row, Peterson, 1957).
3. Abraham H. Maslow, *Motivation and Personality* (New York: Harper & Row, 1954), 80–92.
4. Speech given in Speech class, University of Cincinnati. Printed by permission of Kathleen Sheldon.

SIXTEEN

CRITICALLY EVALUATING ARGUMENTS: SPEECHES OF REFUTATION

When people are confronted with a speech that makes a claim, they can accept it, reject it, or perhaps suspend judgment. *Critical thinking* is the process used to make such judgments; it involves examining the arguments upon which judgments are based.

For each of the earlier assignments, you have prepared a speech, delivered it to the audience, and returned to your seat to listen either to another speech or to an evaluation of your speech. You probably have not had to defend your position or attack a position taken by another student. Yet to excel in social, legislative, vocational, and other decision-making groups, you must develop some confidence in your abilities to attack and defend. To do so, you must be able to think critically.

In the first part of this chapter, we lay the groundwork for thinking critically. In the latter part, we show how to use the results of your critical thinking to prepare a speech of refutation.

THINKING CRITICALLY: ANALYZING ARGUMENTS IN SPEECHES

To think critically about an argument, you must have an accurate representation of that argument. When you evaluate written sources the entire argument is on paper in front of you. To evaluate an oral argument, however, you need to outline the argument carefully to preserve its essence. After you have outlined an argument or a series of arguments, you can begin to examine the reasoning used.

Outlining Arguments

Good outlining requires that you get the key material down on paper accurately. Throughout this book you have been working on your outlining skills. Keep in mind that a good outline is not a transcription of the entire argument. For a persuasive argument, an outline will contain the reason or reasons presented in defense of a conclusion or proposition and the data used in support of the reason or reasons with notations of whether the data were documented.

Let's look at an abbreviated written version of an oral argument:

> Public schools have been criticized during the past few years, but the results of some schools in the city show that public schools are capable of high levels of achievement. Park Hills, a public school on the west side, is an excellent example. Three years ago Park Hills raised its standards in all academic courses. It forced its students to work much harder to achieve good grades. According to an article in the June 26 issue of the *Post,* in June, Park Hills had three merit scholars, more than any year in its history. Moreover, student SAT scores were up 20 points from student scores just three years ago. Linden, a public school on the east side, is another example. Four years ago, Linden began increasing homework assignments and now requires two hours per evening of homework as well as three major papers a year of all students. According to that same *Post* article, in June, Linden had 85 percent of its graduating class accepted to college, up 30 percent from four years ago.

The following is the kind of outline you would write to analyze the argument.

Outline

I. Public schools are capable of high levels of achievement.
   A. Park Hills
   1. Raised standards in all courses
   2. Forced students to work harder for grades
   3. Three merit scholars (more than ever)
   4. SAT scores up 20 points in three years

B. Linden
   1. Two hours of homework per night
   2. Three papers a year of all students
   3. 85 percent of graduates accepted to college (up 30 percent in four years)

Once you have the substance of the speech (or argument) written in outline form, you can begin to test the data and the reasoning from the data.

Testing the data. For a logical conclusion to follow, the data must be sound. For each item, consider the following:

1. *What is the source of the data?* Is the source a newspaper article? a journal article? a government report? Just because something appeared in print does not make it true. If the data come from a poor source, an unreliable source, or a biased source, no reliable conclusion can be drawn from them. In the abbreviated version above, one source, the *Post,* was cited. If no sources are cited, you have the right to ask for sources. When you get the sources, you can raise questions about their quality.

2. *Are the data fact or opinion?* Factual data are usually worth more than opinion, and expert opinion is worth more than inexpert opinion. Can we document that Park Hills raised standards, had three merit scholars, and improved SAT scores 20 points in three years? Can we document that Linden increased homework time, required three papers a year, and sent 85 percent of its graduates (up 30 percent) to college?

3. *Are the data recent?* Products, ideas, and statistics may be obsolete as soon as they are produced. You must ask when the data were true. Five-year-old data may not be true today. Furthermore, even a current article from last week's news magazine may be using old data.

4. *Are the data relevant?* You may find that the data have little to do with the point being presented. This question of relevance leads you into an analysis of the reasoning process itself.

If you are satisfied with the quality of the data (that the examples

Testing the Oral Argument

for Park Hills and Linden are accurate), then you can move to the second step.

Testing the reasoning (warrants).   To test the reasoning, you must understand the link between the data and the conclusion drawn. In the above example, the speaker presents data from two schools and concludes that public schools are capable of high levels of achievement. In this case, the warrant, or reasoning link, is not stated. Before you can test the warrant, you must write it out. The speaker is saying, "What has been accomplished in two public schools can be accomplished in most or all." To test the warrant, phrase it as a yes-or-no question: "Is it true that the results in these two examples (Park Hills and Linden) are possible in most or all public schools? If the answer is yes, the reasoning is sound; if the answer is no, the reasoning is fallacious. As you will recall from our discussion of reasoning in Chapter 14, this argument is illustrative of reasoning by example (generalization). In the next section, we look at the specific tests of this and other types of arguments.

Evaluating Reasoning

You will recall that reason is either inductive or deductive. *Inductive reasoning* means working from specifics to some conclusion. In inductive reasoning you discover what is true or what was true in the past, and then you predict that something is true or will be true in the future. The conclusions of inductive arguments are tested on the basis of probability. That is, we predict that the conclusion will be true most of the time. The higher the probability (the closer to 100 percent), the better the argument.

Deductive reasoning is a form that moves from premises to conclusions. If the premises are true, then the conclusion is not just probable, as in an inductive argument, but *certain.*

Now let's consider the evaluation of inductive reasoning (generalization, analogy, causation, and sign) and deductive reasoning. To enable you to build upon what you have learned, in each of the following discussions we refer back to arguments that we used in Chapter 14 in support of the prediction that Paula Larson will win the senior class election.

Critically evaluating generalization warrants.   Recall that in reasoning by generalization, we drew a conclusion based on several related individual items of information. In support of the proposition that Paula Larson will win the senior class election, the speaker based his or her argument on the three examples: "Paula was successful in her campaign for treasurer of her high school junior class, in her campaign for chairperson of her church youth group, and in her campaign for president of her sorority." This is reasoning from example or generalization. The warrant might be phrased, "Her success in three other campaigns may be used to predict her success in this campaign."

A *generalization warrant* (the verbal statement of the reasoning process) may be tested by asking the following questions.

1. *Are enough instances cited?* Are three campaigns (junior class treasurer, youth group chairperson, and sorority president) enough examples? Since the instances cited should represent most to all possibilities, enough must be cited to satisfy the listeners that the instances are not isolated or handpicked.

   One of the most common thinking fallacies is called *hasty generalization,* which results from a shortage of data. Conclusions from hasty generalization fail to meet the test of sufficient instances cited. In real-life situations, we are likely to find people making generalizations based on only one, or at most a few, examples. For instance, in support of the argument that teenagers favor marijuana decriminalization, a person might cite the opinions of two teenagers who live next door. Yet, the cross-section for that sample is neither large enough nor representative enough. In a speech, the argument may sound more impressive than it is, especially if the speaker dramatizes the one example. But you can refute the argument as a hasty generalization.

   So, if a speaker presents a generalization with no data, or with very little data, you will want to question the reasoning on that basis alone. Although students in a public speaking class shouldn't make the mistake of hasty generalization in a speech, you may find opportunities to refute arguments on that basis.

2. *Are the instances typical?* Are the three instances typical of all of her campaigns for office? *Typical* means that the instances cited must be similar to or representative of most or all within the category. If instances are not typical, they do not support the generalization. For instance, if these three successes came in very small organizations, they would not be typical of all organizations. If you do not believe that three instances are typical, then you would question the logic of the argument on that basis.

3. *Are negative instances accounted for?* In looking at material we may find one or more exceptions to the generalization. If the exceptions are minor or infrequent, then they do not necessarily invalidate the generalization. For instance, Paula may have run for chairperson of the chess club but was defeated. That one failure does not necessarily invalidate the generalization. If, however, the exceptions prove to be more than rare or isolated instances, the validity of the generalization is open to serious question. For instance, if we found that Paula ran for office twelve times and was successful on only the three occasions cited, then the generalization would be fallacious. If you believe that negative instances were not accounted for, then you would question the logic of the argument on that basis.

Critically evaluating analogy warrants. Recall that an *analogy* is a comparative generalization. In reasoning by analogy, we say that what is true of something with one set of circumstances will be true of something else with a similar set of circumstances. In support of the proposition that Paula Larson will win the senior class election, the speaker based his or her argument on the similarity between Paula and Heather Nelson, who won two years ago, by showing that "Paula and Heather are both bright, both have a great deal of drive, and both have a track record of successful campaigns." This is reasoning from analogy. The warrant might be phrased, "Paula's similarity to Heather, who was successful two years ago, can be used to predict her success in this campaign."

An *analogy warrant* (the verbal statement of the reasoning process) may be tested by asking these questions.

1. *Are the subjects being compared similar in all important ways?* Are Heather and Paula similar in intelligence, drive, and track records in elected offices? If subjects do not have significant similarities, then they are not comparable. If you believe that the subjects being compared are not really similar in important ways, then you can question the reasoning on that basis.

2. *Are any of the ways that the subjects are dissimilar important to the outcome?* Is Paula's dissimilarity in sorority affiliation a factor? Is her dissimilarity in religion a factor? If dissimilarities exist that outweigh the subjects' similarities, then conclusions drawn from the comparisons may be invalid. If you believe that the ways the

subjects are dissimilar have not been considered, then you can question the reasoning on that basis.

Critically evaluating causation warrants. Recall that *causation* is a form of reasoning that proves a conclusion on the basis of a special connection between the data and the conclusion. When we say that a causal relationship exists, we mean that one or more of the circumstances cited always (or at least usually) produce a predictable effect or set of effects. In support of the proposition that Paula Larson will win the senior class election, the speaker based his or her argument on the points that "Paula has campaigned intelligently, and Paula has key endorsements—both of which result in election." This is reasoning from causation. The warrant might be phrased, "Intelligent campaigning and the presence of key endorsements, major causes of success in elections, can be used to predict her success in this campaign."

A *causation warrant* (the verbal statement of the reasoning process) may be tested by asking these questions.

1. *Are the data alone sufficient cause to bring about the particular conclusion?* Are intelligent campaigning and getting key endorsements themselves important enough to result in winning elections? If the data are truly important, it means that if we eliminate the data, we would eliminate the effect. If the effect can occur without the data, then we can question the causal relationship.

   Another common thinking fallacy, *questionable cause,* is marked by the failure to meet this test. It is human nature to look for causes for events. If we are having a drought, we want to know the cause; if the schools are in financial trouble, we want to know the cause; if the crime rate has risen during the year, we want to know the cause. In our haste to discover causes for behavior, we sometimes identify something that happened or existed before the event or at the time of the event, and label that something as the cause of the event. This tendency leads to the fallacy of questionable cause.

   Think of the people who blame loss of money, sickness, and problems at work on black cats that ran in front of them, or mirrors that broke, or ladders they walked under. You recognize these as superstitions. Nevertheless, they are excellent examples of attributing cause to unrelated events.

   Superstitions are not the only examples of questionable cause. Consider a situation that occurs yearly on many college campuses.

One year a coach's team has a winning year, and the coach is lauded for his or her expertise. The next year the team does poorly and the coach is fired. Has the coach's skill deteriorated that much in one year? It is quite unlikely. But it's much easier to point the finger at the coach as the cause of the team's failure than it is to admit that the entire team or the program itself is inferior. The fact is that examples of this kind of argument are frequent.

If you believe that the data alone are not important or significant enough to bring about the conclusion, then you can question the reasoning on that basis.

2. *Do some other data that accompany the data cited cause the effect?* Are there some other factors (like luck, drive, friends) that are more important in determining whether a person wins an election? If the accompanying data appear equally or more important in bringing about the effect, then we can question the causal relationship between cited data and conclusion. If you believe that some other data really caused the effect, then you can question the reasoning on that basis.

3. *Is the relationship between cause and effect consistent?* Do intelligent campaigning and key endorsements always (or usually) yield winning elections? If there are times when the effect has not followed the cause, then we can question whether a causal relationship exists. If you believe that the relationship between the cause and effect are not consistent, then you can question the reasoning on that basis.

Critically evaluating sign warrants. Recall that a *sign* is a form of reasoning that proves a conclusion on the basis of a connection between the symptoms and the conclusion. Signs are indicators. When certain events, characteristics, or situations always or usually accompany something, we say that these events, characteristics, or situations are signs.

In support of the proposition that Paula Larson will win the senior class election, the speaker based his or her argument on the points that "Paula has more campaign posters than all other candidates combined, and students from all segments of campus are wearing her campaign buttons." This is reasoning from signs. The warrant might be phrased, "The presence of campaign posters and the wearing of campaign buttons are signs or indicators of the likelihood of success in this campaign."

A *sign warrant* (the verbal statement of the reasoning) may be tested by these questions.

1. *Do the signs cited always or usually indicate the conclusion drawn?* Do large numbers of posters and campaign buttons always (or usually) indicate election victory? If the data can occur independently of the conclusion, then they are not necessarily indicators. If you believe that the data cited do not usually indicate the conclusion, then you can question the reasoning on that basis.

2. *Are sufficient signs present?* Are campaign posters and buttons enough to indicate a victory? Events or situations are often indicated by several signs. If enough of them are not present, then the conclusion may not follow. If you believe there are insufficient signs, then you can question the reasoning on that basis.

3. *Are contradictory signs in evidence?* Are posters being torn down in great numbers? If signs that usually indicate different conclusions are present, then the stated conclusion may not be valid. If you believe that contradictory signs are in evidence, then you can question the reasoning on that basis.

Critically evaluating deductions. As we have mentioned, *deduction* is a form of reasoning that is used in moving from statements that are true to a related statement that must be true. A deductive warrant may be stated, "If two related premises are true, then a conclusion based on those two premises must be true." If the speaker argued that Paula must have won the election for she is giving a victory speech and only winners are entitled to such speeches, you would identify this as a deductive argument.

A *deduction warrant* (the verbal statement of the reasoning process) may be tested by asking these questions.

1. *Are the premises true?* If it is not true that people must win in order to give a victory speech or if Paula is in fact not giving such a speech, then the conclusion would not be true. A sound conclusion cannot be drawn from untrue premises. If the premises are not true, then you can question the reasoning on that basis.

2. *Is the conclusion based on the premises?* Does the conclusion concern itself with Paula or with the election? If the conclusion is not based on the premises, then you can question the reasoning on that basis.

As you study your outlines of oral arguments, you may discover other ways that speakers have tried to reason. Let's consider three additional common patterns that are considered to be fallacies of reasoning that you must learn to recognize.

Recognizing Fallacies

Appeal to authority. An *appeal to authority* is a fallacy based on the quality of the data. When people support their arguments with the testimony of an authority, you can refute it as being fallacious if the use of the testimony fails to meet either of two tests: (1) if the source is not really an authority on the issue or (2) if the content of the testimonial is inconsistent with other expert opinion.

Let us consider cases where the source is not really an authority. Advertisers are well aware that because the public idolizes athletes, movie stars, and television performers, people are likely to accept their word on subjects they may know little about. So when an athlete tries to get the viewer to purchase perfume, the athlete's argument is a fallacy.

Although the fallacy of authority may be easy to recognize in a television ad, other examples of the fallacy may not be so easy to recognize. Economists, politicians, and scientists often comment on subjects outside their areas of expertise; sometimes neither they nor we realize how unqualified they are to speak on such subjects. A scientist's statement is good evidence only in the science in which he or she is an expert. Thus, a geneticist's views on the subject of the world food supply may or may not be fallacious, depending on the point he or she is trying to make.

The other test is whether the content of the testimonial is contrary to other expert opinion. Even when an authority states an opinion relevant to his or her area of expertise, that opinion may be fallacious if the opinion is one that is not supported by a majority of other authorities in that field. If a space biologist says that there must be life like our own on other planets, his or her opinion is no more logical proof than any other opinion; it is not even an authoritative opinion if a majority of other equally qualified space biologists believe otherwise. If you look long enough you can always find someone who has said something in support of even the most foolish statement. Try to avoid the mistake of accepting any statement as valid support just because some alleged authority is cited as the source.

Appeals based on statistics. Fallacies in the use of statistics may be based on the quantity of data, quality of data, or reasoning from data. Statistics are nothing more than large numbers of instances; but statistics seem to have a bewitching force—most of us are conditioned to believe that instances cast in statistical form carry the weight of authority. Yet, the potential fallacies from statistics are so numerous that there is no way I can do total justice to the subject in this short analysis. The old saying, "Figures don't lie, but liars figure," is so applicable to the general use of statistics that you need to be particularly careful with their use. To be safe, you should look at any statistical proof as potentially fallacious. Even statistics that are used honestly and with the best of motives may still be fallacious, because the clear, logical use of statistics is so difficult.

As you examine arguments supported with statistics, look for the following:

1. *Statistics that are impossible to verify.* If you are like me, you have read countless startling statements such as, "Fifteen million mosquitoes are hatched each day in the Canadian province of Ontario" or "One out of every seventeen women in ancient Greece had six fingers." Now, don't go around quoting these—I made them up; but they are no more unlikely than many other examples I have seen. The fact is we have no way of verifying such statistics. How does anyone count the number of mosquitoes hatched? How can we test whether anyone counted the fingers of ancient Greek women? Statistics of this kind are startling and make interesting conversation, but they are fallacious as support for arguments.

2. *Statistics used alone.* Statistics by themselves do not mean much. For example, "Last season the Cincinnati Reds drew about 1.7 million fans to their seventy home games." Although at face value this sounds like (and it is) a lot of people, it does not tell much about the club's attendance. Is this figure good or bad? Was attendance up or down? Often, statistics are not meaningful until they are compared with other data.

3. *Statistics used with unknown comparative bases.* Comparisons of statistics do not mean much if the comparative base is not given. Consider the statement, "While the Zolon growth rate was dawdling along at some 3 percent last year, Allon was growing at a healthy 8 percent." This statement implies that Allon is doing much better than Zolon; however, if Zolon's base was larger, its 3 percent increase could be much better than Allon's 8 percent. We cannot know unless we understand the base from which the statistic was drawn.

Ad hominem argument. An *ad hominem argument* is a fallacy occurring with an attack on the person making the argument rather than on the argument itself. Literally, *ad hominem* means "to the man." For instance, if Bill Bradley, the highly intelligent and very articulate former New York Knicks basketball player, presented the argument that athletics are important to the development of the total person, the reply, "Great, all we need is some jock justifying his own existence" would be an example of an ad hominem argument.

Such a personal attack is often made as a smokescreen to cover up for a lack of good reasons and evidence. Ad hominem, name-calling, is used to try to encourage the audience to ignore a lack of evidence. Make no mistake, ridicule, name-calling, and other personal attacks are at times highly successful, but they are almost always fallacious.

Although books written about argument list other valid types of reasoning and often discuss ten or twenty common fallacies, we do not have the space to cover all of them here. What can you do when you encounter an argument that does not fit one of the patterns we have discussed? Outline the argument, test the data, and test the reasoning link. Even if you are unable to identify the type of argument, you can probably still judge its relative strength or weakness.

**EXERCISE 3
Evaluating
Arguments**

For each of the following (1) write the conclusion that the speaker has drawn and (2) write a warrant that explains the link between the data and the conclusion and identify the type of warrant (generalization, analogy, cause, sign). The first one is done for you to serve as an example of how you should proceed.

> I see that Ohio has stiffened its penalties for drunk driving and has begun applying them uniformly. I don't think there is any doubt that we are going to see instances of drunk driving dropping in Ohio.

1. The number of instances of drunk driving in Ohio will drop.

2. Stiff penalties and uniform application will result in lower numbers of drunk drivers. (Causation)

> Assaults against teachers by students have reached epidemic proportions. The situation is getting out of hand. In Los Angeles a teacher had her hair set on fire by students angry over low grades.

Can you imagine that? In New York a teacher required hospitalization after being beaten by a gang. In Chicago a teacher resigned after being terrorized by midnight phone calls and threats against his family.

1.

2.

If you have been watching indicators lately, you'll notice that interest rates have been creeping upward again. During the past two years, interest rates were flat. For each of the last four months, however, we have seen increasingly higher interest rates. Also, according to an article in *Time,* people are keeping more of their money in savings accounts. I hate to say this, but it seems that we are heading for another recession.

1.

2.

I don't think there is any doubt that we will have bumper corn and wheat crops this year. In each of the past several months, rainfall has been plentiful—average or above for each month. In addition, we haven't had any wild fluctuations in temperature. For the most part, temperatures have been near normal.

1.

2.

PRESENTING A SPEECH OF REFUTATION

Once you have evaluated an argument used as the basis for a speech, you may want, or you may be called upon, to speak to the argument or arguments you have evaluated. The speech that you will give is called a *speech of refutation.*

Refutation is the process of proving that an argument or series of arguments, or the proposition based upon that argument or arguments, is false or erroneous—or at least doubtful. Someone says, "Chris Evert

Trial lawyers must master the art of oral argument and refutation to be successful.

will win the match," and you say, "No, she is no longer able to compete at top levels"; what you have said in reply is refutation.

Refutation, like all other aspects of speech making, can and should be handled systematically.

1. *Prepare with material on both sides of the proposition.* A speech of refutation requires anticipation of what the opposition will say. For any controversial issue, you should know the material on both sides. If you have an idea how an opponent will proceed, you will be in a much better position to reply.

2. *Take careful notes of what your opponent says.* The key words, phrases, and ideas should be recorded accurately and as nearly as possible in the actual words used. You do not want to run the risk of being accused of distorting what your opponent really said.

3. *Note your reactions to what is said.* Thoughts will come to mind as you are outlining. If you sketch your reactions as you listen, you will be in a much better position to respond.

Divide your note paper in half vertically and outline your opponent's speech in one column. Use the other column to note your refutation of each particular point. Figure 16.1 illustrates notes on one point of the speaker's argument. Notice that the proposition is written in full, the main point is written as a complete sentence, and the subpoints include enough words to reflect the content. In the Comments column, you sketch your thoughts related to each point made.

4. *Plan your procedure.* At this stage you will have a reasonably accurate account of all your opponent said. Now, how are you going to reply? You can base your refutation on your opponent's amount of data, quality of data, or reasoning.

If the opposition's case is built on an assertion with little or no evidence to support the assertion, you can refute the argument on that basis.

A better procedure is to attack the quality of the material. If sheer amount of evidence were the most important criterion in proving a point, the person with the most material would always win. However, there is often no direct relationship between amount of material and quality of proof. A statement by a judge who has studied the rights of individual citizens to privacy would be worth far more than several opinions on privacy rights from athletes, musicians, or politicians who have not studied the subject.

For every bit of evidence presented, you should ask the four questions that we outlined earlier (page 319): What is the source? Are the data fact or opinion? Are the data recent? Are the data relevant?

5. *Practice using the four-step method.* Although you do not have as long to consider exactly what you are going to say, your refutation must be organized nearly as well as your planned speeches. If you think of refutation as units of argument, each of which is organized by following four definite steps, you will learn to prepare and to present refutation effectively.
   a. State the argument you are going to refute clearly and concisely.
   b. State what you will prove; you must tell the audience how you plan to proceed so that they will be able to follow your thinking.

c. Present the reasons and data completely and with documentation (a brief reference to source).
d. Draw a conclusion; do not rely on the audience to draw the proper conclusion for you. Never go on to another argument before you have drawn your conclusion.

To illustrate the process of refutation, let us examine a short unit of refutation directed to one particular argument that is presented in Figure 16.1. In the following abbreviated statement, notice how the four

Figure 16.1. *Notes recorded by opponent while listening to advocate's speech.*

Outline of Argument

Proposition (Specific Purpose):
To prove that students should purchase insurance while they are young.

I. Buying insurance while you are young provides systematic compulsory savings.

A. Each due period you get a notice -- banks, etc., don't provide service

B. Once money is invested it is saved -- there's no deposit and withdrawal with insurance

Comments

True, but are these necessarily beneficial?

True, but what if you miss a payment?

True, but what if you need money? You can borrow, but you have to pay interest on your own money! Cash settlement results in loss of money benefits.

steps of refutation (stating the argument, stating what you will prove, presenting proof, and drawing a conclusion) are incorporated (for purposes of analysis, each of the four steps is enumerated):

> (1) Mr. Horan has said that buying insurance provides systematic, compulsory savings. (2) His assumption is that systematic, compulsory savings is a benefit of buying insurance while you are young. But I believe just the opposite is true; I believe that there are at least two serious disadvantages resulting from this. (3) First, the system is so compulsory that if you miss a payment you stand to lose your entire savings and all benefits. Most insurance contracts include a clause giving you a thirty-day grace period, after which the policy is canceled (evidence). Second, if you need money desperately, you have to take a loan against your policy. The end result of such a loan is that you have to pay interest in order to borrow your own money (evidence). (4) From this analysis, I think you can see that this systematic, compulsory saving is more disadvantageous than advantageous for people who are trying to save money.

1. Working with a classmate, select a debatable proposition and clear the wording with your professor. Phrase the proposition so that the first speaker is in favor of the proposal. Speaker A presents a four- to six-minute speech in support of the proposal; Speaker B presents a four- to six-minute speech of conviction in refutation of the proposal.

2. Write a critique of one or more of the speeches you hear in class using the list of questions provided for analyzing a speech of conviction in Chapter 14, pages 291–292. Outline the speech. As you are outlining it, answer the following questions, which relate specifically to refutation:

**ASSIGNMENT
Speech of
Refutation**

Refutation

_____ Did the speaker examine the data presented?

_____ Did the speaker examine the reasoning presented?

_____ Did the speaker document his/her evidence?

_____ Did the speaker follow the steps of refutation?

Evaluate the speech as (check one) ____ excellent, ____ good, ____ average, ____ fair, ____ poor.

Use the information from your check sheet to support your evaluation.

SPEECHES

The following two speeches are presented to illustrate the debate format. The first speech is a speech of conviction with two reasons in support of the proposition. The second is a speech of refutation.[1]

Instead of analyzing this first speech on the basis of its effectiveness as a speech, analyze it as if you were to give the speech of refutation. That is, consider its strengths and weaknesses, but do so in a context of how you would develop your refutation. After you have determined a strategy for refuting the speech, read the analysis.

ANALYSIS

The negative speaker should outline as clearly as possible the key affirmative points.

Special care should be taken to write affirmative reasons accurately.

Accuracy of tests is very important. Is there confirmation for this estimate? If so, accept it and/or work around it. If not, correct it. A decision on how to deal with "misleading" will depend on development.

SPEECH OF CONVICTION: Use of Lie Detector Tests

Lie detector or polygraph tests used either to screen job applicants or to uncover thefts by employees have become a big business. Hundreds of thousands are given each year, and the number is steadily rising. What I propose to you today is that employers should be prohibited from administering lie detector tests to their employees either as a condition of employment or as a condition of maintaining their job. I support this proposition for two reasons. First, despite technological improvement in equipment, the accuracy of results is open to question; and second, even if the tests are accurate, use of lie detector tests is an invasion of privacy.

First, let's consider their accuracy. Lie detector tests just have not proved to be very accurate. According to Senator Birch Bayh, tests are only about 70 percent accurate. And equally important, even the results of this 70 percent can be misleading. Let's look at two examples of the kinds of harm that come from these misleading results.

One case involves a young girl named Linda Boycose. She was at the time of the incident a bookkeeper for Kresge's. One day she reported $1.50 missing from the previous day's receipts. A few weeks later the store's security man gave her a lie detector test. He first used the equipment with all its intimidating wiring and then he used persuasion to get information. He accused her of deceiving him and actually stealing the money. After this test, Boycose was so upset she quit her job—she then spent the next two years indulging in valium at an almost suicidal level. Last year a Detroit jury found Boycose's story so convincing that they ordered the department store chain to award her $100,000. Now, almost six years later, she is still afraid to handle the bookkeeping at the doctor's office she manages.

The next example is of a supermarket clerk in Los Angeles. She was fired after an emotional response to the question, "Have you ever given discount groceries to your mother?" It was later discovered that her mother had been dead for five years, thus showing that her response was clearly an emotional one.

These two examples are very emotional and may be persuasive. But, (1) only two examples have been given. Nothing has been presented to show that the examples are representative. (2) The examples do not necessarily indicate a problem with the mechanics of testing.

Much of the inaccuracy of the tests has to do with the examiner's competence. Jerry Wall, a Los Angeles tester, said that out of an estimated three thousand U.S. examiners, only fifty are competent. Some polygraph operators tell an interviewee that he or she has lied at one point even if the person has not, just to see how the person will handle the stress. This strategy can destroy a person's poise, leading to inaccuracies. With these examples of stress situations and inefficient examiners, the facts point to the inaccuracy of polygraph test results.

Assuming that testers are relatively incompetent, how does this information affect the negative case? Can this be either admitted or ignored? If not, how can it be refuted?

Reemphasis of importance of level of accuracy.

My second reason for abolishing the use of these tests is that they are an invasion of privacy. Examiners can and do ask job applicants about such things as sexual habits and how often they change their underwear. The supposed purpose of lie detector tests is to determine whether an employee is stealing. These irrelevant questions are an invasion of privacy, and not a way to indicate whether someone is breaking the law.

Can instances of abuse be admitted without concluding that tests should be abolished? How?

Excesses are such that the federal government has been conducting hearings on misuse. Congress is considering ways to curtail their use.

That they are an invasion of privacy seems to be admitted by the companies that use them. Employers are afraid to reveal too much information from tests because they have a fear of being sued. Because of an examiner's prying questions on an employee's back-

This material demonstrates a threat of government intervention. But has government intervened? Has government determined what constitutes "invasion of privacy"?

ground, and because government has shown such a concern about the continued use of polygraphs, we can conclude that they are an invasion of privacy.

Strong emotional appeal in this summary. How can the effect of this be countered?

In conclusion, let me ask you how, as an employee, you would feel taking such a test. You'd probably feel nervous and reluctant to take the test. Couldn't you see yourself stating something that would be misconstrued, not because of the truth, but because of your nervousness? Also, how would you feel about having to answer very personal and intimate questions about yourself in order to get a job.

Because lie detector tests are inaccurate and an invasion of privacy, I believe their use should be prohibited.

In this speech, we would expect the speaker to say something about the two reasons that were presented in the first speech. In your analysis, look to see how the groundwork for refutation is laid; then look for the use of the four-step method of refutation.

ANALYSIS

Good opening. Speaker has clearly stated her position.

Speaker has clearly laid the groundwork for her negative position. This material establishes a need for some measures to be taken against theft. It shows that tests are not being used without good reason.

This represents further clarification of what affirmative has done and what negative proposes to do. It

SPEECH OF REFUTATION:
Use of Lie Detector Tests

My opponent has stated that the use of lie detector tests by employers should be abolished. I strongly disagree; I believe employers have to use these tests.

Before examining the two reasons she presented, I'd like to take a look at why more than 20 percent of the nation's largest businesses feel a need to use these tests and why the number is growing each year. Employers use lie detector tests to help curb employee theft. According to the National Retail Merchants Association, employees steal as much as $40 billion of goods each year. Moreover, the figure increases markedly each year. The average merchant doesn't recognize that he loses more to employees than to outsiders—50 to 70 percent of theft losses go to employees, not to shoplifters. This use of lie detector tests is a necessity to curb this internal theft.

Now, I do not believe that my opponent ever tried to show that there is not a problem that lie detector testing solves; nor did she try to show that lie detector testing doesn't help to deter internal theft.

Notice that the two reasons she presented are both about abuses. Let's take a closer look at those two reasons.

First, my opponent said that the accuracy of results is open to question; in contrast, I would argue that these tests are remarkably accurate. She mentioned that Senator Bayh reported a 70-percent level of accuracy. Yet the literature on these tests as reported by Ty Kelley, vice president of government affairs of the National Association of Chain Drug Stores, argues that the level is around 90 percent, not 70 percent.

She went on to give two examples of people who were intimidated and/or became emotional and upset when subjected to the test. And on this basis she calls for them to be abolished. I would agree that some people do become emotional, but this is hardly reason for stopping their use. Unless she can show a real problem among many people taking the test I think we'll have to go along with the need for the tests.

If these tests are so inaccurate, why are one-fifth of the nation's largest companies using them. According to an article in *Business Week*, "Business Buys the Lie Detector," more and more businesses each year see a necessity for using the tests because they deter crime. These tests are now being used by nearly every type of company—banks, businesses, drug stores, as well as retail department stores.

Her second reason for why the tests should be abolished is that they are an invasion of privacy. I believe, with Mr. Kelley, whom I quoted earlier, that there must be some sort of balance maintained between an individual's right to privacy and an employer's right to protect his property. In Illinois, for instance, a state judge ruled that examiners could ask prying questions—there has yet to be any official ruling that the use is "an invasion of privacy."

My opponent used the example of asking questions about sexual habits and change of underwear. In that regard, I agree with her. I think that a person is probably pretty sick who is asking these kinds of questions—and I think these abuses should be checked. But asking questions to screen out thieves, junkies, liars, alcoholics, and psychotics is necessary. For instance, an Atlanta nursing home uses polygraph tests to screen out potentially sadistic and disturbed nurses and orderlies. Is this an invasion of privacy? I don't think so.

helps to place the affirmative attack in proper perspective.

Good direct attack on level of accuracy. Notice she states opponent's point, states her position on the point, and then presents the evidence. She needs a concluding statement to tie the unit of refutation together.

But why are Kelley's figures better than Bayh's? She needs to show us.

Good job of debating the conclusion to be drawn from the example. Still, I would like to have heard her make a closer examination of the examples themselves.

That businesses use the tests does not prove that businesses are convinced they are accurate. Need more factual data here.

This is a further attempt to put the affirmative argument into proper perspective. Judge's ruling gives strong support to her position.

Good line of argument. Any attempt at refuting alleged abuses would be damaging to the negative position.

Here speaker does a nice job of bringing emphasis back to the need for the tests.

Good summary.

This is a good speech of refutation. It illustrates the importance of showing the negative position before launching into refutation; it illustrates good form for refutation; and it provides several approaches to refutation.

It is obvious to me that some type of lie detector test is needed. Too much theft has gone on and something must be done to curtail this. I say that lie detector tests are the answer. First, they are accurate. Companies have been using them for a long time, and more and more companies are starting to use them. And second, it is only an invasion of privacy when the wrong types of questions are asked. I agree that these abuses should be curbed, but not by doing away with the tests. Employers cannot do away with these tests and control theft; the benefits far outweigh the risks.

NOTE

1. These two speeches are based on a debate between Sheila Kohler and Martha Feinberg presented at the University of Cincinnati, and are printed with their permission.

Huff, Darrell, and Irving Geis. *How to Lie with Statistics.* New York: W. W. Norton, 1954. This older book is still an excellent source— not for showing you how to use statistics, but for showing you what to look for in their use.

Kahane, Howard. *Logic and Contemporary Rhetoric.* 4th ed. Belmont, Calif.: Wadsworth, 1984 (paperback). This excellent source gives you some outstanding pointers on the use and development of logical argument and a considerable emphasis on identifying and eliminating the fallacies of reasoning.

Kiesler, Charles A., Barry E. Collins, and Norman Miller. *Attitude Change.* New York: John Wiley, 1969. A comprehensive analysis of theories of attitude change pointing out strengths, weaknesses, similarities, and differences.

Larson, Charles U. *Persuasion: Reception and Responsibility.* 4th ed. Belmont, Calif.: Wadsworth, 1986. A solid textbook that places more emphasis on the receiver of the persuasive message than on the persuader.

Moore, Brook Noel, and Richard Parker. *Critical Thinking: Evaluating Claims and Arguments in Everyday Life.* Palo Alto, Calif.: Mayfield, 1986. One of the best of the recent paperback books that focus on evaluating everyday arguments.

Packard, Vance O. *The Hidden Persuaders.* New York: Pocket Books, 1975 (paperback). This popular book, first published in the 1950s, still makes for excellent reading about the problems and excesses of persuasion.

Smith, Mary John. *Persuasion and Human Interaction.* Belmont, Calif.: Wadsworth, 1982. An excellent review and critique of theories of persuasion.

**Part Four
SUGGESTED
READINGS**

ADAPTING TO OTHER OCCASIONS AND FORMATS

You will, at times, have to apply your skills to group contexts and ceremonial occasions, sometimes using different delivery modes. The material in this unit provides you with the means to meet the challenge of these different goals.

SEVENTEEN

SPEAKING IN PROBLEM-SOLVING GROUPS

Despite the many jokes about committees and the often justified impatience with them, the committee system and the group discussion it encourages can and should be an effective way of dealing with common problems. For our purposes, *problem-solving group discussion* is defined as a systematic form of speech in which two or more persons meet face to face and interact orally in order to accomplish a particular task or to arrive at a solution to a common problem. To speak effectively in groups you must prepare carefully and understand the responsibilities of both the leader and the group members.

PREPARATION FOR PROBLEM-SOLVING DISCUSSION

To prepare for either public or private discussion, you will need to state the problem, analyze the problem, suggest possible solutions, and select the best solution.

Stating the Problem

In many groups, the wheel-spinning that takes place during the early discussion stages results from members' questions about the function, purpose, or goal of the group. As soon as possible, the group needs to clarify its goal. Usually the person, agency, or parent group that forms a particular work group indicates what the group should do. For example, a group may be formed "to determine the nature of the curriculum" or "to prepare a guideline for hiring at a new plant." If the goal is not this clear, it is up to the group leader or representative to find out exactly why the group was formed and what its goals are. If stating the problem is up to the group, then the group should move immediately to get it down on paper; until everyone agrees on what they have to do, they will never agree on how to do it.

Since the goal of discussion is to stimulate group thinking, the discussion problem should be stated as a question. Questions elicit responses. In phrasing a question, make sure that it (1) considers only one subject, (2) is impartially worded, and (3) uses words that can be defined objectively. "Should the United States cut back its foreign aid program and welfare?" considers two different questions; "Should the United States recognize those wretched Palestinians?" would be neither impartial nor definable.

Discussion topics may be stated as questions of fact, questions of value, or questions of policy.

1. *Questions of fact* concern the truth or falsity of an assertion. Implied in such questions is the possibility of determining the facts by direct observation or by spoken or recorded evidence. For instance, "How much rain fell today?" is a question of fact because rain can be measured and recorded. Likewise, "Is Smith guilty of robbing the warehouse?" is also a question of fact. Smith either committed the crime or he did not.

2. *Questions of value* concern subjective judgments of quality. They are characterized by the inclusion of some evaluative word such as *good, reliable, effective,* or *worthy.* The purpose of questions of value is to compare a subject with one or more members of the same class. "What was the best movie last year?" is a question of value. Although we can set up criteria for "best" and measure our choice against those criteria, there is no way of verifying our findings. The answer is still a matter of judgment, not a matter of fact. Similarly, questions like, "Is socialism superior to capitalism?" and "Is a small-college education better than a large-college education?" are also questions of value. Although questions of value are widely discussed in social groups, they are not as likely to be the ultimate goal of work groups.

3. *Questions of policy* judge whether or not a future action should be taken. The question is phrased to arrive at a solution or to test a

tentative solution to a problem or a felt need. "What should we do to lower the crime rate?" seeks a solution that would best solve the problem of increased crime. "Should the university give equal amounts of money to men's and women's athletics?" provides a tentative solution to the problem of how we can achieve equity in financial support of athletics. The inclusion of the word *should* in all questions of policy makes them the easiest to recognize and the easiest to phrase of all discussion questions.

Analyzing the problem is the second step in preparation. *Analysis* means determining the nature of the problem: its size, its causes, the forces that create or sustain it, and the criteria for evaluating solutions. Sometimes analysis takes only a few minutes; often it takes much longer. In preparing for problem solving and in the discussion itself, analysis is too often ignored because most groups want to move directly to possible solutions. For instance, if your goal is "to determine what should be done to solve the problem of thefts of library books," the group may want to start by immediately listing possible solutions. However, a solution or a plan can work only if it solves the problem at hand. Before you can shape a plan, you must determine what obstacles the solution must overcome and what obstacles the solution must eliminate, as well as whom your plan has to satisfy. Before you begin to suggest a solution, you must check to make sure that the following questions about the problem have been answered:

Analyzing the Problem

1. What is its size and scope?
   a. What are its symptoms? (What can we identify that shows that something is wrong or needs to be changed?)
   b. What are its causes? (What forces created it, sustain it, or otherwise keep it from being solved?)

2. What criteria should be used to test the solution? Specifically, what checklist must the solution meet to best solve this problem? Must the plan eliminate the symptoms, be implemented within present resources, and so on?

Most problems have many possible solutions. You should not be content with your work until you have listed as many as you can find.
   How do you find solutions? One way is for you or the group to

Suggesting Possible Solutions

brainstorm. *Brainstorming* is free-association; that is, it involves stating ideas in random order as they come to mind until you have compiled a long list. In a good ten- to fifteen-minute brainstorming session, you may think of several solutions by yourself. Depending on the nature of the topic, a group may develop a list of ten, twenty, or more possibilities in a relatively short time. Other possible solutions will come from your reading, your interviews with authorities, or your observations.

If your goal is phrased as a yes-or-no question, suggesting solutions is simplified. For instance, the question, "Should financial support for women's sports be increased?" has only two possible answers.

Selecting the Best Solution

If the group has analyzed the problem carefully and listed a number of potential solutions, then the final step involves only matching each proposed solution against the criteria. For instance, if you have determined that hiring more patrols, putting in closed-circuit TV, and locking outside doors after 9 P.M. are three possible solutions to the problem of increased crime in dorms, then you can begin to measure each against the criteria. The solution that meets the most criteria or the one that meets several criteria most effectively would be the best selection.

The Outline Agenda

Now let's put together some questions with a sample (and somewhat abbreviated) outline agenda that would help the group proceed logically. The group has been convened to discuss "meeting the needs of women on campus."

1. State the problem (suggested wording):
   What should be done to equalize social, athletic, and political opportunities for women on campus? (Assume that the group has agreed upon this wording.)

2. Analyze the problem of meeting the needs of campus women:
   I. What is the size and scope of the problem?
      A. How many women are there on campus?
      B. What is the ratio of females to males on campus?
      C. What opportunities are currently available to women?
         1. What social organizations are available? What is the ratio of women to men who belong?
         2. Are women involved in political organizations on campus? To what extent?

3. What athletic opportunities are open to women? Are they intramural or intercollegiate?
II. What are the causes of the problem?
   A. Do women feel discriminated against?
   B. Does the institution discriminate?
   C. Do societal norms inhibit women's participation?
   D. Do certain groups discriminate against women?
III. What criteria should be used to test solutions?
   A. Will women favor the solution?
   B. Will it cope with discrimination if discrimination does exist?
   C. Will it be enforceable?
   D. Will it comply with Title IX?

3. State possible solutions:
   (This list can only be started at this point; other possible solutions will be revealed as the discussion progresses.)
   Should a women's center be initiated?
   Should a special-interest seat on all major committees be given to women?
   Should women's and men's athletic teams be combined?
   Etc.

4. Determine best solution:
   (To be completed during discussion.)

LEADERSHIP IN PROBLEM-SOLVING GROUP DISCUSSION

A problem-solving group discussion will not work well without effective leadership. Ordinarily, we think of an appointed or elected person acting as leader and all others in the group acting as contributors of content. Although it is often done that way, it does not have to be. A group can be so organized that everyone shares leadership. Thus, a group can have leadership whether or not it has a designated leader.

Leadership may be defined as exerting influence to help a group achieve a goal. Let us explore the two key ideas in this definition.

What Is Leadership?

1. *Leadership means exerting influence. Influence* is the ability to bring about changes in the attitudes and actions of others. When you influence those in your group, you show them why an idea, a decision, or a means of achieving a goal is superior in such a way that members of the group will follow those ideas of their own free will. Members of your group will continue to be influenced as long as they are convinced that what they have agreed to is right, in their own individual best interest, or in the best interest of the group.

2. *Leadership results in reaching a goal.* In the context of a task or problem-solving discussion, this element of leadership means accomplishing the task or arriving at a solution that tests out to be the best solution available at that time.

Who Will Lead?

Should a group have an appointed or elected leader? Or should everyone in the group share the responsibility for leadership? When someone is appointed or elected leader, the group looks to him or her for leadership. If the individual is a good leader, the group will benefit. Each participant can concentrate on considering the issues being raised, confident that the leader will guide the group justly. The disadvantages of having an appointed or elected leader are seen when the person is so unsure that the group rambles about aimlessly; when the leader is so dominant that participants do not feel free to contribute spontaneously and the discussion follows a path predetermined by the leader; and when the leader is so unskilled that the group flounders and becomes frustrated and short-tempered. Good leadership is a necessity; when the appointed leader cannot provide it, the group suffers.

When the group has no appointed leader, everyone has the right and the obligation to show leadership. Ordinarily, leadership will emerge from one, two, or perhaps three members of the group. Since no one has been given the mantle of leadership, everyone is on an equal footing, and the discussion can be more spontaneous. Disadvantages occur if no one assumes leadership or if a few compete for leadership. In such situations, the discussion becomes "leadershipless." Depending on the qualities of the participants, leaderless discussions can arrive at truly good decisions, or they can be a rambling, meaningless collage of facts and opinions. If you have only one round of discussion, begin with the method in which the group has the most confidence.

Numerous researchers have looked for those particular traits that would enable us to predict leadership ability and account for leadership success. Although traits research does not provide the answers, studying traits does give us some indicators of leadership.

Marvin Shaw, a leading authority in group research, found some correlation between individual traits and leadership measures.[1] He cited four traits: ability, sociability, motivation, and communication skills. In group studies, he found that relative to ability, leaders exceed average group members in intelligence, scholarship, insight, and verbal facility. Relative to sociability, leaders exceed group members in such things as dependability, activity, cooperativeness, and popularity. Relative to motivation, leaders exceed group members in initiative, persistence, and enthusiasm. Finally, relative to communication, leaders exceed group members in various communication skills. This does not mean that people with superior intelligence, or those who are most liked, or those with the greatest enthusiasm, or those who are the best communicators will necessarily be leaders. We believe it does mean that people are unlikely to be leaders if they do not exhibit at least some of these traits to a greater degree than do those they are attempting to lead.

Do you perceive yourself as having any or many of these traits? If you see these traits in yourself, then you are a potential leader. Since several individuals in almost any group of people have the potential for leadership, determining who ends up actually leading depends on many things other than the possession of these traits.

To some extent, whether you will be permitted to lead again may well depend upon how you lead when you have the opportunity. Since leadership requires exerting influence, how you lead may well depend upon whether this influence is a product of power and persuasion, or some combination of both. In effect, who will lead may well be a matter of style.

The collection of a person's behaviors is called *style.* A casual examination of groups in operation will reveal a variety of leadership styles. Some leaders give orders directly; others look to the group to decide what to do. Some leaders appear to play no part in what happens in the group; others seem to be in control of every move. Some leaders constantly seek the opinions of group members; other leaders do not seem to care what individuals think. Each person will tend to lead a group with a style that reflects his or her own personality, needs, and inclination. Although people have a right to be themselves, an analysis of operating groups shows that they work better and feel better about the work they do depending upon the style of leadership.

What are the major leadership styles? Most recent studies define leadership styles as task-oriented (sometimes called authoritarian) or maintenance (sometimes called democratic).

The task-oriented leader exercises more direct control over the group. Task-oriented leaders determine the statement of the question, analyze the procedure, state how the group will proceed to arrive at a decision, and usually outline specific tasks for each group member and suggest the roles they desire members to play.

The maintenance leader *suggests* phrasings of the question, *suggests* procedure, and *suggests* tasks or roles for individual members. Yet in every facet of the discussion, maintenance leaders encourage group participation to determine what actually will be done. Everyone feels free to offer suggestions to modify the leader's suggestions. What the group eventually does is determined by the group itself. Maintenance leaders listen, encourage, facilitate, clarify, and support. In the final analysis, it is the group that decides.

Which is best? According to the definition of leadership as exerting influence to reach a goal, we can see that, by definition, an effective style is one in which the leader takes an active role in the discussion in order to influence its outcome. If that's the case, then why isn't the task-oriented style the ultimate leadership form? Although there are situations in which a task-oriented style may be more desirable, other situations exist in which the maintenance style is more desirable.

At times, the maintenance or democratic style is inappropriate and may lead to chaos. Participatory democracy has its limits. For instance, during a closely contested basketball game, coaches who call a time-out have one minute to help their players handle a particular defensive alignment the other team is using. They will not use their minute in democratic processes—asking their players if they have any ideas or suggesting a plan and giving the players the opportunity to evaluate it. They will tell the players how to proceed, make a substitution if necessary, and give the players encouragement. When accomplishment of the task is, or appears to be, more important than the members' feelings, then task-oriented or authoritarian leadership may be appropriate. (This is not to say that basketball coaches or any other leaders who adopt this style can disregard group feelings.) Ralph White and Ronald Lippitt have shown that a job gets done as fast or faster and often with fewer errors under the task-oriented or authoritarian leader.[2] Authoritarian leadership also seems to work well when the authority is much superior in knowledge and skill to the participants. Again, the basketball example bears this out. Coaches are coaches because of what they know; as long as players respect their superior knowledge, they will work well under the authoritarian style.

There is at least one other advantage of task-oriented or authoritarian leadership—it is easier. Learning to be a good democratic leader sometimes ends in the frustrations of nonleadership. In other words, some people confuse being a democratic leader with not leading at all. Since there is little ambiguity in authoritarian leadership—the leader gives directions and the group follows them—it is far easier to understand and administer.

If authoritarian leadership appeals to you—and many authoritarian leaders do exist, are effective, and win the approval of their groups—perhaps you should consider one other point. The best authoritarian model seems to be "benevolent dictatorship." If authority arises out of the need to control—and perhaps even to crush dissent—it leads to tyranny.

Examine your style very closely. What is your natural inclination? How has it worked in the past? Would it be useful to blend some of the characteristics of another style with what comes naturally to you? Remember, these categories are not necessarily hard and fast. Still, the style you adopt is your own. Once you have determined your approach, you must consider your leadership responsibilities.

RESPONSIBILITIES OF THE LEADER

Group leadership carries several responsibilities. To be an effective leader, you should learn to accomplish each of the following.

Planning the Agenda

As leader, your first responsibility is to plan the agenda. An *agenda* is an outline of what needs to be accomplished during the meeting. In a problem-solving discussion, the agenda should include a suggested procedure for handling the problem. In essence, it is an outline of the problem-solving steps discussed earlier in this chapter. You may prepare the agenda alone or in consultation with the group. When possible, the agenda should be in the hands of the group several days before the meeting. You can't expect group members to prepare if they do not have an agenda beforehand. When a group proceeds without an agenda, discussion is often haphazard, frustrating, and generally unproductive.

If you are leading a discussion on what should be done to better integrate the campus commuter into the social, political, and extracurricular aspects of student life, the following would be a satisfactory agenda:

I. What is the size and scope of the commuter problem?
II. What are the causes for commuters' not being involved in social, political, and extracurricular activities?
III. What criteria should be used to test possible solutions to the problem?
IV. What are some of the possible solutions to the problem?
V. What one solution or combination of solutions will work best to solve the problem?

Establishing a Climate

Before the group begins talking, you will want to set up a comfortable physical environment that will encourage interaction. You are in charge of such physical matters as heat, light, and seating. Make sure the room is at a comfortable temperature, that the room is well lit, and, most important, that the seating arrangement will help lead to spirited interaction.

Too often, seating is too formal or too informal for the best discussion. By "too formal," we mean a board-of-directors style. Imagine the long polished oak table with the chairperson at the head, the leading lieutenants at the right and left, and the rest of the participants seated down the line. Since seating may be an indication of status, how it is arranged can help or hinder real interaction. In the board-of-directors style, a "boss-and-subordinates" pattern emerges. People are unlikely to speak until they are asked to do so. Moreover, no one has a good view of all the people present. However, an excessively informal seating may also limit interaction—especially if people sit together in small groups or behind one another.

The ideal is a circle. Everyone can see everyone else. At least physically, everyone has equal status. If the meeting place does not have a round table, you may be better off with either no table at all or a setting of tables that make a square at which the members can come close to the circle arrangement.

You need to direct the flow of discussion to ensure that everyone has an equal opportunity to speak. Decisions are valid only when they represent the thinking of the entire group. In discussions, however, some people are more likely or more willing to express themselves than others. For instance, if a typical eight-person group is left to its own devices, two or three people may tend to speak as much as the other five or six put together; furthermore, one or two members may contribute little if anything. At the beginning of a discussion you must operate under the assumption that every member of the group has something to contribute. To ensure opportunity for equal participation, those who tend to dominate must be held somewhat in check, and those who are content to observe must be brought into the discussion.

Accomplishing this ideal balance is a real test of leadership. If ordinarily reluctant talkers are embarrassed by a member of the group, they may become even more reluctant to participate. Likewise, if talkative yet valuable members are constantly restrained, they may lose their value to the group.

Let's first consider the handling of shy or reluctant speakers. Often, apparently reluctant speakers want to talk but cannot get the floor. As leader you may solve this problem by clearing the road for them. For instance, Mary may give visual and verbal clues of her desire to speak; she may move to the edge of her seat, she may look as if she wants to talk, or she may even start to say something, but pull back when a more aggressive speaker breaks in. To pave the way for her you might say, "Just a second, Jim, I think Mary has something she wants to say here." Of course, if Mary is sitting back in her chair with a somewhat vacant look, such a statement would be inappropriate.

A second method of drawing out reluctant speakers is to phrase a question that is sure to get some answer and, perhaps, some discussion. The most appropriate question is one requiring an opinion rather than a fact. For instance, "Mary, what do you think of the validity of this approach to combating crime?" is much better than, "Mary, do you have any additional statistics?" Not only is it specific, but it also requires more than a yes or no answer. Furthermore, such an opinion question will not embarrass Mary if she has no factual material to contribute. Tactful handling of shy or reluctant persons can pay big dividends. You may get some information that would not have been brought out in any other way; moreover, when Mary contributes a few times, it builds her self-confidence, which in turn makes it easier for her to respond later when she has more to say. Of course, there are times when some members do not have anything worth saying because they just are not prepared. Under such circumstances, it is best for you to leave them alone.

As a leader, you must also use tact with overzealous speakers. Remember that Jim, the talkative person, may be talkative because he has done his homework—he may have more information than any other member of the group. If you turn him off, the group may suffer immensely. After he has finished talking, try statements such as, "Jim, that's a very valuable bit of material; let's see whether we can get some reactions from other members of the group on this issue." Notice that a statement of this kind does not stop him; it suggests that he should hold off for a while. Difficult participants to deal with are those who must be heard regardless of whether they have anything to say. If subtle reminders are ineffective with these individuals, you may have to say, "Jim, I know you want to talk, but you're just not giving anyone else a chance. Would you wait until we've heard everyone else on this point?" Of course, the person who may be the most difficult of all to control is the leader. Leaders often engage in little dialogues with each member of the group. They sometimes exercise so much control that participants believe they can talk only in response to the leader.

There are three common patterns of group communication (see Figure 17.1; the lines represent the flow of discussion among the eight participants). Discussion A represents a leader-dominated group. The lack of interaction often leads to a rigid, formal, and usually poor discussion. Discussion B represents a more spontaneous group. Since three people dominate and two are not heard, however, conclusions will not represent group thinking. Discussion C represents something close to the ideal pattern. It illustrates a great deal of spontaneity, a

Figure 17.1. *Patterns of group discussion.*

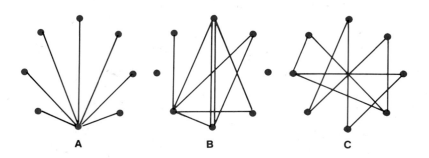

A   B   C

total group representation, and—theoretically at least—the greatest possibility for reliable conclusions.

Perhaps one of the most effective leadership tools is the ability to question appropriately. You need to know when to ask questions and you need to know the kinds of questions to ask.

Ask Appropriate Questions

By and large, a leader should refrain from questions that can be answered yes or no. To ask group members whether they are satisfied with a point that was just made will not lead very far; because after the yes or no answer, you must either ask another question to draw the people out or change the subject. The two most effective types of questions are those that call for supporting information and completely open-ended questions that give members complete freedom of response. For instance, rather than asking John whether he has had any professors who were particularly good lecturers, you could ask, "John, what are some of the characteristics that made your favorite lecturers particularly effective?"

When to ask questions is particularly important. Although we could list fifteen to twenty circumstances, let's focus on four purposes of questioning.

1. *To initiate discussion.* At the beginning of the discussion and when each of the individual units of discussion have been resolved, you will need to suggest a starting point for further discussion. For instance, "Okay, we seem to have a pretty good grasp of the nature of the problem, but we haven't looked at any causes yet. What are some of the causes?"

2. *To probe for information.* Too often group members accept statements without probing further. When an idea seems important, you should see to it that the group does something with it. For instance, on a question of source, you might ask, "Where did you get that information, Jack?" or to develop a point, "That seems pretty important; what do we have that corroborates the point?" To test the strength of a point you might ask, "Does that statement represent the thinking of the group?" or to generate discussion, "That idea sounds rather controversial; should we accept it as stated?"

3. *To focus discussion.* You can use questions to determine speakers' points or to determine the relationship of the points to the issue or

agenda item. For instance, "Are you saying that the instances of marijuana leading to hard-drug use don't indicate a direct causal relationship?" or to what has just been said, "How does that information relate to the point that Mary just made?" or to ask about an issue or an agenda item, "In what way does this information relate to whether or not marijuana is a health hazard?"

4. *To deal with interpersonal problems that develop.* In any discussion, interpersonal frictions may occur. Sometimes you may need to help members ventilate very personal feelings. For instance, "Ted, I've heard you make some strong statements on this point. Would you care to share them with us?" At times, you may need to shield a member from personal attack. Here you can say, "I know Charley presented the point, but let's look at the merits of the information presented. Do we have any information that goes counter to this point?"

Questions by themselves are not going to make a discussion. In fact, some questions can hurt the discussion that is taking place. An effective leader uses questions sparingly but decisively.

Summarize Frequently

A good problem-solving discussion group should move in an orderly manner toward intermediate conclusions represented by summary statements seeking group consensus. For instance, on the question, "What should be done to lower the crime rate on campus?" the group should answer each of the following questions:

1. What is the problem?

2. What are the symptoms of the problem? (Draw intermediate conclusions; ask whether the group agrees.)

3. What are the causes? (Draw an intermediate conclusion on each cause separately or after all causes have been considered; ask whether the group agrees.)

4. What criteria should be used to test the solutions?

5. What is one criterion? (Draw conclusions about each criterion.)

6. What are some of the possible conclusions? (Determine whether all possible solutions have been brought up.)

7. What is the best solution?

8. How does each of the solutions meet the criteria? (Discuss and draw conclusions about each; ask whether the group agrees.)

9. Which solution best meets the criteria? (The conclusion to this final question concludes the discussion; ask whether all agree.)

You need to see to it that the group does not arrive at the final conclusion until each of these subordinate questions are answered to the satisfaction of the entire group.

In addition, you must point out these conclusions by summarizing what has been said and seeking consensus on the wording. If left to its own devices, a group will discuss a point for a while, then move on to another *before a conclusion is drawn.* You must sense when enough has been said to reach a consensus. Then you must phrase the conclusion, ask whether it is correct, and move on to another area. You should become familiar with phrases such as the following that can be used during a discussion:

"I think most of us are stating the same points. Are we really in agreement that . . . ?" (State the conclusion.)

"We've been discussing this for a while, and I think I sense an agreement. Let me state it, and then we'll see whether it does summarize the group's feelings." (State the conclusion.)

"Now we're getting into another area. Let's make sure that we are really agreed on the point we've just finished." (State the conclusion.)

"Are we ready to summarize our feelings on this point?" (State the conclusion.)

Maintain Necessary Control

Finally, you must maintain control of the discussion. Remember, absence of leadership leads to chaos. Group members need to feel that someone is in charge. If the group has a set of formal rules, be sure that the rules are followed; bending is necessary at times, but a total breakdown does not help the group. As leader, remember that some members will be playing negative roles in the discussion; do not let them spoil the outcome. You are in charge. You are responsible. You have authority. Occasionally, you will need to exercise it for the benefit of the group. If John is about to talk for the fortieth time, it is up to you to harness him. If Jack and Mary are constantly sparring with each other, it is up to you to harmonize their differences. If something internal or external threatens the group's work, it is up to you to deal with it. Also, when the group has solved its problem, end the discussion smoothly. Some discussion groups meet by time instead of by problem. Just because you are scheduled to discuss for an hour does not mean that you cannot stop in forty-five minutes if you have done the job.

RESPONSIBILITIES OF DISCUSSANTS

Although good leadership is essential, a discussion group will fail if its members do not fulfill their responsibilities. Good discussion is characterized by members' accomplishing various task and maintenance roles and avoiding various negative roles.

Fill Positive Roles

Everyone in the group has a responsibility to fill certain roles within the group. A *role* is a behavior that you determine for yourself or that is determined for you by the expectations of the group. Sometimes a person plays only one role throughout the duration of the discussion. At other times, a person may play several roles simultaneously or alternately; and, of course, more than one person can play a given role in a discussion.

Positive group roles fulfill both task and maintenance functions. The *task function* involves those roles that contribute to meeting the group's goal; the *maintenance function* involves those roles that contribute to how well the group handles the way they talk about their task, the nature of the interaction, and dealing with the feelings of the group. Thus, when we analyze a discussion, we look first to see how and whether the group solved the problem; second, we look to see how well the group worked together and whether members liked, respected, and understood other members of the group.

Task roles. In most groups there are at least four major identifiable task roles: the information-giver, information-seeker, expediter, and analyzer.

1. *The information- or opinion-giver provides content for the discussion.* Giving information or opinions comprises about 50 per-

cent of a work group's comments. Without information and well-considered opinions, the group will not have the material from which to draw its decisions. Probably everyone in the group plays this role during the discussion. Nevertheless, there are usually one or more persons who have really done their homework. As a result of their past experience with this or a related problem, their conversations with people who have worked with similar problems, or a great deal of reading, these persons are prepared to provide the facts. In some groups, a designated resource person or consultant is called in solely to fulfill the information-giving role. In most groups, one or more persons take it upon themselves to be especially well prepared.

To be well prepared, you should have considerably more information than you could get into the discussion. It is not uncommon for discussants to be familiar with information from eight or ten sources. Since you cannot predict all of the ideas that will be covered in the discussion, you cannot prepare speeches ahead of time. Nevertheless, you should be familiar enough with the material that you can find any item you need when you need it. Usually you will bring your sources with you to the discussion.

In addition to presenting information, you should also be prepared to draw conclusions from information that has already been presented. That information serves as the building blocks for conclusions, and unless you draw conclusions, the information itself will serve little purpose.

To be a valuable contributor, your material must be presented objectively. Let us focus on two recommendations for ensuring objectivity of approach. First, report data, don't associate yourself with it. If you report that crime has risen 33 percent in the past five years, don't feel that because you presented the data you must defend it. An excellent way of presenting data with a degree of disassociation is illustrated by the following: "According to *U.S. News and World Report,* crime has risen 33 percent in the past five years. That seems like a startling statistic. I wonder whether anyone else found either any substantiating or any contradictory data?" Presenting data in this way tells the group that you want a discussion and that, whether the data are substantiated or disproven, you have no personal relationship to the data.

A second recommendation for ensuring objectivity is to look for material representing different viewpoints. Suppose you were discussing the question, "Should financial support of women's sports be increased?" And suppose that after extensive reading you believed that it should. If in the discussion you spoke only to support your position and took issue with every bit of contrary material, you would not be responding objectively. If during the discussion the group draws a conclusion that corresponds to your tentative conclusion, fine. At least the group has had the opportunity to hear all views. If the group draws the opposite conclusion, you are not put in a defensive position. By being objective, you may find that your views will change many times during the discussion. Remember, if the best answer to the topic question could be found without discussion, the discussion would not be necessary.

Information-givers identify themselves by such statements as, "When Jones Corporation considered this problem, they found . . ."; or, "That's a good point you made—just the other day I ran across these figures that substantiate your point"; or, "According to Professor Smith, it doesn't necessarily work that way. He says. . . ."

2. *The information-seeker knows when the group needs data to function.* In most groups, more than one person takes this role during the discussion; one or more are often especially perceptive in knowing when more information is needed.

The information-seeker raises questions about and probes into the contributions of others. Your obligation does not end with reading items of information into the record. Once an item has been submitted, it is the obligation of the membership to determine whether the item is accurate, typical, consistent, and otherwise valid. Suppose that in a discussion on reducing crime, a person mentioned, "According to *U.S. News and World Report,* crime had risen 33 percent in the past five years." The group should not leave this statement until they have explored it fully. What was the specific source of the data? On what were the data based? What years are being referred to? Is this data consistent with other material? Is any countermaterial available? The purpose of these questions is not to debate the data, but to test them. If the data are partly true, questionable, or relevant only to certain kinds of crime, a different conclusion or set of conclusions would be appropriate.

Information-seekers may be identified by such questions as, "What did we say the base numbers were?"; or, "Have we decided how many people this really affects?"; or, "Well, what functions does this person serve?"; or, "Have we got anything to give us some background on this subject?"

3. *The expediter perceives when the group is going astray.* Whether the group meets once or is an ongoing group, almost invariably some remarks will tend to sidetrack the group from the central point or issue in front of them. Sometimes apparent digressions are necessary to get background, to enlarge the scope, or even to give people an opportunity to get something off their chest. Often in a group these momentary digressions lead to tangents that take the group far afield from their assignment. Because a tangent is sometimes more fun than the task itself, the group often does not realize what it is and discusses it as if it were important to the decision. Expediters are the people who help the group stick to its agenda; they help the group stay with the problem at hand. When the group has strayed, they help lead it back to the mainstream. Expediters are revealed by such statements as, "Say, I'm enjoying this, but I can't quite see what it has to do with whether permissiveness is really a cause"; or, "Let's see, aren't we still trying to find out whether these are the only criteria that we should be considering?"; or, "I've got the feeling that this is important to the point we're on now, but I can't quite get hold of the relationship— am I off base?"; or, "Say, time is getting away from us and we've only considered two possible solutions. Aren't there some more?"

4. *The analyzer is the master of technique.* Analyzers know the problem-solving method inside out. The analyzer knows when the group has skipped a point, has passed over a point too lightly, or has not taken a look at matters they need to. More than just expediting, analyzers help the group penetrate to the core of the problem they are working on. In addition, analyzers examine the reasoning of various participants. Analyzers may be recognized from such statements as, "Tom, you're generalizing from only one instance. Can you give us some others?"; or, "Wait a minute, after symptoms, we have to take a look at causes"; or, "I think we're passing over Jones too lightly. There are still criteria we haven't used to measure him by."

Maintenance roles. In most discussion groups at least three major maintenance roles help good working relationships: the supporter, the harmonizer, and the gatekeeper.

1. *The supporter rewards members for valuable contributions.* People participating in groups are likely to feel better about their participation when their thoughts and feelings are recognized. Although we expect nearly everyone to be supportive, sometimes people get so wrapped up in their own ideas that they may neglect to reward the positive comments. The supporter responds verbally or nonverbally whenever a good point is made. Supporters give such nonverbal cues as a smile, a nod, or a vigorous head shake and make statements like, "Good point, Mel"; "I really like that idea, Susan"; "It's obvious you've really done your homework, Peg"; "That's one of the best ideas we've had today, Al."

2. *The harmonizer brings the group together.* It is a rare group that can expect to accomplish its task without some minor if not major conflict. Even when people get along well, they are likely to get angry over some inconsequential points in heated discussion. Most groups experience some classic interpersonal conflicts caused by different personality types. Harmonizers are responsible for reducing and reconciling misunderstandings, disagreements, and conflicts. They are good at pouring oil on troubled waters and encouraging objectivity; and they are especially good as mediators for hostile, aggressively competing sides. A group cannot avoid some conflict, but if there is no one present to harmonize, participation can become an uncomfortable experience. Harmonizers may be recognized by such statements as, "Bill, I don't think you're giving Mary a chance to make her point"; or, "Tom, Jack, hold it a second. I know you're on opposite sides of this, but let's see where you might have some agreement"; or, "Lynne, I get the feeling that something Todd said really bugged you, is that right?"; or, "Hold it, everybody, we're really coming up with some good stuff; let's not lose our momentum by getting into a name-calling thing."

3. *The gatekeeper helps keep communication channels open.* If a group has seven people in it, the assumption is that all seven have something to contribute. However, if all are to feel comfortable contributing, those who tend to dominate need to be held in check and those who tend to be reticent need to be encouraged. The gatekeeper is the one who sees that Jane is on the edge of her chair, ready to talk, but just cannot seem to get in, or that Don is rambling a bit and needs to be directed, or that Tom's need to talk

so frequently is making Cesar withdraw from the conversation, or that Betty has just lost the thread of discussion. As we said earlier, a characteristic of good group work is interaction. Gatekeepers assume the responsibility for helping interaction. Gatekeepers may be recognized by such statements as, "Joan, I see you've got something to say here"; or, "You've made a really good point, Todd; I wonder whether we could get some reaction on it"; or, "Bill and Marge, it sounds like you're getting into a dialogue here; let's see what other ideas we have."

The following are the four most common negative roles that group discussants should avoid.

Avoid Negative Roles

1. *Aggressors work for their own status by criticizing almost everything or blaming others when things get rough.* An aggressor's main purpose seems to be to deflate the ego or status of others. One way of dealing with aggressors is to confront them. Ask them whether they are aware of what they are doing and of the effect it is having on the group.

2. *Jokers clown, mimic, or generally disrupt by making a joke of everything.* Jokers, too, are usually trying to call attention to themselves. They must be the center of attention. A little bit of a joker goes a long way. The group needs to get the jokers to consider the problem seriously, or they will constantly be an irritant to other members. One way to proceed is to encourage them when tensions need to be released, but to ignore them when there is serious work to be done.

3. *Withdrawers refuse to be part of the group.* Withdrawers are mental dropouts. Sometimes they are withdrawing from something that was said; sometimes they are just showing their indifference. Try to draw them out with questions. Find out what they are especially good at and rely on them when their skill is required. Sometimes compliments will bring them out.

4. *Monopolizers need to talk all the time.* Usually they are trying to impress the group that they are well read, knowledgeable, and valuable to the group. They should, of course, be encouraged when their comments are helpful. However, when they are talking

too much or when their comments are not helpful, the leader needs to interrupt them or draw others into the discussion.

WHEN THE GROUP GOES PUBLIC

When the problem-solving group goes public in the form of a panel discussion, the group is discussing for the benefit of the audience as much as for the satisfaction of the group members.

Although most of your group problem solving will be done in private without the presence of an onlooking or participating audience, occasionally your group will be called upon to go public. At times this means conducting your deliberations in public; at other times this means presenting your group's conclusions to another group. In a public discussion, the group is discussing to provide information for the listening audience, as much as they are to analyze or to solve a

problem. As such, public discussions have much in common with traditional public speaking. Two common forms of public discussion are the symposium and the panel discussion.

A *symposium* is a discussion in which a limited number of participants (usually three to five) present individual speeches of approximately the same length dealing with the same subject. After delivering their planned speeches, the participants in the symposium may discuss their reactions with each other or respond to questions from the audience. Despite the potential for interaction, a symposium is often characterized by long, sometimes unrelated speeches. Moreover, the part designated for questions is often shortened or deleted because "our time is about up." A symposium often omits the interaction necessary for a good discussion. If the participants make their prepared speeches short enough so that at least half of the available time can be spent on real interaction, a symposium can be interesting and stimulating. A good symposium that meets the goals of discussion is much more difficult to present than it appears; however, as a public speaking assignment, the symposium may be very beneficial. Rather than solving a problem, a symposium is more effective in shedding light on or explaining various aspects of a problem.

Symposium

A *panel discussion* is one in which the participants, usually from four to eight, discuss a topic spontaneously, under the direction of a leader and following a planned agenda. After the formal discussion, the audience is often encouraged to question the participants. So the discussion can be seen and heard by the audience, the group is seated in a semicircle, with the chairperson in the middle, to get a good view of the audience and the panelists. Since the discussion is for an audience, the panelists are obliged to make good use of traditional public speaking skills. Because a panel discussion encourages spontaneity and interaction, it can be very stimulating for both the audience and the participants themselves. The panel works as a form of problem-solving discussion.

Panel Discussion

More often than not, after a group has finished its deliberations, the leader is asked to present the group's conclusions in a report or in a public presentation. The spokesperson for the group reviews the

Presenting Conclusions

group's goal, discusses the analysis of the problem, mentions potential solutions, gives a summary of strengths and weaknesses of each solution, and then presents the group's conclusion.

ASSIGNMENT
Group Decision
Making

1. Participants select a question of fact, value, or policy for a twenty- to forty-minute discussion. Determine the method of leadership and establish an agenda. Criteria for evaluation of the discussion will include quality of participation, quality of leadership, and ability to arrive at group decisions.

2. Select a single spokesperson for the group. This person will prepare a five- to seven-minute summary of the group's process to explain how the group conducted its deliberations. Consider the question, the analysis of the question, and your key conclusions.

NOTES

1. Marvin E. Shaw, *Group Dynamics: The Psychology of Small Group Behavior,* 3d ed. (New York: McGraw-Hill, 1981), 325.
2. Ralph White and Ronald Lippitt, "Leader Behavior and Member Reactions in Three Social Climates," reprinted in Dorwin Cartwright and Alan Zander, eds., *Group Dynamics,* 3d ed. (New York: Harper & Row, 1968), 334.

EIGHTEEN

ADAPTING TO SPECIAL OCCASIONS

Although most of your speeches will be informative or persuasive, at times you will be called upon to speak under circumstances that are best described as ceremonial. In these speeches, you will not only give information or persuade, but also you must meet the conventions of the particular occasion. This chapter is short, but the skills discussed will serve you well when you speak on such special occasions.

Even though no speech can be given by formula, certain occasions require at least the knowledge of conventions that various speakers observe and that audiences may expect. Because speakers should always use their own imagination to determine how to develop the theme, they should never adhere slavishly to those conventions. Still, you must know the conventions before you can decide whether to deviate from them or ignore them entirely.

This chapter gives the basics for accomplishing five common types of special speeches: introductions, presentations, acceptances, welcomings, and tributes. In addition, the chapter considers alternate forms of delivery for these and other speeches.

INTRODUCTIONS

This occasion calls for a short but very important speech.

Purpose

The purpose of this speech is to pave the way for the main speaker. If you make the introduction in such a way that the audience is psychologically ready to listen to the speech, then you have accomplished your purpose.

Procedure

An audience wants to know who the speaker is, what the person is going to talk about, and why they should listen. Sometime before the speech you should consult with the speaker to ask what he or she prefers to have said. Usually, you want the necessary biographical information that will show who the speaker is and why he or she is qualified to talk on the subject. The better known the person is the less you need to say about him or her. For instance, the introduction of the president is simply, "Ladies and gentlemen, the president of the United States." Ordinarily, you will want enough information to allow you to talk for at least two or three minutes. Only on rare occasions should a speech of introduction go more than three or four minutes; the audience is assembled to hear the speaker, not the introducer. During the first sentence or two, then, establish the nature of the occasion; in the body of the speech, establish the speaker's credibility. The conclusion should usually include the name of the speaker and the title of the talk.

Considerations

There are some special cautions concerning the speech of introduction. First, do not overpraise the speaker. If expectations are too high, the speaker will never be able to live up to them. For instance, over-zealous introducers may be inclined to say: "This man [woman] is undoubtedly one of the greatest speakers around today. You will, I am sure, agree with me that this will be one of the best speeches you've ever heard." Although this statement may appear complimentary, it is doing the speaker a disservice by emphasizing comparison rather than speech content. A second caution is to be familiar with what you have to say. Audiences question sincerity when introducers have to read their praise. Many of us have been present when an introducer said, "And now, it is my great pleasure to present that noted authority. . ." and then had to look at some notes to recall the name. Finally, get your facts straight. The speaker should not have to spend time correcting your mistakes.

Prepare a two- to three-minute speech of introduction. Assume that you are introducing the featured speaker for some specific occasion. Criteria for evaluation will include creativity in establishing speaker credibility and presenting the name of the speaker and the speech title.

**ASSIGNMENT
Speech of
Introduction**

PRESENTATIONS

Next to introductions, presentations are the ceremonial speeches you are most likely to give.

The purpose of a speech of presentation is to present an award, prize, or gift to an individual or group. Sometimes, a presentation accompanies a long tribute to an individual. Usually, the speech of presentation is a fairly short, formal recognition of an accomplishment.

Purpose

Your speech usually has two goals: (1) to discuss the nature of the award, including its history, donor, or source, and the conditions under which it is made; and (2) to discuss the accomplishments of the recipient. If a competition was held, describe what the person did in the competition. Under other circumstances, discuss how the person has met the criteria for the award.

Procedure

Obviously, you must learn all you can about the award and about the conditions under which such awards are made. Although the award itself may be a certificate, plaque, or trophy that symbolizes some achievement, the contest may have a long history and tradition that must be mentioned. Since the audience wants to know what the recipient has done, you must know the criteria that were met. For a competition, you must know the number of contestants and the way the contest was judged. If the person earned the award through years of achievement, you need to know the particulars of that achievement.

Ordinarily, the speech is organized to show what the award is for, to give the criteria for winning or achieving the award, and to state how the person won or achieved the award. If the announcement of the name of the recipient is meant to be a surprise, what is said should build up to the climax, the naming of the winner.

Considerations

For the speech of presentation there are only two special considerations: (1) During the speech avoid overpraising; do not explain everything in such superlatives that the presentation lacks sincerity and honesty. (2) If you are going to hand the award to the recipient, you should be careful to hold the award in your left hand and present it to the left hand of the recipient. At the same time, you want to shake the right hand in congratulations. If you practice, you will find that you can present the award and shake the person's hand smoothly and avoid those embarrassing moments when the recipient does not know quite what he or she is supposed to do.

ASSIGNMENT
Speech of
Presentation

Prepare a three- to five-minute speech in which you present a gift, plaque, or award to a member of the class. Criteria for evaluation will include showing what the award is for, the criteria for winning, and how the person met the criteria.

ACCEPTANCES

When an award is presented, it must be accepted. This speech is a response to a speech of presentation.

Purpose

The purpose of the speech of acceptance is to give brief thanks for receiving the award.

Procedure

The speech usually has two parts: (1) a brief thanks to the group, agency, or people responsible for giving the award; and (2) if the recipient was aided by others, he or she gives thanks to those who share in the honor.

Considerations

Unless the acceptance is the lead-in to a major address, the acceptance should be brief. (A politician accepting a gift from the Chamber of Commerce may launch into a speech on government, but the audience will probably be expecting it.) As the Academy Awards program so graphically illustrates, however, when people are honored, the tendency is to give overly long and occasionally inappropriate speeches.

When accepting an award, your speech should be brief and to the point.

The audience expects you to show your gratitude to the presenter of the award; they are not expecting a major address.

ASSIGNMENT
Speech of Acceptance

This assignment may well go together with the speech-of-presentation assignment. Prepare a one- to two-minute speech of acceptance in response to another speaker's speech of presentation. Criteria for evaluation will be how imaginatively you can respond in a brief speech.

WELCOMINGS

Another common ceremonial speech is the welcoming.

Purpose

The purpose of a speech of welcome is to express pleasure in the presence of a person or organization. In a way, the speech of welcome is a double speech of introduction. You introduce the newcomer to the organization or city, and you introduce the organization to the newcomer.

Procedure

You must be familiar with both the person or organization you are welcoming and with the situation to which you are welcoming the person. It is surprising how little many members of organizations, citizens of a community, and students at a college or university really know about their organization or community. Although you may not have the knowledge on the tip of your tongue, it is inexcusable not to find the material you need to give an appropriate speech. Likewise, you want accurate information about the person or organization you are introducing. Although the speech will be brief, you need accurate and complete information on which to draw.

After expressing pleasure in welcoming the person or organization, tell a little about your guests and give them the information about the place or the organization to which they are being welcomed. Usually the conclusion is a brief statement of your hope for a pleasant and profitable visit.

Considerations

Again, the special caution is to make sure the speech is brief and honest. Welcoming guests does not require you to gush about them or their accomplishments. The speech of welcome should be an informative speech of praise.

ASSIGNMENT
Welcoming Speech

Prepare a speech welcoming a specific person to your city, university, or social organization. Criteria for evaluation will include how well you explain the nature of the institution and how well you introduce the person being welcomed.

TRIBUTES

The final ceremonial speech we will consider is the tribute.

The purpose of a speech of tribute is to praise someone's accomplishments. The occasion may be, for example, a birthday, the taking of an office, retirement, or death. A formal speech of tribute given in memory of a deceased person is called a *eulogy*.

The key to an effective tribute is sincerity. Although you want the praise to be apparent, you do not want to overdo it.

You must have in-depth biographical information about your subject. Since audiences are primarily interested in new information and specifics that characterize your assertions, you must have a mastery of much detail. You should focus on the person's laudable characteristics and accomplishments. It is especially noteworthy if you find that the person had to overcome some special hardship or meet some particularly trying condition. All in all, you must be prepared to make a sound positive appraisal.

One way of organizing a speech of tribute is to focus on the subject's accomplishments. How detailed you make the speech will depend on whether the person is well known. If the person is well known, be more general in your analysis. If the person is little known, provide many more details so the audience can see the reasons for the praise. In the case of very prominent individuals, you may be able to show their influence on history.

Remember, however, no one is perfect. Although you need not stress a person's less glowing characteristics or failures, some allusion to this kind of information may make the person's positive features even more meaningful. Probably the most important guide is for you to keep your objectivity. Overpraise is far worse than understatement. Try to give the person his or her due, honestly and sincerely.

Prepare a four- to six-minute speech paying tribute to some person, living or dead. Criteria for evaluation will include how well you develop the person's laudable characteristics and accomplishments.

TWO ALTERNATE FORMS OF DELIVERY

Throughout this course we have been stressing the value of extemporaneous speaking, a form of speaking that depends on careful preparation but leaves the actual wording until the time of delivery. There will also be times when you must speak without preparation or times when the way you phrase your ideas is as important or perhaps more important than the message itself. To help with these two situations, let us look at impromptu speeches and speeches from manuscripts.

Impromptu Speeches

There is no question that by far the greatest number of "speeches" you give are impromptu. When you answer a question posed by a professor in class, when you rise to speak on a motion made at a club meeting, or when you talk about the events of your vacation at a party, you are giving an impromptu speech. Just because a speech is impromptu (given on the spur of the moment) does not mean that it need not be prepared; it means only that the preparation time is reduced to a matter of seconds or at most a matter of minutes.

If all the time we spent on information exchange and persuasion is going to be worthwhile, we must carry over some of what we have learned into these impromptu settings. Even in a few seconds you can form a specific purpose—or at least a line of development; you can determine two or three points you will pursue in the development, and if time permits, you may even be able to think of a good one-line opening. Just as extemporaneous speaking improves with practice, so does impromptu speaking. The following assignment can be used to help test your preparation and delivery facility even when preparation time is minimal.

ASSIGNMENT
Impromptu Speech

Present a two- to three-minute impromptu speech.

Topics: The best topics for impromptu speeches are those that each of you in class will be able to discuss without going beyond your own knowledge and experience. Your instructor will have words and phrases on 3-by-5-inch cards, such as "Today's television," "Feminism," "Astroturf," "Does the end justify the means?" "The ideal male (or female)," "Sex in the movies."

Procedure: At the beginning of the round, a student (usually a volunteer) draws three topics, selects one, and begins preparation. The first person in the round has three minutes to prepare. The second person in the round draws three cards just before the first person begins talking. The second person, and each subsequent speaker, has the same length of time to prepare as the previous speaker, and does so while the previous speaker is talking.

Throughout this book, we have been emphasizing extemporaneous speaking. I believe that no speaker should face an audience without thorough preparation; yet, I believe that neither the manuscript speech nor the memorized speech provides the speaker with the opportunity to adapt directly to his audience as well as the extemporaneous speech. Nevertheless, you may be called upon to speak on occasions when the wording of the speech is far more important than the spontaneity or potential for audience adaptation.

The final draft of your manuscript should be extremely well worded. You will want to show all that you have learned about making ideas clear, vivid, and appropriate. In your preparation you should proceed as if you were giving an extemporaneous speech. Then record what you would ordinarily consider your final speech practice. Type the manuscript from your recorded practice and work on polishing the language. This procedure will ensure your working from an oral style rather than from a written essay style.

After the manuscript has been completely written, you should practice using it effectively. You should be sufficiently familiar with the material so that you do not have to focus your full attention on the manuscript as you read. Go over the manuscript at least three times in these final stages of practice. You will discover that even when you are reading you can have some eye contact with your audience. By watching audience reaction, you will know when and if to deviate from the manuscript.

So that the manuscript will be of maximum value to you, I suggest the following tips for preparing it.

1. The manuscript should be typed, preferably on a typewriter that has print that is pica-sized or larger. Some radio, television, or student newspaper rooms are equipped with typewriters that have extra large type. You may be able to gain access to such a machine. Whatever size type you use, it is wise to double- or even triple-space the manuscript.

2. For words that you have difficulty pronouncing, you should use phonetic spelling, accents, or diacritics to help your pronunciation.

3. Make marks that will help you determine pauses, places of special emphasis, or where to slow down or speed up. Also make sure that the last sentence on each page is completed on that page to ensure no unintended pauses.

Speeches from Manuscripts

4. Number pages boldly to keep them in their proper order. You may also find it valuable to bend the corner of each page slightly to help you turn pages easily.

5. Make sure to double-check that there will in fact be a lectern or speaker's stand on which the manuscript can be placed.

ASSIGNMENT
Manuscript Speech

Prepare a four- to six-minute manuscript speech (your professor will indicate the kind of speech by purpose or occasion). Criteria for evaluation will include clarity, vividness, emphasis, and appropriateness.

NINETEEN

SPEECHES FOR EVALUATION

Throughout this textbook we have been considering the issue of speech criticism. In Chapter 2, "Listening Critically to Speeches," we outlined an overall approach to speech criticism that could be applied to any speech; throughout the remainder of the book, we presented critiques of student speeches and called for you to compare them with your own analyses. It seems fitting in this final chapter that we return to the subject of speech criticism and give you one final chance to exercise the critical judgments that you have been developing as you have been improving your own speech preparation and presentation.

The following three speeches illustrate how three contemporary speakers met their challenge of effective speaking. The three speeches consider topics that should be of concern to the contemporary student; moreover, each of the speeches illustrates principles that form the foundation of this textbook. None of the speeches is perfect—no speech ever is. What I ask you to do is to seek out their strengths and weaknesses.

Analyze each of the speeches using the questions asked on pages 35–36.

Morality and Education: To Hold Yourself Accountable

A speech by Stephen Joel Trachtenberg, president, University of Hartford, West Hartford, Connecticut. Delivered at the District VII CASE Conference, Las Vegas, Nevada, January 27, 1987.[1]

In this speech, Trachtenberg supports the proposition that morality matters. Be especially sensitive to the way that Trachtenberg uses the word *morality* and the examples he uses to exemplify it.

1 As someone who is, on occasion, obliged to address large groups of people on difficult subjects, it's a pleasure for me to be here today and to have this opportunity to relax and enjoy myself with an easy topic. My assigned title is—quote—"Morality and Education." I plan to give Morality about six or seven minutes, to polish off Education in another five, and to add two minutes of wrap-up and synthesis for a total of 15!

2 I jest, of course, and the fact that I feel compelled to start with a joke may be a good indication of where we are at the present moment in national and world history. Intellectuals worked hard, in the late 19th and 20th centuries, to get certain categories off their backs, including Religion, Morality, Ethics and Patriotism. The heroes of the time were Charles Darwin, Karl Marx, H. L. Mencken, Clarence Darrow, James Joyce, D. H. Lawrence, and a host of figures—artists and celebrities—who were good at tweaking the noses of those who could be characterized as stuffy, Victorian, prudish and censorious. Taken all together, they made up what the late Lionel Trilling called an "adversary culture" in which the highest virtue was that of being considered scandalous.

3 And now, suddenly, we find ourselves living in a changed and changing world. Like romance and marital fidelity, virtue and morality have returned to our social and cultural scene. It is almost fashionable to discuss the extent to which our education system, at all levels, is or is not helping the student to become—not smarter, not more clever, not a brighter light at cocktail parties—but a *better person* who can actually be relied upon to try to behave in a *decent fashion.*

4 Needless to say, none of the social critics who lambasted middle-class morality back in 1880 or 1920 was capable of preaching outright immorality. What they typically declared themselves to be doing was to preach a *higher* morality—one that could appeal to superior specimens like themselves. The problem back then was seen to be the innate conservatism of the average man, who hated to see a great painter or writer or philosopher getting away with thoughts, images or ideas that he himself found threatening and obscene. The average man, in those days, like the average woman, was thought to be a churchgoing stick-in-the-mud who liked nothing

better than a sermon about God showering prosperity on those who wouldn't give in to their urges for wine, women and song.

5   Our own perspective, I needn't tell you at length, is somewhat different. We can see—though only in historical retrospect—that those preaching a Higher Morality weren't quite the lonely figures they made themselves out to be, even if they *did* suffer their share of unfair police raids and judicial smallmindedness. They were the vanguard.

6   From the 1930's to the present moment, we have had all too much experience of what average men and women can do once they have come to share the conviction that there is a *Higher* Morality that cancels out the requirements of the old-fashioned one—the one that says you ought to treat other people the way you want them to treat *you.*

7   As we slowly work our way back to the notion that Morality matters, and that you ought to hold yourself accountable for the things that you allow yourself to do, the effects are visible in every part of our existence. In a recent film like *The Mission* for example, we are actually asked to sympathize with Robert de Niro when he plays a bad person convinced that he is—quote—"Beyond repentance." His moral reevaluation of his life is the heart of the film, even if the reviewers mainly emphasized its spectacular scenery and gory combats.

8   Indeed, even the *look* of film, and of de Niro in particular, suggests the newness of the world we now inhabit. Traditionally, the hero is the one whose white hat never gets dirty and whose brow is untroubled by the wrinkles that accompany deep thought. The hero is the one who is *naturally* heroic while he or she opposes villains who look conflicted and disgusting. In *The Mission,* on the other hand, we are asked to feel deeply for de Niro when he is looking utterly at odds with himself: first when he is in the process of changing from a cad to a missionary, and then when he is once again killing people on the grounds that they are obvious villains. Nothing whatsoever within the film is truly, simply, ecstatically, *satisfying.* All the choices are difficult, all the outcomes ambiguous, all the morals difficult or impossible to draw—which in turn is what makes the film such a moral experience.

9   There's the rub. Morality isn't morality unless it deals with difficult choices, made under pressure or under duress. That's an especially unpalatable notion within a society that has long admired ease, streamlining, and the connection between wealth in the pocket and

free untrammeled movement on the open road. To be top dog in American life has often been pictured as a million dollars in your wallet, a $50,000 car at your command, and a speed limit of 200 miles an hour. And suddenly we are asked to admire Robert de Niro in a state of suicidal funk because he did a couple of bad things in his life—kidnapped some Indians and turned them into slaves, killed his own brother, etc., etc.

10   Here we are then, surrounded by our New Consensus. We would prefer to take our children and our teenagers and to have them turn out as moral people rather than empty-headed brutes. We actually want our kids to pause and *think* a little before they commit destructive acts, before they outrage the feelings of others, and before they succumb to a variety of self-destructive impulses. The question with which we then proceed to wrestle is how we can begin to approach this happy outcome. Specifically: what, if anything, can formal education contribute to the process? What, if anything, can formal education *not* be expected to do?

11   As I contemplate the mine-fields that must be crossed in search of an adequate answer to these questions, I wonder whether it might not be time for another joke! As I prepared for this talk, I naturally read some recent speeches and articles on the subject of morality and higher education, and I noticed the extent to which some of them made unfavorable comparisons between the present and the past. In the past, they observed, people were obviously *concerned* about morality, and put the subject at the very center of the education. Today we seem to be lost in a maze of hedonism and self-gratification. No wonder kids are committing acts of crime and vandalism that would have been unimaginable in 1780 or 1910.

12   Well, I myself am not oblivious with regard to the difference between past and present, but I see our problems with the inculcation of morality as relatively new ones—problems, if I may be so bold as to say so, that are qualitatively unique.

13   It's very misleading, for example, to cite the systems of virtue inculcated by Socrates and Plato without mentioning that their society practiced slavery on an enormous scale, behaved brutally toward prisoners of war, and was able to inflict the death penalty on Socrates himself—with a democratic rather than a tyrannical system ordering that it be carried out. The fact that the classical philosophers *accepted* the existence of slavery, and sometimes provided an explicit rationale on its behalf, tells us that we are dealing with a very different world when we discuss them—one that cannot easily

be compared to our own. Moreover, the aspect of classical philosophy that was able to join with the Judaeo-Christian tradition in a way that *eventually* led to the condemnation of slavery—as well as infanticide and other unpleasant practices—was the one we would today call religious fundamentalism. Plato's belief in a higher universe that we can only glimpse through reasoning and revelation—the picture of Socrates lost, at one point, in beatific meditation—is the kind of thing that would generate a good deal of skeptical concern if it were to be presented, in 1987, in a court of law.

14   I feel the same way, I must confess, when I am told about the concern for morality, virtue and decency in the Middle Ages, or the Renaissance, or just about any period that preceded our own. I don't think anyone in this room would volunteer to be put into a time machine and sent back to an earlier century—or even an earlier decade—if there were *absolutely no possibility of coming back again.*

15   All of the earlier social systems with which we are familiar, no matter what they claimed on their own behalves, were authoritarian systems within which freedom of a sort—*relative* freedom—was reserved to an elite. Our own system, on the other hand, is one which has practiced a steadily widening radius of empowerment. We have enfranchised and given expressive legitimacy to those without significant amounts of property, to women, to racial and ethnic minorities, to teenagers, to the handicapped, and to other groups once treated as effectively invisible. We have turned self-fulfillment from an exceedingly rare privilege into a goal shared by most of those living within our borders and by more and more of those living on our planet.

16   In the process, we have steadily blurred the line that once seemed to divide the—quote—"masses" from the—quote—"Elite." We live in a world where the latest revolution in art, far from being persecuted by the Justice Department, is quickly reported on in the pages of *Time* and *Newsweek.* We live at a moment in history when the *New York Times*—once compared with the mass-circulation *Daily News* as the kind of paper you couldn't read without a college degree—has left the *News* far behind in its march to becoming America's national tabloid and "paper of record."

17   To the extent, therefore, that calls for the inculcation of morality use the language of nostalgia—of the return to a happier past, when decency was decency and right made might—they are very vulnerable, and will soon prove very tiring. The difficult and therefore

interesting question is how we can begin the discussion of morality and ethics in a world of satellite communications and of censorship systems that simply don't work—a world in which individual experience cracks each of the molds that we design to shape and contain it.

18   Even the Soviets, after all, have had to admit that *trying to keep control*—by seizing typewriters and tracking every printing press—has only sharpened the edge of the cry for self-realization, self-fulfillment, and freedom of expression. If we do design a new system for the inculcation of ethics and a moral sense—one that is appropriate to the stage of psychological development attained by most of our citizens—it will look quite different from those that emphasized exclusion of experience as the basis for right vision. And that, I needn't remind you, includes the proposal that Plato attributed to Socrates, whereby no one arguing a bad cause in a good work of literature would be allowed to speak in poetry or in extended prose. Bad thoughts would only be summed up in paraphrase while good ones could speak at length.

19   Let me begin by saying [the] obvious: morality begins at home. Where the inculcation of virtue is concerned, there is nothing like watching Mom and Dad as they make their way through a typically difficult week in a typically difficult year. How they deal with each other and how they deal with relatives, friends, creditors and strangers—how they do that from minute to minute, 365 days a year, 10 years every decade—is a modeling influence that bears the same relation to what schools can accomplish that the hydrogen bomb does to a handgun. The latter can be quite deadly, but it is possible to miss. The former, by definition, "gets you." It is fool proof.

20   The environment of the home is a template. What elementary school and high school does is to have that template imposed by the students as a *group average* and then to extend or reaffirm or embroider its themes. In a democratic society, and even in those far more concerned with authority and order, school systems do not set themselves the goal of overturning the values that prevail in the homes of their students when those students are between the ages of 5 or 6 and 16 or 17. Only when those students reach what we call "college age" are they exposed to thinkers, philosophers, and theoreticians who *might* be construed as overturning or at least disapproving what those parents once preached or accepted.

21   Right now, I believe, we are seeing a real transition in the values that many children and teenagers absorb within their home environ-

ments. As products of our psychological age, their parents know how closely they are observed by their children and how clearly their children can perceive any gap between preaching and practice. As that transition takes place, the children are arriving at school more *prepared* to hear issues of morality and ethics discussed— more *prepared* for the notion that life is a difficult process in which choices are continuous rather than occasional. Easy radicalism, like easy conservatism, is a thing of the past. These curious young children of ours, who often look so adult, are the first to spot a phony, no matter what the ideological coloring he or she wears.

22   And yes, of course, there are the inevitable exceptions. If a kid is determined to get into trouble, the ways of doing that—in a modern society—are all too easily available. We are, alas, a gun-happy society. We make alcohol available in huge quantities at bargain prices. We generate the surplus wealth that can even afford to pay for cocaine. Our roads are filled with roaring tin cans that contain large amounts of highly combustible fluid. We provide our young people with the *physical* care and nutrition that makes certain their hormones are raging to the maximum extent. When we fail to balance that out with *other* kinds of care, the resulting possibilities for destruction make even the automobile look beneficent.

23   All of that is part of the process of empowerment, whereby individual choice, individual self-restraint, and individual humanity plays the roles formerly allotted to judges and police. If you carried an automobile with you in your time machine, and brought it back to the 18th century, no one in his right mind would allow it into the hands of anyone less than the Archbishop of Canterbury or the King himself. "If it got into the hands of the common folk," someone or other would exclaim, "it would surely result in mass murder!"

24   We ourselves have reached the point where we are capable of trusting, to a remarkable extent, the good judgment of most human beings most of the time. That includes, inevitably, their good judgment in matters of education and the educational curriculum. As quite ordinary people make that good judgment felt—having learned many difficult lessons in recent years—the curriculum will continue to change. Our children and our teenagers will be asked to consider difficult issues—and asked to do it not *only* in special courses on ethics but pervasively, throughout the curriculum, by teachers who themselves do not pretend to have easy answers. And when those children and teenagers come home, they will ask their parents hard questions that may lead even Mom and Dad to recon-

sider their behaviors and the gap that separates their preaching from their practice.

25　At which point we will begin to find ourselves living in a much, much better world.

26　I thank you!

Working in a Man's World: Are Women Making Progress?

A speech by Carol Crosthwaite, division staff manager, Corporate Relations, Southwestern Bell Corporation. Delivered to the National Council of Jewish Women, St. Louis, Missouri, October 23, 1985.[2]

In this speech, Crosthwaite speaks to the progress that women have made in the working world. Notice how she contrasts the management approaches of men and women and what she concludes is the way that women should behave to obtain their full potential.

1　I want to compliment whoever it was who came up with the topic for tonight. When I started thinking about it, I'd jotted down four pages of ideas in no time. So it's a fertile subject, for sure.

2　And the title is accurate: It *IS* a man's world, in terms of who sits at the top of American business and government . . . and no doubt it will continue to be for some time to come.

3　John Naisbitt predicts otherwise. He's the author of *Megatrends,* and he's made mega*bucks* consulting with business on how to respond to current and coming trends. He told a group of Southwestern Bell managers that he thinks many American institutions will be run by women in the not-too-distant future.

4　There are certainly signs in that direction. Women mayors in Houston and San Francisco and elsewhere . . . a woman on the bench of the U.S. Supreme Court . . . Geraldine running for the roses . . . women officers and board members at some *Fortune* 500 companies . . . women heading up 30 percent of new business starts each year. Twenty years ago, women held only 14 percent of managerial and administrative jobs; now they hold 33 percent.

5　But there are also signs to the contrary. Women hold a minute portion of the officer and CEO positions in business. And women CEOs of major corporations are as hard to find as a birth control pill in Jerry Falwell's medicine cabinet.

6　Another sign that we won't be taking over any time real soon is based on a decidedly non-random sample of women friends of mine. Many of them are concluding that life in the corporate world is not the paradise of adventure it appeared to be when they were on the outside looking in.

7   They've decided they don't want equal opportunity for alcoholism or divorce or cardiac arrest. They've decided the halls of corporate America aren't the only place where they can make a meaningful contribution to life its ownself. And so they're dropping out.

8   That's certainly one way of dealing with working in a man's world. I'm not here to praise them *or* bury them for their decision. What I *am* here to praise is what their decision seems to represent.

9   What it seems to me they've done is think through their own definition of success—that is, what goals they want to achieve in life—rather than lapping up Pavlov-style the goals their culture might press upon them.

10   Clearly not everyone can *afford* to drop out. But I also see more men *and* women in the corporate world deciding that success for them doesn't necessarily equal moving up the corporate ladder . . . especially when moving *up* requires moving *out* to a distant company location, and leaving their entire support group behind. They're choosing quality of life over size of office or paycheck.

11   As I said before, any choice is valid, so long as it's consciously made with personal goals and values in mind.

12   You asked me to talk about my experiences as a woman working in a man's world. I've been working for a dozen years now, and I've seen some sizeable changes in that time.

13   What I've seen was quantified and supported in some research results in the fall issue of *Harvard Business Review*. Twenty years ago they did a survey of attitudes about working women, and they repeated it this year. The results show how attitudes have changed.

14   For example, the number of men who owned up to having an unfavorable attitude toward women executives fell from *41 percent* in 1965 to *5 percent* in 1985. The number of men who think having women in management improves both *employee morale* and *profits* rose from *25 percent* in '65 to more than *70 percent* in '85.

15   Not that all's golden. The majority of men still think a woman must be exceptional to make it in the business world. One respondent out of three still thinks women will never be totally integrated into corporate life. And while men perceive that women are comparably paid, salary data show the truth is far from it.

16   Even so, the research says some old myths are finally dying out.

The myth that women are "temperamentally unfit" for management, for example. And the myth that a woman has to be "like a man" to succeed (whatever that means!).

17   The latter is the single biggest shift I've seen in my career. When I started in business in the early '70s, women managers were still something of a novelty.

18   We were strangers in a strange land, and we had no female role models. So we compared ourselves to the natives. Not being stupid, we noticed right off that we weren't like them in many ways, and we spent the next decade trying to rectify that.

—We boned up on the games our mothers never taught us.

—We pledged allegiance to John Molloy, and mastered the fine art of getting the ends to come out even on a bow tie.

—We read about power offices, and power bases, and power lunches, and power power.

—Not to be done in by the good old boy's networks, we started networks (scanty though they were) of good old girls.

—We learned how to consume quantities of liquor, and tell dirty jokes, and play golf and poker, and talk jock talk.

19   In short, we wore pinstripes, and we got tough.

20   It wasn't obvious then, but it's all-too-obvious now what was wrong with this picture. We were trying to be something we weren't—namely, men. We were saying there was only one right answer, only one way to win. So we were setting ourselves up for frustration and failure.

21   Fortunately for your sanity and mine, that's becoming past history now. We're moving on to the next step. I think women today realize we don't need a sex change operation to succeed. Even more, I think we realize that, just as there are strengths to being a man in the workplace, there are strengths to being a woman, too.

22   We're learning what those strengths are, and we're learning how to leverage them—to our personal advantage, and to the benefit of our employers and the task at hand.

23   We're still exercising our "masculine" muscles in some ways. But we're no longer letting our "feminine" muscles go slack.

24   Which reminds me of a point I want to make before I go further. By definition the subject you've asked me to address requires doing

something I don't like to do—and that is, make generalizations about women and men.

25   So as a caveat to all of what I'm about to say, please remember we're all individuals with various blends of so-called "male" and "female" traits. And each of us deserves *more* than to be lumped indiscriminately with the other 100-plus million men or women in America today.

26   Having said that, let me proceed to generalize.

27   If you doubt that the workplace needs women's strengths, just read the latest trends described in John Naisbitt's new book, *Reinventing the Corporation*.

> —He talks about people as the determining resource in a competitive world, and thus the need for human values in the workplace. *Women are strong on people awareness and skills.*

> —He talks about managers as facilitators, not order-givers. That's our style. *Women operate through mutual interest rather than manipulation.*

> —He talks about the increasing role of intuition, versus strictly "the numbers," in making management decisions. *Women have been using their intuition all along.*

> —On a somewhat different note, he talks about the shift from an industrial- to an information-based economy. The *Harvard Business Review* study says *women are perceived to have easier access to opportunities in information than we had in industry.*

28   No doubt you've read a lot about how society is moving from a fragmented, specialized view of the world to a wholistic, interdependent view. The larger our population and institutions become, the more interdependent we'll be, and the more we'll have to rely on others.

29   Which means we'll have to negotiate more to achieve our goals. That's another strength women possess. For centuries we've been the equalizers, the mediators, the keepers of the peace. In today's world, people are badly needed who can reconcile divergent interests and find creative solutions where everyone "wins."

30   A friend of mine in Strategic Planning negotiates with companies Southwestern Bell is thinking about joint partnering with or acquiring. He thinks a woman would be an asset to the staff, because we're

"generally less threatening and often downright disarming" in a way it's more difficult for men to be.

31   One last example. Some sociologists just wrote a book called *Habits of the Heart*. They're worried about signs of what they call "radical individualism"—a declining sense of community, and the negative effect it could have on our society. To quote the authors, "We think all those things that strengthen relationships between people, that give a sense that we need each other, that we belong to each other and are responsible for each other are healthy at this point."

32   Does that sound familiar? Does it sound like the way women think? It does to me.

33   What all of this says to me is that, in many ways, *our time is now*. The business and political worlds right now need more of the exact skills and points of view which women possess. But our skills and ideas will go to waste unless we *realize* their value and *put them to use*.

34   To tie back to my earlier point, there's more than one way to win the game . . . more than one right answer. Organizations need the so-called masculine traits today. But they need the so-called feminine traits every bit as much.

35   I think what's happening in business today is analogous to the parenting concept of Tough Love. At one time families led only with the gut—authority ruled. Then in the '50s and '60s we went to the other extreme, and led only with the heart—and anarchy ruled. And neither approach worked well, because each was out of balance.

36   Today we realize the best place to be is not at either extreme, but somewhere in the middle. Children need some freedom, but not total freedom. They need firm discipline, but they need it to be delivered against a backdrop of love.

37   The workplace is no different. Individuals who know how to use the best of masculine *and* feminine traits will bring the greatest value to their organization. And organizations which know how to tap the talents of both men and women will be the ones to thrive.

38   That's my premise. For those of you who were looking for some practical tips on working in a man's world, I'll briefly list a few. Any that interest you we can talk more about in the Q&A.

39 1.   First, *give up thinking you can change other people*. You will still encounter people who stereotype and dislike working women. Some you may win over, but many you won't.

40   The harder you try to be accepted by these people, the more their acceptance will elude you. You cannot control what they think. Don't waste your time: Focus instead on what you *can* control.

41 2.   In the same vein, *don't make an issue of being a woman.* If you send "us-versus-them" signals, you'll never reach your goal—unless your goal is to shore up forever the barriers between the sexes which are starting to come down.

42   I think women are best served by not setting themselves apart. For this reason I'm generally not a supporter of women's business groups. It can be helpful to compare notes. But if your objective is professional rather than social, I would suggest you could grow more by joining a coed group.

43   You have just two shots at professional contacts with men outside of work. One is informal (golf games, "the club," and such), and that one's still largely closed to women. It makes sense to take advantage of the formal organizations where you do have access.

44 3.   Third, *keep yourself above any tactics which men—or other women—may use against you.* I'm not saying roll over and play dead, or be dumb about politics. *Be aware* of these tactics, and don't be sideswiped. But guard your integrity and your self-respect, and remain above reproach.

45   Also be aware that the standards here are much higher for women than for men.

46 4.   *Help other women.* The Harvard study showed that barely half of the females surveyed and only one-third of the males think women feel comfortable working for other women. Both numbers are down significantly from twenty years ago. As one respondent said, "It's been my experience that women in general are the greatest detriment to the success of other women."

47   A grim commentary. Certainly we should also help competent *men* to get ahead, and certainly we shouldn't promote women who are less than capable. But neither can we afford to be our own worst enemy. So lend a helping hand.

48 5.   *Be competent.* Awesome conclusion, huh. But solid performance, along with the passage of time, is what will wear away the gender barriers in the end, like a river wears away the toughest rock.

49   Just as you're held up against higher ethical standards, you'll be held up against higher *performance* standards. You will have to prove yourself over and over again. Get used to it. And, in Buddhist terms, stay focused on the right doing of the next task at hand.

50 6.   Sixth, *know your strengths, and use them.* With apologies again for generalizing (because these strengths do *not* apply to some women, and *do* apply to some men), women are often sensitive to the people around them . . . intuitive . . . good listeners and communicators . . . good facilitators and negotiators . . . and dedicated, hard workers.

51   Whatever your strengths, feel good about them, and don't keep them a secret.

52 7.   And finally, *have some fun.* Don't dwell too much on the male/female issue, and don't let it get you down.

53   I hardly ever think of myself by gender at Southwestern Bell. I don't sense it's an issue. That may have to do with my profession: Public relations has long been known as the velvet ghetto. And it may have to do with my company, which has been ahead of its time in giving women opportunities to advance.

54   So maybe I'm not the norm, and maybe I'm luckier than most. Even so, I can't see how bemoaning our "plight" gets us anywhere.

55   I showed this talk to several men today, and got some useful feedback. My favorite was from a man who's short. He said studies show that short men are paid and promoted less than tall men. So he said, "I have a choice. I can go through life blaming everything on my height.

56   "The laws of nature work so simply. You set up a game like that (you let yourself be stereotyped), and that's the game that will be played. Everywhere you look, you'll see evidence to support the game. Then again, if you *don't* set up that game, it *won't* be played. We all have a choice."

57   This man may be short on height, but not on wisdom.

58   That's all I have prepared to say.

59   Are women making progress? Sure.

60   Do we have a ways to go? You bet.

61   How will we know when we get there? The workplace will be gender blind. Gender won't be an issue, because we'll all be seen as people first.

Think Strawberries

This final speech by James Lavenson, president of the Plaza Hotel, was delivered before the American Medical Association on February 7, 1974.[3]

I have included this speech in five editions of *The Challenge of Effective Speaking*. As you read the speech, I believe you will agree with me that it is a truly excellent informative speech—one of the best you will find. Notice how Lavenson blends humor, excellent specific instances, informal language, and clear, vivid language to form an extremely interesting and very informative speech about the hotel business.

1   I came from the balcony of the hotel business. For ten years as a corporate director of Sonesta Hotels with no line responsibility, I had my office in a little building next door to The Plaza. I went to the hotel every day for lunch and often stayed overnight. I was a professional guest. You know nobody knows more about how to run a hotel than a guest. Last year, I suddenly fell out of the corporate balcony and had to put my efforts in the restaurants where my mouth had been, and in the rooms and nightclub and theater into which I'd been putting my two cents.

2   In my ten years of kibitzing, all I had really learned about the hotel business was how to use a guest room toilet without removing the strip of paper that's printed "Sanitized for Your Protection." When the hotel staff found out I'd spent my life as a salesman and that I'd never been a hotelier, never been to Cornell Hotel School, and that I wasn't even the son of a waiter, they were in a state of shock. And Paul Sonnabend, President of Sonesta, didn't help their apprehension much when he introduced me to my executive staff with the following kind words: "The Plaza has been losing money the last several years and we've had the best management in the business. Now we're going to try the worst."

3   Frankly, I think the hotel business has been one of the most backward in the world. There's been very little change in the attitude of room clerks in the 2,000 years since Joseph arrived in Bethlehem and was told they'd lost his reservation. Why is it that a sales clerk at Woolworth asks your wife, who points to the pantyhose, if she wants three or six pairs—and your wife is all by herself—but the maître d' asks you and your wife, the only human beings within a mile of the restaurant, "How many are you?"

4   Hotel salesmanship is retailing at its worst. But at the risk of inflicting cardiac arrest on our guests at The Plaza when they first hear shocking expressions like "Good Morning" and "Please" and "Thank you for coming," we started a year ago to see if it was possible to make the 1,400 employees of The Plaza into genuine hosts and hostesses. Or should I say "salesmen"?

5   A tape recorder attached to my phone proved how far we had to go. "What's the difference between your $85 suite and your $125 suite?" I'd ask our reservationist, disguising my voice over the phone. You guessed it: "$40!"

6   "What's going on in the Persian Room tonight?" I asked the Bell Captain. "Some singer" was his answer. "Man or woman?" I persisted. "I'm not sure" he said, which made me wonder if I'd even be safe going there.

7   Why is it, I wondered, that the staff of a hotel doesn't act like a family playing hosts to guests whom they've invited to their house? It didn't take too long after becoming a member of the family myself, to understand one of the basic problems. Our 1,400 family members didn't even know each other! With that large a staff, working over eighteen floors, six restaurants, a nightclub, a theater, and three levels of subbasement, including a kitchen, a carpentry shop, plumbing and electrical shops, a full commercial laundry—how would they ever know who was working there, and who was a guest or just a purveyor passing through? Even the old-timers who might recognize a face after a couple of years would have no idea of the name connected to it. It struck me that if our own people couldn't call each other by name, smile at each other's familiar face, say good morning *to each other,* how could they be expected to say amazing things like "Good Morning, Mr. Jones" to a guest? A year ago The Plaza name tag was born. The delivery took place on my lapel. And it's now been on 1,400 lapels for over a year. Everyone, from dishwashers to the General Manager, wears his name where every other employee, and of course every guest, can see it. Believe it or not, our people say hello to each other—by name—when they pass in the halls and the offices. At first our regular guests thought The Plaza was entertaining some gigantic convention, but now even the old-time Plaza regulars are able to call our bellmen and maids by name. We've begun to build an atmosphere of welcome with the most precious commodity in the world—our names. *And* our guests' names.

8   A number of years ago, I heard Dr. Ernest Dichter, head of the

Institute of Motivational Research, talk about restaurant service. He had reached a classic conclusion; when people come to a fine restaurant, they are hungrier for *recognition* than they are for food. It's true. If the maître d' says, "We have your table ready, Mr. Lavenson," then as far as I'm concerned the chef can burn the steak and I'll still be happy.

9   When someone calls you by name and you don't know his, a strange feeling of discomfort comes over you. When he does it twice you *have* to find out *his* name. This we see happening with our Plaza name tags. When a guest calls a waiter by name, the waiter wants to call the guest by name. It will drive him nuts if he doesn't know. He'll ask the maître d', and if he doesn't know he'll ask the bellman, who will ask the front desk . . . calling the guests by name has a big payoff. It's called a *tip*.

10   At first there was resistance to name tags—mostly from the old-time, formally trained European hoteliers. I secretly suspect they liked being incognito when faced with a guest complaint. We only had one staff member who said he'd resign before having his dignity destroyed with a name tag. For sixteen years he'd worn a rosebud in his lapel and that, he said, was his trademark and everyone knew him by it. His resignation was accepted along with that of the rosebud. Frankly, there are moments when I regret the whole idea myself. When I get on a Plaza elevator and all the passengers see my name tag, they know I work there. Suddenly, I'm the official elevator pilot, the host. I can't hide, so I smile at everybody, say "good morning" to perfect strangers I'd ordinarily ignore. The ones that don't go into shock, smile back. Actually, they seem to mind less the fact that a trip on a Plaza elevator, built in 1907, is the equivalent of commuting to Manhattan from Greenwich.

11   There are 600 Spanish-speaking employees at The Plaza. They speak Spanish. They don't read English. The employee house magazine was in English. So was the employee bulletin board. So were the signs over the urinals in the locker rooms that suggest cigarette butts don't flush too well. It was a clue as to why some of management's messages weren't getting through. The employee house magazine is now printed one side in English, the other in Spanish. The bulletin board and other staff instructions are in two languages. We have free classes in both languages for departmental supervisors. It's been helping.

12   With 1,400 people all labeled and smiling we were about ready

last June to make salesmen out of them. There was just one more obstacle to overcome before we started suggesting they "ask for the order." They had no idea what the product was they would be selling. Not only didn't they know who was playing in the Persian Room, they didn't know we had movies—full-length feature films without commercials—on the closed-circuit TV in the bedrooms. As a matter of fact, most of them didn't know what a guest room looked like, unless they happened to be a maid or a bellman.

13   The reason the reservationists thought $40 was the difference between two suites was because they'd never been in one, much less actually slept there. To say our would-be salesmen lacked product knowledge would be as much an understatement as the line credited to President Nixon if he had been the Captain of the Titanic. My son told me that if Nixon had been Captain of the Titanic, he probably would have announced to the passengers there was no cause for alarm—they were just stopping to pick up ice.

14   Today, if you ask a Plaza bellman who's playing in the Persian Room he'll tell you Ednita Nazzaro. He'll tell you because he's seen her. In the contract of every Persian Room performer, there's now a clause requiring him to first perform for our employees in the cafeteria before he opens in the Persian Room. Our employees see the star first, before the guests.

15   And if you ask a room clerk or a telephone operator what's on the TV movies, they'll tell you because they've seen it—on the TV sets running the movies continuously in the employees' cafeteria.

16   Believe me, if you are having your lunch in our cafeteria and watch "Female Response" or "Swedish Fly Girls" on the TV set, you won't forget the film. You might, however, suspect the chef has put Spanish fly in your spaghetti.

17   Our new room clerks now have a week of orientation. It includes spending a night in the hotel and a tour of our 1,000 guest rooms. They can look out the windows and see the $40 difference in suites, since a view of the Park doesn't even closely resemble the back of the Avon building.

18   As I mentioned, about six months ago, we decided it was time to take a hard look at our sales effort. I couldn't find it. The Plaza had three men with the title "salesman"—and they were good men. But they were really sales-*service* people who took the orders for functions or groups who came through the doors and sought us out. Nobody, but nobody, ever left the palace, crossed the moat at Fifth

Avenue, and went looking for business. We had no one knocking on doors, no one asking for the order. The Plaza was so dignified it seemed demeaning to admit we needed business. If you didn't ask us we wouldn't ask you. So there! Our three sales-service people were terrific once you voluntarily stepped inside our arena. You had to ring our doorbell. We weren't ringing yours or anyone else's.

19   This condition wasn't unique to our official Sales Department. It seemed to be a philosophy shared by our entire staff—potentially larger sales staff of waiters, room clerks, bellmen, cashiers, and doormen. If you wanted a second drink in the Oak Bar, you got it by tripping the waiter. You asked for it. If you wanted a room you were quoted the minimum rate. If you wanted something better or larger, you had to ask for it. If you wanted to stay at the hotel an extra night, you had to ask. You were never invited. Sometimes I think there's a secret pact among hotelmen. It's a secret oath you take when you graduate from hotel school. It goes like this: "I promise I will never ask for the order."

20   When you're faced with as old and ingrained a tradition as that, halfway countermeasures don't work. We started a program with all our guest contact people using a new secret oath: "Everybody sells!" And we meant everybody—maids, cashiers, waiters, bellmen—the works. We talked to the maids about suggesting room service, to the doormen about mentioning dinner in our restaurants, to cashiers about suggesting return reservations to departing guests. And we talked to waiters about strawberries.

21   A waiter at The Plaza makes anywhere from $10,000 to $20,000 a year. The difference between those two figures is, of course, tips. When I was in the advertising agency business, I thought I was fast at computing 15 percent. I'm a moron compared to a waiter. Our suggestions for selling strawberries fell on responsive ears when we described a part of the Everybody Sells program for our Oyster Bar restaurant. We figured, with just the same number of customers in the Oyster Bar, that if the waiters would ask every customer if he'd like a second drink, wine, or beer with the meal, and then dessert—given only one out of four takers we'd increase our sales volume by $364,000 a year. The waiters were way ahead of the lecture—they'd already figured out that was another $50,000 in tips! And since there are ten waiters in the Oyster Bar, even I could figure out it meant five grand more per man in tips. It was at that point I had my toughest decision to make since I've been in this job. I had to choose between

staying on as President or becoming an Oyster Bar waiter.

22   But, while the waiters appreciated this automatic raise in theory, they were quick to call out the traditional negatives. "Nobody eats dessert anymore. Everyone's on a diet. If we served our chocolate cheesecake to everybody in the restaurant, half of them would be dead in a week."

23   "So sell 'em strawberries!" we said. "But sell 'em." And then we wheeled out our answer to gasoline shortages, the dessert cart. We widened the aisles between the tables and had the waiters wheel the cart up to each and every table at dessert time. Not daunted by the diet protestations of the customer, the waiter then went into raptures about the bowl of fresh strawberries. There was even a bowl of whipped cream for the slightly wicked. By the time our waiters finish extolling the virtues of our fresh strawberries flown in that morning from California, or wherever he thinks strawberries come from, you not only have had an abdominal orgasm but one out of two of you order them. In the last six months we show our waiters every week what's happening to strawberry sales. This month they have doubled again. So have second martinis. And believe me, when you get a customer for a second martini you've got a sitting duck for strawberries—with whipped cream. Our waiters are asking for the order.

24   "Think Strawberries" is The Plaza's new secret weapon. Our reservationists now think strawberries and suggest you'll like a suite overlooking Central Park rather than a twin-bedded room. Our bellmen are thinking strawberries. Each bellman has his own reservation cards, with his name printed as the return addressee, and he asks if you'd like him to make your return reservation as he's checking you out and into your taxi. Our Room Service order takers are thinking strawberries. They suggest the closed-circuit movie on TV ($3.00 will appear on your bill) as long as you're going to eat in your room. Our telephone operators are even thinking strawberries. They suggest a morning Flying Tray breakfast when you ask for a wake-up call. You just want a light breakfast, no ham and eggs? How about some strawberries?

25   We figure we've added about three hundred salesmen to the three-man sales-service team we had before. But most important, of course, is that we've added five pure sales people to our Sales Department. Four of them are out on the street calling—mostly cold—on the prospects to whom they're ready to sell anything from a cocktail in the Oak Bar to a Corporate Directors meeting to a Bar Mitzvah. The chewing gum people sell new customers by sampling

on street corners. The Plaza has chewing gum licked a mile. Our sales people on the street have one simple objective: get the prospect into the hotel to sample the product. With the Plaza as our product, it isn't too difficult. And once you taste The Plaza, frankly, you're hooked.

26   In analyzing our business at the hotel we found, much to my surprise, that functions—parties, weddings, charity balls, and the like—are just about three times more profitable than all our six restaurants put together. And functions are twice as profitable as selling all 1000 of our rooms. Before we had this analysis, we were spending all our advertising money on restaurants, our nightclub, and our guest rooms. This year we're spending 80 percent of our advertising money to get function business—weddings instead of honeymoons, banquets instead of meals, annual corporate meetings instead of a clandestine romantic rendezvous for two. We've added a fulltime Bridal Consultant who can talk wedding language to nervous brides and talk turkey to their mothers. Retailers like Saks and Bonwit's and Bergdorf's have had bridal consultants for years. Hotels have Banquet Managers. Banquet Managers sell wedding dinners. Bridal Consultants sell strawberries—everything from the bridal shower, the pictures, the ceremony, the reception, the wedding night, to the honeymoon, to the first anniversary.

27   When you fight a habit as long-standing as the hotel inside salesman, you don't just wave a wand and say, "Presto: now we have four outside salesmen." We want our new salespeople to know how serious we are about going after business. We started an Executive Sales Call program as part of our "Everybody Sells" philosophy. About forty of our top and middle-management executives, ones who traditionally don't ever see a prospect, are assigned days on which they make outside calls with our regular salesmen. People like our Personnel Director, our Executive Housekeeper, our Purchasing Director, and our General Manager are on the street every day making calls. Our prospects seem to like it. Our salesmen love it. And our nonsales "salesmen" are getting an education about what's going on in the real world—the one outside the hotel.

28   As a matter of fact, that's why I'm here today. I made a sales call myself with one of our salespeople. We called on your program chairman and tried to sell him strawberries. He promised that if I showed you a strawberry he'd book your next luncheon at The Plaza. I'm looking forward to waiting on you myself. Thank you very much.

NOTES

1. Reprinted from *Vital Speeches*, March 15, 1987, 333–335. By permission.
2. Reprinted from *Vital Speeches*, January 1, 1986, 178–180. By permission.
3. Reprinted from *Vital Speeches*, March 15, 1974, 346–348. By permission.

Bormann, Ernest G. *Discussion and Group Methods: Theory and Practice,* 2d ed. New York: Harper & Row, 1975. This is a comprehensive textbook on group discussion.

Brilhart, John K. *Effective Group Discussion,* 5th ed. Dubuque, Iowa: Wm. C. Brown, 1986. This paperback is a very popular textbook.

Hare, Paul A. *Handbook of Small Group Research.* 2d ed. New York: Free Press, 1976. This may be the single most complete survey of small-group research available. The extensive bibliography includes every important work on leadership published prior to 1976.

Rogge, Edward, and James C. Ching. *Advanced Public Speaking.* New York: Holt, Rinehart & Winston, 1966. This comprehensive book on public speaking formats has a good section on speeches for special occasions.

Verderber, Rudolph F. *Working Together.* Belmont, Calif.: Wadsworth, 1982. This paperback gives a complete discussion of analyzing and resolving various types of discussion questions.

**Part Five
SUGGESTED
READINGS**

Ethos. *See* Credibility
Ettensohn, Frank, "Definition of Fossils, A," 216–218
Etymology, 212
Eulogy, 373
Evaluating speeches, 35–36, 142–143, 377
  actuation, 310–311
  conviction, 261–262
  criteria for, 33–36
  definition, 214–215
  description, 205
  expository, 235–236
  informative, 166–167
  persuasive, 270–271
  process, 193–194
  refutation, 333
Evaluation, propositions of, 251
Evidence. *See* Data
Examples, 62–63, 115–116
Expediter, 361
Expository speeches, 219–241
  assignments, 235
  citing material, 231–232
  creativity in, 232–234
  defined, 219
  interviewing for, 224–230
  library sources, 220–224
  outline, 236–237
  questions for evaluation, 235–236
  speech and analysis, 238–241
  testing material, 230–231
  topics, 220
Extemporaneous speaking, 133–134
Eye contact, 123

Facial expression, 131
Facts, 254, 255
  propositions of, 251
  questions of, 344
Fallacies, 326–328
  ad hominem, 328

authority, appeals to, 326
hasty generalization, 321
questionable cause, 323
statistics, 326–327
Fear of speaking, 138–142
Feedback, 8–9
Feinberg, Martha, "Use of Lie Detector Tests," 334–336
Festinger, Leon, 299, 315n
Figures of speech, 107–108
Films, 180–181
Fisher, Hilda, 149
Floyd, James J., 40
Francis, W. Nelson, 100, 119n
Freese, Arthur S., 39n

Gadzella, Bernadette M., 183n
Garwood, John D., 64, 70n
Gatekeeper, 353–355, 362–363
Geis, Irving, 339
Generalization, 280–281
  fallacy, 320
  testing, 320–322
Gesture, 131
Gibson, James, 149
Gilgoff, Andy, 39n
Grant, Nancy, "Juggling," 195–199
Graphs, 177–180
Group discussion, 343–366
  agenda, 346–347
  assignment, 366
  defined, 343
  forms, 364–366
  leadership, 347–358
  outline, 346–347
  preparation, 343–347
  roles, 358–364
Guth, Hans P., 242

Haefele, John W., 162, 171n
Hanna, Michael, 149
Hare, Paul A., 399
Harmonizer, 362

Hasty generalization, 320
Hearing, 20, 22
Heintz, Mary, "Television and Children," 273–275
Huff, Darrell, 339
Humanities Index, 222
Humor, 87–88, 165–166

Illustrations, 62–63
Impromptu speaking, 133, 374–375
Inductive reasoning, 280–285
  analogy, 281–282
  causation, 283
  defined, 280
  generalization, 280–281
  sign, 284–285
Inferences, 277
Information, 358–360
Informative speaking, 153–175
  definition, 216–218
  descriptive, 207–208
  expository, 219–241
  goals, 153–154
  organization, 158–160
  principles, 154–166
  process, 195–198
  questions for evaluation, 166–167
  source material, 230–231
  specific purposes, 154–158
  speech and outline, 166–171
Intention, 265–266
Interviewing, 60
  conducting the interview, 228–229
  interpreting results, 229
  purpose, 224
  questions, 226–228
  selecting interviewee, 225–226
  survey, 60–61
Introductions, speeches of, 367–369

Visual aids *(continued)*
  pictures, drawings, and
    sketches, 175–176
  speaker as, 173–174
  speech assignment, 182
  use, 181–182
Vital Speeches, 398n
Vividness, 106–109
Vocabulary, and listening,
  22–23
Vocal folds, 124
Voice, 124–129
  pitch, 126
  production, 124–126
  quality, 127

rate, 127
variety and expressiveness,
  127–128
Volume, 126–127

Warrants, 278–279. *See also*
  Reasoning
Weaver, Richard, 209, 218n
Webster's New World Dictionary,
  99, 119n
Weiler, Ernest, 39n
Welcomings, 371
White, Ralph, 350, 366n
Whitehead, Deborah A., 183n
Withdrawer, 363

Woistmann, Susan,
  "Classifications of Nursery
  Rhymes," 145–147
Wolff, Florence I., 40
Wording. *See* Language
"Working in a Man's World: Are
  Women Making Progress?"
  Carol Crosthwaite,
  384–390

Yes-Response, 309

Zimmer, Karen, "The Cape
  Hatteras Lighthouse,"
  207–208